Beyond Silenced Voices

Beyond Silenced Voices

Class, Race, and Gender in United States Schools

REVISED EDITION

edited by

Lois Weis and Michelle Fine

STATE UNIVERSITY OF NEW YORK PRESS

Published by
State University of New York Press, Albany

Printed in the United States of America

For information, address State University of New York Press,
194 Washington Avenue, Suite 305, Albany, NY 12210-2384

Production by Christine L. Hamel
Marketing by Fran Keneston

Library of Congress Cataloging-in-Publication Data

Beyond sileneced voices : class, race, and gender in United States schools / editred by Lois
Weis and Michelle Fine.—Rev. ed.
       p. cm.
    Includes bibliographical references and index.
    ISBN 0-7914-6461-X (alk. paper) — ISBN 0-7914-6462-8 (pbk. : alk. paper)
       1. Discrimination in education—United States. 2. Sex discrimination in education— United
States. 3. Sexism in education—United States. 4. Minorities—Education—United States. 5.
Women—Education—United States. 6. Working class—Education—United States. 7.
Educational equalization—United States. I. Weis, Lois. II. Fine, Michelle.

LC212.2B49 2005
371.82—dc22
                                                                                    2004062592

10   9   8   7   6   5   4   3   2

Contents

Acknowledgments   ix

Introduction   xi
Michelle Fine and Lois Weis

SECTION ONE
STRUCTURING EXCLUSIONS:
EDUCATIONAL POLICIES, POLITICS, AND PRACTICES

1   Segregation 50 Years after *Brown:* A Metropolitan Change   3
    Gary Orfield and Chungmei Lee

2   The Education Pipeline in the United States, 1970–2000:
    Trends in Attrition, Retention, and Graduation Rates   21
    Walter Haney, Lisa Abrams, George Madaus, Anne Wheelock,
    Jing Miao and Ileana M. Gruia

3   Reform as Redefining the Spaces of Schools:
    An Examination of Detracking by Choice   47
    Susan Yonezawa and Amy Stuart Wells

4   Hollowing the Promise of Higher Education:
    Inside the Political Economy of Access to College   63
    Janice L. Bloom

5   Subtractive Schooling, Caring Relations, and Social Capital
    in the Schooling of U.S.-Mexican Youth   83
    Angela Valenzuela

6 The Ideology of "Fag": The School Experience of Gay Students   95
   George W. Smith
   (completed for publication by Dorothy E. Smith)

                          SECTION TWO
               LISTENING HARD: SILENCE AND DISSENT

7 Race, Suburban Resentment, and the Representation
   of the Inner City in Contemporary Film and Television   117
   Cameron McCarthy, Alicia Rodriguez, Shuaib Meecham,
   Stephen David, Carrie Wilson-Brown, Heriberto Godina,
   K. E. Supryia, and Ed Buendia

8 Learning about Race, Learning about "America":
   Hmong American High School Students   133
   Stacey J. Lee

9 In the Bad or Good of Girlhood:
   Social Class, Schooling, and White Femininities   147
   Lyn Mikel Brown

10 The Culture of Black Femininity and School Success   163
    Carla O'Connor, R. L'Heureux Lewis, and Jennifer Mueller

11 Speech and Silence:
    An Analysis of the Cultural Practice of Talking   181
    Heejung S. Kim and Hazel Rose Markus

                         SECTION THREE
                   EDUCATING FOR CHANGE

12 Global Politics, Dissent, and Palestinian American Identities:
    Engaging Conflict to Reinvigorate Democratic Education   199
    Thea Renda Abu El-Haj

13 Risky Business: Teaching about the Confederate Flag
    Controversy in a South Carolina High School   217
    Dennis Carlson and Susan L. Schramm-Pate,
    with Richard R. Lussier

14   Popular Culture, Pedagogy, and Urban Youth:
     Beyond Silenced Voices   233
         Greg Dimitriadis

15   The Alchemy of Integrated Spaces:
     Youth Participation in Research Collectives of Difference   251
         Mariá Elena Torre

Notes   267

References   279

Contributors   309

Index   315

Acknowledgments

This volume could not have been accomplished without the help of key individuals. Priscilla Ross of the State University of New York Press supported the idea of a revised edition and offered immeasurable support along the way. A long-term friend and colleague, we could not have asked for a better editor than Priscilla. Michelle Meyers, graduate student in Buffalo, held the entire project together, keeping Lois and Michelle on track as well as being in constant contact with contributors. Catie Lalonde, also a graduate student in Buffalo, offered much-needed assistance as we pulled the final pieces together. Amy Ferry, once again, produced the final product with great dedication and skill. We could not have done this without her.

Numerous students and teachers worked with researchers and appear anonymously on the pages of this book. It is your strength, courage, and determination that make our labor worthwhile, and we simultaneously honor you as we honor the researchers who appear in this volume. Our final thanks are reserved for readers of the earlier edition. *Beyond Silenced Voices* has been taught in a large number of education courses both in and outside the United States since its publication in 1993. It is your sustained engagement with the original text that ultimately convinced us to produce a second edition.

With thanks,

Lois and Michelle
April 2004

Permissions

Chapter 5 originally appeared in *Reflexiones 1998: New Directions in Mexican American Studies,* published by The Center for Mexican American Studies at the University of Texas, Austin.

Chapter 6 originally appeared in *The Sociological Quarterly,* Vol., 39, no. 2, 1998, published by University of California Press.

Chapter 7 originally appeared in *Off White: Readings on Race, Power, and Society,* edited by M. Fine, L. Weis, L.C. Powell, and L.M. Wong, published by Routledge, 1997

Parts of Chapter 9 were excerpted from *Raising Their Voices: The Politics of Girls' Anger* by Lyn Mikel Brown, published by Harvard University Press, 1998.

Introduction

Michelle Fine and Lois Weis

Beyond Silenced Voices: Class, Race, and Gender in U.S. Schools (revised edition) rests on the belief that educators must be at the center of informing educational policy as we are the ones who are both able to listen to youth and design classrooms. Across the chapters of this volume, we raise tough questions that simultaneously haunt and invigorate preservice educators and those already in schools. We ask our readers to engage with us through chapters that explore the structuring of exclusions, listening hard to youth, and educating for change. Written from the perspective of researchers, policy analysts, teachers, and youth workers, these chapters reveal a shared belief in education that "could be" and a shared worry about schools that currently reproduce class, race, and gender relations and privilege.

The chapters in this volume commit to the values of participation and change—a belief in the power of educators to think broadly and work intimately, and a belief in the power of youth to wrestle with questions of intellect, power, voice, dissent, and hope in schools and community. Section 1, "Structuring Exclusions" takes a close look at a series of significant late-twentieth-early twenty-first-century policies and practices that have significantly narrowed poor and working-class students' access to rigorous and democratically based educational opportunity. Section 2, "Listening Hard" turns our attention to the microdetails of voice, desire, anger, dreams, and struggles that characterize students living at the margins of race, class, ethnicity, and gender. Finally, in Section 3 "Educating for Change," we hear from researchers and educators who have dared to create spaces in schools and communities that wrestle with fundamental inequalities.

Structuring Exclusions

"Structuring Exclusions: Educational Policies, Politics, and Practices" focuses on a set of federal, state, and local policies, as well as social and discursive practices, that systematically exclude students of color, those from poverty, and those from the working class from rigorous, engaging, challenging, and integrated educational opportunities. In this section we examine the "dismantling of desegregation" (Gary Orfield and Chungmei Lee), the proliferation of high-stakes testing (Walter Haney, Lisa Abrams, George Madaus, Anne Wheelock, Jing Miao, and Ileana M. Gruia), increasingly rigidly enforced within-school tracking systems that determine who enjoys access to rigor and who does not (Susan Yonezawa and Amy Stuart Wells), and substantially narrowed access to tertiary level education (Janice L. Bloom) for low-income students. By looking deeply and across these select federal, state, and locally based policies and practices, we witness the systematic restructuring of educational opportunities, as such opportunities are increasingly out of reach for large groups of students.

We would be remiss, however, if the only mechanisms of exclusion included in this section were policy and/or structurally based. For we know well that social relations and discursive practices in schools dramatically and fundamentally rust students' souls or, in contrast, invite them to engage with creative intellectual imagination. Thus the final two chapters in this section address the school culture that Angela Valenzuela calls "subtractive schooling" and the discursive practices surrounding homophobia that function to isolate and dehumanize lesbian, gay, bisexual, and today transgender students (George W. Smith, chapter completed by Dorothy Smith). The chapters in Section 1, diverse in method, focus, and style, work as a force to reveal the long and devastating reach of federal and state policies, school relations, and everyday discourses as they excise the personal, local, and intimate lives of students on the margins. Section 1 is a cautionary tale: these chapters ask us to bear witness and simultaneously act, as policies, politics, and practices shrink the educational horizon for so many youth.

Listening Hard: Silence and Dissent

Section 2 consists of chapters that introduce voices not typically heard. Most powerfully, these chapters reveal the complex negotiations by which and through which youth on the margins negotiate with/against normalized representations of whiteness, "being American," femininity, and even "talk." In so doing, the chapters educate readers as to how we might "listen" to the voices of our youth. Beginning with Cameron McCarthy and colleagues' chapter on popular media, black youth, and the production of "resentment," we begin to understand the importance of listening closely to messages embedded within media. The authors offer up a cultural critique of media representations of black youth and at the same time ask us, in this chapter, to listen to how such youth contend with and interpret these perverse representations. In the next chapter, Stacey J. Lee guides us into the diverse worlds of Hmong youth, as they grapple with mandates to Americanize, endure racist assault, contend with popular culture, survive under the weight of the myth of the "model minority," and navigate the faultlines of family and schooling.

Lyn Mikel Brown continues this line of inquiry as she escorts us into the worlds of white working- and middle-class girls living in rural Maine, following the lightning rod of anger along which wisdom, pain, and desire emanate from the bodies of young women. In cross-chapter conversation with Brown, Carla O'Connor, R. L'Heureux Lewis, and Jennifer Mueller offer lessons learned from the culture of black femininity and school success. O'Connor, et al. ask their informants—successful African American women—to journey backward so as to elaborate the critical family, social, personal, and political commitments that fashioned their success. Finally Heejung S. Kim and Hazel Rose Markus educate readers as to the cultural significance of "silence" in Asian American communities, challenging us to understand the local politics of culture before assuming that spoken voice is the primary vehicle of communication and that speech must necessarily be privileged over respectful silence.

The chapters in Section 2 are a gift; through these chapters we hear voices not normally heard, as we gather respect for those on the margins. These chapters offer a hand as we wander into relations with youth whom perhaps we have never met before or have refused to meet on their terms.

EDUCATING FOR CHANGE

In this section we read from a series of researchers who are themselves educators, youth workers, theorists, and those engaged in educating for justice. Thea Abu El-Haj opens the section with a theoretical chapter on schooling and global politics. Moving between political theory and the everyday lives of Palestinian American students Abu El-Haj not only introduces a group of youth largely unknown to U.S. readers but also interrogates the processes by which global conflicts are embodied within schools and at the same time miscast as "discipline problems." Here, like all the other chapters in this section, she helps readers imagine what could be, if schools were interested in "educating for change."

Dennis Carlson and Susan L. Schramm-Pate with Richard R. Lussier move us into a southern school, where we eavesdrop on a classroom discussion revolving around the Conferderate flag controversy. Using their insights as both educators and researchers, the authors examine how differently positioned youth view the flag, the pedagogical possibilities built into the controversy, and our responsibility as educators to interrogate conflict rather than paper it over. Greg Dimitriadis assumes a similar stance in relation to critical pedagogy, moving into an afterschool program in an African American community, where he examines how African American youth connect up civil rights history as represented in the film *Panther*, with contemporary conditions of police surveillance and brutality. With an eye on popular culture, community curriculum, and the rhythms of youth culture, Dimitriadis allows educators to see the links that are often missed—or severed—within traditional classrooms.

Finally Mariá Elena Torre escorts readers into a "free space" in which diverse groups of youth have come together to craft critical research on race, ethnicity, social class, and the opportunity gap, designing a spoken word/dance performance as "public scholarship." As the chief architect of this "space," Torre allows us to witness the power of what can happen when very differently positioned youth come together to undertake a project larger than self.

Building off serious analyses of social inequality such as those chapters offered in Section 1, and deep understandings of student generated "voice" as reflected in the chapters in Section 2, Section 3 offers a vision. Writers in Section 3 provide guidance, wisdom, and real cases of critically based education, as they/we are determined to take back the Deweyian and Freirian vision of what must be, recognizing at one and the same time that good schooling sits at the foundation of a strong nation, a democratic society, and an educated, engaged, and active community for hope and justice.

Structuring Exclusions: Educational Policies, Politics, and Practices

ONE

Segregation 50 Years after *Brown*

A Metropolitan Challenge

Gary Orfield and Chungmei Lee

INTRODUCTION

A HALF-CENTURY AFTER the Supreme Court found that segregated schools are "inherently unequal," there is growing evidence that the Court was correct. Desegregated schools offer tangible advantages for students of each racial group. Our work, however, shows that U.S. schools are becoming more segregated in all regions for both African American and Latino students. We are celebrating a victory over segregation at a time when schools across the nation are becoming increasingly segregated.

This study reviews the broad sweep of segregation changes nationally, regionally, and by state since the 1954 *Brown* decision, including a decade of resegregation since the 1991 Dowell decision, which relaxed desegregation standards in many districts and authorized a return to neighborhood schools, even if that would result in segregation. It considers the very different desegregation levels in communities of differing sizes and shows the impact of segregation in schools in the Boston metropolitan area. Boston has been a center of conflict for desegregation efforts in the urban North. Typically, the issues have been focused in the city and not the larger metropolitan area as a whole in the 1960s and 1970s. Boston was the first major city in the country whose population growth was cut off by surrounding cities, and it has had a constantly shrinking share of the metropolitan population for generations. Like other metropolitan areas in the country, most of this growth has been fueled by the growth of the suburbs (Logan, 2001). While suburbs remain predominantly white, they are becoming more diverse as minority families move into them. However, despite a growing presence of minorities in the suburbs, most of the minority families are settling in a limited number of communities and are segregated from white homeowners (Stuart, 2000). Thus, segregation is no longer an urban issue, as it is a metropolitan one (Clotfelter, 1999; Reardon & Yun, 2002). Furthermore, as public schools across the nation are becoming steadily more nonwhite, there is a dramatic trend toward school district resegregation in both suburbs and central cities (Frankenberg & Lee, 2002).

The increasing levels of segregation must be considered in the context of the strong correlation between race and poverty. Children in these schools often experience conditions of concentrated disadvantage, including less experienced or unqualified teachers, fewer demanding precollegiate courses and more remedial courses, and higher teacher turnover (Young & Smith, 1997; Freeman, Scafidi, & Sjoquist, 2002; Orfield & Eaton, 1996). The strong correlation between race and poverty shows that a great many black and Latino students attend these schools of concentrated poverty.

THE DATA AND THE QUESTIONS EXPLORED

This chapter looks at the changing nature of enrollment in U.S. schools, the dynamic patterns of segregation and desegregation of various groups, regions,[1] and community types by using data from 1968 until the present day, as well as the demographic changes in the Boston metropolitan area and the implications of these changes on educational opportunity.[2] We examine both the changes over the last decade (1991–2002) and those over a much longer period (1968–2001) and explore the relationship between racial and economic segregation, discussing the implications of these trends, and possible policy alternatives.

Using data collected by National Center for Education Statistics (NCES), the study examines the composition of public schools for the years 1988, 1991, and 2001 and the distribution of students between regions for each racial group.[3] The term *white* means non-Hispanic white, and the term *Latino* or *Hispanic* means children of Latino origin, whatever their race or multiracial background may be.[4] The statistics on income (free and reduced price lunch eligibility) are less complete, though these data are available for the great majority of U.S. schools. The metropolitan area studied, formally known as the Boston New England County Metropolitan Area (NECMA), includes the counties of Bristol, Essex, Middlesex, Norfolk, Plymouth, Suffolk, and Worcester with a total student population of 767,601 in 2001.[5] For the purposes of this study, the metropolitan area will be divided into five regions: Boston, inner satellite cities, outer satellite cities, inner suburbs, and outer suburbs. Inner satellite cities include Brockton, Cambridge, Chelsea,

Everett, Lynn, Malden, Somerville, Gloucester, and Waltham.[6] Cities such as Worcester, Leominster, Attleboro, Fall River, Fitchburg, Lawrence, Leominster, Lowell, and New Bedford are outer satellite cities. The suburbs are all other cities in the Boston NECMA that are not satellite cities.

We rely on two kinds of measures to examine the dimensions of segregation (Massey & Denton, 1988; Orfield, et al., 1997; Reardon & Yun, 2001). The exposure index gives the proportion of a particular group present in the school of the average member of another racial group. We also examine the distribution of students in schools with different racial compositions: predominantly minority (defined as 50–100 percent minority), predominantly white (defined as 50–100 percent white), intensely segregated minority schools (defined as schools with more than 90 percent minority), and intensely segregated white schools (defined as schools with more than 90 percent white). In some tables we include calculations of the number and percent of students in "apartheid schools" or schools with 0 to 1 percent white students. These schools are almost as isolated as schools in the South and Border states before *Brown*.

THE CONTINUING RACIAL TRANSFORMATION OF AMERICAN SCHOOLS

In the last decade, the nation's schools have undergone substantial demographic change. Due to high birth rates and increased migration, the number of Latino students in the country is increasing much faster than the number of white students, and the total growth of black and Latino students is more than twice that of whites (Orfield & Lee, 2004). Census Bureau population projections suggest that by the middle of this century less than half of the school age youth will be white.[7]

The scale and significance of these changes have been obscured because much of this growth has been uneven (Table 1.1) The changes are most apparent in the Sunbelt where Latino communities have traditionally been large.[8] In the last decade, the schools of the western United States changed from being 59 percent white to less than half white, becoming the first region with a white minority in its total public school enrollment (Orfield & Lee, 2004). In this region, the multiracial character of the future is apparent in the fact that the Asian enrollment is now larger than the black enrollment, and Latinos are more than one third of total enrollment.

The South, a region with the second smallest share of whites (53 percent) in 2001, has had a very small increase in the percentage of black students but a substantial growth in Latino enrollment, from 14 percent in 1991 to 17 percent in 2001 (Orfield & Lee, 2004). There is a net migration of both African Americans and whites to the South from other regions.

TABLE 1.1
Public School Enrollments by Race/Ethnicity and Region, 2001–02

Region	Total Enrollment	% White	% Black	% Latino	% Asian	% Native American
South	14,572,198	52.8	27.3	17.4	2.1	0.4
West	10,969,842	49.3	6.6	34.0	8.0	2.1
Northeast	8,248,568	67.0	15.4	12.7	4.6	0.3
Border	3,483,448	70.3	20.7	3.7	2.0	3.4
Midwest	9,854,759	75.6	14.6	6.5	2.4	0.9
Alaska	134,367	60.4	4.7	3.6	5.9	25.5
Hawaii	184,546	20.3	2.4	4.5	72.3	0.4
Bureau of Indian Affairs	46,476	0	0	0	0	100.0
U.S. Total	**47,494,204**	**60.3**	**17.1**	**17.0**	**4.2**	**1.2**

Source: 2000–01 and 2001–02 NCES Common Core of Data

For those who argue that the declining share of whites in public schools was a result of desegregation, it is interesting to note that the West, the region with the greatest drop in the percentage of white students, now has very little court-ordered desegregation.[9] The ending of court orders and the return to neighborhood schools in many areas in the last decade coincided with sharp drops in the proportions of white students. Immigration, age structure, and fertility levels are all factors that contributed to these changes in racial composition (Logan, 2001).

RACIAL VARIATIONS IN SEGREGATION

Because white students are often isolated residentially, they have very little interracial exposure to other groups of students in much of the United States (Logan, 2001). Although whites made up two thirds of U.S. students in 2001, the typical white student attended a school where almost 80 percent of the students were white (Table 1.2). The typical Latino student, at the other extreme, attended a school where only 28 percent of students were white, and the typical black student attended a 31 percent white school. Black and Latino students attended schools where two thirds of the students were black and Latino, and most students were from their own group. Asian students, in contrast, attended the most integrated schools where, on average, only one fourth (22 percent) of the other students in their school were Asian. The typical American Indian student was in a school where one third of the students were Indian.[10]

TABLE 1.2
Racial Composition of Schools Attended
by the Average Student of Each Race, 2001–02

	Racial Composition of School Attended by Average				
Percent Race in Each School	White Student	Black Student	Latino Student	Asian Student	Native American Student
% White	79.0	30.5	28.2	45.4	45.0
% Black	8.6	53.8	12.0	11.8	6.7
% Latino	8.1	12.2	54.2	19.8	10.3
% Asian	3.2	3.0	4.9	22.3	2.5
% Native American	1.0	.5	.8	.7	35.5
Total	**100.0**	**100.0**	**100.0**	**100.0**	**100.0**

Source: 2001–02 NCES Common Core of Data

The clear progression of desegregation and resegregation for black students is apparent in Table 1.3, which shows, by region, the percentage of black students in schools with different levels of segregation at four different points in time: at the end of the civil rights era in 1968, at the high point of desegregation in 1988, at the time the Supreme Court authorized resegregation in 1991, and a decade later in 2001. During the period from 1968 through 1988 there was a very dramatic drop in the percentage of black students in intensely segregated schools in all regions except the Northeast and a very substantial increase in the percentage of black students in majority white schools in the southern and border states, where most of the segregation orders were being implemented.

Since 1988, with strong opposition to desegregation from the courts and inaction or opposition by executive agencies, segregation has increased substantially in all regions on both measures, except in the Northeast where there were never significant desegregation efforts by comparison to other regions of the country. In many districts where court-ordered desegregation was ended in the past decade, there has been a major increase in segregation (Orfield & Lee, 2004). The courts assumed that the forces that produced segregation and inequality had been cured. Clearly, the patterns of segregation, desegregation, and resegregation for black students reflected the direction of social policy and are the result of government inaction and court rulings.

The data in Table 1.3 indicate several important points. One is that the claim that we have made no progress since *Brown* is simply not true. Before *Brown* virtually all black students in the southern and border states were in completely segregated schools. Today, the vast majority is not, in spite of a decade of increasing segregation. In other words, we may be regressing in

TABLE 1.3
Percentage of Black Students in 50–100% and 90–100%
Minority Schools 1968, 1988, 1991, and 2001

Percentage of Black Students in 50–100% Minority Schools

	1968	1988	1991	2001
South	80.9	56.5	60.1	69.8
Border	71.6	59.6	59.3	67.9
Northeast	66.8	77.3	75.2	78.4
Midwest	77.3	70.1	69.7	72.9
West	72.2	67.1	69.2	75.8
Total	**76.6**	**63.2**	**65.5**	**72.0**

Percentage of Black Students in 90–100% Minority Schools

	1968	1988	1991	2001
South	77.8	24.0	26.1	31.0
Border	60.2	34.5	34.5	41.6
Northeast	42.7	48.0	49.8	51.2
Midwest	58.0	41.8	39.9	46.8
West	50.8	28.6	26.6	30.0
Total	**64.3**	**32.1**	**33.7**	**37.9**

Source: 1991–02 and 2001–02 NCES Common Core of Data

terms of the progress made during the height of the desegregation era, but we are nowhere near the situation that existed in seventeen of our states and the nation's capital 50 years ago before the civil rights revolution.

The absence of a current desegregation effort is most apparent for Latino students. The increase in segregation for Latinos in the West where most Latinos live has been very substantial in the past decade and extremely dramatic since the 1960s. The percent of Latino students in predominantly minority schools in the West has almost doubled from 42 percent in 1968 to 80 percent in 2001 (Table 1.4). It is fast approaching the level in the Northeast, previously the most segregated region in the nation. In addition, the share of Latino students in 90 to 100 percent minority schools has more than tripled during the same period, from 12 percent to 37 percent. Overall, in all regions of the country, Latino segregation has increased fairly consistently since 1968.

SEGREGATION AND POVERTY CONCENTRATION

Segregation by race and ethnicity is severe and growing, but many Americans ask why it makes such an educational difference. One basic reason is the link between segregation by race and segregation by poverty. In the 2001 through

TABLE 1.4
Percentage of Latino Students in 50–100% and 90–100%
Minority Schools 1968, 1988, 1991, and 2001

Percentage of Latino Students in 50–100% Minority Schools

	1968	1988	1991	2001
South	69.6	80.2	76.4	77.7
Border	***	***	38.2	52.8
Northeast	74.8	79.7	77.4	78.2
Midwest	31.8	52.3	53.6	56.6
West	42.4	71.3	72.6	80.1
Total	54.8	71.5*	72.8	78.4

Percentage of Latino Students in 90–100% Minority Schools

	1968	1988	1991	2001
South	33.7	37.9	38.6	39.9
Border	***	***	11.0	14.2
Northeast	44.0	44.2	46.8	44.8
Midwest	6.8	24.9	20.9	24.6
West	11.7	27.5	28.6	37.4
Total	23.1	32.2*	33.6	42.0

* These numbers are from the 1986–87 school year.
** The enrollments were too small in these years to make accurate comparisons.
Source: 1991–92 and 2001–02 NCES Common Core of Data

2002 school year, 43 percent of all U.S. schools were intensely segregated white schools or schools with less than one tenth black and Latino students (see Table 1.5). Only 15 percent of these intensely segregated white schools were schools of concentrated poverty or schools with more than half of the students on free or reduced price lunch. In contrast, 88 percent of the intensely segregated minority schools (or schools with less than 10 percent white) had concentrated poverty, with more than half of all students getting free lunches. That means that students in highly segregated neighborhood schools are many times more likely to be in schools of concentrated poverty.

Concentrated poverty turns out to be powerfully related to both school opportunities and achievement levels. The average black or Latino student attends a school where close to half of the students are poor (Frankenberg, Lee, & Orfield, 2003). Past research has shown that segregated schools tend to have high concentrations of poverty, low parental involvement, and high dropout rates.[11] Students attending these schools are exposed to less credentialed teachers, higher teacher turnover, and lower educational aspirations and career options than students in more desegregated settings.[12] In contrast, suburban schools, which tend to be majority white, usually provide a more rigorous curriculum, have more highly skilled and experienced teachers and tougher academic competition than their urban counterparts.[13] Exposure to

TABLE 1.5
Relationship between Segregation by Race and by Poverty, 2001–02

Percent Black and Latino Students in Schools

% Poor in Schools	0–10%	10–20%	20–30%	30–40%	40–50%	50–60%	60–70%	70–80%	80–90%	90–100%
0–10%	24.7	20.2	9.5	5.1	5.5	4.2	4.9	4.2	3.8	4.3
10–25%	27.6	28.3	25.4	15.9	9.2	4.8	3.8	2.4	2.0	2.0
25–50%	32.9	35.4	40.3	42.9	38.2	30.4	19.9	12.0	8.8	6.1
50–100%	14.8	16.2	24.8	36.2	47.1	60.7	71.4	81.4	85.4	87.6
Total	100.0	100.0	100.0	100.0	100.0	100.0	100.0	100.0	100.0	100.0
% of U.S. Schools	**43.2**	**11.7**	**7.8**	**6.2**	**5.5**	**4.6**	**4.0**	**3.7**	**3.8**	**9.6**

* Numbers may not add up to 100 due to rounding.

more desegregated settings can break the tendency for racial segregation to become self-perpetuating for all students, regardless of race, later in life (see Braddock & McPartland, 1989; Wells & Crain, 1994). Furthermore, students of all races who are exposed to integrated educational settings are more likely to live and work among people of diverse racial and ethnic backgrounds.[14]

DESEGREGATION BY COMMUNITY SIZE

Most Americans would probably guess that the most progressive places in the country were the nation's sophisticated big cities and the most reactionary were the rural areas, which historically were the breeding ground of racial violence, the Ku Klux Klan, and some of the worst incidents in the civil rights era (Kluger, 1994). When we examine racial patterns in 2001, however, the data show that integration for black public school students is highest in the rural schools, mostly in the rural South (Table 1.6). The average black and Latino student in rural schools attends a school that is half white. One possible explanation is that residential segregation is often much less in the rural areas, and there may be only a single school for a large geographic area.

Unfortunately the vast majority of black and Latino students live and go to school in the nation's metropolitan areas, where the most severe segregation affects the 2.5 million black and 2.6 million Latinos in the central cities of the large metropolitan areas and another 1.9 million black and 2.7 million Latino students in the suburbs of the large central cities (Orfield & Lee,

TABLE 1.6
Exposure Rates to Whites, by Racial Group and Metro Region, 2001–02

	White/ White	Black/ White	Latino/ White	Asian/ White	Native American/ White
Large Metro					
Central city	52.7	12.6	13.8	25.0	35.1
Suburb	76.8	34.7	30.9	50.3	60.2
Small Metro					
Central city	68.2	31.6	30.6	49.8	57.9
Suburb	83.4	50.8	36.8	67.1	58.7
Other					
Small cities	76.8	43.8	41.4	70.8	61.5
Towns	83.6	42.9	44.7	74.2	56.7
Rural Areas	88.2	49.9	51.5	58.6	39.1

Source: 2001–02 NCES Common Core of Data

2004). Central city black students typically attend schools with 87 percent minority students; for Latinos it is 86 percent (Table 1.6). In the suburbs of large metropolitan areas, where a huge migration of middle-class minority families is well underway, the typical black student is in a school that is 65 percent minority, and the typical Latino student is in an even more segregated school with 69 percent minority students. Obviously high residential segregation and the fragmentation of most of our large metropolitan regions into many separate school districts produce the most severe segregation in American education (see, for example, Logan, 2003).

The Supreme Court's 5 to 4 decision drawing a line between city and suburbs for desegregation purposes and the failure to seriously address housing segregation build severe isolation of children into the life of our metro regions and mean that even minority families who can afford housing choice often end up in segregated, poorly performing schools.[15] The Boston metropolitan area is an example of the severe segregation experienced by students in large metropolitan areas.

BOSTON METROPOLITAN DEMOGRAPHICS

The Boston metropolitan area is overwhelmingly white and suburban. Of the 772,490 students attending 1,457 public schools in 2001 and 2002, 76 percent of the students are white, and almost three out of every five students attend schools in the suburbs (Table 1.7). By contrast, Boston's central city school district (Boston Public Schools) enrolls just 8 percent of public school students in the metropolitan area. Satellite cities are all cities (excluding Boston)

TABLE 1.7
Enrollment and Racial Composition of
Public Schools by Location and Race, 2001–02

	White (%)	Black (%)	Latino (%)	Asian (%)	Percent of Total Entrollment by Region (Column Percentages)
Boston	15	47	28	9	8
Inner Satellite Cities	47	22	22	8	9
Outer Satellite Cities	55	8	28	9	13
Inner Suburbs	82	5	4	9	11
Outer Suburbs	91	2	3	3	59
Total Enrollment	**76**	**9**	**10**	**5**	**100**

* Totals may not add up to 100 due to rounding.

within the Boston New England County Metropolitan Area (NECMA) that are defined by the Census Bureau as "central cities" and places with a population density greater than 10,000 per square mile. Suburbs are all cities or towns in the Boston NECMA, excluding Boston and the satellite cities. Latino students are the largest minority group in the metropolitan area at 10 percent, followed closely by black students (9 percent). About 5 percent of students enrolled in public schools are Asian.[16]

The differences in the distribution of white students across the metropolitan area are quite marked. Eighty-two percent of the public school student population in the inner suburbs and 91 percent of the outer suburb students are white. In contrast, only 15 percent of the public student enrollment is white in Boston, and close to half of the students are black. White students are also heavily underenrolled in the satellite cities, where more than one fifth of the student enrollment is Latino.

DEMOGRAPHIC TRENDS OVER TIME

There are two strong trends in metropolitan demographic changes since 1989.[17] At the same time that enrollment of students is growing in the metropolitan area, the city of Boston is enrolling a shrinking share of the students. While enrollment in every region has increased, only the outer suburbs enroll a growing percentage of total students. The city of Boston has the slowest rate of growth (5 percent) in a little over a decade and now enrolls just 8 percent of the students. The outer suburbs experienced the most growth (31 percent) and now enroll three out of every five students.[18]

The second trend is the growing presence of minority students in the satellite cities. The proportion of the total student population who were black increased substantially from 13 percent in 1989 to more than one fifth of the total student population in the inner satellite cities. In a little more than 10 years, Latino presence has doubled from 11 percent to 22 percent in the inner satellite cities. The growth of Asian students is more evenly spread: except for the outer suburbs, Asian students now constitute about 10 percent of the student population in each of the regions.

The demographic shift in the different regions increasingly exacerbates the uneven distribution of students across the metropolitan regions: white students are disproportionately enrolled in the suburbs: more than four out of every five white students in the Boston metropolitan area attend schools in the inner and outer suburbs (Table 1.8). Only 2 percent of all white students in the metropolitan area attend schools in Boston compared to 71 percent in the outer suburbs.

In contrast, black students are disproportionately concentrated in Boston: the city itself accounts for more than 40 percent of the total black public

TABLE 1.8
Distribution of Public School Students across the Boston Metropolitan Area,
by Race 2001–02 (in Percent)

	White	Black	Latino	Asian
Boston	2	44	23	14
Satellite Cities				
Attleboro	1	0	0	1
Brockton	1	11	2	1
Cambridge	0	4	1	2
Chelsea	0	1	5	1
Everett	1	1	1	1
Fall River	2	1	1	1
Fitchburg	1	1	2	2
Gloucester	1	0	0	0
Lawrence	0	1	13	1
Leominster	1	0	2	1
Lowell	1	1	4	11
Lynn	1	3	6	5
Malden	1	1	1	3
New Bedford	2	3	3	0
Somerville	0	1	2	1
Worcester	2	4	9	5
Waltham	1	1	1	1
Inner Suburbs	12	6	4	19
Outer Suburbs	71	16	19	30
Total	**100**	**100**	**100**	**100**

school enrollment in the metropolitan area, and more than half of the black population in the metro area attend schools in just two cities: Boston and Brockton (Table 1.8). Of all the groups, the share of black students enrolled in the suburbs is the smallest (22 percent).

Latino student population is also concentrated in a few cities. Close to half of all Latino students in the state attend schools in just three cities: Boston, Lawrence, and Worcester. About 20 percent of Latino students in the metropolitan area attend schools in Boston (Table 1.8).

The Asian student population provides an interesting contrast to both black and Latino distribution through the metropolitan area (Table 1.8). In general, Asians are more spread out than either blacks or Latinos. On the other hand, 11 percent of the Asian students attend schools in just one city, Lowell, which has high concentrations of Cambodians (Census, 2000).

The high fragmentation that characterizes the metropolitan area, in which many independent incorporated cities and towns have their separate school districts, leads to greater sorting among students and very little overlap between minority students and white students. We define high fragmentation to mean the many independent incorporated cities and towns within the metropolitan area, each with separate school districts, instead of large consolidated districts.

Furthermore, segregation in the housing market may also contribute to the intense concentration of minorities. Outside of Boston, close to half of the homes purchased by black and Latino buyers from 1993 through 1998 were located in 7 out of 126 communities: Chelsea, Randolph, Everett, Lynn, Somerville, Milton, and Malden (Stuart, 2000).[19] In addition, people of different incomes are buying homes in different communities, resulting in income isolation. A more recent report found that black and Latino families are living in segregated communities regardless of affordability (McArdle, 2003).

It is interesting to note that despite the high levels of segregation in the public schools, both private schools and charter schools are more segregated than the public schools. A study on private schools found that although private schools in the 20 largest metropolitan areas are 70 percent white, the average white student attends private schools that are typically 85 percent white, while black and Latino students attend private schools that are less than half white. In the Boston metropolitan area, the average white student attends private schools that are 89 percent white. In addition, while charter schools in Massachusetts are on average 54 percent white, the average white student attends charter schools where almost 80 percent of the students are white (Frankenberg & Lee, 2003). In contrast, the average black and Latino charter school students in Massachusetts attend schools that are only 22 and 26 percent white, respectively.

EXPOSURE OF STUDENTS ACROSS THE
BOSTON METROPOLITAN AREA

The high levels of school segregation among the different regions result in schools with differing racial compositions. For example, in the outer suburbs, over 70 percent of white students attend intensely segregated white schools as opposed to Boston, where there are no schools that are more than 60 percent white.[20] While one might expect that, given the fact that only 15 percent of the student body in Boston is white, schools in Boston will have lower shares of white students. However, despite the low white share of enrollment, there are still white students in Boston attending schools where more than half of the student body is white. In other words, even in places with a small share of white students, white students remain highly isolated.[21]

Data also suggest that 61 percent of the black students attend intensely segregated minority schools.[22] Places where minority or white students are disproportionately concentrated (such as Boston and the outer suburbs) are also places where students attend schools that are either overwhelmingly white or overwhelmingly minority. In contrast, where there are no such concentrations such as the satellite cities for black and white students, blacks and whites attend schools with higher levels of diversity. In other words, there can be no meaningful interracial exposure if substantial numbers of students from several racial groups are not present in the same school system.

As in the case of black students, Latinos are highly segregated in Boston. Furthermore, Latinos are also highly segregated in the satellite cities, especially the outer satellite cities where almost one out of every four students attends intensely segregated minority schools. In the inner satellite cities, almost half attend schools where less than one third of the students are white. In these regions, Latinos are experiencing high levels of segregation. This is disturbing given that there has been a substantial growth of Latinos in the satellite cities: since 1989, the share of Latino enrollment has grown by 10 percentage points in both inner and outer satellite cities, and these are places, aside from Boston, where Latino students are highly concentrated. In other words, Latinos are highly segregated in regions where they are growing quickly and highly concentrated.

The most striking finding about Asians is that they have a bimodal distribution in Boston and the inner satellite cities. On the one hand, about one third of Asian students attend intensely segregated minority schools in Boston. On the other hand, about 12 percent of the Asians attend schools where more than half of the student body is white, similar to the attendance rate of white students in these schools (13 percent). Aggregated data on Asians tend to mask the substantial variation that exists among different Asian subgroups and obscure the bimodal nature of the Asian population. In other words, there are certain subgroups of Asians that are doing better than others. In summary, the structure of the metropolitan area drives the distribution of students in the different regions. Given the demographic trends and the fragmentation of the metropolitan area, students are becoming most segregated in regions where they are highly concentrated.[23]

RELATIONSHIP BETWEEN POVERTY AND RACIAL SEGREGATION

These trends of increasing segregation for minority students in certain regions in the metropolitan area should be placed in the context of the strong relationship between race and poverty.[24] Schools with high levels of minority segregation from white students are often schools with high levels of poverty. Past research has shown that schools with high levels of poverty are often schools with fewer resources, a lack of credentialed teachers, less parental involvement, and higher teacher turnover, diminishing the educational opportunities available for students attending these schools.[25] At the national level, students in schools with at least 90 percent minority students were almost six times as likely to be in a predominantly poor school as students that attended predominantly white schools.[26]

The correlation between race and poverty is even starker for the Boston metropolitan area (Table 1.9). The numbers in each of the cells represent the percentage of schools with a certain share of black and Latino students that are also of a specific poverty level. For example, 74 percent of the schools with 10 percent or fewer black and Latino students (low minority schools) are also schools where 10 percent or fewer of the students were poor (low poverty schools). Only 1 percent of low minority schools had a student body where the majority of the students qualified for free or reduced lunch (high poverty schools). By contrast, almost all (96 percent) of the intensely segregated black and Latino schools were high poverty schools. In other words, students in schools with at least 90 percent minority students were almost 96 times as likely to be in a predominantly poor school as students that attended predominantly white schools. Compared to the nation as a whole, the relationship between racial and income segregation is dramatically higher in the Boston metropolitan area.[27] Because of this high correlation, there are no low-poverty and high-minority or low-minority and high-poverty schools in the metropolitan area (as shown by the gray areas).[28] Four percent of the students attend high-poverty and high minority-schools.

CONCLUSION

American public schools are now only 60 percent white nationwide, and nearly one fourth of U.S. students are in states with a majority of nonwhite students. However, except in the South and Southwest, most white students have little contact with minority students. Rural and small town school districts are, on average, the nation's most integrated for both African Americans and Latinos, while central cities of large metropolitan areas are the epicenter of segregation, where the vast majority of intensely segregated minority schools face conditions of concentrated poverty, which are powerfully related to unequal educational opportunity. Students in segregated minority schools face conditions that students in segregated white schools seldom experience. In metropolitan areas such as the Boston metropolitan area, there is a growing number of students attending schools in the outer suburbs, which are becoming overwhelmingly white (91 percent), and Boston schools are overwhelmingly minority (85 percent) and places of concentrated poverty.

As our study shows, a half century of struggle for school desegregation has shown large gains and serious reverses for the integration of African American students as the Supreme Court, the Congress, and the president have taken sharply changing postures toward the goal of integrated education

TABLE 1.9
Relationship between Segregation by Race and by Poverty in Boston Metropolitan Area, 2001–02

Percent Black and Latino Students in Schools

% Poor in Schools	0–10%	10–20%	20–30%	30–40%	40–50%	50–60%	60–70%	70–80%	80–90%	90–100%
0–10%	74	16	5	0	0	0	0	0	0	0
10–25%	20	27	19	6	2	4	0	0	0	0
25–50%	5	36	43	42	22	2	0	3	4	4
50–100%	1	20	34	53	77	94	100	97	96	96
Total	100	100	100	100	100	100	100	100	100	100
% of Schools	**60**	**10**	**6**	**5**	**5**	**4**	**2**	**3**	**2**	**4**

* The correlation between percent black and Latino enrollment and percent poor is very strong (r=.85).

** Numbers may not add up to one hundred due to rounding.

and either pushed hard to bring down the color lines in American education or pressed to return to the old order of segregated neighborhood schools. Most of the serious effort was directed at black-white segregation in the South, the region where the highest level of integration was achieved and held for a third of a century. There never was a similar effort to desegregate Latinos, who are now highly isolated by race and poverty. Since the beginning of the 1990s the United States has been moving backward toward growing racial isolation for both African American and Latino students. Those who say that the progress has all been lost, however, are far too pessimistic. The levels of segregation from 2001 through 2002 are nowhere near the levels recorded for the seventeen states with apartheid laws until 1954. Today's centers of segregation are in the industrialized metros of the North, and the states of New York, Michigan, and Illinois have the most segregated schools for black students because of their high residential segregation, large black populations, and fragmentation into many small segregated school districts.

Desegregation has consequences. Schools segregated by race are also segregated by income, which results in many forms of unequal opportunities. *Plessy* has no more viability as a route to equal education now than it did a half century ago. Desegregation is related to academic gains but is also linked to better understanding of people of different backgrounds, a greater receptivity to living and working in diverse settings, and life chances. It has impacts on both minority and white children. Some of these impacts are very similar to the diversity benefits for all students recognized by the Supreme Court in its 2003 decision upholding affirmative action at the University of Michigan. Citing social science research, the Supreme Court held that interracial classes had benefits for all students, that they helped prepare leadership that could function across racial lines, and that they aided major American institutions and our democracy. Recent surveys of high school students have produced very similar findings.

There have been no significant positive policies promoting desegregation at the federal level since the repeal of the federal desegregation aid program in 1981.[29] Recent choice policies such as federal support for charter schools and student transfers in No Child Left Behind (NCLB) have no desegregation elements in contrast to earlier policies such as the federal magnet school program. At their worst, as shown in our recent studies of the No Child Left Behind adequate year progress requirements, the NCLB policies often require more from segregated schools and tend to penalize them for their unequal opportunities. Well-intentioned policies that ignore the profound inequalities between schools risk blaming the victims of the segregation policies and punishing them and their schools for the consequences of segregation.

Obviously, as shown in our national data and in the metro Boston study, the problem for the future of the Brown dream is now in our large metropolitan complexes. We believe that a major challenge for educators, researchers, and policy makers in the coming generations will be to understand, control, and reverse the strong dynamic of spreading segregation in these huge communities and to support the development of new systems of successfully and stably integrated schools and neighborhoods that can prepare young Americans to function effectively in a nation that will have no racial majority by the middle of this century. In an increasingly multiracial society, the need for integrated schooling environments that provide fair educational opportunity for students of all races will become increasingly obvious.

TWO

The Education Pipeline in the United States, 1970–2000

Trends in Attrition, Retention, and Graduation Rates

Walter Haney, Lisa Abrams, George Madaus,
Anne Wheelock, Jing Miao, and Ileana M. Gruia

INTRODUCTION

CLOSE TO 100 years ago, in a book titled *Laggards in Our Schools: A Study of Retardation and Elimination in City School Systems,* Leonard Ayres wrote:

> No standard which may be applied to a school system as a measure of accomplishment is more significant than that which tells us what proportion of the pupils who enter the first grade succeed in reaching the final grade. (Ayres, 1909, p. 8)

Nearly a century later, rates of student progress through elementary and secondary school continue to be recognized as indicators of the quality of educational systems. In the Goals 2000 Act of 1994, the U.S. Congress and President Bill Clinton established as a national education goal that the United States should aspire to a high school graduation rate of 90 percent. In 2002, in the No Child Left Behind (NCLB) law, the Congress and President George Bush set out as a criterion for evaluating secondary education, "graduation rates for public secondary school students (defined as the percentage of students who graduate from secondary school with a regular diploma in the standard number of years)" [Sec 1111(b)(2)(D)(i)].

In this chapter we present results of analyses of data on grade enrollment and graduation over the last several decades both nationally (1968–2000) and for all 50 states (1984–2000) in an effort to assess the progress of public school students as they advance through the education pipeline from kindergarten through high school graduation. State-reported dropout statistics are often unreliable, and most states do not regularly report grade retention data, that is, data on the rates at which students are held back to repeat grades. Therefore, the only way to study long-term rates of student progress through elementary-secondary educational systems is to examine data on grade enrollment and graduates over time. This project grew out of a study of education reform in Texas in which it was found that analyzing enrollment and graduation statistics could show what was really happening when reliable statistics on dropouts were unavailable (Haney, 2000).

These analyses allow us to illustrate how graduation rates, both nationally and for the states, have been changing in recent decades. In addition we are able to examine the education pipeline in the United States and identify key transition points through which students progress, or fail to progress. This chapter first describes the data used and methods via which enrollment and graduation data have been analyzed before presenting the results. Generally the results show that over the last thirty years there have been increases in Grade 9 to Grade 10 attrition, a growing "bulge" of students in Grade 9, and decreases in high school graduation rates—especially in the last decade. Each of these trends will be discussed in turn. Last, the chapter ends with a discussion of the possible causes and consequences of these changes in the education pipeline in the United States over the last three decades.

DATA AND METHODS

The data used in the analyses presented in this chapter are the numbers of students enrolled in public schools by grade for each academic year and the numbers of students graduating each academic year. These data are available from the *Digest of Education Statistics (DES)*, a report issued by the National Center for Education Statistics (NCES) since 1962, and the *Common Core of Data (CCD)*, a federal repository of education statistics available on-line at http://nces.ed.gov/ccd/.

To examine patterns of student progress through the education pipeline, we have conducted cohort progression analyses. These analyses are used to address questions such as the following: If there were 1000 students enrolled in Grade 9 in 1990–91, how many progressed to Grade 10 in 1991–92? We have examined such year-to-year "grade-to-grade" rates of progress for thirteen transition points, from kindergarten through Grade 12 and to graduation. We analyzed such year-to-year transitions nationally from 1968–69 to 2000–01 and for all 50 states from 1984–85 through 2000–01. Additionally, we examined rates of progress over more than one year, for example, by addressing the following question: How many students enrolled in Grade 9 in 1990–91 graduated in 1993–94? This is, of course, exactly the sort of high school graduation rate calculation suggested by the requirements of the 2002 NCLB law. Indeed, we will report such graduation rates, both nationally and for the 50 states.

INCREASING ATTRITION BETWEEN GRADES 9 AND 10

One major finding from our cohort progression analyses is that the rate at which students disappear between Grades 9 and 10 has *tripled* over the last 30 years. Figure 2.1 shows the percent fewer students enrolled in Grade 10 nationally than in Grade 9 the previous year. As shown, during the first half of the 1970s there were less than 4 percent fewer students enrolled in Grade 10 than in Grade 9 the previous year. Attrition between Grades 9 and 10 started increasing in the late 1970s and accelerated from the mid-1980s onward. By the turn of the century there were nearly 12 percent fewer students enrolled in Grade 10 than in Grade 9 the previous year. To provide some sense of the numbers of students being lost between Grades 9 and 10, in 1998–99, there were 3.86 million students enrolled in Grade 9 in public schools in the U.S., but in 1999–2000, there were 3.42 million enrolled in Grade 10. The difference, 440,000 students, means that 11.4 percent of ninth graders in 1998–99 did not show up as enrolled in Grade 10 in 1999–2000. In short, by the end of the century, the transition from Grade 9 to Grade 10 was clearly the largest leak in the education pipeline. Three decades ago, far more students were lost between Grades 11 and 12 than between 9 and 10. In subsequent sections of this chapter we discuss what happened to these missing students, but first we summarize results of state-level analyses of student attrition between Grades 9 and 10.

Analyses of enrollment data at the state level reveal that there has long been substantial variation in rates of student attrition between Grades 9 and 10. Between 1984–85 and 1985–86, when the rate of attrition between Grades 9 and 10 nationally stood at a little less than 5 percent, six states had attrition rates of 10 percent or worse (Georgia 16.5 percent, Texas 14.9 percent, Louisiana 13.2 percent, South Carolina 11.5 percent, Kentucky 11.2 percent, and Virginia 10.0 percent). By comparison, ten states showed Grades 9 to 10 attrition rates of less than 2 percent (California, Minnesota, Nebraska, Nevada, Utah, Kansas, Wyoming, South Dakota, Hawaii, and Wisconsin).

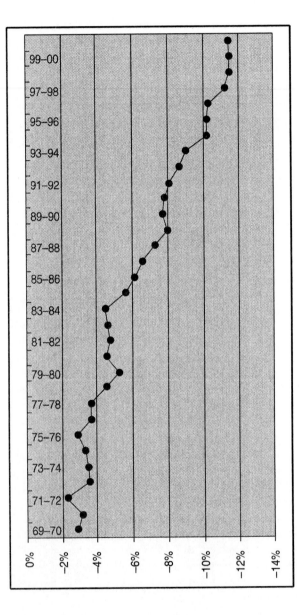

FIGURE 2.1
National Public School Enrollment,
Percent Fewer Students in Grade 10 than in Grade 9 the Previous Year

By the end of the century, however, the list of states with Grade 9 to 10 attrition rates exceeding 10 percent had more than tripled. Table 2.1 lists the 21 states with the worst rates of Grade 9 to 10 attrition between 1999–2000 and 2000–2001. Since the number of states with Grade 9 to 10 attrition rates greater than 10 percent had more than tripled between the mid-1980s and the end of the century, it is hardly surprising that the Grade 9 to 10 attrition rate nationally had more than doubled during the same interval, from less than 5 percent to more than 11 percent. What is striking about the list of states shown in Table 2.1 is that it includes not just southern states (the only ones with such attrition rates of more than 10 percent in the mid-1980s), but also northern and midwestern states such as New York, Massachusetts, Rhode Island, Ohio, and Michigan.

GROWING BULGE IN GRADE 9 ENROLLMENT

The increasing rate of attrition between Grades 9 and 10 may be explained in part by the second key finding from our analyses of enrollment data—that

TABLE 2.1
**States with Worst Attrition Rates between
Grades 9 and 10, 1999–2000 to 2000–01**

State	Grade 9 to 10 attrition 1999–2000 to 2000–01
Florida	–23.8%
South Carolina	–22.7%
Georgia	–20.3%
Texas	–20.0%
Nevada	–18.8%
North Carolina	–18.0%
Louisiana	–17.3%
Hawaii	–15.9%
Alabama	–15.0%
Mississippi	–14.4%
New York	–13.9%
Tennessee	–13.9%
Kentucky	–13.4%
New Mexico	–13.1%
Alaska	–12.6%
Delaware	–12.4%
Maryland	–11.3%
Ohio	–11.0%
Massachusetts	–10.7%
Michigan	–10.6%
Rhode Island	–10.2%

there has been a sharp increase in the "bulge" of students enrolled in Grade 9 in the last 30 years. As a simple way of showing the increasingly critical role of Grade 9 in the education pipeline, we start with a simple graph. Figure 2.2 depicts the numbers of students in U.S. public schools nationwide enrolled by grade in each of two academic years; namely, 1968–69 and 1999–2000. Note that this figure provides a cross-sectional view of grade enrollments in these two years rather than results of cohort progression analyses. In 1968–69 and 1999–2000, there were similar numbers of students enrolled in Grades 1–12 overall, about 42 million across the span of Grades 1–12. From Figure 2.2 we see that there were between 2.5 and 4 million enrolled in each of the twelve grades in both 1968–69 and 1999–2000. In general there were slight declines in both years in the numbers enrolled in Grades 1 through 7, with sharper declines in Grades 9 through 12. Strikingly discrepant from this overall pattern is the Grade 9 enrollment for 1999–2000 which is 440 thousand more than Grade 8 enrollment in the same year, and 520 thousand more than Grade 10 enrollment. This simple graph reflects how Grade 9 has become an increasingly important valve in the education pipeline, as enrollments are "bulging up" in Grade 9 and, as discussed in the previous section, attrition of students between Grades 9 and 10 is increasing.

Figure 2.3 shows another view of how enrollments have been bulging up in Grade 9. As this figure shows, during the 1970s there were only 4 to 6 percent more students enrolled in Grade 9 than in Grade 8 the previous year. However, beginning in the mid-1980s, this percentage began to climb sharply so that by the end of the century, in public schools nationally, there were about 13 percent more students enrolled in Grade 9 than in Grade 8 the previous year. This means that in the last 30 years, the bulge of students in Grade 9 has more than tripled, from around 4 percent to 13 percent.

This combination, of increasing attrition of students between Grades 9 and 10, and increasingly more students enrolled in Grade 9 relative to Grade 8, is surely a reflection of the fact that more students nationally were being held back to repeat Grade 9. This pattern bodes ill for future graduation rates because research suggests that retaining students to repeat a grade is not a sound educational strategy (Shepard & Smith, 1989) for reasons that will be discussed later in the chapter. Indeed, recent evidence from Texas and other states indicates that 70 to 80 percent of students who are required to repeat Grade 9 will not persist in school to high school graduation (Haney, 2001). In the next section we present direct evidence on what has been happening to graduation rates, both nationally and among the states, but first we pause to summarize evidence from state-level analyses of the Grade 9 "bulge."

Analyses of state-level enrollment data from 1984–85 to 2000–01 indicate that the Grade 9 bulge, like attrition between Grades 9 and 10, has long varied across the states. As of 1985–86, one state, New York, had 20 percent more students enrolled in Grade 9 than in Grade 8 the previous year, and

FIGURE 2.2
Number of Students (in 1000's) Enrolled in U.S. Public Schools, by Grade, 1968–69 and 1999–2000

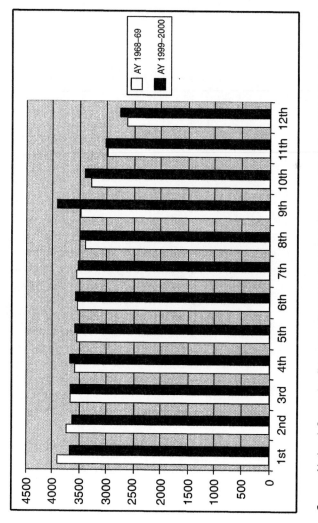

Source: National Center for Education Statistics, *Digest of Education Statistics 1981* (Washington, DC: National Center for Education Statistics), Table 30, p. 40; *Digest of Education Statistics 2001* (Washington, DC: National Center for Education Statistics), Table 40, p. 56.

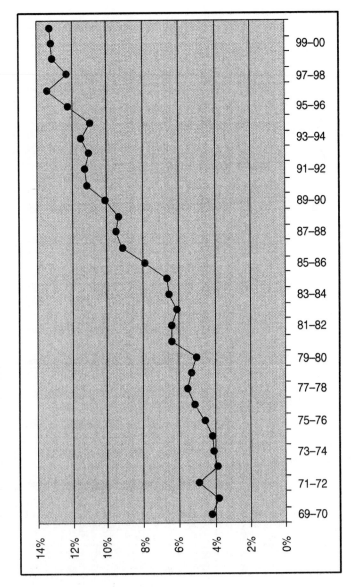

FIGURE 2.3
Percent More Students Enrolled in Grade 9 than in Grade 8 the Previous Year,
U.S. Public Schools, 1969–70 to 2000–01

seven states (California, Delaware, Florida, Georgia, Hawaii, Michigan, and Wisconsin) had a Grade 9 bulge of 10 to 13 percent. In contrast, in 1985–86, twenty-two states had Grade 9 bulges of less than 5 percent.

By the end of the century, however, this pattern had changed dramatically. By 2000–01 more than half the states had 10 percent or more students enrolled in Grade 9 than in Grade 8 the previous year, and *seven* states had Grade 9 bulges of 20 percent or more.

In contrast, by the end of the century just 8 states (Michigan, South Dakota, Montana, North Dakota, Utah, Wyoming, Arkansas, and Maine) had a Grade 9 bulge of less than 5 percent. This sharp reversal—the number of states with Grade 9 bulges greater than 10 percent more than doubled, and the number of states with bulges less than 5 percent fell from 22 to 8—is a clear sign that far more states are requiring far more students to repeat Grade 9 by the end of the century than had been true in the mid-1980s.

FALLING GRADUATION RATES

The combination of findings presented in the last two sections should make our third finding come as no surprise: high school graduation rates have been falling in the United States in recent years. To illustrate this unfortunate development, we begin as usual with a summary of national results, followed by a review of state-level results.

As mentioned previously, the most obvious way to calculate high school graduation rates is simply to divide the number of high school graduates by the number of students enrolled in Grade 9 three and a half years earlier. However, as shown in the last section of this chapter, as more students are being held back to repeat Grade 9, such simple calculations will be affected not just by changes in the numerator (the numbers of graduates) but also by changes in the denominator (the increasing bulge of students enrolled in Grade 9). In an effort to disentangle changes in graduation rates from the increasing bulge in Grade 9 enrollments, in this section we start by focusing on rates of graduation from Grade 8 to graduation four and a half years later.[1]

Graduation rates climbed slightly in the early 1980s and dipped slightly during the late 1980s. Since the early 1990s, however, the Grade 8 to graduation rates have fallen quite steadily, from 78.4 percent in 1991–92 to 74.4 percent in 2000–01. In other words, since a high school graduation rate of 90 percent was set out as a national education priority as part of the Goals 2000 initiatives in the early 1990s, actual graduation rates, instead of increasing toward this goal, have fallen from a little more than 78 percent in the early 1990s to less than 75 percent in 2000–01. A decline in graduation rate from 78.41 percent in 1990–91 to 74.40 percent in 2000–01 may not seem like a huge drop, but three facts help to put the 4.01 percent decline in graduation rate in perspective. First, since there were 3.4 million students enrolled in Grade 8 in 1996–97, a graduation rate of 74.4 percent means that 871,000 of these students did not graduate in 2000–2001. Second, if the graduation rate for the class of 1992 had merely persisted another decade, 135,000 more students would have graduated in 2000–01. Third, if the national education goal of a 90 percent graduation rate by the year 2000 had been achieved, an additional 531,000 students would have graduated with their class in 2000–01 "in the standard number of years." In the concluding section of this chapter we discuss the implications of this loss of 100s of thousands of students from school prior to graduation. But first, we turn from the national level discussion to examine graduation rates at the state level.[1]

Graduation rate results for the 50 states from 1988–89 through 2000–01 are shown in Table 2.2. In summary, only 2 of the 50 states—New Jersey and Wisconsin—appear to have achieved the national education goal of a graduation rate of 90 percent as of the turn of the century. As of 2000–01, just 15 states (Wisconsin, New Jersey, Iowa, Minnesota, North Dakota, Utah, Pennsylvania, Nebraska, Maryland, Virginia, Montana, Connecticut, Massachusetts, Vermont, and Idaho) had graduation rates of 80 percent or more. On the other end of the graduation spectrum, there were 13 states with graduation rates of 70 percent or less (Delaware, New Mexico, Maine, Oregon, North Carolina, Louisiana, Georgia, Arizona, Alabama, Florida, Tennessee, South Carolina, and Mississippi). As of 1990–91, only five states (Louisiana, Mississippi, South Carolina, Alabama, and Florida) had graduation rates of 70 percent or less. So in the last decade the number of states with graduation rates of 70 percent or less has more then doubled (from 5 to 13). The states with the largest declines in graduation rates since 1988–89—all with declines of 5 percent or more—were Hawaii, Maine, Arizona, Delaware, Tennessee, New Mexico, South Carolina, Alabama, South Dakota, Indiana, New York, North Carolina, Minnesota, Florida, and Illinois.

In sum, at the state level, decreases in graduation rates are more apparent than increases between 1988–89 and 2000–01. Over this interval there were just 5 states that consistently showed graduation rates of 85 percent or better (Wisconsin, New Jersey, Iowa, Minnesota, and North Dakota). On the other end of the graduation rate spectrum, by 2000–01 there were 9 states with graduation rates of less than 70 percent (North Carolina, Louisiana, Georgia, Arizona, Alabama, Florida, Tennessee, South Carolina, and Mississippi). Among these states, Arizona posted the largest decline in graduation rate, falling from 75 percent in 1988–89 to 65 percent in 2000–01. The other states showing large declines in graduation rate over the same interval were Tennessee (71 percent to 63 percent), Alabama (72 percent to 65 percent), South Carolina (70 percent to 62 percent) and Florida (68 percent to 63 percent).

Why have high school graduation rates been falling, in effect going in the opposite direction than intended in the 1994 Goals 2000 legislation? We address this question in the next section of this chapter. Before proceeding to that discussion we pause here to discuss possible weaknesses in our graduation rate calculations based on the numbers of graduates divided by Grade 8 enrollments four and a half years earlier.

Cohort progression analyses of the sort discussed so far do not take into account four ways students may disappear from their cohorts or classes other than being held back in grade or dropping out of school. First, they may die. Second, they may move out of the state or country. Third, they may move out of public schools into nonpublic schools. Fourth, they may be withdrawn from public schools to be schooled at home via what is known as "homeschooling." In subsequent portions of this section we discuss each of these possibilities.

Mortality

At least in theory, one possible cause for students disappearing from one grade one year and the next grade the next year is that they may die. However, statistics on mortality rates indicate that death of young people could have only a very small impact on results of cohort progression analyses. Death rates in the United States have been falling for some decades. As of 2000, the rate of death for the general population was 873 per 100,000, or 0.87 percent. For school-aged populations, however, death rates are much, much lower. For those aged 5–9 years in 2000, it was 16 per 100,000; for those aged 10–14 years, 21 per 100,000 and those aged 15–19, 68 per 100,000. Since the mortality rates for the school-aged population are so low—all less than one tenth of 1 percent— outright death, even over a 4-year period is clearly not a major source of leaks in the education pipeline. Moreover, given that death rates for school-aged children in the United States have dropped substantially over the last 20 years, this decreasing death rate for young people would, if anything, have been *decreasing* the leakage from the education pipeline over this interval.[2]

Migration

A second possible influence on results of cohort progression analyses is migration. For example, instead of progressing from Grade 9 to Grade 10, or on to graduation, young people might leave the United States (or in the case of state-level analyses, move from one state to another). Regarding this possibility we are fortunate to have a special tabulation by the U.S. Census Bureau. Census 2000 results show patterns of gross and net migration by age of the U.S. population by region and state. Since results for the total United States are simpler to explain, we start with the United States as a whole before dealing with migration at the state level.

According to census 2000 data, the total population 5 years and older in 2000 was 262 million. Of these, 7.5 million, or 2.9 percent, were immigrants

TABLE 2.2
State High School Graduation Rates, Grade 8 to Graduation Four Years Later, 1988–89 to 2000–01

	88–89	89–90	90–91	91–92	92–93	93–94	94–95	95–96	96–97	97–98	98–99	99–00	00–01
Data Source	2,16	3,17	4,18	5,19	6,20	7,21	8,22	9,23	10,24	11,23	12,25	13,26	14,26
Alabama	72%	69%	68%	68%	65%	63%	64%	62%	61%	63%	61%	63%	65%
Alaska	68%	69%	75%	76%	77%	76%	72%	71%	70%	71%	72%	69%	71%
Arizona	75%	76%	82%	78%	81%	75%	68%	64%	69%	68%	65%	68%	65%
Arkansas	76%	76%	75%	76%	77%	75%	72%	73%	70%	74%	74%	74%	73%
California	75%	77%	77%	79%	78%	76%	73%	73%	74%	74%	77%	78%	78%
Colorado	79%	79%	78%	81%	81%	80%	79%	77%	76%	75%	75%	76%	75%
Connecticut	81%	81%	85%	85%	85%	85%	82%	80%	80%	78%	79%	85%	80%
Delaware	79%	76%	76%	79%	80%	75%	72%	75%	74%	78%	76%	71%	70%
Florida	68%	68%	69%	73%	70%	69%	67%	66%	67%	66%	66%	65%	63%
Georgia	69%	71%	72%	71%	70%	68%	66%	64%	64%	60%	60%	63%	68%
Hawaii	90%	96%	85%	84%	83%	84%	83%	83%	76%	73%	71%	76%	73%
Idaho	77%	78%	80%	82%	82%	82%	82%	82%	82%	81%	80%	80%	80%
Illinois	83%	83%	84%	85%	85%	83%	82%	82%	82%	83%	83%	84%	78%
Indiana	80%	80%	81%	81%	80%	78%	77%	76%	76%	75%	76%	73%	73%
Iowa	89%	90%	89%	92%	92%	91%	90%	89%	89%	89%	88%	88%	87%
Kansas	83%	84%	84%	83%	84%	84%	82%	81%	80%	78%	78%	79%	79%
Kentucky	72%	74%	76%	76%	79%	83%	78%	75%	74%	73%	73%	74%	74%
Louisiana	68%	64%	61%	59%	64%	65%	67%	65%	65%	66%	65%	67%	68%
Maine	84%	88%	86%	86%	81%	75%	73%	74%	76%	73%	71%	71%	70%
Maryland	81%	81%	82%	85%	84%	84%	83%	83%	81%	81%	81%	81%	84%
Massachusetts	79%	85%	82%	85%	83%	83%	81%	81%	81%	81%	80%	81%	80%
Michigan	79%	79%	78%	79%	78%	78%	77%	76%	78%	79%	80%	76%	79%
Minnesota	91%	94%	94%	93%	93%	92%	91%	89%	81%	87%	88%	87%	86%
Mississippi	60%	66%	64%	65%	65%	65%	63%	61%	61%	62%	61%	61%	61%

(continued on next page)

TABLE 2.2 *(continued)*

Missouri	79%	80%	80%	80%	80%	80%	80%	79%	78%	78%	80%	79%	78%
Montana	84%	82%	84%	85%	87%	88%	88%	86%	85%	83%	83%	82%	81%
Nebraska	87%	87%	87%	89%	89%	89%	89%	87%	87%	87%	89%	88%	84%
Nevada	73%	79%	80%	74%	73%	72%	69%	68%	76%	73%	74%	73%	72%
New Hampshire	79%	80%	81%	82%	83%	82%	80%	78%	77%	77%	75%	76%	77%
New Jersey	85%	86%	88%	89%	91%	91%	90%	90%	90%	82%	83%	91%	90%
New Mexico	78%	75%	77%	76%	76%	75%	73%	73%	72%	66%	68%	70%	70%
New York	78%	79%	77%	78%	77%	77%	74%	74%	76%	74%	73%	73%	72%
North Carolina	74%	73%	73%	74%	73%	73%	72%	70%	69%	69%	70%	71%	69%
North Dakota	87%	87%	87%	88%	86%	88%	88%	90%	88%	88%	87%	87%	85%
Ohio	82%	81%	81%	80%	83%	84%	83%	78%	78%	79%	78%	78%	79%
Oklahoma	76%	79%	77%	78%	78%	78%	79%	77%	76%	76%	78%	77%	75%
Oregon	72%	74%	74%	76%	76%	75%	76%	70%	70%	70%	70%	72%	70%
Pennsylvania	85%	86%	86%	88%	88%	88%	87%	87%	86%	85%	85%	84%	84%
Rhode Island	77%	76%	78%	82%	81%	79%	79%	76%	77%	76%	76%	77%	78%
South Carolina	70%	64%	68%	65%	67%	67%	64%	64%	62%	62%	62%	62%	62%
South Dakota	84%	84%	84%	85%	88%	91%	88%	87%	88%	80%	75%	80%	78%
Tennessee	71%	71%	72%	74%	73%	69%	71%	71%	66%	62%	62%	62%	63%
Texas	70%	72%	74%	74%	68%	69%	69%	68%	70%	72%	72%	75%	75%
Utah	82%	79%	78%	81%	81%	81%	80%	79%	84%	83%	84%	85%	84%
Vermont	76%	85%	77%	78%	77%	80%	86%	83%	86%	86%	83%	83%	80%
Virginia	79%	79%	80%	80%	81%	79%	79%	78%	79%	80%	80%	81%	82%
Washington	79%	82%	78%	82%	81%	80%	80%	79%	77%	76%	76%	77%	76%
West Virginia	76%	77%	77%	77%	79%	79%	77%	79%	79%	79%	79%	77%	76%
Wisconsin	93%	96%	94%	94%	95%	93%	92%	91%	91%	89%	89%	89%	90%
Wyoming	76%	76%	79%	84%	86%	86%	80%	78%	79%	78%	77%	78%	73%

from abroad within the previous 5 years. Immigration rates clearly vary substantially by age, with the highest rates evident for the young adult age ranges of 20 to 24 years and 25 to 29 years (both more than 6 percent). For the elementary-secondary school age ranges of 5 to 9, 10 to 14, and 15 to 20 years, immigrants as percentages of the age group population were 2.8 percent, 2.5 percent, and 3.9 percent, respectively. The latter we suspect is slightly higher because it includes 18 and 19 year olds, many of whom were taking up residence in the United States to attend college.

So let us assume that the 2.5 percent rate is a reasonable estimate for immigration in the elementary-secondary school-aged population between 1995 and 2000. Presuming that the immigration for the age group was spread out evenly over the 1995–2000 period, this would imply an annual net immigration of 0.5 percent for elementary-secondary school-aged children during the last half of the 1990s. What this suggests is that immigration from abroad would have been contributing to *increases* rather than leakage in the education pipeline over this interval.

To illustrate, let us consider the high school class of 2001. When this cohort was in Grade 8, in the fall of the 1996–97 school year, it numbered 3.403 million. When this class graduated in 2000–01, graduates numbered only 2.532 million, for a graduation rate (from Grade 8 to graduation four and a half-years later) of 74.4 percent. Yet if the annual rate of immigration of high school aged young people into the United States over this period was 0.5 percent per year, this implies that the cohort ought to have increased in size by at least 2 percent over the interval. Even if only half of these immigrant children entered public high schools and proceeded to graduation, this would have increased the graduation rate over the interval by 1 percent or more. This suggests that the real "immigration-adjusted" graduation rate for children in Grade 8 in 1996–97 may have fallen by the end of the millennium not just to 74.4 percent but to something like 73 percent.

Dealing with migration in analyses at the level of the states is slightly more complex, because here we must deal not just with international but also domestic migration—that is with migration across states. Again, we are fortunate to have a special tabulation by the U.S. Census Bureau of results of the census 2000 showing patterns of gross and net migration by age both from abroad and across the states. These data are quite voluminous, but following the logic outlined above regarding foreign migration for school-age people, let us examine patterns of migration for individuals aged 10 to 14 as of census 2000.

Table 2.3 shows the numbers of children aged 10 to 14 as of April 2000, by state, plus the number who were immigrants to the state either domestically (that is, from within the United States from another state) or from abroad within the five years preceding the April 2000 census. The table also shows the 5-year rate in percent of total migration (that is, the net domestic and foreign migration of 10 to 14 year olds into each state).

TABLE 2.3

Census 2000 Population Aged 10 to 14, by States and Immigration Status

State	Population 10 to 14 Years	5-Year Net Domestic Migration	5-Year Foreign Migration	Total Migration (%)
Alabama	321,569	3,792	3,092	2.1%
Alaska	56,962	−2,599	1,219	−2.4%
Arizona	378,451	15,774	12,968	7.6%
Arkansas	192,450	5,419	2,212	4.0%
California	2,593,337	−85,497	92,896	0.3%
Colorado	311,835	10,942	9,243	6.5%
Connecticut	244,079	−1,640	8,387	2.8%
Delaware	55,703	673	1,056	3.1%
Florida	1,060,724	23,871	48,434	6.8%
Georgia	612,358	27,758	15,401	7.0%
Hawaii	83,316	−7,628	3,221	−5.3%
Idaho	104,807	4,146	1,487	5.4%
Illinois	906,678	−25,049	22,573	−0.3%
Indiana	444,320	7,054	4,014	2.5%
Iowa	210,825	1,378	2,627	1.9%
Kansas	203,606	43	3,406	1.7%
Kentucky	280,178	2,928	2,937	2.1%
Louisiana	351,072	−6,282	3,093	−0.9%
Maine	92,776	1,036	560	1.7%
Maryland	395,472	−174	11,643	2.9%
Massachusetts	431,562	−3,831	14,019	2.4%
Michigan	747,157	−93	10,843	1.4%
Minnesota	375,047	5,286	5,820	3.0%
Mississippi	219,488	2,310	1,349	1.7%
Missouri	413,358	6,779	4,807	2.8%
Montana	69,455	497	493	1.4%
Nebraska	128,215	492	2,010	2.0%
Nevada	139,656	14,904	5,466	14.6%
New Hampshire	93,080	3,295	1,219	4.8%
New Jersey	592,401	−8,291	21,862	2.3%
New Mexico	149,462	−4,013	3,479	−0.4%
New York	1,336,043	−62,955	49,471	−1.0%
North Carolina	556,658	22,617	12,462	6.3%
North Dakota	47,602	−1,892	570	−2.8%
Ohio	831,032	−2,964	8,181	0.6%
Oklahoma	253,488	2,895	3,309	2.4%
Oregon	241,529	5,114	5,248	4.3%
Pennsylvania	867,276	−1,528	11,416	1.1%
Rhode Island	71,811	−71	1,835	2.5%
South Carolina	293,460	8,558	3,540	4.1%
South Dakota	59,883	307	761	1.8%

(continued on next page)

TABLE 2.3 *(continued)*

State	Population 10 to 14 Years	5-Year Net Domestic Migration	5-Year Foreign Migration	Total Migration (%)
Tennessee	397,496	12,410	4,911	4.4%
Texas	1,642,973	12,717	53,430	4.0%
Utah	192,204	2,244	4,291	3.4%
Vermont	44,829	526	463	2.2%
Virginia	499,166	5,662	14,607	4.1%
Washington	435,598	3,140	13,278	3.8%
West Virginia	115,042	225	451	0.6%
Wisconsin	403,421	5,705	3,550	2.3%
Wyoming	38,847	−351	304	−0.1%

As shown in Table 2.3, for most states there was a small positive net in-migration of children aged 10 to 14 between 1995 and 2000. However there were seven states that had in-migrations of more than 5 percent (Nevada +14.6 percent, Arizona, +7.6 percent, Georgia +7.0 percent, Florida +6.8 percent, Colorado +6.5 percent, and North Carolina +6.3 percent). Also, one state showed a net out-migration of more than 5 percent, namely, Hawaii at −5.3 percent. The latter finding may help explain why in Table 2.2 Hawaii appears to have had a falling Grade 8 to graduation rate over the last decade. If school aged children are moving out of Hawaii at the rate of 5 percent between 1995 and 2000, the out-migration may help explain a sizable portion (i.e., 4 to 5 percent) of the 24 percent of Hawaii youngsters in the class of 2000 who did not graduate in the standard numbers of years. Conversely however, for the majority of states with net in-migration of school aged children, and especially for the seven states mentioned above with high rates of in-migration, migration cannot explain the low, and in many cases declining, graduation rates.

Private School Enrollments

A third possible cause of increasing leakage from the public education pipeline (specifically sharp increases in attrition between Grade 9 and 10 and falling graduation rates) is that some students might be leaving public schools to enroll in private schools. By private schools we refer to all nonpublic schools including Catholic and other religious schools as well as nonsectarian private schools. In 1999, for example there were about 8,000 Catholic schools, 13,000 other religious schools, and 6,000 nonsectarian schools in the United States.[3] One way of examining whether flows through the public school pipeline have been affected by patterns of enrollment in nonpublic schools is to look at enrollments in public versus private schools in Grade 9 through 12 over the last three decades. Total enrollments in Grades 9 through 12 have ebbed and flowed somewhat over the last three decades—from close to 15 million in 1970, ebbing to about 12.5 million in 1990 and increasing to almost 15 million in 2000. Enrollments in Grades 9 through 12 in public schools have very closely paralleled these totals. This is hardly surprising since over the last three decades 90 to 92 percent of all students in Grades 9 through 12 have been enrolled in public as opposed to private schools. In contrast, enrollments in private schools have been remarkably stable over the last 30 years, varying only between 1.15 and 1.40 million. As a percentage of total enrollments in Grades 9 through 12, private school enrollments were at a high of just over 10 percent in the early 1980s but since then have declined to just under 9 percent in the late 1990s. This means that leakage from the public education pipeline clearly has not been caused by sharp increases in private school enrollments.

Homeschooling

A fourth and final possible way in which students may leave the public school pipeline is that they leave public schools for homeschooling, that is, children being schooled at home instead of in either public or private schools. Unfortunately statistics on the homeschooling phenomenon are very hard to find. Rudner (1999) estimates that in 1998 there were between 700,000 and 1.2 million students enrolled in home schools. More recently a homeschooling advocacy organization, the Home School Legal Defense Association has reported that the annual rate of growth in numbers of students being schooled at home in the last decade has been 7 percent to 15 percent. The same source estimates that as of the 2001–02 school year there were between 1.7 and 2.2 million children in the United States being schooled at home.[4] Independent analysts, however, indicate that these estimates are somewhat inflated. Citing national survey data, Henke, Kaufman, and Broughman (2000) report that the number of homeschooled children in the United States was estimated at 345,000 in 1994 and 636,000 in 1996. Bielick, Chandler, and Broughman (2001) report that in spring 1999 an estimated 850,000 students nationwide were being homeschooled. They noted however that about 20 percent of homeschoolers were enrolled in public or private schools part-time. More recently, Bauman (2002) of the U.S. Census Bureau reports that the number of homeschooled children was well under 1 million in 1999 and the growth rate from 1996 to 1999 was unlikely to have exceeded 15 percent per year. Both Bauman (2002) and Bielick, Chandler, and Broughman (2001) report data indicating that the number of homeschooled children is relatively evenly divided across the school age span of 6 to 17 years old.

   Thus, overall it seems clear that less than 3 percent of children nationwide are being homeschooled (1 million divided by 42 million enrolled in public schools = 2.4 percent). There is some evidence that homeschooling has been increasing over the last decade, so as a liberal estimate let us suppose that homeschooling had been increasing by 150,000 per year during the late 1990s. Assuming that this number was evenly distributed across the 13 grade levels of kindergarten through Grade 12, this would imply an outflow from the public school system of only about 11.5 thousand per year per grade 150,000/13 = 11,538). Between 1999–2000 and 2000–01, attrition between Grades 9 and 10 was 448 thousand. This indicates that increases in homeschooling—even given the most liberal estimates—could account for only a very tiny share of the attrition between Grades 9 and 10 (11,500/448,000 = 2.6 percent).

In sum, it is clear that high school graduation rates from public schools have been falling, rates of attrition between Grades 9 and 10 increasing, and the Grade 9 bulge (that is, the number of students held back to repeat Grade 9) has been increasing over the last two decades. In this section we have reviewed evidence on possible alternative explanations of these trends, namely, mortality, migration, private school enrollments, and homeschooling. Overall, none of these possibilities can explain the broad trends in public school enrollments and graduates previously recounted.

CAUSES AND CONSEQUENCES

What has been causing these changes in the education pipeline in the United States over the last 30 years, and what are their likely consequences? As to causes the following questions occur: Why has attrition between Grades 9 and 10 increased in the 1980s and 1990s? Why have high school graduation rates from Grade 8 to graduation 4 years later decreased in the 1990s, from 78 percent in 1991–92 to 74 percent in 2000–01?

Before presenting a discussion of these questions we offer a disclaimer. Politicians, researchers, and ordinary citizens often try to make judgments about whether a certain change (such as a piece of federal legislation or an increase in atmospheric carbon dioxide) caused a particular development (such as an economic boom or global warming). But as with the two examples just offered, it is often difficult to make cause-and-effect inferences about complex systems, be they social or physical, with absolute certainty. Indeed, there is no way to prove cause and effect regarding historical matters with absolute certainty. Thus, we readily acknowledge that some of what we suggest in this section about probable causes and consequences of changes in the education pipeline of the United States over the last three decades is somewhat conjectural. Nonetheless, we argue, as did Leonard Ayres a century ago, that rates of student progress through elementary and secondary school are one of the best measures of the health of an educational system. While the news from our analyses of the education pipeline is not altogether bleak, evidence suggests that constrictions in the secondary school pipeline are likely leading to unfortunate negative consequences not just for young people but also for society as a whole.

Constriction of the High School Pipeline

One major change in the education pipeline over the last three decades is that progress through the high school years has become more constricted. By this we refer to the changes in increasing rates of attrition between Grades 9 and 10, an increasing bulge of students in Grade 9, and falling graduation rates. What has been causing such constriction in the high school pipeline?

As stated previously, proving cause and effect regarding historical developments is no easy matter, but what seems clear is that constriction in the high school education pipeline has been associated with three waves of education reform over the last three decades, namely, minimum competency testing, academic standards movement, and high stakes testing.

As shown in Figure 2.1 above, attrition between Grades 9 and 10 was low and relatively stable at around 3 percent during the first half of the 1970s. However during the late 1970s attrition between Grades 9 and 10 increased to around 5 percent. This coincided with the rise of the so-called minimum competency testing movement (Haney & Madaus, 1978). By the late 1980s, studies showed that there was a relationship between state implementation of minimum competency testing and dropout rates (Kreitzer, Madaus, & Haney, 1989). In a study of effects of grade retention, Shepard and Smith (1989) observed that "the percentages of overage students [that is, students older than the modal age for particular grades] began to climb . . . in the late 1970s in response to the minimum competency testing movement" (1989, p. 6).

As shown in Figure 2.1, attrition between Grades 9 and 10 was relatively stable in the early 1980s but began a steady increase, from less than 5 percent in 1983–84 to 8 percent in 1988–89. This happened following publication in 1983 of one of the last century's most publicized education reform reports, *A Nation at Risk*. In this report, the National Commission on Excellence in Education ominously warned, in a much quoted phrase, that "the educational foundations of our society are presently being eroded by a rising tide of mediocrity that threatens our very future as a Nation and a people" (p. 5). To remedy what it saw as declining academic standards, the commission called for increased academic course requirements in high school and for the use of standardized tests at "major transition points from one level of schooling to another" (p. 8).

In a follow-up study to *A Nation at Risk*, entitled *Meeting the Challenge*, the staff of the commission surveyed the 50 states and the District of Columbia on their recent efforts to improve education. Though acknowledging that many reform initiatives were underway prior to the release of *A Nation at Risk*, the follow-up report recounted that among the reform efforts nationwide, "action has been taken or proposals made" with regard to "student evaluation/testing" by 35 states, and with regard to "graduation requirements" by 44 states (p. 6). Thus it seems clear that what might be called the "academic standards movement" of the 1980s was a likely cause of the constriction in the high school pipeline during this period.

Referring again to Figure 2.1, it is apparent that the third period of increase in attrition between Grades 9 and 10 started about 1990 and lasted until the end of the decade. During this period attrition between Grades 9 and 10 increased nationally almost 50 percent from about 8 percent to nearly 12 percent. During the same interval, the Grade 9 to graduation rate fell from about 71 percent (already down from about 77 percent in 1971–72) to only 67 percent. This further constriction in the high school pipeline has been associated with the rise of standards-based reform and high-stakes testing. Others such as Shepard (2002) have combined the education reform movement of the 1990s with reforms immediately following the 1983 *Nation at Risk* report (in what she calls the "excellence movement"). Nonetheless, we think what happened in the 1990s was fundamentally different than what was going on earlier for one key reason, namely, that in the 1990s test results started being used to make decisions not just about students but also about schools.

There is no way in a short chapter such as this that we can describe all that has happened in terms of standards-based education reform in the United States over the last decade. Hence, let us simply describe what is meant by this term and what we see as negative consequences of this reform initiative. Standards-based reform refers to a process by which states have been encouraged to develop grade-level academic "standards," then to develop tests based on those standards, and finally to use results of those tests to make decisions about both students and schools based on test results. For example, it is often advocated that decisions about whether to promote students from one grade to the next or to award them high school diplomas should be made based on results of such standards-based tests. Similarly, it is often recommended that ratings of schools be based on such test results (indeed, such ratings of schools are now mandated in the NCLB law).

Though the idea of such a reform strategy is seductively simple, there are a number of limitations with it. First, even brief reflection ought to make clear that the aims of public education in the United States extend far beyond merely academic learning (much less merely raising scores on a small number of tests of academic subjects).

Second, to base high school graduation decisions on standardized test results in isolation, irrespective of other evidence about student performance in high school, is contrary to recognized professional standards regarding appropriate use of test results. (See for example the statement of American Educational Research Association, http://www.aera.net/about/policy/stakes.htm). A simple way of communicating this point is to note how college admissions test results are used. There is not a single college anywhere in the nation that accepts all applicants who score above a particular point on the SAT (say a combined score of 1,000) and rejects all applicants who score below that point. Colleges make admissions decisions flexibly using test scores, grades, and other information rather than making decisions mechanically based on test scores alone. It is worth adding also that decades of research on college admissions testing show that it is far more sound (more valid and with smaller adverse impact on minorities and females) to use test scores in this way (in what might be called a "sliding scale approach" so that students with high grades may be considered with lower test scores, but students with low grades need higher test scores to be considered for admission).

Third, documentation of widespread errors in test scoring, scaling, and reporting in the testing industry should make clear how unwise it is to make important decisions mechanically based on test scores in isolation (Henriques & Steinberg, 2001; Rhoades & Madaus, 2003). Indeed, in Minnesota, one large testing company was forced into a $10 million settlement after it was shown that hundreds of students had been wrongfully denied high school diplomas when the testing company used the wrong answer key in scoring exams.

Fourth, recent research has demonstrated conclusively that "low-tech" tests such as those being used in all the states (that is, paper-and-pencil tests in which students answer multiple-choice questions or write answers on paper longhand) seriously underestimate the skills of students used to writing with computers (Russell & Haney, 2000; Russell & Plati, 2001). A number of states are beginning to experiment with ways of administering tests via computer, but it will be a long time before twenty-first-century testing (e.g., allowing use of keyboards rather than just longhand composition and rapid feedback of results) becomes available in most schools. And in any case, the aims of education in our society extend way beyond what can be measured via computer, much less via paper and pencil.

Finally, however, it is clear that when the same fallible technology (and all bureaucratic accountability systems and high-stakes testing systems are such fallible technologies, Madaus, 1990) is used to make decisions about children and social institutions, the latter will always be in a better position to protect their interests than the former. For example, when schools are under intense pressure to increase test score averages, and are not given the resources or tools for doing so in an educationally sound manner, the easiest way to make test score averages appear to increase is to exclude "low-achieving" students from being tested, particularly in the grade at which high-stakes tests are administered. One way to exclude them, at least temporarily, is to hold them back to repeat the grade before the grade is tested. Another is to push students out of school altogether.

There is ample historical evidence of this phenomenon. Rapple (1994) found that in England during the latter part of the 19th century, when financial grants to schools were based on examination results, weaker pupils were often kept back in a grade or were told to stay home from school on the exam date. Similarly in Ireland during the mid-20th century, when a primary school exit exam was used and schools' reputations were strongly influenced by student pass rates, teachers would flunk students at higher rates in the grades before the grade in which the high-stakes exam was administered (Madaus & Greaney, 1985).

So as the stakes of test results for schools in the United States increased during the 1990s, it is not surprising, though regrettable, that such practices of student exclusion have reappeared but often in ways so that excluded students are not counted as dropouts. As dismaying as it may be to believe, there is now evidence of such practices from three different states (Texas, Alabama, and New York).

In Texas, it is now clear that some school officials have been actively pushing students out of school, but using contrivances so that such students are not officially counted as dropouts (see Bainbridge, 2003, for example, or the sad story of Crystal Gonzalez, Associated Press, 2003, or even more recently, the exposé of fraud in reporting on dropouts in the Houston Public Schools broadcast on *60 Minutes II,* January 6, 2004).[5]

From Alabama comes the troubling story of Steve Orel and the "Birmingham 500." Orel was a teacher in an adult education program in Birmingham, Alabama, in the spring of 2000 when he discovered that many "low-achieving" students (that is, students who had scored low on the Stanford Achievement Test, 9th Edition or SAT-9) had been administratively dismissed from the Birmingham Public Schools, ostensibly because of "lack of interest." Upon investigation, Orel learned that a total of 522 students had been pushed out of school in this manner in an effort to make school test results look better. Six Birmingham high schools had been placed on "academic alert status" and were thereby threatened with takeover by the state if SAT-9 score averages did not improve (Orel, 2003). Because of his efforts to bring the "push-out" policy to public attention and to end it, Orel was fired from his public school teaching job, but with support from a local charity went on to help organize an adult education program for the students pushed out of Birmingham public high schools.

And from New York, a recent report from Advocates for Children (Gotbaum, 2002) documents the fact that 10s of thousands of students are being "discharged" from New York City high schools but in ways so that they are not counted as dropouts. According to the report, "school officials are encouraging students to leave regular high school programs even though they are of school age or have a right to receive appropriate literacy support, and educational services through the public school system" (Gotbaum, 2002, p. 2). In

2001, according to Gotbaum, 31 New York City high schools "discharged" more students than they graduated. The number of students discharged was more than triple the number officially counted as dropouts. The real number of dropouts may be masked, according to the report, by counting discharged students as transferring to GED preparation programs. In such cases students were not counted as dropouts.

CONCLUSION

Our analyses of the enrollment data concerning the U.S. public school pipeline over the last 30 years have been based on a simple proposition—that in the absence of reliable data on dropouts and rates of student retention in grade, one reasonable way of studying what has been happening to flows of students through public schools in the United States is to analyze annual enrollments by grade, both nationally and for all 50 states. Most of our analyses focused on the simple question of how student enrollment in one grade in one year compares with enrollment in the previous grade the previous year. When considering high school graduation rates we also examined numbers of regular high school graduates in particular years compared with numbers enrolled in Grade 8 four and a half years previously. Such cohort progression rates, especially when considered over longer periods of time, may be affected not just by rates at which students are promoted or not promoted from grade to grade but also by other factors. Hence we digressed to discuss how mortality, migration, private school enrollments, and homeschooling might affect cohort progression rates. In sum, what we found was that these factors do not affect rates much at the national level but that migration may affect rates somewhat for a few states.

The main substantive findings from our analyses of state and national grade enrollment and graduation data suggest that over the last 30 years the public high school education pipeline in the United States has been constricted in three respects. The rate at which students disappear between Grade 10 one year and Grade 9 the previous year has *tripled* over the last 30 years from less than 4 percent to nearly 12 percent. States with the worst attrition between Grade 9 in 1999–2000 and Grade 10 in 2000–01 (as listed in Table 2.1) are Florida, South Carolina, Georgia, Texas, Nevada, North Carolina, Louisiana, Hawaii (perhaps in part due to out-migration of school-age children), Alabama, Mississippi, New York, and Tennessee—all with attrition rates of about 14 percent or more.

Further evidence of constriction in the high school pipeline is that there has been an increasing bulge of students in Grade 9. Nationally, during the 1970s there were only about 4 percent more students in Grade 9 than in Grade 8 the previous year. However by the late 1990s there were more than

12 percent more students nationally in Grade 9 than in Grade 8 the previous year. Bulges in Grade 9 enrollments in 2000–01, as compared with Grade 8 enrollments the previous year were particularly severe in Florida (32 percent), South Carolina (24 percent), Nevada (24 percent, though in this instance, this finding may be partially due to in-migration of school-age children), New York (21 percent), Hawaii (21 percent), Kentucky (20 percent) and Texas (20 percent).

This combination of an increasing bulge of students in Grade 9 relative to Grade 8 the previous year is clear evidence that there has been a sharp increase nationally over the last 20 years in the percentage of students who are being held back to repeat Grade 9. Since being flunked to repeat a grade is a strong predictor of students dropping out of school prior to graduation, it is not surprising that high school graduation rates have been falling nationally, especially in the last 10 years or so. As of 2000–01, the national graduation rate stood at about 75 percent if calculated on the basis of numbers of graduates compared with enrollments in Grade 8 four and a half years earlier, and at only about 67 percent if calculated on the basis of numbers of graduates compared with enrollments in Grade 9 three and a half years earlier. Either result is, of course, appallingly short of the national education goal of a graduation rate of 90 percent.

We also discussed some of the apparent causes and consequences of these changes in the education pipeline in the United States over the last 30 years. Regarding the constriction in the high school pipeline, we noted that increases in attrition between Grades 9 and 10 have been associated with the minimum competency testing movement in the 1970s, the academic standards movement in the 1980s, and so-called standards-based reform and high-stakes testing in the 1990s.

In closing, we should acknowledge that in recent years there has been considerable debate about the merits of high-stakes testing. We do not try to review that debate here (though our position on the matter should by now be clear). Rather we emphasize that whatever has been causing the constriction in the high school pipeline—the increasing rate at which students are being flunked to repeat Grade 9 and the falling rate at which students are graduating from high school—this development should be viewed as a real national emergency. When students are squeezed out of the high school pipeline and do not even graduate from high school, this has dire consequences not just for these young people but for society as a whole. The reason we say this is that recent research shows that there is an increasingly strong link between people's failing to graduate from high school and their ending up in prison.

A recent report from the Bureau of Justice Statistics reports, for example, that "About 41% of inmates in the nation's State and Federal prisons and local jails in 1997 and 31% of probationers had not completed high school or its equivalent. In comparison, 18% of the general population age 18 or older had not finished the 12th grade" (Harlow, 2003, p. 1). In other words, failure to graduate from high school (or its equivalent) appears to double the likelihood of being imprisoned. Moreover, if we discount high school equivalency degree recipients[6] and consider only those who actually graduate from high school, 68 percent of state prison inmates (and 59 percent federal and 62 percent of local prisoners) did not graduate from high school (Harlow, 2003, p. 1). This suggests that failure to graduate from high school is associated with a *tripling* of likelihood of being imprisoned. Moreover, less educated inmates are more likely than the more educated to be recidivists (Harlow, 2003, p. 10).

In short, failure to graduate from high school dramatically increases the odds that young people will end up in prison at least once and perhaps even more than once. Hence in closing we simply observe that it is far less costly to keep young people in schools than in prisons—and not incidentally, much better for them.

THREE

Reform as Redefining the Spaces of Schools

An Examination of Detracking by Choice

Susan Yonezawa and Amy Stuart Wells

OVER THE PAST several decades, researchers, educators, and policy makers have struggled to make American schools places of equity and to close the achievement gap between African American, Latino, and low-income students and white, Asian, and middle-income students. As part of this larger struggle, we find ourselves continually frustrated by well-meaning efforts to produce greater equity in schools, which nevertheless fail miserably because they do not seek to fundamentally redefine power relations in America's schooling. Through our research, we have come to believe that effective educational reforms must radically redefine the spaces within schools—spaces that sort and separate students—and thus redefine the students who fill them in order for constitutive, equity-minded changes to occur.

In this chapter, we use a research study on detracking by choice to illustrate how equity-based reforms must go beyond relying on students and parents' individual agency to facilitate change. We assert that examining detracking by choice is helpful when studying issues of spatial power relations within schools because it is a meso (or middle) level reform that purports to raise academic achievement standards for low-income and minority students without altering the prevailing hierachies within schools. Choice-based detracking asks students to move up the educational hierarchy yet ignores the fact that the spaces low- and middle-track students occupy in tracked educational structures and cultures contain within them powerful barriers and norms that make moving up quite difficult.

In the sections that follow, we describe and define tracking and detracking. Then we describe our research study on schools undergoing detracking and the methods we used to collect and analyze data across the sites we studied. Finally, we present our findings that schools that detracked by choice failed to increase low-income and minority student enrollment in honors courses because the tracked spaces that remained bore powerful norms, beliefs, barriers, and networks that made remaining in lower tracked classes appealing to formerly low- and middle-tracked students.

EXAMINING ONE REFORM MOVEMENT IN DETAIL: DETRACKING AS A MESO-LEVEL REFORM

For the past three decades, researchers have argued that tracking practices reproduce the social order by providing high-income, white, and Asian students greater access to high-status courses and learning opportunities and low-income, Latino, and African American students spaces in low-level classes. (See Oakes, 1985; Oakes, Gamoran & Page, 1992; Gamoran, 1992; Dornbusch, 1994; Oakes & Guiton, 1995.) Largely because of this critique of tracking, educators around the country have embraced various attempts to detrack their schools. Detracking in the research literature is often defined as the process of replacing tracked course programs with mixed-ability classrooms sometimes known as "heterogeneous" classrooms (Oakes, Wells & Associates, 1997a; Wheelock, 1992).

What Is Detracking?

Detracking is a reform concept rather than a prescribed set of practices (Oakes, 1996). The central assumption of detracking reform is that equal learning opportunities for low-achieving students should be provided without sorting and separating them from high-achieving students (Wheelock, 1992). The forces that buttress tracking often must be addressed in ways befitting each school-community's unique context (Wells & Serna, 1996). Moreover, detracking requires rethinking of traditional conceptions of intelligence and merit, particularly as related to race and class (Oakes, et al., 1997a; Oakes, Wells, Datnow, & Jones, 1997b).

In some cases, schools engaged in detracking increase access to curriculum for all students, maintain higher expectations for previously low-track students, and improve the quality of student work in their classrooms (Oakes, et al., 1997a; Wheelock, 1992). Teachers engaged in detracking reflect more on their practice and feel professionally efficacious (Cone, 1990; Ross, McKeiver, & Hogaboam-Gray, 1997). The political nature of detracking, however, makes it difficult to modify despite bold efforts by reformers (Oakes, et al., 1997b; Wells & Serna, 1996).

Our Study

From fall 1992 to spring 1995, our research team[1] studied 10 racially and socioeconomically mixed secondary schools voluntarily engaged in detracking. We discovered that these schools often defined part of their detracking reform as eliminating remedial courses and encouraging previously low-tracked students to "choose" more challenging courses. Although we do not know how extensive this detracking-by-choice model is nationally, we found this model occurred in some form in all 10 of the schools that we studied. This is notable given the geographic and demographic range of these 10 schools. Inevitably, detracking by choice placed the burden of the reform on students rather than tackle the structures and cultural norms supporting ability grouping. Three themes—*institutional barriers, tracked aspirations,* and *choosing respect*—emerged from the voices of students and their advocates to explain why previously low-tracked students refused to move upward when barriers to higher tracked courses had supposedly been eliminated.

METHODS

Detracking by choice at all 10 schools in our study generally meant opening up student access to high-track courses or programs by reducing course prerequisites or recommendation requirements. At the 6 senior highs, which we discuss in this chapter, students could choose honors courses within a few academic departments or self-select courses across the curriculum. Educators assumed low-track students would choose high-track courses if given the opportunity.

The 10 schools we studied were chosen from a group of 200 volunteer schools, for their national geographic distribution, diversity of race, and socioeconomic student body, and stated commitment to detracking. The schools ranged in student populations from over 3,000 to less than 500. They enrolled very different mixes of Latino, white, African American, Asian American, and Pacific Islander students, and all 10 had socioeconomically mixed student populations.

Two to four members of our research team conducted three data collection trips to each school over a two-year period. We conducted a total of 75 classroom and meeting observations and 423 semistructured interviews with school administrators, teachers, counselors, local and state-level policy makers, parents, students, and community members. Additionally, more than 100 documents from the school sites and local communities were collected. All of the interview, observation, and document data were coded and analyzed.[2]

RESULTS

The following sections discuss the three themes—institutional barriers, tracked aspirations, and choosing respect.

Theme One: Institutional Barriers

Students bumped up against several types of institutional barriers to course choice. Information was distributed unevenly from educators to all students. Educators responded selectively to students' requests for higher placements. Students encountered hidden prerequisites when exercising their "options."

Uneven Information. For the past two decades, sociologists have examined how race and class segregation in people's workplaces, schools, and neighborhoods shape the kinds of relationships or networks they form and the type of information they accrue (Granovetter, 1973, 1983; Huckfeldt, 1983; Lin, 1990; Weatherford, 1982). Tracking practices, which sort and separate students along race and class lines, also impact the form and content of networks that students enjoy with their peers and educators (Hallinan & Sorenson, 1985; Stanton-Salazar & Dornbusch, 1995; Stanton-Salazar, 1997). Therefore, students' positions in their community and schools' track hierarchy often shape the information they do (and do not) receive about course options. We found this to be true in schools detracking via choice.

For example, educators at Midwestern Plainview High School relied heavily on their neighborhood networks to inform students of the open access policy for advanced placement (AP) classes. Plainview students could learn about the open access policies from "their brothers or sisters," "through the neighborhood," or at parent "coffees" held by the counseling office. This system of local networks worked well for students and families who lived in the white areas of the district. But it worked less well for the school's black students, half of whom lived in an isolated community within the district, and half of whom were bussed in from the central city.

At West Coast Central High School, where a majority of the students are low income and Latino, most counselors seemed nonchalant about informing their students that they could petition for honors classes. One Central teacher commented that "there is supposed to be a process to get into honors classes. . . . But we've been kind of lax on that." At Union High, a school serving many low-income black and white students in a midsized city in the Southeast, educators also relied on "word of mouth" to acquaint students with their honors petition process.

Selective Flexibility. Past research on tracking shows that schools often selectively alter their course offerings to match the racial and socioeconomic characteristics of their students (Garet & DeLany, 1988; Oakes & Guiton, 1995). While structural aspects of schools such as staff capability and resources influence such decisions, educators' norms and expectations about the abilities of their student population (signaled by race and social class) also sway decisions about course creation.

In the schools we studied, the schools and educators engaged in a kind of selective flexibility—educators readily acquiesced to the course-placement requests of mostly white, Asian, and upper-income, high-track, high-achieving students, while, low-track, low-achieving students, many of whom were Latino, African American, and low income, bumped up against more resistance.

At Central High School, for example, where only 10 to 12 percent of its 60 percent Latino student body attend four-year colleges and high-status students are rare, teachers bent over backward to accommodate requests made by whiter, affluent honors students. For instance, one Central teacher said she willingly taught an extra zero period of honors French to accommodate some high-track students.

> They are my prize kids. They're my kids that take the honors, the honors history, the honors math, and honors is the highest. . . . They take honors everything. And they couldn't fit the extra French in, so they asked me to take them zero period. That's how bright they are. . . . They don't take cooking and sewing and that kind of thing. Their elective is French. I don't want to lose those kids, and I can't tell them no. . . . How could I tell a kid you're so bright, you're motivated, and I can't be flexible enough to help you? I mean, that's insane.

Meanwhile, low-income, low-track Central students experienced choice-based detracking differently. These students, many of whom were Latino, said counselors and teachers denied or delayed their requests to move into higher level courses. One teenager repeatedly approached his counselor for an advanced math course but was never seen and, consequently, never transferred out of Central's lowest math level. Another low-track Central student complained, "It seems like they put you in a class where they feel it's right. They don't listen to your opinion on what classes you want to be in."

Hidden Prerequisites. Low- and middle-track students also confronted hidden prerequisites when exercising course "choice." For example, at the Midwest's highly stratified, Plainview High School, where maintaining a separate elite track is seen by administrators as the best way to stem white flight, "choosing" to be honors was never as easy as educators reported (Wells & Serna, 1996). The school had an open-door policy for honors; however, many students were told that they needed another course or a higher grade before they could use the policy. For instance, an honors math teacher at Plainview initially insisted that all students were welcome to take her class but later qualified the "open access" as contingent on students successfully completing prerequisites that began in junior high:

TEACHER: It's an open class, anybody can be in it. We don't exclude anybody. Anybody who wants to try it, no matter what, they're allowed to do it.

INTERVIEWER: Even if they haven't had . . .

TEACHER: Well, they have to have had Algebra I and Geometry.

INTERVIEWER: Algebra I and Geometry, okay. So beyond that . . .

TEACHER: And so, beyond that, it's strictly . . . I mean, we could recommend that we don't think their skill level is appropriate.

At rural Green Valley High School, where a high number of its students are not proficient in English, the assistant principal in charge of counseling noted that all juniors and seniors were welcome to take AP English. But, he added, before they sign up, they had to go through the English department's screening process to ensure they "know what they're getting into." Although access was technically open, students who desired honors placements had to jump through some hoops: "It is open access, but, you know, there *is* a screening process," said the assistant principal.

Theme Two: Tracked Aspirations

The heights to which students aspire help determine what options students exercise. Yet the factors that shape students' aspirations are multifaceted, including race (Ogbu, 1978; MacLeod, 1987; Hauser & Anderson, 1991), gender (Crowley & Shapiro, 1982; Marini, 1984), parental influence (Stage & Hossler, 1988), peer groups (Hallinan & Williams, 1989), and school structures and cultures (Fine, 1991; Lightfoot, 1983; Metz, 1978; Willis, 1977).

Academic tracks are important structural and cultural modifiers of most secondary schools. Tracks sort and separate students. But they also create within them high-track and low-track cultures that emphasize independence and self-expression on the one hand and control and conformity on the other (Oakes, 1985; Oakes, Gamoran, & Page, 1992). As such, track structures and the places of identity they create within schools help shape students' aspirations and actions and influence whether or not students take advantage of choice-based placement policies.

The Leveled. Social reproduction theorists who examine student agency and societal structures and their interactions with aspirations have argued that "leveled aspirations" are an important aspect of how lower-class students end up disenfranchised from the educational system. Drawing on Bourdieu's notion of students' "habitus,"[3] MacLeod (1987) demonstrates how working-class and poor boys from housing projects became disillusioned with the "American Dream" when the young men's experiences and meaning making resisted and actively rejected the education system's "meritocratic" ideology, which told them that if they worked hard, they would get ahead. Others bought into the promise of social mobility through educational achievement and eventually came to blame themselves for not "making it."

In the schools we studied, we encountered low- and middle-track students whose habitus helped them assess the identity of particular classes and steered them away from higher track classes. At Grant High, for example, where the elite top-tier classes had grown increasingly high status and competitive each year, students from the vocational track—most of whom were African American—were often intimidated by the "aura" of honors courses. These students had little specific information about these courses; still, they assumed that high-track classes were places where they did not belong. They insisted that they were "not good at" honors, despite the fact that they had never taken an honors course and knew few students who did.

While some low-track students operated from leveled aspirations, others held more hope. These students wavered between wanting to try more challenging courses and feeling unsure they would succeed. For instance, at Plainview High, where AP courses abound, a low-track African American freshman expressed his ambivalence about attempting an honors course:

> I think about it once in awhile, but I'm not sure yet. It depends. I'm half and half. One part of my body says go for it, the other part says don't go for it. So I try and listen to the other half of it. Sometimes I try not to listen to the other half, sometimes I go for a challenging thing.

Leaving the low track was not easy for many of these students. Many had experienced school from the bottom of the tracked hierarchy for so long that they had come to identify themselves as "low track" or "slow." When left to their own devices, they chose familiar spaces with familiar faces, resegregating themselves along the same lines and labels.

The Entitled. In drawing on the work of Pierre Bourdieu, Harrison (1993) writes that struggles around domination and oppression are not simply about inequitable distribution of material goods but also involve "the arbitrary principles of social classification." One of the most powerful such social classifications is the entitlement of those with privilege and status. Those with greater economic or cultural capital legitimize their higher status in society by claiming it as their entitlement (Harrison, 1993). The educational system contributes to this legitimization process by labeling certain students as "gifted and talented" or "advanced" at a very young age (Barr & Dreeben, 1983; Gamoran, 1986; Good & Brophy, 1987; Slavin, 1987). The seemingly meritocratic way in which students "earn" these titles and are placed accordingly into their "proper" spaces within the educational system is an important aspect of the social consecration of the intergenerational transmission of privilege. Students who are labeled gifted in elementary school develop a habitus of entitlement. They, unlike the students with leveled aspirations, see high-track classes as their destiny.

In the six high schools we studied, some students saw their honors placement as the result of a natural progression: "Last year I had honors English, so I just took honors English again, and I had honors Algebra, so I'm taking honors Geometry," said one entitled student. Many others could not recall how they had become honors students. As one Plainview High 12th grader commented, honors classes were "just kind of programmed in me."

Yet, despite these students' remarks, the high-track, high-achieving students in the schools we studied did not sit idly by and allow themselves to be passed through the educational system. Rather, these students and their parents operated from their powerful places in the local hierarchy to reinforce existing educational inequities and garner the best teachers and courses. Their actions helped ensure that detracking by choice would assist high-track students in protecting places in elite classes more than it helped low-track students gain access to these same courses. In this way, our findings cohere with past research on the activities of middle- and upper-class parents (Lareau, 1989; David, 1993; Oakes & Guiton, 1995; Useem, 1992).

We found a particularly vivid example of entitled students at Liberty High School, where more than 85 percent of the school's graduates went on to two- and four-year colleges, and academic credentials signaled status in the local community. At this school, high-track students supported the choice-oriented self-scheduling process because it allowed them to select challenging courses taught by the school's most demanding teachers. Self-scheduling, they argued, lessened the risk that they would end up in classes with students who "just didn't want to learn," as one high-track student explained:

> I know that I am getting a good education because I picked the hard teachers. A lot of students just go for the easy teachers. . . . They might [not] get the best education, but at least they might go to class and not mess anybody else up.

Entitled Liberty students and parents also supported freedom of choice policies because these policies allowed the families to actively manipulate the placement process and secure for themselves the best teachers and placements. This would occur most prominently at the school's "tennis shoe registration" each summer where students raced competitively around the school gymnasium to gather enrollment passes, which were distributed by teachers on a first-come, first-served basis. At tennis shoe registration, entitled students and their parents volunteered to dole out enrollment cards to the student body and would often be caught by educators "pulling cards for their friends," allowing them to enroll ahead of other students.

Theme Three: Choosing Respect

This final section reveals why low-income, African American, and Latino students resisted higher track classes, even when they felt capable enough to compete. In some cases, students rejected high-track classes because they believed—or knew from experience—that their contributions in these classes would not be valued. In other cases, students resisted higher placements because they believed that taking such courses would require them to abandon their friends and buy into the existing hierarchy. A smaller number of students consciously critiqued the ideology of privilege in high-track classes. All sought places where they felt respected and valued by their teachers and fellow students and avoided places where they felt disrespected.

Not Wanting to Be with People Who Don't Respect You. Some students of color also remained in lower levels because the way honors teachers taught and how honors students related (or refused to relate) to them told them that their knowledge and presence were not valued in advanced classrooms. Although not every African American or Latino student in advanced or honors classes felt this, way a substantial number of those we spoke to brought up this dilemma that they experienced a sense of isolation in such spaces. This supports Ladson-Billings' (1994) argument that it is not so much what we teach but "the way we teach" culturally diverse students that matters.

A common experience of many of these students was that of unwelcome salience in the honors classrooms. As a minority in majority white classrooms, these students felt compelled to justify their presence in their schools' high-track classes.

> I feel that I have to defend every black person that's in there. Like the token person. So, in general, I feel like I have to prove something extra to the white kids that are in there. Even if I know a piece of literature well, I feel like I have to study it over and over.

This student recalled how he felt in his honors math class:

> I was swearing because I was like, "Oh man, I don't even belong in here," because it was like 30 Caucasian kids and one African student. I felt like I

had to prove myself and prove that blacks aren't stupid. [I felt like] if I were to get a problem wrong and raise my hand, they would look at me and say, "Ah, that black." I was always under pressure, so . . . I transferred to just [the] advanced level.

These formerly low-track students of color carried into honors classes the double burden of having to defend both their capability and the capability of their race. This subtle form of discrimination was even more onerous as these classes were devoid of the race-specific support groups these students had enjoyed in lower-level classes.

Sometimes it made it hard when you needed to study and stuff. A lot of times I found myself studying on my own. Or if there was another black person in there, or two or three other [black] people in there, we could form a study group. But most of the time, if I didn't want to be around those [white] people. I just had to make it on my own.

Formerly low- and middle-track African American and Latino students entered high-track classrooms knowing that their appearance and accents often caused their teachers and classmates to question their presence. The sidelong glances and unkind whispers of the "entitled"—those individuals who have the luxury of never having their positionality questioned—constantly reminded these students of their perpetual "inability to fit in" (Ellis, 1993). Their experiences fit with Weber's (1978) description of the kind of ongoing social estimation that protects high-end status groups (e.g., upper-track classes) from those unable to reflect the "style of life"—the viewpoints and culture—that is the norm in elite circles.

Wanting to Be with People Who You Respect or "The Pull of the Peer Group." Students tend to form friendships within their assigned tracks, and this social separation, and the racial and socioeconomic segregation that often accompanies it, increases as students move from elementary to secondary school (Oakes, Gamoran, & Page, 1992; Hallinan & Williams, 1989; Hallinan & Sorenson, 1985). Thus track structures are believed to increase within-school social segregation (Braddock & Slavin, 1993; Cooper, 1996) and to impede some students' access to rich postsecondary information networks (Wells & Crain, 1994).

Yet students' tendency to make friends with peers of similar racial and socioeconomic backgrounds has also been shown to provide low-income students and students of color with a sense of belonging and identity (Datnow & Cooper, 1997; Eckert, 1989; Fordham, 1996; Mehan, Villanueva, Hubbard, & Lintz, 1996). How racially identifiable peer groups influence students' academic aspirations and achievement is unclear. Research has shown that these race- and class-specific peer cultures can sometimes oppose (Comer 1976;

Fordham, 1996; Ogbu, 1988) and other times support academic achievement (Datnow & Cooper, 1996; Mehan, et al., 1996). Our purpose here is not to enter into this debate per se but rather to suggest that tracks exist as spaces where identity formation and student achievement ideology meet.

We found some evidence that peer pressure against racial mixing made some black students apprehensive to enroll in majority-white honors courses for fear of being ostracized from their black cohort. Black students at some of the schools reported that their black peers used coercive name-calling (e.g., sellout or whitewashed) to deter other black students from developing social relationships with whites. At one school, for example, a black female honors student was labeled "a female version of Clarence Thomas" because of the white company she kept. A teacher at a different school spoke of several black students he knew who "knew they were capable of doing honors work and weren't doing it because they wouldn't want to deal with the grief they would take for leaving their peer groups." These data support Fordham's (1996) argument that blacks sometimes pressure each another to avoid "acting white" and hooks' (1992) discussion of the ways in which black women assert "false authenticity"[4] over one another.

More commonly, black and Latino students at the schools we studied shunned honors courses because they refused to give up supportive peer networks they had within the lower track. Those who decided to leave the lower tracks often felt isolated. For example, at Plainview High School, only 10 of the school's 350 African American students enrolled in any of the 18 AP classes offered. Black students reported that they felt uncomfortable in honors and AP courses where they were the "only black in the room." When counselors encouraged them to enroll in AP courses, they resisted: "I can't be in there. I'm the only black student in there," or "I feel weird in this class because I'm the only black student. None of my friends are there." African American students at Liberty High School voiced similar complaints: "At the beginning of the school year I was in AP chemistry, and that's like first-year college chemistry. I was the only black student in there, and I was uncomfortable," said one Liberty High honors student.

These students teach us that choosing a higher track placement involves more than a simple structural rearrangement of bodies. It requires that students from lower tracks be willing to abandon or suppress the peer group ideologies and identities that they have formed. Because of this, choice-based detracking places the burden of detracking on low-track black and Latino adolescents who might desire high-status courses but who desperately need the respect, admiration, and companionship of students who they respect and who respect them.

Wanting to Be Able to Respect Yourself. Another reason why some low-track students refused high-track courses was their belief that education should reflect their culture, knowledge, and lived experiences. These students critiqued the education they received and sought out "safe spaces" or "homeplaces," where they could explore their identities as racial minorities and strengthen their sense of self-worth, free from the racial domination they experienced in daily life (Hill-Collins, 1991; hooks, 1990).

These students engaged in "placemaking"—the forging of public spaces that shield their members from racist domination and allow critical consciousness and group solidarity to emerge—with educators and peers to turn low-track classrooms and programs targeting particular racial groups into places of resistance. Through their efforts, the students developed identities consistent with an ideology of resistance (Haymes, 1995; Fine, et al., 1997).

At Liberty High School, for example, critically conscious African American students frequently rejected honors courses, opting instead for courses in the African American Studies Department. This department was seen by many African American students as a safe haven where black students could freely express their views without fear of reprisals. Classes such as African American history or African American journalism furnished black students with a place where they could affirm one another.

Because Liberty allowed students to take up to four years of African American literature to satisfy their English and history graduation requirements, black students who felt as though their history and culture were ignored in honors and AP courses could avoid taking these high-status classes. Thus, even after Liberty educators loosened the prerequisites to the honors track, few low- and middle-track black students transferred. For many black students at Liberty, the self-respect they gained by taking African American Studies classes was far more valuable than the weighted grades or college credit of honors or AP classes. As one African American student explained, the difference between taking classes in the African American Studies Department versus other departments was "a sense of self respect."

Black students at Grant told us as well that high-track credentials were a poor exchange for the dignity and respect they felt in majority black classes. For example, one African American girl stated quite passionately that she preferred remaining in Grant's segregated classrooms: "I like the fact that it's segregated. I don't really want to sit next to no white person or in back of a white person or in front of a white person and learn. I want to learn with my own people and with my own teachers." Another Grant student remarked that she elected to remain in majority black classrooms because honors classes focused only on "white history, white this, white that. Everything is European." Grant's assistant principal stated that many low-tracked students, particularly African Americans, rejected honors courses because they believed that the curriculum in these classes did not address where they were "coming from."

At Green Valley High school, Latino students gathered in the school's Mexican American history class where they felt supported by Mr. Rodriguez, the course's Latino teacher, and by their Latino peers. Students signed up for this elective class even though it did not satisfy state college entry requirements, because they wanted, as one Latina student explained, "to learn a little bit more about [their] background, [their] ancestors." Students also found themselves drawn to a teacher who they believed wanted to teach them and curriculum that valued their home lives and cultures. In some cases, Latino students opted out of college-prep electives such as foreign language to make room in their schedules for the Mexican American History class.

The dilemma many minority students found themselves in when forced to choose between high-track courses and these safe spaces often resulted in these students choosing to remain in the places in which they felt comfortable and powerful. For these students, developing strong political ideologies that would help them resist the racist domination they encountered on a daily basis was more important than college credit or extra GPA points.

Detracking by Choice as an Inequitable, Agency-Laden Reform

Our findings in this study of detracking by choice fundamentally critique policies that aim to move students out of low-track classes and into high-track ones, without altering the prevailing hierarchies in schools. Detracking by choice, like the standards movement and high-stakes testing, cannot improve students' educational achievement by simply opening up the doors to advanced placement and honors courses as a way to provide students greater access to learning opportunities. Eliminating remedial course offerings and prerequisites to honors and advanced placement classes are helpful. But they are, by themselves, insufficient to moving students into these courses and, more importantly, making them successful as they tackle more difficult work.

This is because, as we have seen in the discussion of detracking by choice as a case in point, students who have been disadvantaged by the current educational system need far more than reformers have been providing them to be successful. They need far more than teachers who teach "to the standards." They need far more than simply "motivation" to pass a high-stakes test or the occasional afterschool or summer bridge program for additional instructional time. They even need far more than educators' well-intentioned invitations into more rigorous coursework. These students need real, systemic efforts to alter significantly the hierarchical educational system they exist within to provide them ongoing, deep academic and social supports that recognize and value the knowledge they bring with them to school.

Educational Reforms' Final Exam:
Does It Redefine the "Spaces" of Schooling?

Fundamental to our analysis of educational reforms is the extent to which a given reform attempts to reconceptualize the political and hierarchical spaces that exist within schools. Reforms that tack on new requirements, mandates, benchmarks, and goals without altering the prevailing hierarchies within schools, we believe, will do little to help make students more successful in the long run. We believe this because, to us, schools are continually constructed and operate in large measure by the routines and habits that those within and outside them have come to understand as normal, taken-for-granted under-standings of people's identities, worth, and social relations. In order for reforms to experience success with traditionally unsuccessful students, we must work to disrupt these politically and socially significant hierarchical spaces in schools—spaces to which we have assigned meanings and which constantly create and are created by individuals' identities (Haymes, 1995; Keith & Pile, 1993; Rury, 1997).

Our analysis of school reform has a parallel analysis among urban theo-rists who assert that the racial and economic isolation of urban centers and, consequently, urban schools, are the result of the social and political construc-tion of cities as spatially organized arenas of urban life (Anyon, 1997; Gottdi-ener, 1985; Rury, 1997). Black, Latino, and low-income urban centers are cre-ated through the complex interplay of reduced opportunities, political strategizing by power elites, and cultural mythologies of nonwhite spaces as disordered, abnormal, or dangerous. Altering the cycle of poverty, violence, and despair in urban centers cannot be achieved by patchwork reforms that fail to address the ways in which people's identities and social relationships within urban centers intersect with individuals and institutions outside to shape identity and real opportunities. Similarly, low achievement in schools serving racial minorities and poor children is sustained in a similar manner.

Our belief is supported by a small but growing body of research that links spatial arrangements and the creation of identity and opportunity within schools. This research has its roots in prior work on interracial relations within schools (see Hawley & Jackson, 1995) and feminist and social theory. It argues that students need alternative spaces within schools where they can challenge the identities thrust upon them by larger society (Gutierrez, Rymes, & Lar-son, 1995; hooks, 1990). Fine, Weis, and Powell (1997), for example, docu-ment one school's efforts to create "desegregated spaces," places in school where students from different backgrounds can come together and actively resist and critique the cultural and structural forces that seek to identify and to divide them along multiple lines.

We believe that the spatial arrangements of low-achieving schools help shape the relationships and identities of students, parents, and educators. Some of this grows out of the structural aspects of tracking: the segregated nature of tracking hierarchies prevents students from building supportive and informative relationships with diverse groups (Stanton-Salazar, 1996; Yonezawa, 1997). But cultural forces buttressed by tracking and by ideologies surrounding poverty and racial minorities are also important considerations.

Society has constructed "merit" and "ability" to value the experiences and knowledge of some students over others (Oakes, Wells, Datnow, & Jones, 1997). Low-income, black, and Latino students do not often find themselves in classrooms where their culture and understanding of the world are rewarded. They do not experience the kind of supportive, alternative spaces they desperately need in order to redefine themselves in preparation for their encounter with the outside world.

Educational reforms, if they are to be successful with high-minority, low-income populations of students, must redefine the "spaces of schooling" that exist within schools, not simply provide external impetus for improvement. Pressure-based reforms such as standards and testing may show in the short-term improvements in test scores or dropout rates. Structural reforms to make schools smaller and personalize instruction—but leave the hierarchies within them intact—will produce limited gains. Steady, substantial growth in the academic achievements of our most struggling students will remain elusive until reformers, educators, and policy makers provide ongoing supports and redefinitions of the spaces of schooling such that all students see themselves as academically capable and invested learners.

For too long we have tinkered with our schools and then lamented when academic achievement measures indicate little to no change in the achievement gap between students of color and white students and poor and rich students. Yet we remain fearful of eliminating the differentiation among regular-, honors-, and advanced-placement courses because we recognize doing so will anger the most elite populations we serve. So worried are we about white and elite flight, we continue to cater to small percentages of our most powerful student and parent populations to the detriment of all our students. We continue to give elite families the stratified spaces at the top of our schools with our most experienced and powerful teachers just as they want and (we believe) they deserve. We must confront our own notions of meritocracy and deep-seated beliefs about intelligence, deservedness, and privilege. Only then can we provide all our students the equitable and high-quality education they deserve. Only then will we see the kind of academic growth and closing of the achievement gap that we claim to be hoping for in all our schools and communities.

FOUR

Hollowing the Promise of Higher Education

Inside the Political Economy of Access to College

Janice L. Bloom

In testimony before Congress, the National College Access Network asserted that financial barriers prevent 48% of college qualified, low-income students from attending four-year colleges and
22% from attending any college at all within two years of high
school graduation.

—NCAN bulletin, July 15, 2003

IN THE LAST THIRTY YEARS, as the American economy has been transformed by technology and globalization, a college education has become
more than just a "door to the middle class" (Loza, 2003; Tierney & Hagedorn, 2002). Whereas before the 1970s a high school degree was sufficient to
provide access to stable working-class jobs, today, "a college education is fast
becoming indispensable to an individual's economic self-sufficiency" (Fossey,
1998, p. 1).

To what degree do all Americans have access to this, now, deeply important opportunity for higher education? At first glance, it appears that in many
respects equality of access has been achieved. The civil rights movement and

affirmative action have opened higher education to a wider range of racial and ethnic backgrounds than ever before in history. Beginning in the 1960s as well, a federal system of financial aid and a network of local and state colleges and universities (subsidized by the states) widened economic access for those without the means to afford college.

However, while attacks on affirmative action have made national headlines in recent years, this second but equally important avenue of access—ability to afford a college education—has in fact been quietly choked off since the late 1970s. While the cost of college has risen exponentially during this time, viable financial aid for the poor and working class has been steadily eroded—resulting in a 32 percent gap in college-going rates between students from the lowest and highest income families in 2003 (a gap equal to the one that existed in 1970, before many federal financial aid programs were put into place) (Burd, 2002). This retreat from the goal of widening access to—and public responsibility for—higher education through the hollowing of government programs can be seen as part of a larger move toward "the drastic reduction of government responsibility for social needs" (Apple, 2001, p. 65) that has characterized the last quarter century. What it means is that, while the expectations and dreams nurtured by the promise, and necessity, of higher education remain, the means to fulfill them often do not. This is a reality, however, that is not widely recognized by the American public (Carnevale & Rose, 2003).

The place where promise and truth most tellingly collide is in the lives of poor and working-class young people, and it is they who pay the price of our continued national inattention, on the one hand, and our policy choices on the other. In this chapter, I have two goals. First, I chronicle the changing landscape of financial aid policy over the past thirty years. Second, I explore what "access to higher education" looks like from the vantage point of some of these young people. Is financial aid available? How accessible is it, at the points when they actually need it? What are the risks they must take in applying to college and for financial aid? From where they stand, are these risks worth it?

I use a combination of ethnography and policy analysis (see also Anyon, 1997; Duneier, 1999; Newman, 1999; Weis & Fine, 2004) or "multi-level ecological analysis" (O'Connor, Lewis, & Mueller, in press) to map how social class is lived at a crucial moment of transition in the lives of young people coming of age at the beginning of the 21st century. Through this mapping, I document the ways in which, despite many assurances to the contrary—by their teachers, by the media, by the government, by the colleges themselves—the promise of college has been hollowed for many of these students, in ways both large and small. This shift away from providing sufficient financial access to college has important consequences for this country's claims of justice and equal opportunity.

THE RESEARCH

Over the 2002–03 academic year, as part of a larger research study, my research followed the journey of a group of high school seniors in two small urban high schools as they made their plans for life after graduation. Though underexplored in both the literatures on secondary schools and higher education, this time of transition and choices about the future seemed like a crucial one in understanding why high school students do or do not go on to college and how they arrive at particular institutions if they do. As students go through the process of applying to college in their senior year, the abstraction of "going to college" must meet the reality of where and how. This "meeting" is a particularly challenging one for low-income students.

Every week from September to June, I spent a day at each of two high schools in New York City. These schools are unique in several important ways: As members of the Coalition of Essential Schools, they are part of a movement for small high schools with a twenty-five-year history in New York City. Both have enrollments of under 300, and neither tracks its students; all students are assumed to be "college bound." Many of the small schools in New York City were founded to serve predominantly low-income students of color; this was definitely the case at the Vista and Connections schools,[1] where more than 80 percent of students qualify for free lunch, and over 90 percent of students are African American or Latino.[2]

Literature on small schools shows a consistent and often strong relationship between school size and higher graduation and college-going rates (Gladden, 1998). Lindsay (1984) and Sares (1992) both found that, even when controlling for factors such as ability and high school achievement, smaller high school size is related to completing more years of college and graduate education. The Vista Academy and Connections High hold out high academic aspirations for all of their students; all students receive a college-prep curriculum; and at both schools, close to 100 percent of the 2003 graduating cohort of students applied to college.[3] In important ways, therefore, these schools are answering the call for high-quality education and high expectations so that low-income students of color can indeed reach the portals of higher education.

In my year at the Vista Academy and Connections High schools, my research took several forms. I worked closely with a few students—four at Connections and three at Vista—interviewing them separately and together at least once a month, as well as meeting with their parents outside of school. In addition, I tracked them and their classmates more broadly through extensive participant observations, surveys, and interviews with teachers, college counselors, and principals. As the year progressed, my observations and conversations raised questions that led me to research the changing landscape of financial aid policy in both the academic literature and current media (educational, i.e., *The Chronicle of Higher Education* and *Education Week*, and more broadly, newspapers such as the *New York Times* and the *Washington Post*). In this chapter, I draw from all of these sources: focus group and individual interview transcripts, survey data, my field notes, and literature and articles on financial aid and access to higher education.

Throughout the year, I endeavored to connect the setting and situations I was studying to the larger conditions that influenced them, elaborating the effects of the "macro" on the "micro" (Burawoy 1991). This linking of microprocesses with more meso- and macroinfluences (O'Connor, Lewis and Mueller, in press) allows for what I consider an *ethnographic policy analysis* that moves between policy and individual lives, revealing the lived consequences of federal and state policies. In my writing, then, I move back and forth from my data to the larger policy landscape, in order to illuminate the important—if often less visible—ways that they are deeply intertwined.

COLLEGE DREAMS

With three or four exceptions, all 89 of the seniors with whom I came in contact expressed a desire to go to college when I first met them in September. This reflects nationwide data, in which 95 percent of current high school students say they want to go to college (Adelman, 2002; Rosenbaum, 2001). Current economic and educational trends, and thus the importance of a college education in today's economy, are not lost on young people or their parents. The most recent U.S. Department of Labor statistics indicate that college graduates earn an average of $15,000 per year more than students with only a high school diploma (U.S. Department of Labor, 2000); U.S. Census Bureau figures for 2000 put the figure slightly over $16,000.[4] Numerous educational studies confirm this data (Brint & Karabel, 1989; Dougherty, 1994; Grubb, 1999), with declining pay over the last 20 years for students who end their education at high school (Rothstein, 2002; Lafer, 2002) playing a large part in widening the gap. Thus, for high school students to say or plan for anything other than college is to consign themselves to a future of dead-end jobs.

At both the Vista Academy and Connections High, there were specific class periods set aside, at least once a week, for students to research colleges in books and on the internet, and as the fall went on, to actually fill out college applications. Students began the year with clear hopes—and willingness to express them to teachers, in front of peers, and with parents.

In a questionnaire that they filled out in September, I asked a group of students to write a short scenario for "their dream come true" for the first day of September 2004. Of 15 students that filled out the questionnaire at Vista Academy, 12 described their dream as college.

I would be in the college which accepted me.
I would be at Long Island University studying.
I picture myself in college.
After graduating I will be in John Jay College.
I hope I would be at either UConn or the University of Maryland.

Their hopes, however, were tinged with fear. On the same question-naire, I asked students to describe a second scenario. "Your worst fears have come true—this is what you were afraid would happen." Two of the Vista students wrote:

No friends, pregnant, no love, welfare, small apartment.
I have just quit college. I have become a very solitary person. I feel ashamed of myself and my family does also.

In a survey later in the fall, in answer to the question "Is there anything that you worry might get in the way of your plans next year?" students at Connections High wrote:

A lot of things.
Getting the money and things to support myself during college.
Paying for it, but I'm still gonna go.

Undertaking higher education, then, was an endeavor that students at Vista Academy and Connection High approached with some trepidation.

Encountering College

JANICE: Saquina, I'm curious why you chose Assumption as one of the schools you're applying to. I've actually never heard of it. Where is it?
SAQUINA: I don't know. I think it's in Massachusetts? I . . . well . . . it sounded . . . well, I liked the name.

For most of the students, getting themselves to college was an overwhelming process. Many were the first in their family to finish high school or go to college; those who were not had older brothers and sisters who had paved the way, but their parents had not gone. When asked on the fall survey to list the people they knew who had gone to or were in college, many listed cousins, aunts and uncles, friends, or siblings who were attending community colleges in New York City; many others left the list blank. Of 67 students who took the fall survey at the two schools, 5 had parents who had completed a bachelor's degree; others had family members who were in the process of doing so.

For all of them, making their way through a maze of unfamiliar names and choices (What's the difference between Hunter College and Harvard University? What does it mean to "major" in something? What's the difference between "suburban" and "rural"?) was baffling.

And then there was the issue of cost. They knew that college was expensive; most knew that some colleges were really expensive and others were less expensive. But how much, they wanted to know? How much does college cost? On a visit to Columbia University with a group of students from Connections High, the most frequently asked questions were: "How much does the school cost?" "How much does the food in the cafeteria cost?" "Do you have to pay to use the gym?" "What happens if you drop out. Do you get your money back?"

The costs of college, of course, are staggering for most families in America; for these students, many living below the federal poverty line, they are simply fantastical. Thirty-five thousand dollars a year? That may be three times their family's income. Even the sums for CUNY, New York's city university, are far beyond their family's means. An extra $3,200 a year? Where is that going to come from?

"But don't worry," soothed teachers and the college counselor, at both Vista Academy and Connections High (myself among them, when I used to teach 11th and 12th grade). "Don't worry about the money now. You'll get financial aid. You don't actually have to pay that amount. Just figure out where you would want to go and apply, then we'll worry about the money later." In an interview in June 2003, reflecting on the year, a teacher at Connections High remarked,

> I think one thing we didn't do a very good job of dealing with, even this year, with the seniors, was to talk about the costs. Like no one has ever talked to the kids about the cost. We haven't. I don't know that the college counselor has. And no one has really talked to the parents. . . . I think my perception is that there's a reticence to talk about it, because we all know that the costs are so prohibitive, and there's so many other factors that dissuade kids and parents or create ambivalence about going to college, it's like, "Why pile on one more thing?" Let's just wait and see . . . you know, let's not scare them.

On one level, the teachers and college counselors are right. Because they are eligible for federal financial aid, students in need of financial help will never have to pay the full "price tag" of a college; and because substantial financial aid *is* sometimes offered by schools, they should not limit their college search, at least at the beginning, based on money. On another level, however, as I learned over the course of the year, these poor and working-class students are tapping into a reality that eludes their teachers, many of whom grew up middle class and all of whom went to college under different economic circumstances in terms of the costs of higher education.

Though students may not know specific facts and figures, their sense of caution is in fact quite well informed.

SHIFTS IN FINANCIAL AID POLICY

The GI Bill passed after World War II could be officially considered the first federal financial aid for college. As such, it heralded a new commitment to the expansion of access to higher education in the United States. Soon after its passage, President Truman's Commission on Higher Education noted,

> We have proclaimed our faith in education as a means of equalizing the conditions of men. But there is a grave danger that our present policy will make it an instrument for creating the very inequalities it was designed to prevent. If the ladder of educational opportunities rises high at the doors of some youth and scarcely rises at all at the doors of others, while at the same time formal education is made the prerequisite to occupational and social advance, then education may become the means, not of eliminating race and class distinctions, but of deepening and solidifying them. It is obvious, then, that free and universal access to education, in terms of the interests, ability and need of the student, must be a major goal of American education. (President's Commission on Higher Education, 1947)

The 1960s War on Poverty took the next important step toward embodying this belief in policy. The 1965 Higher Education Act (HEA) was intended to provide disadvantaged students with the resources necessary to attend college;[5] and the 1972 Reauthorization of the Higher Education Act enabled financial aid to take its most meaningful form, with the creation of sizable grants (Basic Education Opportunity Grants, BEOG, later renamed Pell Grants) that were specifically targeted to the most needy students.

The impact of these grants on the college going of low-income students is uncontested. In 1975, 76 percent of all federal aid was in the form of gifts such as grants, scholarships, and benefits (Mortenson, 1990b, p. 9). The outcome of these grants was a sharp drop in the gap between college attendance of low-income and high-income students; it fell to its lowest level ever between 1970 and 1980, at 19.6 percent in 1979 (Mortenson, 1990b, p. i).

However, this trend was extremely short lived. In 1978, the Middle Income Students Assistance Act (MISAA) made important changes to the shape of federal financial aid and began a trend that has continued up to the present. Thomas G. Mortenson explains that, since 1978, "Virtually every major change in federal, state and institutional student aid has worked for the benefit of students from middle and high family income backgrounds. Whereas in 1975, 76 percent of aid was given in grants, by 1988 [a much lower percent] was made up of grants (with the rest consisting of loans), and Pell Grant formulas have . . . shifted this money away from low-income students" (Mortenson 1990b).[6]

TABLE 4.1
Distribution of Federal Financial Aid[7]

	1975	1988	2001
% of grants, work-study, scholarships	76%	45%	41%
% loans	21%	52%	58%

Changes in the 1980s and 90s have only moved further in the same direction. In 1992, the government stopped offering federally subsidized loans to all students (meaning the government paid accruing interest costs during the time that borrowers were enrolled as students), creating a whole new category of *unsubsidized* loans. By 1998, about one third of student loans were unsubsidized (Fossey, 1998, p. 11).

The shift of public dollars away from the goal of increasing access to higher education for those most in need has been justified in a variety of ways over the last twenty-five years. Under Reagan, cuts were made in the name of "restoring accountability in the use of federal funds" (Mumpers, 1996). In the 1990s, neoliberal policies championed "rationalizing" and "economizing" in education (as well as in other areas), vigorously attacking the "bloated state" and championing the move of public dollars toward more "rational" market mechanisms, such as school to work and "education for employment" (Apple, 2001). Most recently, calls for "accountability" have attempted to hold schools, students, and families responsible for unequal outcomes in education, and to simply deny the role of money altogether.[8] Whatever the justification, the numbers speak for themselves: students and their families must take increasingly large loans in order to attend college in the 21st century.

"JUST FILL IN ZEROS"

What do these shifts mean in the lives of students? As I spoke with students at the Vista Academy and Connections High over the course of the year—and watched them make the decisions that would shape their lives after high school—I discovered that they knew both much less and much more than I did about the answer to this question. While I—former teacher, college graduate, and now graduate student—knew a great deal of technical information about the landscape of American colleges and the myriad steps of the application process, I lacked an understanding of how deeply money and class "matters" (hooks, 2000) in this process. Applying to college is a moment in which the lived experience of social class—both in terms of money and of subjective ways of experiencing and making sense of the world (Cole & Omari, 2003; Ostrove & Cole, 2003; Sennett & Cobb, 1972; Walkerdine, Lucey, & Melody, 2001)—plays a critical role.

In terms of practical, concrete information, students and their parents were working from a pronounced disadvantage. They did not understand what exactly they were doing as their college counselor and teachers walked them through filling out the FAFSA (Free Application for Federal Student Aid) forms; they were not clear to whom they were applying for money, how the financial aid they might get would be broken down (i.e., grants, loans, work-study), or how that money would get routed to the colleges to which they were applying. Even in May, sitting with three of the four students at Connections High whom I had followed closely, it was clear that they did not understand their financial aid packages.

CARLA: *[showing us a piece of paper, which explains her financial aid package from SUNY Oswego]* This is how much money they're giving me.

JANICE: *[I look at the paper]* It's $5,000 each semester, almost 6,000. And then they're giving you TAP and Stafford loans.

CARLA: So how much will I have to pay?

JANICE: You're taking out almost $3,000 in loans that are unsubsidized.

CARLA: What does that mean?

JANICE: That means that you have to start paying back right away. With subsidized loans, the federal government pays the interest on them while you're in college, but not with unsubsidized. They're giving 1,300 each semester. Plus, then the TAP; you get a grant, you don't have to pay it back.

CARLA: So, wait—they're giving me 1,300 each semester?

JANICE: In loans.

CARLA: Loans, okay. How much do I have to pay?

They found the paperwork—the FAFSA itself, and the many papers that began arriving in the mail in the spring—confusing—and full of questions that made little sense in their universe. Questions about the year and make of their car, mortgage information, net worth of their parents' investments, tax deferred pension plans.

"Do you pay rent?" one Vista Academy teacher translated gently as she helped a student with her FAFSA form in February. "Does your grandmother work?"

"No, she gets disability," the student answered.

"Just fill in zeros, then," the teacher explained quietly.

The students' confusion and these interactions were tinged with other, more painful emotions: doubt, humiliation, a loss of dignity, what Sennett and Cobb call "the hidden injuries of class" (Sennett & Cobb, 1972). "My FAFSA was mad zeros," one student, Jasmine, confided to me in March. Having thought of herself as relatively well off compared to some of her peers, she was taken aback by how her family looked on paper. Zero, zero, zero. Sum total, nothing.

For many, their families could not be squeezed into the neat boxes and ovals that the form offered them. For the many students who live with grandparents, aunts and uncles, or other extended family members, because their parents have died or are in prison, their families were defined right out of existence.

Page seven of the FAFSA form:

Read these notes to determine who is considered a parent on this form. *Answer all questions in Step Four about them,* even if you do not live with them. (Note that grandparents and legal guardians are not parents.)

At Vista Academy, Isabella, who had been brought up by her grandmother, wondered out loud about how to fill out the form. "But I don't know anything about my mom or dad. What do I put?"

One more "not" to add to the list; and one (or two, or four) more pieces of paper that these students must confront. They must make their way through *more* paperwork than middle-class students, with *less* knowledge and support. Moreover, although these papers are "just" bureaucratic forms, for Jasmine and Isabella and others, they speak to so much more—the small print of the wrong contract they seem to have signed at birth. When did they sign away all these things that Americans are supposed to have—cars, mortgages, pensions, the right kind of family? And what, then, does that mean about whether they might possibly "belong" at college? These questions, written in ink invisible to me as I helped them fill out their forms, read all too clearly to their eyes.

Many of the students balked when they realized the costs of applying to college; $40 for a CUNY application, $40 for each SUNY. They had not realized it would *cost* money to apply to college. As I traveled with them around the city to visit colleges, watching them go without lunch because they could not afford to buy a slice of pizza or stop at the subway entrance because they did not have the $2 fare, I caught glimpses of what $40 meant in their world. Slowly, the magnitude of what it meant to leave their neighborhoods and familiar patterns, where expenses were predictable, began to dawn on me. In college, they would have to buy their own lunch every day; they would have to pay their own subway fare; they would need to buy books; who knew what else?

Fine and Burns speak of the importance of tying together the "material *conditions* of inequality, within which class is lived, to those national ideologies, institutional contexts, social relations and psychological dramas through which individuals *experience* class" (Fine & Burns, 2003). Watching these students over the course of the year, I began to understand how deep their worry went, how daily they live on the edge of a financial precipice. What could be called their "well-grounded assessments," their intimate analyses of whether they could "afford" college, was far more based in reality than my or their teachers' or counselors' assurances "not to worry about it."[9]

What Loans Cost

One refrain echoed repeatedly throughout my conversations with students and their overheard conversations with each other. "I'm not taking loans"; "I don't know how I'm going to pay, but I don't want to borrow money!"

Sitting with William at Vista Academy as he filled out his FAFSA, I watched him check off "No" to question 33, "In addition to grants, are you interested in student loans (which you must pay back)?" When I explained that he may need these loans to pay for college he reluctantly changed his answer. But his fear of going into debt spoke volumes about the costs of reaching for mobility in the United States.

The deep aversion to debt that I observed among the students I worked with mirrors that of other low-income students around the country, and there is increasing evidence that higher levels of unmet financial need and greater loan burdens are discouraging applications from them and their peers (Carnevale & Rose, 2003). Many may have watched family members, friends, or neighbors take out loans and then drop out of college and be unable to pay them back (McDonough, 1997, p. 144). Research shows that students educated in inner-city schools (as their families, neighbors, and friends are most likely to have been) are more likely to be underprepared for college (Campaigne & Hossler, 1998; Kane, 1999; Mumpers, 1996), putting them at higher risk of dropping out or needing to take remedial classes in college, increasing their loan costs and delaying their entry into the job market (Fossey, 1998, p. 12).

For this reason, loans for higher education are a much higher risk for low-income students. Mortenson reports that poor students are far less likely to want to assume debt or take financial risks and that therefore loans are not a substitute for grants in terms of convincing low-income students to go to college (1990a).

And yet, with the financial aid system as it currently exists, the amount of debt a college education incurs has risen enormously. The average students' cumulative indebtedness grew dramatically between 1985 and 2003, while annual gross income grew by only 5.5 percent.

TABLE 4.2
Average Debt of Student Borrowers

1985	1991[10]	2003[11]
$6,488	$16,417	$27,600

Meanwhile, "students with the most financial need have increased their debt-burden faster than have traditional college-age students" (Fossey, 1998, p. 12).

This is *most* true for students with the most need and the least chance of paying off that debt. Not only are these students the least able to forgo income that would have been earned if they were not in school (Kane, 1999, p. 92); they must also borrow *more* than higher income students, thus increasing the amount that they pay overall for a college education (given interest payments).[12]

This trajectory is being reinforced by current changes in federal and state higher education financing. As students at the Vista Academy and Connections High weighed their options, the ground was shifting under their feet. Around the country, responding to growing budget gaps, almost every state raised tuition and fees for public universities in 2002, some by 20 percent or more (Winter & Medina, 2003).[13] In New York state specifically, CUNY and SUNY tuitions were raised by 25 percent and 28 percent respectively, and New York state's governor, George Pataki, attempted to cut Educational Opportunity Programs for low-income students.

What all of this means is that those most in need are sure to be hardest hit by the rising cost of college. Carnevale and Rose (2003) note that financial barriers to higher education are significant and growing, with unmet financial need, which was equivalent across classes in 1974–75, remaining the same for high-income students, while it has doubled for low-income students.

Is It Worth the Risk?

Is it worth the risk? While they are convinced of the importance of college on one level, when students look around them, current economic signals send mixed messages. Even for those students who do succeed in finishing college, it is unclear if their earnings after college will justify the money they must borrow (Freeman, 1999; Perna, 1998). Students from low-income backgrounds, on average, earn less postcollege than higher income students (Mortenson, 1990a; Mumpers, 1996, p. 131); likewise, according to the most recent census data, African Americans and Latinos earn less than their white counterparts even when they hold equivalent degrees.

TABLE 4.3
Full-Time Workers Median Income for 1999[14]

	H.S. Dropout	H.S. Graduate	Bachelor's Degree
White Men	21,696	32,269	53,557
Black Men	20,812	26,682	41,442
Hispanic Men	18,372	23,373	42,311
White Women	16,111	22,486	37,454
Black Women	15,925	20,611	35,634
Hispanic Women	14,013	19,448	32,469

Though reports may emphasize that "70% of the 30 fastest-growing jobs will require an education beyond high-school" (Haycock & Huang, 2001), Rothstein (2002) points out that the Bureau of Labor Statistics projects an increase of only 1.1 percent from 2000 to 2010 in the share of occupations requiring a bachelors degree. Similarly, Lafer (2002) notes that no economist predicts that the total demand for college-educated workers will exceed 25 to 30 percent of the labor force at any point in the foreseeable future.[15]

At Vista Academy and Connections High, this reality seemed to travel as an electric undercurrent whose voltage seemed to get stronger as the year wore on. In spring surveys at both schools, when asked again about their worries for next year, the most frequent answer was once again about paying:

That I will fail and all that money go down the drain.
How will I pay?
The price.
Money.
Worrying about paying.
Money, Money, Money: dealing with loans/financial aid.

In one group discussion toward the end of the year, several Connections High students pointed out,

Even if you go to college, you're not the only one who has an education. Just because you graduated doesn't mean you've got a guaranteed job. You're not going to start off at the top, and you're going to have loans to pay.

Mickelson (1990) posits that attitudes towards education are multidimensional; for African American (and I would add, Latino) youth, their abstract beliefs about the achievement ideology and equal opportunity in the United States coexist with concrete attitudes that reflect the empirical realities of returns on education for many low-income people of color. And while data from the 1988 National Educational Longitudinal Survey (NELS) and other surveys show that on average, African Americans in particular complete more years of schooling than whites from similar socioeconomic backgrounds (Karen, 1991; Ludwig, 2001; see also Hochschild, 1995), these class-based experiences and wariness—students' grounded assessments—necessarily play a crucial role at the moment when students must make hard decisions about the bets they take on their futures.

As the year progressed, students' dreams of college as a hopeful next step with wholly positive outcomes had begun to look far less certain. It seemed that college appeared increasingly out of reach the more it came into focus as a reality rather than an abstraction. At the Vista Academy, some students who had spoken hopefully of studying accounting, auto mechanics, English, and forensic science, came later and later to the 8:00 college class as the fall wore on; in the spring, though their attendance in other classes was still good, they stopped coming at all.

Sennett and Cobb (1972) help to make sense of these students' choice not to come to class. They point out that, in order to retain their dignity, people prefer to frame their actions as choices rather than necessities. By refusing to pursue college, some Vista Academy students protected themselves from being denied something they wanted but believed they could not attain. Though Willis (1977) might (perhaps rightfully) call this response "partial penetration," in that students' taking on of agency acts to reproduce the existing social order, these were *not* students who did not aspire to college (and four-year college, at that). Rather, they had struggled their way to its doorstep, only to find another staircase still to climb.

Despite these obstacles, many others continued coming faithfully to class. For them, it was dragging themselves through the FAFSA form in February that brought them up short. Those zeroes said it all: How could they afford to go to college? And yet how could they afford not to? A future that was all too familiar stared back at them down this road. Several withdrew their applications to four-year CUNY schools, declaring their intention to attend community college instead.

Though all but two or three of the students at Vista Academy and Connections High School applied to and were accepted at some type of college in their senior year, by May it felt as though many of them did not really believe they were going.

WHEN THE END IS JUST THE BEGINNING

Of the seven students whom I followed closely through the year, five were accepted to four-year colleges, and two were accepted into two-year programs. And yet, as they soon discovered, their acceptance letters were not the end of their journey to college; because they needed substantial financial help to be able to go, they found themselves up against an even more challenging set of obstacles.

Jasmine and Saquina, both African American young women, were two of the students from Connections High that I followed through the year, checking in with them in depth every few weeks. I watched as their list of colleges evolved, talked about SAT strategies the night before they took the test in November, spoke to their parents. Unlike many of their peers, both students were adamant that they wanted to go to private liberal arts colleges: they were applying to CUNY and SUNY as back-ups, but that was not their dream for themselves. Through their high school experiences, they understood the benefits of attending a small school.

"Being at a small school is really good, because you get a lot of help and attention from your teachers," Saquina explained when I asked her how she had decided what she wanted to do the next year.

"I wouldn't like a big school where there are so many people," Jasmine concurred. "Because that really helped me in high school, that I know all the teachers and they're always there to help you."

Though neither has parents who attended college, these two young women approached the process with a quiet, determined energy. They spent lunch periods in the library, looking at colleges on the College Board website; they completed their essays early and stopped by the college counselor's office frequently. In the spring, Saquina arranged weekend visits for herself to Bucknell and Connecticut College; Jasmine went with her father to visit Hampton, Clark-Atlanta, and Virginia Union, the historically black colleges she was most interested in attending. When I asked if they were worried about the cost or how they would pay, both answered, "Not really." They wanted desperately for this decision *not* to be about money, to reach out for a future that could take them away from their lives in the city. "Bucknell was like an episode of *Friends*," Saquina described wistfully. "It was really nice."

Reaching out toward this vision, these students and others at the Vista Academy and Connections High found themselves both exposed and rendered invisible. In order to be eligible for financial aid and scholarships, the colleges demanded access to the reaches of their private lives. When Saquina called Wheaton to ask why she had not gotten her financial aid package, a week before the May 1 deadline to notify the school if she was planning to attend there, she was told that she needed a letter of attestation that her father was not in contact with her in any way. "I haven't seen him since I was little," she explained to me. "What do I give them?" Another student was required to furnish proof of her parent's death in order to be eligible for a small scholarship.

And yet, at the same time that the college application process relentlessly commits these students' class position to paper, it simultaneously and consistently denies the material and lived realities that *result* from this class position. There are no accommodations made for Saquina to travel to Accepted Students Day at Wheaton, no recognition that she will have nowhere to stay overnight in order to get there when the day begins at 8:30 A.M., no understanding that the bus fare for the visit will eat up all the money she and her mother have put aside, save the $350 she needs to hand them for her deposit.

> *Field note:* Saquina planned to take the 3:00 A.M. bus from Port Authority in order to be at Wheaton on time for Accepted Students Day, all 92 pounds of her, alone in the New York City bus station in the middle of the night. Only her sister's boyfriend, who was supposed to take her down there, didn't show up. At 2:30 A.M., her mother arrived home from work—too late to get her to the bus. At 3:00 A.M., instead of getting on the bus, she got into bed, defeated.[16]

SO MANY STEPS ON THE WAY

And as they climb towards their hoped-for futures, there are many steps on the way to trip them up. Many of them seem to come back to money. In the third week of July, Jasmine is still waiting to get her financial aid package from Hampton, the school she handed over a precious $600 to on May 1. Now it is unclear if, in fact, she will be able to actually go. There was a discrepancy between the financial aid forms she filled out for FAFSA and those she did for the college. They still do not know how much aid she will get and how much her father will need to pay.

All the plans are made: she has been saving money all summer; she has told everyone that she is going to Hampton. When I speak to her father a few days later, however, he is not so sure.

> She might need to stay in the city, start college here and then go away the next year. But I worry—that's what happened to me. The city is expensive, things happen; and then you find it's too hard to go back.

I wonder what it will mean to Jasmine if that comes to pass: so much effort has gone into escaping the pull of gravity and breaking out into a different orbit. Will she have the energy to do it twice?

Kane calls the arcane financial aid system that has evolved over the years "a byzantine and discouraging process" (Kane, 1999, p. 95). And Nora and Horvath aptly quote D. M. Windham: "The very students most needy of financial assistance have the most difficulty in accommodating to the complex and arbitrary demands of the student assistance income reporting and documentation required" (1989).

A bill arrives in Saquina's mail, due August 1 for $1,400, for health insurance, telephone and internet access, a "general fee." Much more than she has saved from her summer job, more than she will have by the end of the summer. And school has not even begun yet.

CLOSING THE COLLEGE-GOING GAP

Despite the intensive efforts of teachers and counselors at Vista Academy and Connections High School, national statistics paint a discouraging picture of how many students will make it from high school graduation to college enrollment. A 2002 report by the Advisory Committee on Student Financial Aid, an independent counsel to Congress and the U.S. Department of Education, says that high costs prevent almost half of all college-qualified low-income students from going to a four-year college (Cavanagh, 2002); this means that 80,000 to 140,000 of qualified students from the poorest families do not pursue college degrees each year because they believe they cannot afford to do so (Burd, 2002). The use of ethnographic policy analysis allows us to meet students who have overcome all of the other barriers in their way—who have graduated from high school and applied to college, against all the odds—and thus both confirms and explains these figures. These young people point out the ways, both large and small, that economics pose a substantial barrier to college attendance for low-income students.

The fact that the college-going gap between high- and low-income students was at its lowest between 1970 and 1980, when financial aid to low-income students reached its peak, makes it easy to argue that current statistics are the outcome of policy decisions made in this country over the past thirty years. Though much current political rhetoric would have it otherwise, there has been a steady retreat, through successive administrations, both Democratic and Republican, from the commitment to providing equal opportunity for students from a range of economic backgrounds (Lavin & Hyllegard, 1996). As we strive to understand why students do not attend college, then, we must reexamine federal financial aid policy and the ways that its transformation over the last quarter century has hollowed, leaving the appearance but not the substance of, the promise of access to higher education for low-income students.

Over the last decade, a range of scholars and economists have proposed new formulations that would reconfigure state and federal financial aid policies toward greater equity in access (see Kane, 1999; McPherson & Shapiro, 1991; Mumpers, 1996); most recently, a "National Dialogue on Student Financial Aid" run by the College Board concluded,

The fundamental purpose of student financial assistance at federal, state, institutional, and philanthropic levels is to assist financially needy students . . . the centerpiece must be closing the gap between the cost of attending college and family resources available to financially needy students. (The College Board, 2003)

In a recent article in *The Chronicle of Higher Education,* the late U.S. Senator Paul Simon made an even more pointed suggestion.

In 2001, under the leadership of President Bush, Congress enacted a 10-year tax cut of $1.35 trillion. What if, instead of that, a decision had been made to use a small portion of that tax cut to shift back to a three-fourths grant, one-fourth loan program, bringing the total available to students— regardless of need—to something approaching what the GI Bill provided? (Simon, 2003)[17]

At a much more local level—in classrooms, counselors' offices, and after-school programs that do work around access to college[18]—my research would also suggest the importance of speaking out loud about the role of money to low-income students and parents as they go through the college application process. Though there may be a sense that this will "scare" students and parents away from college, my conversations and observations indicate that young people and their families carry a deeply grounded assessment of the expense of college; they are making calculations based on this whether or not schools feel comfortable enough to broach the topic. In fact, it is exactly by speaking about students' fears, by acknowledging the importance of the very real difficulties and risks of reaching for mobility through the avenue of college, and by providing technical information early on, that teachers can help students to feel in control of their futures. It is by understanding the specific ways that the multiple and confusing layers of the college application process confounds them, and sends the silent message that "college isn't for them," that teachers and counselors can help to build a bridge that will carry students to higher education.[19]

CONCLUSION

What my research this year suggests—what Saquina and Jasmine and all the other students I have worked with have discovered is that, approaching the oasis of college from a distance, far too many low-income students discover it to be a mirage. In this, as in so many other arenas of American public life, access to the "goods" of the American dream is becoming increasingly polarized, with the rich getting richer and the poor getting poorer (Carnevale &

Rose, 2003). We ask those who can least afford to take risks to take the most; we ask those who can least afford to pay for college to pay significantly *more* for their higher education.

The students I have worked with this past year rarely speak out loud about the disappointment or frustration of watching their college dreams dissolve; they do not voice the shame and indignity of watching others take a place at a table where they cannot afford to eat. They speak by their absence, by the tone of longing in their voices, and by the hardness in their eyes as they stare down a long bleak road, one they have watched their parents travel, one they know all too well. There was a time in our history—not very long ago— in which the nation committed to helping these young people gain access to higher education. It is a commitment, however, that is yet to be fulfilled.

FIVE

Subtractive Schooling, Caring Relations, and Social Capital in the Schooling of U.S.-Mexican Youth

Angela Valenzuela

SCHOOLS SUBTRACT RESOURCES from youth in two major ways. The first involves a process of "de-Mexicanization," or subtracting students' culture and language, which is consequential to their achievement and orientations toward school. The second involves the role of caring between teachers and students in the educational process. De-Mexicanization erodes students' social capital (Coleman 1988, 1990; also see Stanton-Salazar, 1997), by making it difficult for constructive social ties to develop between immigrant and U.S.-born youth. By *social capital*, I mean the social ties that connect students to each other, as well as the levels of resources (like academic skills and knowledge) that characterize their friendship groups. This dynamic is of special conse- quence to regular-track, U.S.-born Mexican youth, who often lack a well- defined and effective achievement orientation.

Regarding caring, teachers expect students to *care about* school in a tech- nical fashion before they *care for* them, while students expect teachers to *care for* them before they *care about* school. By dismissing students' definition of education—an orientation thoroughly grounded in Mexican culture and advanced by caring theorists (e.g., Noddings, 1984, 1992)—schooling sub- tracts resources from youth.

After describing the study I undertook at Seguín High School,[1] I explain
how I derived the concept of 'subtractive schooling.' This description incorporates my concerns about current theorizing (especially see Portes, 1995)
that narrowly casts achievement differences between immigrant and U.S.-
born youth as evidence of "downward assimilation." I then elaborate on how
culture and caring relations are involved in the process of subtractive schooling. Throughout, I draw selectively on both quantitative and qualitative evidence that lends support to my thesis.

THE SEGUÍN HIGH SCHOOL STUDY

Seguín High is a large, comprehensive, inner-city high school located in the
Houston Independent School District. Its 3,000-plus student body is virtually all Mexican and generationally diverse (45 percent immigrant and 55
percent U.S. born).[2] Teachers, on the other hand, are predominantly non-
Latino. Currently, 81 percent are non-Latino, and 19 percent are Latino
(mostly Mexican American).

Seguín's failure and dropout rates are very high. In 1992 a full quarter of
the freshman class repeated the grade for at least a second time, and a significant portion of these were repeating the ninth grade a third and fourth time.
An average of 300 students skip daily. Between 1,200 and 1,500 students enter
the 9th grade each year and only 400 to 500 students graduate in any given
year. Low expectations are virtually built into this school: Were students to
progress normally from one grade to the next, there would be no space to
house them. As things stand, Seguín's 3,000-plus student body is crammed
into a physical facility capable of housing no more than 2,600. Because of the
school's high failure and dropout rates, the freshman class makes up more
than half of the school population.

An ethnic brand of politics that has focused on problems in the school has
made for a contentious relationship between Seguín and its surrounding community. Although local community activists have historically supported
numerous causes, including legal challenges against segregation during the
early 1970s, a massive student walkout in October 1989, and a number of
school reforms such as site-based management, little has changed to significantly alter its underachieving profile. Seguín is locked in inertia. Steeped in a
logic of technical rationality, schooling centers on questions of how best to
administer the curriculum rather than on why, as presently organized, it tends
to block the educational mobility of huge segments of its student body. Except-
ing those located in the privileged rungs of the curriculum—that is, honors
classes, the magnet school program, and the upper levels of the Career and
Technology Education (CTE) vocational program[3]—the academic trajectories
of the vast majority are highly circumscribed. Because as a group, 9th graders

are especially "at risk," I tried to talk to as many of them as possible and to incorporate their voices and experiences into this ethnographic account.

Although my study makes use of quantitative data, the key modes of data collection are based on participant observation and open-ended interviews with individuals and with groups of students. Group interviews enabled me not only to tap into peer-group culture but also to investigate the social, cultural, and linguistic divisions that I observed among teenagers at Seguín. Before elaborating my framework, I will first address relevant survey findings that pertain to parental education, schooling orientations, and generational differences in achievement.[4]

First, students' parental education levels are very low, hovering around nine years of schooling completed for third-generation students.[5] Though higher than the average for parents of first-generation respondents (i.e., six years of schooling), a "high" of nine for the U.S.-born population means that parents have little educational "advantage" to confer to their children (Lareau 1989). That is, most parents have either no high school experience or a negative one to pass on to their progeny. Rather than aberrant, this finding is consistent with Chapa (1988), who found that third-generation Mexican Americans in the state of Texas complete an average of 9.3 years of education and that the dropout rate is 56 percent.[6]

These data indicate that with such low average attainment levels, the major responsibility for education falls on the school by default. School officials, however, tend not to see it this way. They tend to blame the students, their parents, their culture, and their community for their educational failure. This tendency on the part of teachers and administrators to blame children, parents, and community has been amply observed in ethnographies of minority youth in urban schools (Fine, 1991; Peshkin, 1991; Yeo, 1997; McQuillan, 1998).

Complicating matters—and reinforcing many teachers' and other school officials' opinion that students "don't care" about school—is that a significant proportion of students, mostly U.S. born, have become adept at breaking school rules. For example, they skip class and attend all three lunch periods knowing that the numbers are on their side and that they are unlikely to get processed even if they get spotted by school officials. A common scenario is the presence of several administrators in the school cafeteria alongside scores of students whom they know are skipping class. The sheer amount of time, paperwork, and effort that would be required to process every offender discourages massive action. In short, violations of school policies are so common that they outstrip the administration's capacity to address them, making Seguín a capricious environment that minimizes many students' sense of control, on the one hand, and their respect toward authority, on the other. Despite the fact that certain types of students, discussed shortly, consistently succeed, the prevailing view is that students "don't care."

Another finding from survey data corroborated in the ethnographic account is that immigrant youth experience school significantly more positively than do their U.S.-born peers. That is, they see teachers as more caring and accessible than do their U.S.-born counterparts, and they rate the school climate in more positive terms as well. They are also much less likely to evade school rules and policies. These students' attitudes contrast markedly with those of their second- and third-generation counterparts, whose responses in turn are not significantly different from one another. Particularly striking is how generational status—and not gender or curriculum track placement—influences orientations toward schooling.

Because of its relevance, I interject at this point how ethnographic evidence additionally reveals that immigrant, more than U.S.-born, youth belong to informal peer groups that exhibit an esprit-de-corps, proschool ethos. Immigrants' collective achievement strategies, when combined with the academic competence their prior schooling provides, directly affect their level of achievement. Academic competence thus functions as a human-capital variable that, when marshaled in the context of the peer group, *becomes* a social-capital variable (Coleman, 1988, 1990). This process is especially evident among females in Seguín's immigrant student population (see Valenzuela, 1999). In contrast, and borrowing from Putnam (1993, 1995), regular-track, U.S.-born youth are "socially decapitalized." Through a protracted, institutionally mediated process of de-Mexicanization that results in a de-identification from the Spanish language, Mexico, and things Mexican, they lose an organic connection to those among them who are academically oriented. U.S.-born youth are no less solidaristic; their social ties are simply devoid of academically productive social capital.

Finally, quantitative evidence points to significantly higher academic achievement among immigrants than among U.S.-born youth located in the regular track. Though not controlling for curriculum track placement, other scholars have observed this tendency among Mexican and Central American students (Buriel, 1984; Buriel & Cardoza, 1988; Matute-Bianchi, 1991; Ogbu, 1991; Suárez-Orozco, 1991; Vigil & Long, 1981). This finding has been primarily interpreted from an individual assimilationist perspective rather than from a critical analysis of assimilating institutions.

Invoking a generational analysis of change, classic assimilation theory (Gordon, 1964) suggests that achievement should improve generationally if assimilation worked for Mexicans in the way that it has worked for European-origin immigrant groups in the United States. Though unintended, this generational model encourages a construction of U.S.-born youth as "deficient" and as fundamentally lacking in the drive and enthusiasm possessed by their immigrant counterparts. Drawing on several works that examine the phenomenon of oppositionality among minority youth (Fordham & Ogbu, 1986; Matute-Bianchi, 1991; Ogbu, 1991), Portes and Zhou (1993, 1994) conclude that U.S.-born minority youth are members of "adversarial cultures" (or "reactive subcultures"). They convey the imagery of a downward achievement spiral that accompanies the assimilation process, culminating, often by the second generation, in a devaluation of education as a key route to mobility. Sorely lacking in their account is an understanding of the myriad ways in which powerful institutions such as schools are implicated in both the curtailment of students' educational mobility and, consequently, in the very development of the alleged "adversarial culture" about which Portes and Zhou express concern.

My data show that institutionalized curricular tracking is a good place to begin assessing the academic well-being of the would-be socially ascendant. That is, the previously observed pattern of higher immigrant achievement vis-à-vis U.S.-born underachievement is *only* evident among youth within the regular, noncollege-bound track. In other words, as one would expect, location in the college-bound track erases these differences. At Seguín, however, the vast majority of youth are located in the regular academic track. Only between 10 and 14 percent of the entire student body is ever located in either honors courses, the magnet school program, or the upper-levels of the Career and Technology Education (CTE) vocational program (see Oakes, 1985; O'Connor, Lewis, & Mueller, this volume; Olsen, 1997).

To categorically characterize U.S.-born Mexican youth as emanating from cultures that do not value achievement is to at once treat them as if they were a monolith and to promote an invidious distinction. Key institutional mechanisms such as tracking—and, as I shall shortly argue, subtractive schooling—mediate and have always mediated achievement outcomes. That most minority youth, however, are not located in the college-bound track should not keep us from recognizing the power of such placement: It is there where they acquire privileged access to the necessary skills, resources, and conditions for social ascendancy within schools, and ultimately, within society.

Beyond the "blind spot" in the assimilation literature overlooking the significance of tracking, the limitations of assimilation theory to account for differences in achievement between immigrant and U.S.-born youth becomes further apparent through a close examination of the subtractive elements of schooling. The theoretical question that emerges from the framework I have elaborated is not whether we bear witness to "downward assimilation," as Portes (1995) suggests, but rather *how schooling subtracts resources from youth*.

THE CONCEPT OF SUBTRACTIVE SCHOOLING

I derive the concept of 'subtractive' in the phrase *subtractive schooling* from the sociolinguistic literature that regards assimilation as a nonneutral process (Cummins, 1981, 1986; Gibson, 1988; Skutnabb-Kangas & Cummins, 1988). Schooling involves either adding on a second culture and language or subtracting one's original culture and language. An additive outcome would be fully vested bilingualism and biculturalism. Whenever Mexican youth emerge from the schooling process as monolingual individuals who are neither identified with Mexico nor equipped to function competently in the mainstream of the United States, subtraction can be said to have occurred.

There is no neutral category for schooling because the status quo is subtractive and inscribed in public policy: the Texas Bilingual Education Code is a transitional policy framework.[7] The state's English as a Second Language (ESL) curriculum is designed to impart to nonnative English speakers sufficient verbal and written skills to effectuate their transition into an all-English curriculum within a three-year time period. Under these circumstances, maintaining and developing students' bilingual and bicultural abilities is to swim against the current.

Though 'subtractive' and 'additive bilingualism' are well-established concepts in the sociolinguistic literature, they have yet to be applied to either the organization of schooling or the structure of caring relationships. Instead, the bulk of this literature emphasizes issues pertaining to language acquisition and maintenance. Merging these concerns with current evidence and theorizing in the nascent comparative literature on immigrant and ethnic minority youth— as I do in this chapter—is fruitful, broadening the scope of empirical inquiry. Currently, the literature addresses differences in perceptions and attitudes toward schooling among immigrant and ethnic minority youth, as well as the adaptational coping strategies they use to negotiate the barriers they face in achieving their goals (e.g., Gibson, 1988, 1993; Matute-Bianchi, 1991; Suárez-Orozco & Suárez-Orozco, 1997). While I address this in my work as well, it is also worthwhile to investigate how the organizational features of schooling relate to the production of minority status and identities, on the one hand, and how these productions relate to achievement and orientations toward schooling, on the other.

I derive the concept of 'schooling' in 'subtractive schooling' from the social reproduction literature, which views schools as actually "working"— that is, if their job *is* to reproduce the social order along race, class, and gender lines (e.g., Callahan, 1962; Giroux, 1988; Olsen, 1997). Academic success and failure are presented here more as products of schooling than as something that young people do. Of course, the manifest purpose of schooling is not to reproduce inequality, but the latent effect is that with which we must contend.

Segregated and generationally diverse, Seguín proved to be a natural laboratory for investigating reproduction theory. One can see what students are like when they enter school as immigrants and what they look like after having been processed. The combined terms 'subtractive' and 'schooling' thus bring the school into greater focus than has much of the previous literature on ethnic minority, but especially Mexican, schooling.

The Process of Subtractive Schooling

Language and Culture

"No Spanish" rules were a ubiquitous feature of U.S.-Mexican schooling through the early 1970s (San Miguel, 1987). They have been abolished, but Mexican youth continue to be subjected on a daily basis to subtle, negative messages that undermine the worth of their unique culture and history. The structure of Seguín's curriculum is typical of most public high schools with large concentrations of Mexican youth. It is designed to divest them of their Mexican identities and to impede their prospects for fully vested bilingualism and biculturalism. The single (and rarely taught) course on Mexican American history aptly reflects the students' marginalized status in the formal curriculum.

On a more personal level, students' cultural identities are systematically derogated and diminished. Stripped of their usual appearance, youth entering Seguín get "disinfected" of their identifications in a way that bears striking resemblance to the prisoners and mental patients in Goffman's essays on asylums and other "total institutions" (1977). ESL youth, for example, are regarded as "limited English proficient" rather than as "Spanish dominant" and/or as potentially bilingual. Their fluency in Spanish is construed as a "barrier" that needs to be overcome. Indeed, school personnel frequently insist that once "the language barrier" is finally eliminated, Seguín's dismal achievement record will disappear as well. The belief in English as the panacea is so strong that it outweighs the hard evidence confronting classroom teachers every day: The overwhelming majority of U.S.-born, monolingual, English-speaking youth in Seguín's regular track do not now, have not in the past, and likely will not in the future prosper academically.

Another routine way in which the everyday flow of school life erodes the importance of cultural identity is through the casual revisions that faculty and staff make in students' names. At every turn, even well-meaning teachers "adapt" their students' names: *Loreto* becomes *Laredo; Azucena* is transformed into *Suzy*. Because teachers and other school personnel typically lack familiarity with stress rules in Spanish, surnames are especially vulnerable to linguistic butchering. Even names that are common throughout the Southwest, like Martinez and Perez, are mispronounced as MART-i-nez and Pe-REZ. Schooling under these conditions can thus be characterized as a mortification of the self in Goffman's terms—that is, as a leaving off and a taking on.

Locating Spanish in the Foreign Language Department also implicates Seguín in the process of subtraction. This structure treats Mexicans as any other immigrant group originating from distant lands and results in course offerings that do not correspond to students' needs. Because Spanish is conceived of as similar to such "foreign languages" as French and German, the

majority of the courses are offered at the beginning and intermediate levels
only. Very few advanced Spanish-language courses exist. Rather than designing the program with the school's large number of native speakers in mind,
Seguín's first- and second-year Spanish curriculum subjects students to material that insults their abilities.

Taking beginning Spanish means repeating such elementary phrases as
"Yo me llamo María." (My name is María.) "Tú te llamas José." (Your name
is José.) Even students whose linguistic competence is more passive than
active—that is, they understand but speak little Spanish—are ill served by this
kind of approach. A passively bilingual individual possesses much greater linguistic knowledge and ability than another individual exposed to the language
for their first time. Since almost every student at Seguín is either a native
speaker of Spanish or an active or passive bilingual, the school's Spanish program ill serves all, though not even-handedly. To be relevant, the curricular
pyramid would have to be reversed, with far fewer beginning courses and
many more advanced-level courses in Spanish.

Subtraction is further inscribed in Seguín's tracking system. That is, the
regular curriculum track is subdivided into two tracks—the regular, English-
only, and the ESL track. This practice of nonacademic "cultural tracking" fosters social divisions among youth along cultural and linguistic lines and limits
the educational mobility of all youth. A status hierarchy that relegates immigrant youth to the bottom gets established, enabling the development of a
"politics of difference" (McCarthy, 1993). That is, immigrant and U.S.-born
youth develop "we-they" distinctions that sabotage communication and pre-
clude bridge building.

The sharp division that exists between immigrant and U.S.-born youth is
a striking feature, particularly when one considers that many of the U.S.-born
students have parents and grandparents who are from Mexico. However, such
divisions have been observed among Mexican adults as well (Rodriguez &
Nuñez, 1986). This discussion should not be taken to mean that immigrants
should not be accorded their much-needed, and often deficient, language support systems. I simply want to express that the broader Mexican community's
collective interest to achieve academically gets compromised by a schooling
process that exacerbates and reproduces differences among youth.

Regarding mobility, time-honored practices make it virtually impossible
for ESL youth to make a vertical move from the ESL to the honors track.
Never mind that many immigrant youth attended *secundaria* (known more
formally as *educación media*) in Mexico. Since only 16.9 percent of the total
middle school–age population in Mexico attends *secundaria,* any *secundaria*
experience is exceptional (Gutek, 1993). Though members of an "elite" group,
they are seldom recognized or treated as such by school officials, including
counselors who either do not know how to interpret a transcript from Mexico
or who are ignorant about the significance of a postprimary educational expe-

rience. Such negligent practices helped me understand immigrant youth who told me, "I used to be smarter." "I used to know math."

Ironically, the stigmatized status of immigrants—especially the more *"amexicanados"*—endures vis-à-vis their Mexican American peers, enhances their peer group solidarity, and protects them from the seductive elements of the peer group culture characteristic of their U.S.-born counterparts. Immigrant students' proschool, esprit-de-corps ethos (that explains their ESL teachers' affectionate references to them as "organized cheaters") finds no parallel in the schooling experiences of U.S.-born youth. Immigrants' collective achievement strategies, when combined with the academic competence their prior schooling provides, translate into academically productive social capital.

Disassociation and deidentification with immigrant youth and Mexican culture have no such hidden advantage for Mexican American youth. The English-dominant and strongly peer-oriented students who walk daily through Seguín's halls, vacillating between displays of aggressiveness and indifference, are either underachieving or psychically and emotionally detached from the academic mainstream. Hence, for U.S.-born youth, to be culturally assimilated is to become culturally and linguistically distant from those among them who are academically able. Thus eroded in the process of schooling is students' social capital. Within a span of two or three generations, "social decapitalization" may be said to occur. Under such conditions, teachers become highly influential and even necessary gatekeepers. Hence the significance of caring relations.

Caring Relations

Regardless of nativity, students' definition of education, embodied in the term *educación*, gets dismissed. Interestingly, the concept of *'educación'* approximates the optimal definition of education advanced by Noddings (1984) and other caring theorists. Being an educated person within Mexican culture carries with it its own distinctive connotation (Mejía, 1983; Reese, Balzano, Gallimore, & Goldenberg, 1991). *Ser bien educado/a* (to be well educated) is to not only possess book knowledge but to also live responsibly in the world as a caring human being, respectful of the individuality and dignity of others. Though one may possess many credentials, one is poorly educated *(mal educado/a)* if deficient in respect, manners, and responsibility toward others, especially family members.

Following from students' definition of education is the implicit notion that learning should be premised on *authentic* caring, to use Noddings' (1984) terminology. That is, learning should be premised on *relation* with teachers and other school adults having as their chief concern their students' entire well-being. In contrast to their teachers' expectations, Seguín youth prefer to be *cared for* before they *care about* school, especially when the curriculum is impersonal, irrelevant, and test driven. U.S.-born students, in particular, display psychic and emotional detachment from a schooling process organized around *aesthetic,* or superficial, caring. Such caring accords emphasis to form and nonpersonal content (e.g., rules, goals, and "the facts") and only secondarily, if at all, to their students' subjective reality.

The benefit of profound connection to the student is the development of a sense of competence and mastery over worldly tasks. In the absence of such connectedness, students are not only reduced to the level of objects; they may also be diverted from learning the skills necessary for mastering their academic and social environment. Thus, the difference in the ways in which students and teachers perceive school-based relationships can have direct bearing on students' potential to achieve.

Caring becomes political, however, when teachers and students hold different definitions of caring and the latter are unable to insert their definition of caring into the schooling process because of their weaker power position. Mexican American youth frequently choose clothing and accessories such as baggy pants and multilayered gold necklaces that "confirm" their teachers' suspicions that they really do not care about school. Withdrawal and apathy in the classroom mix with occasional displays of aggression toward school authorities. This makes them easy to write off as "lazy underachievers."

U.S.-born youth indeed engage in what Ogbu calls "cultural inversion" whereby they consciously or unconsciously oppose the culture and cognitive styles associated with the dominant group (Fordham & Ogbu, 1986). However, they do so mainly in the realm of self-representation. In contrast to what Fordham and Ogbu (1986) and Matute-Bianchi (1991) have observed among African American and Mexican American youth in their studies, strong achievement orientations among youth at Seguín are never best interpreted as attempts on their part to "act white." Instead, proschool youth are simply dismissed as "nerdy" or "geeky." Rather than education, it is *schooling* they resist—especially the dismissal of their definition of education.

Some of the most compelling evidence that students do care about education despite their rejection of schooling lies with the great number of students who skip most classes chronically but who regularly attend that one class that is meaningful to them. Without exception, it is the teacher there who makes the difference. Unconditional, authentic caring resides therein.

Seguín's immigrant students often share their U.S.-born peers' view that learning should be premised on a humane and compassionate pedagogy inscribed in reciprocal relationships, but their sense of being privileged to attend secondary school saps any desire they might have to insert their definition of education into the schooling process. Immigrant students therefore respond to the exhortation that they "care about" school differently from U.S.-born youth. Immigrant students acquiesce and are consequently seen by their teachers as polite and deferential. Their grounded sense of identity further combines with their unfamiliarity with the Mexican American experience to enable them to "care about" school without the threat of language or culture loss or even the burden of cultural derogation when their sights are set on swiftly acculturating toward the mainstream. U.S.-born youth in Seguín's regular track, on the other hand, typically respond by either withdrawing or rebelling. *Caring about* threatens their ethnic identity, their sense of self.

Frank's story illustrates one student's resistance to schooling, the productive potential of a caring relationship at school, and the debilitating effects of a curriculum that fails to validate his ethnic identity. He is an unusually reflective ninth-grader. As a "C-student," he achieves far below his potential. His own alienation from schooling accounts for his poor motivation:

> I don't get with the program because then it's doing what *they* [teachers] want for my life. I see *mexicanos* who follow the program so they can go to college, get rich, move out of the *barrio*, and never return to give back to their *gente* (people). Is that what this is all about? If I get with the program, I'm saying that's what it's all about and that teachers are right when they're not.

Frank resists caring about school not because he is unwilling to become a productive member of society, but rather because to do so is tantamount to cultural genocide. He is consciously at odds with the narrow definition of success that most school officials hold. This definition asks him to measure his self-worth against his ability to get up and out of the *barrio* along an individualist path to success divorced from the social and economic interests of the broader Mexican community. With his indifference, this profoundly mature young adult deliberately challenges Seguín's implicit demand that he derogate his culture and community.

Frank's critique of schooling approximates that of Tisa, another astute U.S.-born, female student whom I came across in the course of my group interviews. When I ask her whether she thinks a college education is necessary in order to have a nice house and a nice car and to live in a nice neighborhood, she provided the following response: "You can make good money dealing drugs, but all the dealers—even if they drive great cars—they still spend their lives in the 'hood. Not to knock the 'hood at all. . . . If only us *raza* (the Mexican American people) could find a way to have all three, money . . . *clean* money, education, and the 'hood."

In a very diplomatic way, Tisa took issue with the way I framed my question. Rather than setting up two mutually compatible options of being successful and remaining in one's home community, Tisa interpreted my question in *either/or terms*, which in her mind unfairly counterposed success to living in the 'hood. That I myself failed to anticipate its potentially subtractive logic caused me to reflect on the power of the dominant narrative of mobility in U.S. society—an "out-of-the-*barrio*" motif, as it were (Chavez, 1991).

Thus, for alienated youth such as Frank and Tisa to buy into "the program," success needs to be couched in additive, both/and terms that preserve their psychic and emotional desire to remain socially responsible members of their communities. These findings bring to mind the ethos that Ladson-Billings (1994) identifies as central to culturally relevant pedagogy for African American youth. Specifically, effective teachers of African American children see their role as one of "giving back to the community." For socially and culturally distant teachers, such discernment and apprehending of "the other" is especially challenging and can only emerge when the differential power held by teachers of culturally different students is taken fully into account (Noddings, 1984, 1992; Paley, 1995; Ladson-Billings, 1994).

Conclusion

Schools such as Seguín High School are faced with a special challenge. To significantly alter the stubborn pattern of underachievement, they need to become authentically caring institutions. To become authentically caring institutions, they need to at once stop subtracting resources from youth and deal with the effects of subtraction. Although it is up to each school to determine what a more additive perspective might entail, my study suggests that an important point of departure is a critical examination of the existing curriculum.

The operant model of schooling structurally deprives acculturated, U.S.-born youth of social capital that they would otherwise enjoy were the school not so aggressively (subtractively) assimilationist. Stated differently, rather than students failing schools, schools fail students with a pedagogical logic that not only assures the ascendancy of a few but also jeopardizes their access to those among them who are either academically strong or who belong to academically supportive networks.

Although the possession of academically productive social capital presents itself as a decided advantage for immigrant youth, analytical restraint is in order here as well. However "productive" it may be, social capital is still no match against an invisible system of tracking that excludes the vast majority of youth. Strategizing for the next assignment or exam does not guarantee that the exclusionary aspects of schooling will either cease or magically come to light. Even should it come to light, the power to circumvent regular-track placement remains an issue, especially for the more socially marginal. Most sobering is the thought that in some ultimate sense, schooling is subtractive for all.

SIX

The Ideology of "Fag"
The School Experience of Gay Students

George W. Smith
(completed for publication by Dorothy E. Smith)

Gay and lesbian youth attend schools throughout the nation. . . .
These students—from every ethnic and racial background, in
urban, suburban, and rural schools—have sat passively through
years of public school education where their identities as gay and
lesbian people have been ignored and denied. They have done this
because of their own fears and isolation, and because of the failure
of gay men and lesbians to effectively take up their cause.
—E. Rofes, "Opening Up the Classroom Closet"

THE IDEOLOGY OF "FAG" is key to the organization of the heterosexist/homo-
phobic dimensions of the school regime. It is a practice in language. Mikhail
Bakhtin's work is used to devise ways of "seeing" social organization in the
speech and graffiti in which the ideology of "fag" is realized in schools. His
conception of the dialogic explicates the relationship between researcher and
informants, as well as the dialogues internal to informants' narratives.
Excerpts from their stories create windows into the local practices of the ideology of fag as they experienced it and made available the social organization
of their everyday school lives. Analysis focuses on how speech, whether as verbal abuse or homophobic graffiti, concerts antigay activities, articulating to the
wider organization of gender and the school as a regime.

Informants' stories describe how fag as a stigmatized object is constituted in "gossip." Aspects of youths' appearance are interpreted with reference to fag as an underlying pattern. Everyday practices of "fag-baiting," such as poking fun, teasing, name calling, scrawling graffiti on lockers, insulting and harassing someone, produce the fag as a social object. The language intends a course of action isolating the gay student and inciting to physical violence. Verbal abuse both is and initiates attack. As a form of public speech, graffiti constitutes a depersonalized form of threat and harassment. Whether a gay student is identified as fag or not, he acquires a gay identity/consciousness through the practices of the ideology of fag.

What this chapter describes is a normal part of school organization. The social relations of heterosexuality and patriarchy dominate its public space. Being gay is never spoken of positively (in these informants' experience). Teachers are reported as being generally complicit by their silence if not actively participating in the ideology. Attacks on and ostracism of gay students are taken for granted. The heterosexism of the regime makes fag the stigmatized other, and reflexively, "fag" as stigmatized other feeds into the regime's heterosexism. Thus, the gay students' stories show the school's complicity in the everyday cruelties of the enforcement of heterosexist/homophobic hegemony.

This study investigates and reports on the treatment gay youth receive in school and on the effect this has on their education and ultimately on their lives. It is part of a collaborative project, funded by the Ontario Ministry of Education, researching the everyday school experiences of gay and lesbian teenagers. My colleague, Didi Khayatt (1994, 1995), researched the school experience of lesbians, and I investigated the situation of gay males. This chapter is a report on what I learned from the gay youth I talked to. My interest in this topic comes out of my own educational history as a gay youth who went through high school and then on to a career in elementary and secondary school teaching before going on into graduate studies. It has also been influenced by my involvement, during the 1970s and 1980s, in the Canadian Gay Liberation Movement.

THE RESEARCH DESIGN

I interviewed gay young men about their school experiences. I talked to individuals who were either still in school or who had left school just recently. I wanted my information to be current and sufficiently detailed in order to describe how they were actually treated in contemporary schools. The informants whose stories are the data for this study were treated not as objects of study but as individuals knowledgeable about how schools work, at least as far as students are concerned (Devault, 1990).

The research approach is that of institutional ethnography, which rests on the ontological presupposition that an actual world exists that people actively bring into being and that can be studied and described. The part of this world I was interested in was the current educational regime—a particular system of education based on a specific set of social norms. The interviews opened various windows on different aspects of the organization of this regime. Each informant provides a partial view; the work of institutional ethnography is to put together an integrated view based on these otherwise truncated accounts of schools. The aim is to describe the heterosexist/homophobic social relations of the current educational regime in schools.

The interviews were designed reflexively to create a dialogue between two gay individuals, myself and my informant, about the school experiences of gay students. The dialogic character of the interviews was essential to this reflexivity. I located myself as someone who, after a thirty-year hiatus, was catching up on how schools treated gay students. Critical to establishing a dialogue was, first, that my informant was assured that he was not the object of study—schools were—and second, that he felt in this situation that he was someone who knew more about his school than I did. *I* was there to learn from *him*. These and similar procedures organized taking up schools from the standpoint of gay students.

In locating informants, I started with a community organization in Toronto, Lesbian and Gay Youth Toronto (LGYT), as a source of informants. The group met each Tuesday evening at a community center in the heart of Toronto's gay community. At the beginning of each meeting there was an opportunity for me to advertise for informants. This I did on three or four occasions. The contacts I made sometimes referred other students to the study. I also recruited informants from my contacts in the gay community. Didi Khayatt, my research colleague, also referred gay students to me from her contacts with her lesbian interviewees. Last, I recruited some "street youths" from a Toronto community service agency, the Street Outreach Services (SOS).

Very few of my informants were still attending secondary school at the time they were interviewed. Some were university undergraduates who had recently graduated from high school. They were bright, articulate, self-selected individuals who had often given considerable thought to their high school experience. Some of them arrived for their interview prepared to give witness to their school experiences. For example, one brought in his high school notebook with the pages marked where he had recorded, as part of a very systematic practice of note-taking, the homophobic remarks made by one of his teachers. It became clear, however, that most of these students had been "in the closet" during high school. They had finished high school and gone on to a university. Nonetheless they could describe the harassment of gay students who were "out" at school and who eventually for the most part "dropped out" before completing high school.

This latter group bore the violence of high school homophobia. It became clear to me that the school experiences of students who were "out" would be different from those who were "in the closet." I wanted to capture this difference as part of my work. To do so, I arranged to interview "street kids" who were SOS clients. Unlike the LGYT interviewees, the agency staff selected these young men. Whom I interviewed depended on who turned up that day, provided they were willing to be interviewed. All of the young people I talked to from this agency had "dropped out" of school, and one reportedly had attempted suicide. All but one of these individuals "dropped out" because they were discriminated against for being gay. Interestingly enough, like their college counterparts, most of these young men had been enrolled in an academic program. They were bright, engaged, and engaging.

The gay and bisexual students interviewed were clear, at this point in their lives, about their sexual orientation. Some realized from an early age that they were "different," while others had only recently determined their orientation for sure. One student said categorically that he had always known he was gay. Another said he had "funny feelings around age nine" and "that by age twelve [he] knew without a shadow of a doubt" that he was gay. What struck me about these young men was the positive attitude they had about being gay, although this was probably tied to the fact that they were largely self-selected and all were "out" at the time of interview. It was equally clear, however, that they had this attitude in spite of their schooling. Here is an example, a story told by one of the informants.

INTERVIEWEE: So when I was reading my speech [in class], the principal happened to walk in just as I admitted that I was, in fact, gay. As far as I can remember his chin hit the floor, he was so flabbergasted . . . and called me to the office afterwards.

RESEARCHER: He called you to the office. And what happened there?

INTERVIEWEE: Basically he warned me that if I didn't keep my sexual preference under wraps that I'd be suspended. And I said, "Well it's my business, and if I want to share it with people it's up to me; nobody can tell me not to tell other people who I am . . . 'cause I'm not afraid of it, so why should I be?" That's basically what my attitude was back then and still is. I was suspended for being rude and insubordinate.

What was typical of these young men, in the end, was their straightforward attitude toward their sexuality. What emerged over and over again was a strong belief that they were not the horrible people others made them out to be simply because they were gay. My informants, whether high school students, university students, or "street kids," viewed their sexual orientation as a normal, natural part of themselves. This self-knowledge and clarity of identity stood in stark contrast to the popular conception most teachers, administrators, and fellow students held of homosexuals and homosexuality.

●Gossip and the Ideology of "Fag": The Social Organization of Stigma

The fag as stigmatized object is constituted in "gossip." Gossip projects the fag as object of the ideology's activities; a fag is pivotal to their actualization even if one has to be invented.

> RESEARCHER: How often would they occur? Who was beaten up? People they just thought were fags?
>
> INTERVIEWEE: Yeah. I would say the last point is really the most important. It's quite often that they were only people perceived to be fags. I don't think that half the time, they ever really were. Or, half the time what people . . . if people really knew what a fag was, to be that intent on determining whether that person's sexual orientation was one way or the other. What it would entail was, depending on the circumstances, I mean, I . . . there was a few times where fights would break out in the cafeteria I recall, but more often it would happen after school. Somebody would be sort of systematically singled out, and a group of people would harass that person, and if a fight ensued, then usually it wasn't in the individual's favor. There would usually be a number of people involved, even if it was only one person who was actually physically beating on that person.

Within the ideology of fag, characteristics made visible by the organization of gender are seen as documenting the "underlying pattern" of fag. Here the documentary method of interpretation enforces the difference, required by heterosexual hegemony, between what is properly male or female. Characteristics that blur this boundary (e.g. effeminacy, being "bookish" or unathletic) document the underlying pattern of fag. This is not just a mental activity, as the documentary method of interpretation seems to imply. Rather, it forms a social course of action contextualized by the relations of gender. Identifying a fag, and thereby engaging the ideology, is an activity usually organized within a group of male heterosexual students.

> INTERVIEWEE: I mean, it was assumed that you were heterosexual, and I think that more than anything was my biggest problem. So maybe it's more productive to talk about heterosexism than homophobia, because it was just assumed that you were, and if you went to a school dance and you

knew more than one or two steps then you were a fag. If you made any conscious attempt to look well dressed or were perceived to dress "funny"—you know, in quotations—you were a fag.

The above interview excerpt points to the social character of being labeled "fag." Finding the fag is socially, indeed dialogically, organized in speech, primarily through gossip, and, as we see below, sometimes textually in the form of graffiti. The interpersonal organization of gossip as the activities of speakers and listeners, writers and readers, makes this a piece of social organization there to be described.

> RESEARCHER: What about this kind of gossip or that kind of thing, what form did that take?
>
> INTERVIEWEE: Primarily it would be comments overheard in the halls as people were at their lockers and someone would walk by and either an explicit comment would be yelled at them, such as "fag," "queer," or "cocksucker," sometimes, and either that or you'd hear little whispers like, "She's a dyke," or "I hear she lives with another woman," or whatever, or "Avoid her in the showers," whatever, something like that, so it was to my mind very, very petty backbiting sort of . . .

I want to examine more carefully two informants' accounts of activities in which the fag as stigmatized object operates as a coordinative device. The first is a report of graffiti scrawled near a men's toilet; the second reports an English teacher's routine comments to students hanging out near the men's toilet at an alternative high school. The similarities of these accounts—the same rhetoric is in both—points again to the generalized character of the ideology of fag.

> RESEARCHER: Was there any sort of graffiti on the walls or any jokes or anything like that? Can you tell me anything about that?
>
> INTERVIEWEE: Okay, in this one washroom in the school, it was like downstairs, there was like graffiti written on the walls and, "Anyone found going in this washroom, we will know is . . ."
>
> RESEARCHER: Is queer?
>
> INTERVIEWEE: "Anyone caught going in this washroom, we know is a faggot."
>
> INTERVIEWEE: Even the English teacher . . . [who] was really the most open-minded, the most nonconformist, in the sense that he dressed always in whatever he wanted to. No other school would see a teacher dressed like that. The thing is he went to the students' . . . the lounge for

the alternative school was right . . . outside the lounge there were two doors—one for the women's washroom, one for the men's washroom—and therefore a lot of students would just . . . instead of going into the lounge to talk to other students, they'd just stand outside, as they were passing each other by, and they'd just talk. So the men would be standing beside the men's washroom, and the English teacher would walk by and often say, "Oh you know what they say about guys who hang out by the washroom." So they have things like that constantly.

Both of these accounts show how producing fag is organized in language among writers and readers, speakers and hearers, active in particular social settings. In the first excerpt above, the social character of the activity is textually mediated in the writing and reading of graffiti. The exchange that produces a fag connects the writer and readers of the text. Reading the graffiti "activates" the text, coordinating a social course of action—a form of consciousness: Even if nobody was seen using this toilet, everyone is alerted to be on the look out for a possible fag. Every reader has learned from the text one way of identifying a fag. Every reader has been given a basic lesson in homophobia in learning how to produce a fag as a stigmatized object. Thus, the social organization generated by the text shapes the consciousness of students, setting up this course of action as potential, waiting to be actualized, waiting for the opportunity to produce a "fag" on some appropriate occasion.

In the second excerpt, producing the "fag" is locally organized in the talk between teacher and students. In this instance, the teacher's remarks engage the process and coordinate it as a course of action. Most probably the teacher is using this "joking" form of queer baiting as a method of control—that is, to stop the students from congregating in the hallway. His remarks deploy the same rhetorical device as the graffiti. In this case, the dialogic organization is striking. Students are hooked as listeners into a discourse already being carried on by others—"Oh, you know what they say. . . ." The teacher's remarks teach the documentary method of interpretation that produces the fag as a stigmatized object.

Informants reported a range of antigay abuse and violence. These activities, as with finding the fag, were organized through utterances, whether as talk or text. Informants could not describe what had gone on in their schools without remembering or reconstructing comments, snatches of conversations, or graffiti scrawled on students' lockers, toilet cubicles, or school walls. The utterances they recalled included their own internal conversations. My informants were caught up in the organization of these ideological practices and how they were located by them as gay men. Through them, they came to identify themselves as gay, if they had not already done so, and to experience being gay in school as isolation.

VERBAL ABUSE: ACCOMPLISHING THE
IDEOLOGY OF "FAG" IN TALK

The peculiar form of social organization I have called the "ideology of fag" is assembled reflexively: The language used intends a course of action, and the resulting course of action actualizes what is latent in the rhetoric of fag, for example, by isolating the gay student or subjecting him to physical violence. Carrying out such a course of action accomplishes what speech has already intended. The pivotal role of language in this process displays the reflexivity of the course of action. Verbal abuse identifies the stigmatized object, thereby marking him for attack, but is itself part of the attack. The organization of the activity is both in and coordinated by talk.

In the following accounts, informants make use of their knowledge of how antigay speech works and how the social organization of homophobic courses of action unfold in school settings, starting with talk and ending in physical violence. Each of the following examples gives a different account, but all reflect the same social organization. It is the ubiquity of this form of organization that locates the generalized form of the ideology of fag. This property does not rely on the procedures for arguing from a sample to a population (in a sense, I am not concerned with individuals here) but on the actual recursive organization of constituent practices. The generalized ideology of fag is part of the real world, there to be described.

RESEARCHER: Can you give me some examples of how you determined that it [homosexuality] was "fiercely taboo," as you put it?

INTERVIEWEE: I think just the language, and what you would overhear in the hallways, just being very negative. Okay, if a few people did talk about people being gay, then that would be immediately followed by not associating with this person, ostracizing this person, often actually following through and doing that, harassing the person on a regular basis, to their face.

The practical work of identifying gay students and attacking them is a course of action with a distinctive social organization. I have described how the ideology of fag is put in place through the use of language. Its effect is to isolate the individuals identified in a variety of ways. This process I call "entering" the ideology of fag. One student, at the time in the closet and so with no problems at school arising from his sexual orientation, described how an "out" gay friend was treated to what he calls "ignorant comments." He reported that his friend "didn't have that many friends. People just kept away from him." The use of what one informant called "negative" language is followed by not associating with him or by outright ostracism.

INTERVIEWEE: So what would happen if people flaunted it [i.e., did not hide the fact that they were gay]?

RESEARCHER: People like George, for example, they'd call him "faggot." He would be ostracized. People would exclude him from different things. You know students, generally I guess, wouldn't go out of their way for him. They might drop a door on him or . . . wouldn't talk to him. He felt very excluded. Actually I think he ended up feeling so excluded that he left school. He thinks he was driven out of the school.

A further intensification is regular harassment "to [his] face," a confrontational form of abuse that foreshadows violence. Harassment builds into borderline or actual physical attacks.

RESEARCHER: Oh they'd pick on you, in the cafeteria?

INTERVIEWEE: I had one incident when I was going up for a meal, one of the junior kids at the school decided that—he walked by and he tripped me and [spilled] my tray and said something like "a faggot needs to be on his knees."

Antigay violence is, as one informant described it, the "logical conclusion" to the antigay abuse. Another said it was "kind of odd" when this outcome did not materialize. Thus the sequence organized within the ideology of fag goes from naming that identifies the fag through verbal abuse and ostracism to harassment in which verbal attacks are combined with petty violence and finally to outright violence.

GRAFFITI: THE TEXT-MEDIATED
ACCOMPLISHMENT OF THE IDEOLOGY OF FAG

The ideology of fag may also be coordinated by the practice of scrawling antigay graffiti on toilet stalls, on someone's locker, or on the walls of the school. Graffiti are a form of public speech but with a permanence lacking in speech. Antigay graffiti are sometimes used to identify a fag as when the word *fag* is written on someone's locker, and in such instances they serve to isolate gay students and incite harassment of them. As with verbal abuse, graffiti both identify the stigmatized object and are a form of attack upon the fag. They also set up a dialogic process, linking writers and readers. In these respects, there is little difference between talk and text in coordinating the ideology of fag. However, the text's relative permanence gives them a powerful role. Detaching utterance from author, they speak to every passerby who cares to look and read. A depersonalized form of threat and harassment against an individual is produced, coming from no one in particular, but inciting readers in general to marginalize and attack the gay student they identify. Their relative permanence gives them a powerful role in organizing the ideology of fag.

Accounts of homophobic graffiti figured prominently in how my interviewees were treated at school. Again their accounts display the ubiquity and generalized character of the ideology of fag.

RESEARCHER: So was there any other incident that comes to your mind about that period that was sort of homophobic? You said that the school was really homophobic in a "people way." What other kind of things . . . how would you describe that?

INTERVIEWEE: Among other things, spray painting fag on a locker, the person's locker; going off and carving into the school . . . you know how some people love to carve hearts with J. H. or something. Well, they'd scrawl the person's name and then put "queer" or "gay" or something like that.

INTERVIEWEE: I said that homosexuals are people too. "Look at me. I am one." And I think the whole school just about died. *[laughter]* The next day I had "faggot," "queer," and "homo" and all sorts of junk like that all over my locker to which I just drew a big pink triangle and said, "I am so, and I'm proud of it." Didn't seem to bother me at all. But the ridicule I got from people physically and verbally was a little bit much. So I ended up quitting school.

The work done by graffiti reflexively coordinates and directs the ideology of fag. A writer uses graffiti to make public statements that he cannot make publicly himself, perhaps because he fears official censure or because he has no access to a medium of public communication. Graffiti claim the authority of the public space. Though they may not always be successful in accomplishing what they intend within the ideology of fag, they are read, even if reinterpreted or read ironically. But often they do work. Over and over again the young men I interviewed described how the graffiti isolated them at school, in some instances forcing them to leave school altogether. The patriarchal forms of heterosexism graffiti coordinate are not exclusively the writers'. Though graffiti as a medium are ordinarily identified as speaking from an underground, antigay graffiti trade on the general patriarchal relations that are the basis of school life. Lack of administrative intervention is tacit acceptance of the ideology of fag. It is a measure of the school administration's heterosexism and its complementary homophobia.

The Dialogic of the Stigma of Fag:
Gay Consciousness and Self-Identification

Students first learn to identify fags and how to treat them through the social organization of talk and text in school. This is equally true for homosexual and bisexual as well as for "straight" students. Indeed, it is in part out of the dialogic of the ideology of fag that some gay students come to see themselves as gay and take on gay identity. Though presumably not intentionally, the ideology of fag thus accomplishes gay identity/consciousness. As informants describe the process, consciousness emerges dialogically in the characteristic sequence of the ideology of fag, beginning with gossip and foreshadowing if not actually concluding in violence. A gay consciousness is formed dialogically in this socially isolating process.

The antigay rhetoric enters these students into the ideology of fag as a form of consciousness for them, whether or not they are subject to direct attack. Many of my informants reported that they knew they were "different" early in life but that entering the ideology of fag during their high school years identified and shaped their consciousness of difference. School gossip and sometimes verbal abuse were the dialogic context in which some homosexual students develop fully fledged gay identities:

INTERVIEWEE: [W]hen I was in elementary school, I did a lot of ballet. I was at the National Ballet School one summer. And that sort of stigma *[laugh]* which I never thought was a stigma, or could be a stigma, but which became a stigma, followed me into high school. And that was followed with comments continually—"fag," you know, "fag." I think that was actually . . . one of the reasons why I eventually gave up ballet was just because of the constant harassment and also pursuing other interests. But I think that was at the back of my mind a lot of the time with the harassment, and realizing that they're right. That's what I was. I knew that that's what I was.

The organizing effects of fag rhetoric on the gay consciousness of my informants was profound. This use of language, this naming within the patriarchy, sets up an internal dialogue within individuals.

INTERVIEWEE: I never really thought about it [passing]. I just acted like the way I always did—normal. I didn't put up a front to say I wasn't gay or whatever. People always called me "homo," and I said, "If that's what you want to think, go ahead." And in the back of my mind I'd think, "I wish you knew how right you were."

Some gay students took up the ideology of fag as a set of practices and activities for protecting themselves:

RESEARCHER: What did you then do to hide it [being gay]?

INTERVIEWEE: I had to lie, like, "Hey man, so what if I know gay people, doesn't mean I'm gay." And like one guy goes, "I know you are. Just admit it." I said, "I ain't no faggot!" And the way I came on to him . . . I came on strong, and he goes, "I'm just kidding, relax." And I said, "Relax! You called me a fucking faggot, and I'm going to relax about it?" And so I said, "Just get out of my. . . ." Then after he left, I'd be laughing to myself.

Some became preoccupied with being identified as gay or almost compulsively concerned with avoiding stereotypical fag behavior.

INTERVIEWEE: Well, . . . it would have been just everything, from being, like, nervous about, am I walking the right way? Am I talking the right way? Do I move my hands too much? I mean, that sort of thing. I mean, that's just sort of general paranoia.

The contradictions one informant experienced made self-isolation a forced choice.

INTERVIEWEE: I just stayed to myself in school . . .

RESEARCHER: How long were you there in that school?

INTERVIEWEE: Almost three months. I just stayed really to myself.

RESEARCHER: Yes, and then you left?

INTERVIEWEE: Yes . . . I had like, kids in my own class would come up to me and start talking like, "Do you want to go . . . ?" or, "What are you doing on noon hour . . . ?" and I said, "Oh I don't know." And like, "So you want to go and smoke a [inaudible] somewhere?" . . . "Oh no, I don't do anything like that. I've got to meet somebody at noon hour."

RESEARCHER: So then you just left that school. Did it have anything to do with your being gay?

INTERVIEWEE: I didn't like the thought of me just having to ignore everyone. I could have played like the straight guy, like, "Check that baby out, uh huh." I could have done that, but I just like, stayed to myself, did my school work, left school. I wouldn't take the bus home either. I didn't want to meet anybody.

The gay consciousness of my informants was organized by the ideology of fag. This view of consciousness as social activities based in language contrasts to the conception of consciousness as a private mental state. The social organization of gay consciousness is visible in social activities that are ordinarily available to be described. Its dialogic creates for gay students a breach in everyday consciousness through which they come to see themselves as marginalized, isolated, and other.

THE IDEOLOGY OF FAG AND RELATIONS OF GENDER

The ideology of fag is embedded in and organized by contemporary heterosexual relations of gender. Take, for example, one informant's description of the work of passing as heterosexual in order to avoid the stigma of fag. On this occasion, it is the gendered organization of the setting that initiates fag baiting. Passing in this and in every other instance depends on knowing how to assemble heterosexuality. So, in describing the work of passing, my informant reveals how the ideology of fag is embedded in the social organization of heterosexuality. Lack of interest in the opposite sex can trigger fag baiting and fag-baiting gossip.

> RESEARCHER: How was it when you were in the closet in school? How would you go about passing? What sorts of things would you have to do to make sure that you stayed in the closet? How did you . . . ?
>
> INTERVIEWEE: Okay, well I'm happy you asked that. It's unreal what people have to do. You know when all the guys would be making the girl jokes, you'd have to go along with them, as much as you tried not to, you still had to chuckle here and there to not raise suspicion . . . very frequently, jokingly, some students would say to other students—when they didn't necessarily conform to all the jokes and the way of thinking of women students—they'd say, "What, you're not gay, are you?" just jokingly . . . it was said jokingly but half seriously, so you didn't want that accusation left about you. If it was, you'd know you'd be ready to deny it wholeheartedly, and to that extent you'd even talk about other female students at school that you said you were interested in. When in reality you weren't . . . and you had to make sure you did stuff like that.

In this description, the language of "girl jokes" coordinates a particular set of gender relations and a particular form of male consciousness. My informant describes this as a "way of thinking about women students." On one level these jokes express an interest in the opposite sex. But this says little about how they work as jokes among students. As social organization, they create for the students involved a heterosexual masculinity defined by treating women as objects of heterosexual humor and as inferior to men. The ideology of fag is used to coerce a male student who "didn't necessarily conform."

Activities that define heterosexual masculinity are activities of men in groups. Failure to join in risks initiating the cycle organized by the ideology of fag. Informants' accounts often distinguish between such group displays of heterosexual masculinity and associations of other kinds with students, including genuine friendships. Thus, informants' accounts show the ideology of fag operating at the level of public or "popular" relations among students. It organizes males as groups but not necessarily the practices of single individuals. Fag baiting at school was described almost invariably as launched by groups of students and under pressure from peers.

> INTERVIEWEE: It [avoiding me] depended on whether they were in a group or if they were by themselves. If they were in a group they would be much more homophobic and stick together as a group, and whereas alone they might not . . . they might still talk to me. It would vary. They might realize that since they weren't in a group and the peer pressure wasn't an influence on them and so that changed.

Gay students are located differently from their heterosexual counterparts in the gender relations of the school. The social consciousness in which they participate is differentiated from the heterosexist domination of the public space and hence is embedded in different social relations.

One of my informants who was "out" at school described how his friendly association with girls could trigger the ideology's sequence of harassment and violence.

> RESEARCHER: How does that work? How does the violence come in and what was it like?
> INTERVIEWEE: Well the violence comes in because now you get a bunch of guys who . . . "Oh my God, there's a fag," or if they're associating with girls or whatever or other friends of theirs, the jealousy . . . they can't see how I get along so good with these girls and so the jealousy and the fact that you're gay that's a turn off for them, and they say, "Oh, we can't see this happening," and they don't think, they're just . . . they start with the names and then with the pushing and . . .

A distinctive feature of the ideology of fag is that it is basically the work of males. Informants' accounts suggest that gay students would be more likely to be out to women than to men in school. Moreover none of my informants described being verbally abused or harassed by women students, though this does not mean that it never occurred or that the girls were not to some degree homophobic. In interview after interview, informants made visible how the ideology of fag enforced the rule of heterosexual males and hence the relations of patriarchy in their schools. Among males, behavior subverting these relations brought the ideology into play to coerce conformity.

HETEROSEXIST HEGEMONY IN THE SCHOOL

With the help of my informants, I have been describing the antigay activities that are a normal, everyday part of school social organization. I have identified these activities as the ideology of fag. In their ubiquity, they are independent of any particular individual and of any particular school. Informants' lives were shaped by the ideology of fag no matter where they went to school. Virtually all the schools that the interviews investigated were organized as local iterations of these generalized ideological practices. The recursive properties of the ideology constitute it as a general phenomenon. A gay student might have genuine friends, male or female (though more often female), but heterosexism had hegemony in the public consciousness.

Popularity in school is a publicly defined status. The social relations of heterosexuality and patriarchy dominated the public space of the school, and popularity was defined within that public space. Students identified as gay, whether by themselves or by others, could not be "popular" in schools. Public status among students in the school meant being straight or acting straight. One sixteen-year-old youth, a member of the student council, had just quit school because he was afraid of the social repercussions when his fellow students found out he was gay. What triggered this set of events was simply that a young woman from his school saw him going into a gay club in downtown Toronto.

"Passing" is generally understood in terms of the individual, but in relation to the heterosexist hegemony over the public spaces of the school, it must also be understood as it affected the possibility of the formation of gay groups or open gay friendships in schools.

> INTERVIEWEE: Yes, and another thing, I found out, when we were talking with my friends now, who live in . . . they also thought other people were gay but they never went up to that person to say, "Are you gay?" because they were scared to do that in case they might be wrong, and everyone would know for sure that they were gay, and also, it's a problem hanging out with each other, because if everyone thinks you're gay and like individuals who are gay, and then those individuals hang out together, you know it's like a confirmation, so . . .

Many of my informants who were closeted in school claimed that, as far as they knew, they were the only gay person in their high school; later, they learned of many high school contemporaries who were also gay. Over half of the young men mentioned, after having left school, meeting or hearing about high school contemporaries who turned out to be gay.

Not knowing who else was gay at school made any form of support and solidarity among the gay students virtually impossible. This isolation of gay students as individuals was a major feature of the social organization of "passing" as straight at school. Though gay students might find individual support from friends and teachers, no school is reported as challenging the heterosexist hegemony of its public space.

The Official Silence of the School

At best, the official organization of the school assumes that all students are heterosexual; at worst, it implies that it is professionally appropriate to attack and isolate gay students on the basis of their sexual orientation. When my informants got support from teachers, it was always a personal matter and not the result of official school policy or professional responsibility.

One informant had kept a notebook recording the heterosexism of teachers. Notebook in hand, he described to me the ideological practices of his history teacher, constituting homosexuals as beyond the pale of moral society.

INTERVIEWEE: I have all the quotations of all the homophobic comments and so, like off the top of my head, the one like . . . he did talk about homosexuals but only in very negative context, so he talked about when the Nazis, Ernst Roehm . . . like we were talking about Nazi Germany and Hitler and all that, and he was talking about the Nazi system, the storm troops, and how Roehm was head of that, and he was making fun, the history teacher was making fun, of him. Like how he was from an aristocratic background, but was really into leather and young boys. And it was the night of the long knives in 1934, and he was found in bed with his chauffeur, or something, and killed. And this history teacher was much more homophobic in making light of it, and he would do imitations of homosexuals . . .

The patriarchal context makes fag the stigmatized other. Such ideological practices are supported by and support the social relations of gender pervasive in the wider society. In school, this is visible in how school authorities—teachers, counselors, and principals—give tacit support and sometimes even approval to the local practices of the ideology of fag. Tacit approval of the ideology was given when teachers pretended not to hear and, hence could ignore, the use of fag-baiting language in the corridors and classrooms.

RESEARCHER: Now the staff and the school would never have access to this kind of gossip [in the corridors of the school]?

INTERVIEWEE: They might have. They could walk up and down the halls and hear it the same as anyone else. Generally however, I think that most of the staff either ignored it or pretended to ignore it. They simply would refuse to give comments.

Counteracting homophobia or heterosexism was not part of the professional responsibilities of teachers, as it might be in curbing the ideology of "race."

INTERVIEWEE: But when you're in a general classroom, when you hear somebody up front say, "Oh ya, fucking faggots," or something to that effect, you couldn't do anything, whereas if they'd said, "Those fucking niggers," the teacher would probably say something, most likely . . .

Worst of all were teachers who would encourage or even join in the anti-gay talk. One student, whose teachers generally were supportive, described some teachers who, when he was verbally abused, laughed along with the students. Some teachers were openly homophobic. This seemed particularly true of physical education teachers. Indeed, physical education programs were notable in this respect and were especially alienating for gay students. Like public sporting events, physical education operates as an organizational nod-ule coordinating patriarchal relations in our society, authorizing the male teachers' participation in the ideology of fag. Beer advertisements on televi-sion, for example, or the way wars are described, the use of sports metaphors in managerial occupations, and the topic of sports as a kind of male lingua franca all trade on the relations of male hegemony.

INTERVIEWEE: I find that's probably one of the most intimidating things about phys ed, (a) how competitive it was, and (b) always being exposed to phys ed teachers and particularly this one that I can recall, who con-stantly poked fun at people who were not informed, and part of poking fun is this notion of "sissy" and then you know, whether they carried that over into something that I would label homophobic or not, and I seem to recall that he did on several occasions. Often students would, after class, carry on and taunt you and that would, you know, if this authority figure said, it's okay to call you a sissy and determines that you're a sissy then, wow, talk about carte blanche, we have freedom to basically feel . . . make you feel shitty about yourself and did often.

RESEARCHER: The phys ed instructor was . . .

INTERVIEWEE: Definitely very homophobic, and I even suspected him of being gay at times . . .

Some informants reported that teachers would attack fellow teachers who were gay (and must have done so where they could be overheard by students).

RESEARCHER: What happened around that?

INTERVIEWEE: He led a very straight lifestyle, and he was also very well liked by the student body, although behind his back, there were tons of jokes, even from the other teachers or the other faculty, making jokes about it [the fact that he was a homosexual].

Some reported teachers who were supportive on an individual basis.

INTERVIEWEE: I found that with the teachers, because you get some kind of relationship with the teachers, so the teachers are more understanding because you see them every day and talk to them. I'm not saying with all teachers but the teachers that you get along with, they would help you out, they would ask you if you were having problems, but with the principal, I don't think so. Although there are large numbers of homosexuals in the society, homosexuality is a forbidden topic of instruction in most schools. This means that most students remain ignorant of a substantial minority of people in contemporary society.

One informant described consulting a counselor whose response made it clear that the school's hands-off policy toward homosexuality was official.

INTERVIEWEE: And also, at one time, I was very confused about my sexuality, and I felt the need to talk to someone, and I went to the school guidance counselor, and he responded with, he's not allowed to talk to us about the subject because he'd get in trouble with the school board. He didn't give me a phone number, he didn't give me the stress number or LGYT or anything like that. He just sort of just left it at that and closed the subject before it was really open, so that was another piss off, and that made me stay in the closet a little longer than I had to.

Consistently, these stories in various ways make visible the official tolerance of the local practices of the ideology of fag as an implementation of the hegemony of heterosexism in the schools.

CONCLUSION

That the ideology of fag is primarily a practice of (some) male students seems to divest teachers and counselors as well as the school administration of responsibility. But the foregoing analysis and the accounts of the experiences of gay students in schools shows the power and effectiveness of a public regime of heterosexism. The ideology of fag dominates the public space of schools and defines its public discourse. Teachers may overtly participate in or just go along with its local practices. Those who may be supportive of gay students as individuals lack a public voice. Curriculum materials in social studies, literature, and health avoid the topic of homosexuality. Counselors appear to be untrained in providing the kinds of support that gay students need and act merely as buffers that individualize the "problem." The local practices of the ideology of fag are never penalized or publicly condemned. Explicitly homophobic ridicule in sports contexts goes unremarked. Effective toleration of the ideology of fag among students and teachers condemns gay students to the isolation of passing or ostracism and sometimes to a life of hell in school.

Those who were "in the closet" were consigned by the official tolerance of the ideology of fag to a dialogue with it in which they sorted out their sexuality in isolation, ignorance, and fear. For students who were "out" in high school the ideology of fag conducted a sequence in which verbal abuse, ostracism, and harassment culminated in the conclusive isolation of dropping out. The occasional hero who sought a gay appropriation of the public space of the school suffered heavy penalties. Schools must be held responsible for the arbitrary suffering of gay students as well as for the barrier to education that it creates, at least for those who are driven to the final exclusionary logic of the ideology of fag. The experiences of gay students as they have spoken them in the examples recorded in this chapter show schools as complicit in the everyday cruelties of the ideology's enforcement of heterosexist hegemony. This is a school-created environment and an act of government.

Listening Hard:
Silence and Dissent

Race, Suburban Resentment, and the Representation of the Inner City in Contemporary Film and Television

Cameron McCarthy, Alicia Rodriguez,
Shuaib Meecham, Stephen David,
Carrie Wilson-Brown, Heriberto Godina,
K. E. Supryia, and Ed Buendia

Introduction

MUCH CONTEMPORARY MAINSTREAM and radical theorizing on race and popular culture places television, film, and advertising outside the circuits of social meanings, as though these practices were preexisting, self-constituting technologies that then exert effects on an undifferentiated mass public (Parenti, 1992; Postman, 1986). This chapter counters that tendency. We see television and film as fulfilling a certain bardic function, singing back to society lullabies about what a large hegemonic part of it "already knows." Like Richard Campbell (1987), we reject the vertical model of communication that insists on encoding/decoding. We are more inclined to theorize the operation of communicative power in horizontal or rhizomatic terms. Television and film, then, address and position viewers at the "center" of a cultural map in which suburban, middle-class values "triumph" over practices that drift away from mainstream social norms. In this arrangement, the suburb, in the language of

Christopher Lasch (1991), becomes "The True and Only Heaven": the great incubator and harbinger of neoevolutionary development, progress, and modernity in an erstwhile unstable and unreliable world.

Suburban dweller here refers to all those agents traveling in the covered wagons of postsixties white flight from America's increasingly black, increasingly immigrant urban centers. White flight created settlements and catchment areas that fanned out farther and farther away from the city's inner radius, thereby establishing the racial character of the suburban-urban divide (Wilson, 1994). As tax-based revenues, resources, and services followed America's fleeing middle classes out of the city, a great gulf opened up between the suburban dweller and America's inner-city resident. Into this void contemporary television, film, and popular culture entered, creating the most poignantly sordid fantasies of inner-city degeneracy and moral decrepitude. These representations of urban life would serve as markers of the distance the suburban dweller had traveled away from perdition. Televisual and filmic fantasies would also underscore the extent to which the inner-city dweller was irredeemably lost in the dystopic urban core. Within the broad vocabulary of representational techniques at its disposal, the preference for the medium shot in television tells the suburban viewer, "We are one with you," as the body of the television subject seems to correspond one-for-one with the viewer.

As Raymond Williams (1974) argues in *Television: Technology, and Cultural Form*, television, film, advertising, textbooks, and so forth are powerful forces situated in cultural circuits themselves—not outside as some pure technological or elemental force or some fourth estate, as the professional ideology of mainstream journalism tends to suggest. These are circuits that consist of a proliferation of capacities, interests, needs, desires, priorities, and commitments—fields of affiliation and fields of association.

One such circuit is the discourse of resentment or the practice of defining one's identity through the negation of the other. This chapter will call attention to this discourse in contemporary race relations and point to the critical coordinating role of news magazines, television, the Hollywood film industry, and the common sense of black filmmakers themselves in the reproduction and maintenance of the discourse of resentment, particularly its supporting themes of crime, violence, and suburban security.

Drawing on the theories of identity formation in the writings of C. L. R. James (1978, 1993) and Friedrich Nietzsche (1967), we argue that the filmic and electronic media play a critical role in the production and channeling of suburban anxieties and retributive morality onto its central target: the depressed inner city. These developments deeply inform race relations in late-twentieth-century society. These race relations are conducted in the field of simulation as before a putative public court of appeal (Baudrillard, 1983).

STANDING ON THE PYRES OF RESENTMENT

I feel deadly faint, bowed and humped, as though I were Adam,
staggering beneath the piled centuries since Paradise.
—Ahab in Herman Melville's *Moby Dick*, 1851, p. 535

These words uttered in a moment of crisis in the nineteenth-century canon-
ical text of Herman Melville's *Moby Dick* (1851) might well have been
uttered by Michael Douglas as D-fens in the contemporary popular cultural
text of *Falling Down* (1993), or by Douglas as Tom Sanders in the antifemi-
nist, protoresentment film *Disclosure* (1995). Douglas is the great twentieth-
century suburban middle-class male victim, flattened and spread out against
the surface of a narcotic screen "like a patient etherized upon a table" (Eliot,
1964, p. 11).

    In two extraordinary texts written in the late forties, *Mariners, Rene-
gades, and Castaways: The Story of Herman Melville and the World We Live In*
(1978) and *American Civilization* (1993), C. L. R. James made the provoca-
tive observation that American popular cultural texts—popular film, popular
music, soap operas, comic strips, and detective novels—offered sharper intellectual lines of insight into the contradictions and tensions of modern life in
postindustrial society than the entire corpus of academic work in the social
sciences. For James, comic strips such as *Dick Tracy* (first published in 1931)
and popular films such as Charlie Chaplin's *Modern Times* (1936) and John
Huston's *Maltese Falcon* (1941, based on the novel by Dashiell Hammett)
were direct aesthetic descendants of Melville's *Moby Dick*. These popular
texts removed the veil that covered twentieth-century social relations "too
terrible to relate," except in the realm of fantasy and imagination (Morrison,
1990, p. 302).

    For James, these popular texts foregrounded the rise of a new historical
subject on the national and world stage: the resentment-type personality.
This subject was a projection of the overrationalization and sedimented
overdeterminations of the modern industrial age ("the fearful mechanical
power of an industrial civilization which is now advancing by incredible
leaps and bounds and bringing at the same time mechanization and destruction of the human personality," [1978, p. 8]). James's new subject articulated
an authoritarian populism: the mutant, acerbic, and emotionally charged
common sense of the professional middle class (Douglas with a satchel of
hand grenades in *Falling Down*, Harry and Louise of the antihealth care
reform ads). This authoritarian personality was, in James's view, willing to
wreck all in the hell-bent prosecution of his own moral agenda and personal
ambition. According to James, what was unusual and egregious about the
resentment personality type in *Moby Dick* and the nineteenth-century world
of Melville had become pseudonormative by the time of *The Maltese Falcon*

in the 1940s—a period marked by the rise of what James (1993) called "non-chalant cynicism" (p. 125).

Thus in *The Maltese Falcon* (1941), detective Sam Spade (Humphrey Bogart) puts the woman he loves in jail for the murder of his corrupt partner, Miles Archer. Their love is overridden by the ideology of professionalism and the socionormative priority of making wrongdoers pay. As the paranoid Spade says plaintively to his lover, "I don't even like the idea of thinking there might be one chance in a hundred that you'd played me for a sucker" (Spade quoted in James, 1993, p. 125). In Sam Spade's world, lovers do not have any special privileges beyond the domestic sphere. Spade is playing by his own ethics and chucking human relations and feelings as encumbering eruptions of irrationality. This is a tart dish of public common sense. As the eternal proxy for middle-American values, Spade holds the line against the threat of invasion by the morally corrupt other, the socially different and the culturally deviant and deprived.

Contemporary popular discussion of crime and violence also follows this logic of closed narrative where the greatest fear is that the enemy will be let into our neighborhoods. And the greatest stress on public policy may be how to keep the unwanted off the tax payer–dependent welfare rolls and out of our town, safely in prisons, and so forth. Sam Spade's worries have had a meltdown in our time, at late century. And they have become a potent paranoid resentment brew that spills over from the fantasy land of television and film into the social world in which we live.

What James's astute comments point us toward is the fact that the filmic and televisual discourse of crime and violence is not simply about crime or violence. Art is not here simply imitating life in some unthinking process of mimesis. Art is productive and generative. Televisual and filmic discourses about crime and violence, as Gerbner (1970) and others argue, are fundamentally urban fables about the operation of power and the production of meaning and values in society. They are about moral reevaluation, about our collective tensions, crises, and fears. They are about how we as a society deal with the social troubles that afflict us: sexism, racism, and the like. In this sense, popular culture—the world of film noir and the grade B movie, of the tabloids, and of the mainstream press—constitutes a relentless pulp mill of social fictions of transmuted and transposed power. In the late twentieth century, Sam Spade was replaced by the towering popular and preternatural intelligence of Sweeney Erectus, our guide into the moral inferno. James wrote almost prophetically about resentment mutations and the time lag in the modern world in the late forties (Bhabha, 1994). The aim of this chapter is to describe the operation of resentment a half century later in our time—a time in which racial antagonism has been the host of a parasitic resentment stoked in the media and circulating in popular culture.

DANGER IN THE SAFETY ZONE

The crisis of the middle class is of commanding gravity. . . . The crisis is hardening the attitude of the middle class toward the dependent poor, and to the extent that the poor are urban and black and Latino and the middle class suburban and white, race relations are under a new exogenous strain . . .

—Jack Beatty, 1994, p. 70

Within the past year or so, *Time* magazine published two articles that together document the contemporary rise of suburban middle-class resentment. In these articles, crime and violence are fetishized, transmuted in the language of the coming invasion of the abstract racial other. According to the first article, "Danger in the Safety Zone," murder and mayhem are everywhere outside the suburban home: in the McDonald's restaurant, in the shopping mall, in the health club, in the courtroom (Smolowe, 1993, p. 29). The article also quoted and displayed statistics indicating that crime in the major cities had been declining somewhat while residents of the suburbs—the place where the middle classes thought they were safest—were now increasingly engulfed in random violence.

The second article is entitled "Patriot Games." It is about the mushrooming of heavily armed white militias in training, preparing for the war of wars against the federal government and nameless invading immigrants and foreign political forces that the Clinton administration somehow, unwittingly, encouraged to think that America is weak and lacking in resolve to police its borders. About these armed militias we are told:

In dozens of states, loosely organized paramilitary groups composed primarily of white men are signing up new members, stockpiling weapons and preparing for the worst. The groups, all privately run, tend to classify themselves as "citizen militias." . . . On a home video promoting patriot ideas, a man who gives his name only as Mark from Michigan says he fears that America will be subsumed into "one big, fuzzy, warm planet where nobody has any borders." Samuel Sherwood, head of the United States Militia Association in Blackfoot, Idaho, tells followers, absurdly, that the Clinton Administration is planning to import 100,000 Chinese policemen to take guns away from Americans. (Farley, *Time,* December 19, 1994, pp. 48–49)

What does all of this mean? These articles announce a new mood in political and social life in the United States: a mood articulated in suburban fear of encirclement by difference and increasingly formulated in a language and politics of what James and Nietzsche called "resentment." The dangerous inner city and the world "outside" are brought into the suburban home through television and film releasing new energies of desire mixed with fear. As we enter a new century, conflicts in education and popular culture are increasingly taking the form of grand panethnic battles over language, signs, and the occupation and territorialization of urban and suburban space. These conflicts intensify as the dual model of the rich-versus-poor city splinters into fragmentary communities signified by images of the roaming homeless on network television. For our late-twentieth-century Sweeney Erectus, standing on the pyres of resentment in the culturally beleaguered suburbs, the signs and wonders are everywhere in the television evening news. Sweeney's cultural decline is registered in radically changing technologies and new sensibilities, in spatial and territorial destabilization and recoordination, in the fear of falling, and in new and evermore incorrigible patterns of segregation and resegregation (Grossberg, 1992). Before his jaundiced eyes, immigrant labor and immigrant petty bourgeoisie now course through suburban and urban streets—the black and Latino underclasses after the Los Angeles riots, announces one irrepressibly gleeful news anchor, are restless. The fortunes of the white middle classes are, in many cases, declining. And the homeless are everywhere.

This new world order of mobile marginal communities is deeply registered in popular culture and in social institutions such as schools. The terrain to be mapped here is what Hal Foster (1983) in the *Anti-Aesthetic* calls postmodernism's "other side"—the new centers of the simulation of difference that loop back and forth through the news media to the classroom, from the film culture and popular music to the organization and deployment of affect in urban and suburban communities—Sweeney's homeground.

THE POLITICS OF AFFECT

The America of the diverging middle class is rapidly developing a
new populist anti-politics.
                                                                —Beatty, 1994, p. 70

You will recall that Fredric Jameson (1984), in his now famous essay "Postmodernism, or, the Cultural Logic of Late Capitalism," maintained that a whole new emotional ground tone separated life in contemporary postindustrial society from previous epochs. He described this ground tone as "the waning of affect," the loss of feeling. While we agree with Jameson that emotions, like music, art, film, literature, and architecture, are historically determined and culturally bound, we disagree with his diagnosis that contemporary life is overwhelmingly marked by a certain exhaustion or waning of affect. We maintain that a very different logic is at work in contemporary life, particularly in the area of race relations. Postmodernism's other side of race relations—of the manipulation of difference—is marked by a powerful concentration of affect, or the strategic use of emotion and moral reevaluation.

Like James, Nietzsche regarded the deployment of retributive morality as central to the organization and mobilization of power in modern industrial society. He also called this use of retributive morality "resentment." In his *Genealogy of Morals* (1967), Nietzsche defined resentment as the specific practice of defining one's identity through the negation of the other. Some commentators on Nietzsche associate resentment only with "slave morality." We are here taken genealogically back to "literal slaves" in Greek society, who being the most downtrodden had only one sure implement of defense: the acerbic use of emotion and moral manipulation. But we want to argue along with Robert Solomon (1990) that contemporary cultural politics is "virtually defined by bourgeois resentment" (p. 278). As Solomon maintains: "Resentment elaborates an ideology of combative complacency—a 'levelling' effect that declares society to be 'classless' even while maintaining powerful class structures and differences" (p. 278). The middle class declares there are no classes except itself, no ideology except its ideology, no party, no politics, except the politics of the center, the politics of the middle, with a vengeance.

A critical feature of discourses of resentment is their dependence on processes of simulation (Baudrillard, 1983). For instance, the suburban middle-class subject knows its inner-city other through an imposed system of infinitely repeatable substitutions and proxies: census tracts, crime statistics, tabloid newspapers, and television programs. Last, the inner-city other is known through the very ground of the displaced aggressions projected from suburban moral panic itself: it is held to embody what the center cannot acknowledge as its own (Beatty, 1994; Reed, 1992). Indeed, a central project of professional middle-class suburban agents of resentment is their aggressive attempt to hold down the moral center, to occupy the center of public discourse, to stack the public court of appeal. The needs of the suburbs therefore become "the national interests." By contrast, the needs of the inner city are dismissed as a wasteful "social agenda." Resentment is therefore an emotion "distinguished, first of all, by its concern and involvement with *power*" (Solomon, p. 278). Moreover, it is a power with its own material and discursive logic. In this sense it is to be distinguished from self-pity. If resentment has any desire at all, it is the "total annihilation . . . of its target" (p. 279). Sweeney offers his own homemade version of the final solution: take the homeless and the welfare moms off general assistance. Above all, build more prisons!

A new moral universe now rides the underbelly of the beast—late capital's global permutations, displacements, relocations, and reaccumulations. The effect has meant a material displacement of minority and other dispossessed groups from the landscape of contemporary political and cultural life. That is to say that increasingly the underclass or working-class subject is contemporaneously being placed on the outside of the arena of the public sphere as the middle-class sub-ject-object of history moves in to occupy and to appropriate the identity of the oppressed, the radical space of difference. The center becomes the margin. It is as if Primus Rex had decided to wear Touchstone's fool's cap, Caliban exiled from the cave as Prospero digs in. Resentment operates through the processes of simulation that usurp contemporary experiences of the real, where the real is proven by its negation or its inverse. Resentment has infected the very structure of social values.

This battle over signs is being fought in cultural institutions across the length and breadth of this society. We are indeed in a culture war. We know this, of course, because avatars of the right such as Patrick Buchanan (1992) and William Bennett (1994) constantly remind us of their books of values. As Buchanan put it bluntly, some time ago, "The GOP vote search should bypass the ghetto" (quoted in Omi & Winant, 1986, p. 124). From the cultural spiel of the 1992 and 1994 election campaigns, from family values to Murphy Brown, to the new corporate multicultural advertising, from rap music to the struggle over urban and suburban space, from the Rodney King beating, to Charles Stu-art, to Susan Smith, to O. J. Simpson, a turf battle over symbolic and material territory is under way. The politics of resentment is on the way as the suburbs continue to draw resources and moral empathy away from the urban centers.

Of course, a fundamental issue posed by the theories of resentment of James and Nietzsche is the challenge of defining identity in ways other than through the strategy of negation of the other. This, we wish to suggest, is the fundamental challenge of multiculturalism, the challenge of "living in a world of difference" (Mercer, 1992). Education is a critical site over which struggles over the organization and concentration of emotional and political investment and moral affiliation are taking place. The battle over signs, that is resentment, involves the articulation and rearticulation of symbols in the popular culture and in the media. These signs and symbols are used in the making of identity and the definition of social and political projects. Within this framework the traditional poles of left versus right, liberal versus conservative, democrat ver-sus republican, and so forth are increasingly being displaced by a more dynamic and destabilizing model of mutation of affiliation and association. A further dimension of this dynamic is that the central issues that made these binary oppositions of race and class conflict intelligible and coherent in the past have now collapsed or have been recoded. The central issues of social and economic inequality that defined the line of social conflict between left and right during the civil rights period are now, in the postcivil rights era, inhabited by the new adversarial discourses of resentment. Oppositional discourses of identity, his-tory and popular memory, nation, family, the deficit, and crime have displaced issues concerning equality and social justice. New Right publisher William Rusher articulates this displacement by pointing to a new model of material and ideological distinctions coming into being since the 1980s:

> A new economic division pits the producers—businessmen, manufacturers, hard-hats, blue-collar workers, and farmers [middle America]—against a new and powerful class of non-producers comprised of the liberal verbalist elite (the dominant media, the major foundations and research institutions, the educational establishment, the federal and state bureaucracies) and a semi-permanent welfare constituency, all coexisting happily in a state of mutually sustaining symbiosis. (Rusher quoted in Omi & Winant, 1986, p. 124)

Let us examine some manifestations of one of the principal articulations of resentment: the discourse of crime, violence, and suburban security. In the next section of this chapter, we will discuss examples from television evening news, film, and popular magazine and newspaper features that show the variability, ambiguity, and contradiction in this discourse of conflict. We will see that signifiers of the inner city as the harbinger of violence, danger, and chaos loop into the mass media and the suburbs and Hollywood and back again in the constructions of black male directors of the reality of the "hood."

"REFLECTING REALITY" AND FEEDING RESENTMENT

> Too often, black artists focus on death and destruction arguing that it is what's out there so we got to show it! Please!! What needs to be shown is the diversity and complexity of African American life.
>
> —*The Syracuse Constitution*, August 2, 1993, p. 5

The logic of resentment discourse does not proceed along a straight line in a communication system of encoding/decoding. It does not work one way from text to audience. Its reach is more diffuse, more rhizomatic, deeply intertextual. Resentment processes work from white to black and black to white, from white to Asian and Asian to white, and so on, looping in and out and back again as second nature across the bodies of the inhabitants of the inner city— the black world available to the black director who delivers the black audience to Hollywood. The inner city is thereby reduced to an endless chain of recyclable signifiers that both allure and repel the suburban classes.

But there is also the shared ground of discourses of the authentic inner city in which the languages of resentment and the reality of "the" hood commingle in films of black realism of black directors such as John Singleton and the Hughes brothers. This is a point that Joe Wood (1993) makes somewhat obliquely in his discussion of the film *Boyz 'N the Hood* (1992), which is set, incidentally, in South Central, Los Angeles. In a recent article published in *Esquire* magazine entitled "John Singleton and the Impossible Greenback Bind of the Assimilated Black Artist," Wood notes the following:

Boyz's simplified quality is okay with much of America. It is certain that many whites, including Sony executives and those white critics who lauded the film deliriously, imagine black life in narrow ways. They don't want to wrestle with the true witness; it might be scarier than "hell." Sony Pictures' initial reaction to *Boyz* is instructive: John confides that the studio wanted him to cut out the scene in which the cops harass the protagonist and his father. "Why do we have to be so hard on the police?" they asked. An answer came when Rodney King was beaten; the scene stayed in—it was suddenly "real." (Wood, August 1993, p. 64)

Here we see the elements of repeatability, the simulation of the familiar, and the prioritization of public common sense that evening television helps to both activate and stabilize. Hollywood drew intertextually on the reality code of television. Television commodified and beautified the images of violence captured on a street-wise camera. Singleton's claim to authenticity, ironically, relied not on endogenous inner-city perceptions but, exogenously, on the overdetermined mirror of dominant televisual news. *Boyz 'N the Hood* could safely skim off the images of the inner city corroborated in television common sense. For these Hollywood executives, police brutality became real when the Rodney King beating became evening news. As Wood argues:

> What Sony desired in *Boyz* was a film more akin to pornography . . . a safely voyeuristic film that delivered nothing that they did not already believe. . . . But how strenuously will they resist his showing how Beverley Hills residents profit from South Central gangbanging, how big a role TV plays in the South Central culture. (p. 65)

Of course, what even Joe Wood's critical article ignores about a film like *Boyz 'N the Hood* is its own errant nostalgia for a world in which blacks are centered and stand together against the forces of oppression; a world in which black men hold and practice a fully elaborated and undisputed paternity with respect to their children; a world that radically erases the fact that the location of the new realist black drama, Los Angeles, South Central, the memories of Watts, et cetera, are now supplanted by an immigrant and migrant presence in which, in many instances, black people are outnumbered by Latinos and Asian Americans (Davis, 1992; Fregoso, 1993; Lieberman, 1992).

Like the Hollywood film industry, the mainstream news media's address to black and brown America directs its gaze toward the suburban white middle class. It is the gaze of resentment in which aspect is separated from matter and substance undermined by the raid of the harsh surfaces and neon lights of inner-city life. In the sensation-dripping evening news programs of the networks—CBS, NBC, ABC, and CNN—as they pant to keep up with the inflamed journalism of the tabloids, black and Latino youth appear metonymically in the discourse of problems: "kids of violence," "kids of welfare moms," "car jackers," the "kids without fathers," "kids of illegal aliens," "kids who don't speak 'American.'" The skins of black and brown youth are hunted down like so many furs in the grand old days of the fur trade. The inner city is sold as a commodity and as a fetish, a signifier of danger and the unknown that at the same time narrows the complexity of urban working-class life. You watch network evening news, and you can predict when black and brown bodies will enter and when they will exit. The overwhelming metaphor of crime and violence saturates the dominant gaze on the inner city. News coverage of the cocaine trade between the United States and Columbia routinely suggests that only poor and black inner-city residents use cocaine, not rich suburban whites who are actually the largest consumers of the illegal drug.

The mass media's story of inner-city black and Latino people pays short shrift to the stunning decline of opportunity and social services in the urban centers within the last fifteen years: poor public schools, chronic unemployment, isolation, the hacking to death of the public transportation system, the radical financial disinvestment in the cities, and the flight of jobs and resources to the suburbs. All of these developments can ultimately be linked to government deprioritization of the poor as middle-class issues of law and order, more jail space, and capital punishment usurped the Clinton administration's gaze on the inner city. Instead, the inner city exists as a problem in itself and a problem to the world. The reality of the inner city is therefore not an endogenous discourse. It is an exogenous one. It is a discourse of resentment refracted back onto the inner city itself.

It is deeply ironic, then, that the images of the inner city presented by the current new wave of black cinema corroborate rather than critique mainstream mass media. Insisting on a kind of documentary accuracy and privileged access to the inner city, these directors construct a reality code of "being there" after the manner of the gangster rappers. But black film directors have no a priori purchase on the inner city. These vendors of chic realism recycle a reality code already in the mass media. This reality code operates as a system of repeatability, the elimination of traces, the elaboration of a hierarchy of discourses— the fabrication and consolidation of specular common sense.

Menace II Society (1993), created by Allen and Albert Hughes, is the capstone on a genre that mythologizes and beautifies the violent elements of urban life while jettisoning complexities of gender, ethnicity, sexuality, age, and economy. Instead of being didactic, like *Boyz 'N the Hood*, the film is nihilistic. The reality of the hood is built on a trestle of obviousnesses. Its central character, Caine Lawson (Tyrin Turner), is doomed to the life of drug running, car stealing, and meaningless violence that claims young men like himself (and before him, his father) from the time they can walk and talk. It is a world in which a trip to the neighborhood grocery can end in death and destruction, and gangbangers demand and enforce respect at the point of a gun. This point is made at the very beginning of the movie when Caine and his trigger-happy buddy, O-Dog (Larenz Tate), feel disrespected by a Korean store owner. The young men had come to the grocery to get a beer but are provoked into a stand-off when the store owner hovers too close to them. The young men feel insulted because the Korean grocer makes it too obvious that he views them with suspicion. In the blink of an eye, O-Dog settles the score with a bout of unforgettable violence. When Caine and O-Dog leave, the store owner and his wife are dead. And one act of violence simply precipitates another: by the end of the film, Caine too dies in a hail of bullets, a payback by the gang of a young man that Caine had beaten up mercilessly earlier in the film.

This film sizzles with a special kind of surface realism. There is a lot of blood and gore in the 'hood in *Menace II Society*. Shot sequences are dominated by long takes of beatings or shootings, almost always shot in extreme close-ups. Caine's life is supposed to be a character sketch of the inevitability of early death for inner-city male youth reared in a culture of violence. We have already seen it on television evening news before it hits the big screen. Black filmmakers therefore become pseudonormative bards to a mass audience, who, like the Greek chorus, already knows the refrain. These are not problem-solving films. They are films of confirmation. The reality code, the code of the 'hood, the code of blackness, of Africanness, of hardness, has a normative social basis. It combines and recombines with suburban middle-class discourses such as the deficit and balancing the federal budget; taxes; overbearing, overreaching, squandering government programs; welfare and quota queens; and the need for more prisons. It is a code drenched in public common sense. The gangster film has become paradigmatic for black filmic production out of Hollywood. And it is fascinating to see current films such as Singleton's *Higher Learning* (1995) glibly redraw the spatial lines of demarcation of the inner city and the suburbs onto other sites such as a university town: *Higher Learning* is *Boyz 'N the Hood* on campus.

It is to be remembered that early in his career, before *Jungle Fever* (1991), Spike Lee was berated by mainstream white critics for not presenting the inner city realistically enough—for not showing the drug use and violence. Lee obliged with a vengeance in *Jungle Fever* in the harrowing scenes of the drug addict Vivian (Halle Berry) shooting it up at the "Taj Mahal" crack joint and the Good Doctor Reverend Purify (Ossie Davis) pumping a bullet into his son (Samuel Jackson) at point-blank range (Kroll, 1991).

By the time we get around to white-produced films such as *Grand Canyon* (1991) or *Falling Down* (1993), the discourse of crime, violence, and suburban security has come full circle to justify suburban revenge and resentment. In *Falling Down*, directed by Joel Schumaker, we now have a white suburban male victim who enters the 'hood to settle moral scores. Michael

Douglas as the angst-ridden protagonist, D-fens, is completely agnostic to the differences within and among indigenous and immigrant inner-city groups. They all should be exterminated as far as he is concerned, along, of course, with his exwife, who will not let him see his infant daughter. D-fens is the prosecuting agent of resentment. His reality code embraces Latinos, who are supposedly all gangbangers, and Asian store owners, who are portrayed as compulsively unscrupulous. In a bizarre parody of gang culture, he becomes a one-man gang, a menace to society. In a calculated cinematic twist, the world of D-fens is characterized by a wider range of difference than the world of the films of black realism. However, ironically, blacks are for the most part mysteriously absent from this Los Angeles (Douglas apparently feels more confident beating up on other racial groups). On this matter of the representation of the "real" inner city, the question is, as Aretha Franklin puts it, "Who's zooming who?"

What is fascinating about a film such as *Falling Down* is that it too is centered around a kind of hypernormative, anomic individual, who is "out there." He is the purveyor of what Jacques Lacan calls "paranoiac alienation" (1977, p. 5). Singlehandedly armed with more socio-normative fire power than any gangbanger could ever muster, D-fens is ready to explode as everyday provocations make him seethe to the boiling point. We learn for instance that he is a disgruntled laid-off white-collar employee, a former technician who worked for many years at a military plant. Displaced as a result of the changing economy in the new world order, displaced by the proliferation of different peoples who are now flooding Los Angeles in pursuit of the increasingly elusive American dream, D-fens is part of the growing anxiety class that blames government, immigrants, and welfare moms for its problems. He is the kind of individual we are encouraged to believe a displaced middle-class person might become. As Joel Schumaker, the film director, explains:

> It's the kind of story you see on the six o'clock news, about the nice guy who has worked at the post office for twenty years and then one day guns down his co-workers and kills his family. It's terrifying because there's the sense that someone in the human tribe went over the wall. It could happen to us. (Morgan, 1993)

D-fens is a kind of Rambo nerd, a Perot disciple gone berserk. *Newsweek* magazine, that preternatural barometer of suburban intelligence, tells us that D-fens is the agent of suburban resentment. D-fens's actions while not always defensible are "understandable":

> *Falling Down*, whether it's really a message movie or just a cop film with trendy trimmings, pushes white men's buttons. The annoyances and menaces that drive D-fens bonkers—whining panhandlers, immigrant shopkeepers who

don't trouble themselves to speak good English, gun-toting gangbangers—are a cross section of white-guy grievances. From the get-go, the film pits Douglas—the picture of obsolescent rectitude with his white shirt, tie, specs and astronaut haircut—against a rainbow coalition of Angelenos. It's a cartoon vision of the beleaguered white male in multicultural America. This is a weird moment to be a white man. (David Gates, March 29, 1993, p. 48)

D-fens's reactions are based on his own misfortunes and anger over the anticipated disempowerment of the white middle class. Despite his similarities with the neo-Nazi, homophobic army surplus store owner in the movie, they are not the same type of social subject. Unlike the neo-Nazi, D-fens reacts to the injustices he perceives have been perpetrated against him. Like his alter ego Tom Sanders in *Disclosure* (1995), he is the postcivil rights scourge of affirmative action and reverse discrimination.

With *Falling Down*, Hollywood places the final punctuation marks on a discursive system that is refracted from the mainstream electronic media and the press onto the everyday life of the urban centers. Unlike D-fens in *Falling Down*, the central protagonist in *Menace II Society*, Caine, has nothing to live for, no redeeming values to vindicate. He is preexistentialist—a man cut adrift in and by nature. What *Menace II Society* and many other black new wave films share with *Falling Down* are a general subordination of the interests and desires of women and a pervasive sense that life in the urban centers is self-made hell. Resentment has now traveled the whole way along a fully reversible signifying chain as black filmmakers make their long march along the royal road to a dubious Aristotelian mimesis in the declaration of a final truth. The reality of being black and inner city in America is sutured up in the popular culture. The inner city has no interior. It is a holy shrine to dead black and brown bodies—hyperreal carcasses on arbitrary display.

CONCLUSION

There is a country-western song popular, we are told, among the rural suburban dwellers of the Southwest. Its refrain is an urgent plea to God to keep the penitent middle American on the straight and narrow. "Drop kick me Jesus through the goal posts of life," the song goes. Here, the importunate penitent draws down lines of social location in an edict of moral specificity and separateness from the contagion of all that dwells outside the security of the home and the neighborhood. The fictive goal posts morally keep the unwanted out. The trope of resentment exists in the empty space of the center, between the homoerotic legs of the goal posts, so to speak.

In many respects, then, the resentment discourse of crime, violence, and suburban security that now saturates American popular cultural forms, such as the country-western song quoted above, indicates the inflated presence of suburban priorities and anxieties in the popular imagination and in political life. It also indicates a corresponding circumscription of the control that blacks and Latinos (particularly black and Latino youth) and other people of color have over the production of images about themselves in society—even in an era of the resurgence of the black Hollywood film and the embryonic Latino cinema. The discourse of crime, violence, and suburban security also points to deeper realities of abandonment, neglect, and social contempt for the dwellers in America's urban centers registered in social policies that continue to see the inner city as the inflammable territory of "the enemy within" and the police as the mercenary force of the suburban middle classes. Those who articulate the anxieties repressed in and by their own privileged access to society's cornucopia of rewards—dwellers of the suburban city and the parvenu masters of the fictive hyperrealisms of the 'hood—bear some responsibility to the urban city, which their practices of cultural production and overconsumption both create and displace. In these matters, to use the language of the Guyanese poet Martin Carter, "All of us are involved, all of us are consumed" (1979, p. 44).

EIGHT

Learning about Race, Learning about "America"

Hmong American High School Students

Stacey J. Lee

AS THE CHILDREN of immigrants, second-generation youth gather much of their information about "America"[1] and "being American" from their experiences attending school. Messages about race permeate the curriculum, school policies (e.g., tracking), relationships with teachers, and interactions with peers. One of the most powerful lessons that second-generation youth learn concerns the existence of a racial hierarchy that places whites at the top (Lee, 2001; Olsen, 1997). Directly related to this lesson is the powerful message that whiteness is equated with Americanness. As Hurtado and Stewart (1997) have argued, "In the United States, national identity has been construed as white" (p. 305). Finally, the children of immigrants learn that being nonwhite and immigrant leads to a second-class citizenship in the United States.

This chapter explores how ideas about race, particularly as they are expressed in teachers' racialized constructions of students, inform the school experiences of a group of second-generation Southeast Asian American students. In particular, the chapter will focus on how school experiences inform the way second-generation Hmong American students interpret race in the United States. Questions to be addressed are: What are the racialized messages that Hmong American students learned through their experiences at school? How do messages about race inform the students' understanding of what it means to be Hmong in America?

Data for this chapter were collected as part of a one-and-a-half-year ethnographic study of Hmong American students at a public school I call "University
Heights High School" (UHS). Located in a midsized city in Wisconsin, UHS
enjoys an excellent academic reputation in the city and throughout the state. In
1985 UHS was awarded a School of Excellence Award by the U.S. Department
of Education. UHS enrolled 2,023 students during the 1999–2000 academic
year, with 29 percent of these students classified as students of color and 14 percent identified as receiving free or reduced lunch. According to estimates made
by the various school staff, there were 54 Hmong students enrolled at UHS during the 1998–1999 school year and approximately 65 Hmong students enrolled
during the 1999–2000 academic year.[2] Hmong is the first language in the homes
of all of the Hmong American students at UHS, and most students' parents
speak limited English. Most of the Hmong American students are from low-
income families and receive free or reduced lunch. Many live in low-income
housing in the poorer sections of the city where low-income African American
and Latino families also live. A majority of Hmong American students at UHS
were born in the United States and are second generation. Most of these students are in mainstream classes and do not have official connections to the English as a Second Language (ESL) department at the school.

The fieldwork for the study included participant observation of Hmong
American students during lunch periods and study halls, interviews with Hmong
American students and school staff, classroom observations, analysis of site documents, observations at school district–sponsored meetings for Southeast Asian
parents, and observations of local Hmong community events. As in all ethnographic work, the identity of the researcher influenced the research process. Early
in my research at UHS I discovered that Hmong American students were assessing me for trustworthiness and would not share their stories with me until I
earned their confidence. In my first encounters with students, I was asked questions about my ethnicity, age, marital status, occupation, and place of birth. As a
third-generation Chinese American woman, I share a racial category with the
Hmong students, but I am not an "insider." Students who expressed a panethnic
identity (Espiritu, 1992) were the ones most likely to view me as a potential ally.
Most Hmong American students, however, remained relatively cautious in my
presence until they confirmed that I could be trusted. For the first few months at
UHS, for example, the students would often switch to speaking Hmong when
discussing potentially sensitive topics (e.g., marriage, funerals, etc.).

UHS AND THE CULTURE OF WHITENESS

UHS has a reputation throughout Wisconsin for academic excellence and for
having a diverse student population. The ninth-grade principal, Mr. Smithson, described UHS like this:

I indicate to people that this is an extremely diverse school. We have students here at any given time from over 50 countries throughout the world. We have probably the most diverse student population in terms of ethnicity and national origin and most any other parameter you can think of, of any school I know of, certainly of any other school in the city. It is also a school with an extremely strong academic tradition, although we have programs that provide training and the possibility of careers in many areas including business, tech ed, and so forth. In other words we are a comprehensive high school; however, our main emphasis has always been academic postsecondary preparation, and that is primarily because that is what our community has demanded of us. That is the expectation of the community.

Although UHS faculty and staff claim to be committed to both academic excellence and diversity, there is little evidence that the school is truly committed to serving the increasingly diverse student population. Cultural differences were certainly tolerated, but they were not truly valued. The school organization, Eurocentric curriculum, racial composition of the staff, and school culture reflect and favor students from white middle-class/highly educated families. In short, the school did little to change in response to the growing diversity of the student population.

Faculty and staff of color suggested that most of their colleagues view students from white, highly educated families to be the most important students at the school. They noted that white, middle-class parents made their voices heard and that the school responded to their desires and structured the school environment to match their interests. In fact, it is this white, highly educated community that Mr. Smithson referred to as "our community" in his description of UHS. Ms. Bowman, an African American woman who was a member of the support staff, asserted that many teachers see any efforts to address issues of diversity as unnecessary and even threatening to the elite culture of the school that white, middle-class parents demanded.

In their explanations of the advantages that students from white, middle-class backgrounds possessed, white educators emphasized the significance of class over race. Class and educational background thus became codes for whiteness. In discussing the relationship between middle-class status and constructions of whiteness, Kenny (2000) writes that

> whiteness is also, among other things, a classed position, tempered through and recognizable as "cultural capital" (Bourdieu 1984): the ability to have access to and make optimum use of things like higher education and the learned social graces, vocabularies and demeanors that allow one to prosper among the elite or at least compete within the dominant culture. (p. 7)

By focusing on class, white educators at UHS helped to keep whiteness largely invisible. This virtual invisibility served to normalize whiteness and thereby maintain its dominance (Dyer, 1993).

Teachers' definitions of the "talented" and "good" student reflected the assumptions of the culture of whiteness. For example, students who scored high on standardized tests such as the SAT and were actively involved in school-sponsored activities were identified as "good" and "talented." Children from immigrant families who master English as their second language and help with family responsibilities are not referred to as "talented" even though the challenge of these accomplishments is equal to, if not greater than, that of the white students.

As in other U.S. high schools, teachers at UHS defined good students as those who expressed a proschool attitude. There was no room in this definition for explicit or implicit criticism of the school culture or structure. Good students engaged in school-sponsored extracurricular activities, got good grades, and enjoyed friendly relationships with teachers and other school authorities (Eckert, 1989). In classes, "good" students expressed their opinions and felt entitled to question the teacher's ideas. The ability to engage in this type of discourse requires a specific style of speech that reflects educated middle-class norms (Heath, 1983). It also requires a level of cultural entitlement necessary to assert this speech.

While teachers take a positive view of participation in any school-sponsored activity, not all activities have equal status. High-status activities were those that attracted positive publicity to the school (e.g., jazz band, orchestra, theater, varsity sports) as well as activities that impress college admissions officers, especially those at elite private colleges and universities (e.g., student government). Not insignificantly, high-status students (i.e., white, middle class) know which activities carry the highest status. By seeking out and participating in these activities, the high-status students at UHS confirm their own high status in the school community and serve to confirm the status of the activities in which they participate as high. Thus, the relationship between student status and participation in high-status extracurricular activities is circular and self-perpetuating.

In short, whiteness set the standards by which students were made either insiders or outsiders at UHS. Many East Asian American students achieved the status of good students by also excelling at academics and participating in high-status extracurricular activities. They were thus marked as model minorities and "honorary whites" (Lee, 1996; Tuan, 1998). Most Hmong American students, however, fall short of teachers' definitions of good or talented students. Although some Hmong American students are managing to do well academically, an increasing number of students are falling into academic trouble. In addition to academic marginalization, most Hmong American students are socially isolated from the mainstream of the school. In my observations, for example, there were only three Hmong American students who participated in any of the higher status extracurricular activities (e.g., athletic teams, music, theater, or student government) at UHS. Hmong American students who did participate in extracurricular activities were most likely to join either the Hmong Club or the Asian Club. It is significant, however, that both of these clubs were seen as peripheral to the school.

TEACHERS' REPONSES TO HMONG AMERICAN STUDENTS

In my conversations with UHS faculty I was struck by the fact that most mainstream teachers (i.e., those outside of the ESL department) were largely uneducated about their Hmong American students. When I asked mainstream teachers about their experiences working with Hmong American students I was repeatedly instructed to talk to ESL teachers in order to find out about Hmong students. Several mainstream UHS educators observed that Hmong American students appeared to be struggling, and they assumed that their struggles were related to culture. The first version of the cultural explanation advanced by many UHS educators focused on the *cultural differences* between Hmong culture and mainstream American culture. UHS educators who reflected this perspective echoed many of the assumptions advocated by cultural difference/discontinuity theorists (e.g., Au & Jordan, 1981; Erickson & Mohatt, 1982; Heath, 1983; Philips, 1982). According to cultural difference/discontinuity scholars, the problems that many children of color face in school are due to cultural differences/mismatches between the students' home culture and the school culture. Significantly, cultural difference theorists do not negatively judge the home cultures of nonmainstream children but instead argue that while their cultures are inherently valuable they do not match the mainstream culture represented in schools. Furthermore, they suggest that schools need to adopt culturally sensitive pedagogy to accommodate the cultural differences of the students.

Like the cultural difference scholars, many UHS educators suggested that cultural differences (e.g., language, attitudes towards education, family structure, gender roles) created difficulties for Hmong American students. Many teachers, for example, asserted that the issues that Hmong American students faced were related to language. Although UHS educators who advanced this explanation did not explicitly judge the Hmong culture, many used the cultural explanation to free themselves of any responsibility for serving Hmong American students. Unlike cultural difference theorists, these teachers assumed that once Hmong American students became more "Americanized" (i.e., like white, middle-class students) that they would be integrated into the mainstream of UHS culture. Here, the assumptions seemed to be that Hmong American students will inevitably assimilate into the dominant culture and that once they do they will no longer have problems.

Many of these educators believed that the ESL department should handle any educational issues that involved culture. Their implicit assumption seemed to be that the ESL department was best equipped to work with culturally different students. Ms. Heinemann, the chair of the ESL department, complained that most non-ESL teachers at UHS have abdicated responsibility for students they view as culturally different. According to Ms. Heinemann, many teachers refer Hmong students—even those who were not enrolled in the ESL department—to ESL as soon as they experience academic difficulties. She argued that

> the school needs to recognize the population of students who are born and educated here and still don't feel part of the mainstream curriculum, the mainstream school activities. . . . I don't think those students should be counted as ESL students, because that makes them more different, that separates them more.

The practice of referring all Hmong students to ESL reflects the idea that cultural issues fall outside the purview of the regular educational program. These teachers seemed to assume that nonmainstream students were the only ones affected by cultural issues. Once again, the culture of white/middle classness remained invisible. Culture was understood to be embodied in the other. Furthermore, the culture of whiteness implicitly associates whiteness with "Americanness."

As nonwhites, the issues which Hmong Americans face are viewed as culturally different (i.e., foreign) and therefore un-American. Viewed as culturally different "foreigners," Hmong American students are understood to be outside the responsibility of the regular educators. Although it might appear that Hmong American students at UHS are viewed as foreigners simply because they are relative newcomers to the United States, it is important to note that Asian Americans have historically been cast as perpetual foreigners in the United States (Lei, 2001; Lowe, 1996; Tuan, 1998). At UHS, foreigners were understood to be the responsibility of the ESL department.

While many UHS educators characterized Hmong American students as culturally different (i.e., foreign), a few members of the UHS staff characterized Hmong students as *culturally deficient*. These educators reflected the position of the cultural deficiency literature of the 1960s and the "at risk" literature of the 1980s and 1990s (Hess & Shipman, 1965). Unlike cultural difference/discontinuity theorists who support a culturally relativistic perspective, scholars who focus on cultural deficiency/deprivation argue that nonmainstream children are disadvantaged/deprived by their home cultures (e.g., Hess & Shipman, 1965; Lewis, 1966). According to this perspective, poor and minority children were trapped in a "culture of poverty," which prevents them from taking advantage of educational opportunities (Lewis, 1966). Implicit in this argument is the assumption that poor and minority cultures are inherently inferior to mainstream white, middle-class culture.

In contrast to their colleagues who emphasized cultural differences, the UHS educators who advanced the cultural deficit discourse made more explicitly negative judgments about Hmong students' culture. Their descriptions of Hmong culture reflected much of the scholarly and popular literature on Hmong immigrants that has cast Hmong culture as preliterate, traditional, clannish, rural, and patriarchal. According to this literature, the economic and social problems faced by the Hmong American community are almost exclusively rooted in their culture. The practice of early marriage and early child-bearing for girls has been identified as the major barrier to girls' educations (Goldstein, 1985; Rumbaut & Ima, 1988; Walker-Moffat, 1995).

Similarly, many UHS educators identified early marriage as the primary reason that Hmong American girls could not take advantage of the educational opportunities at UHS. These educators constructed the practice of early marriage as "backward." Mrs. Smith, a guidance counselor, suggested that Hmong girls who followed the path of early marriage were doomed to economic failure beyond the control of the schools. Although early marriage does in fact create obstacles for some Hmong American female students, the suggestion that early marriage is the proximate cause of the educational troubles faced by some Hmong American girls fails to consider the role that schools play in their school experiences. Furthermore, this explanation fails to recognize that the Hmong American adults and youth hold complex and diverse attitudes toward the practice of early marriage. The majority of Hmong parents now encourage the postponement of marriage until after high school. Most of the girls in my study asserted that they planned to wait until after high school to marry. Interestingly, girls who are estranged from their families and from school are the ones most likely to view early marriage as a form of escape. Some of these girls marry against their family's wishes. Thus, marriage becomes a form of resistance to family and school authority (Lee, 2001a).

Some UHS educators who advanced the cultural deficit perspective believed that many Hmong students were falling into negative patterns as a result of living in poverty. Here, the problem was seen as being related to social class and not the Hmong culture. These educators asserted that some Hmong students had become Americanized in a "bad way" and were "at risk" for becoming the "new underclass." Several teachers and administrators expressed fears about what they perceived to be the growing gang problem in the Hmong community. Although there was no evidence of widespread gang involvement among Hmong American students at UHS, the baggy pants and baseball caps worn by many of the youth were seen as evidence of possible gang affiliation. Additionally, the fact that many Hmong American students spoke English in a dialect associated with urban youth of color led some educators to conclude that Hmong American youth were being pulled into the "bad aspects of American culture." These UHS educators suggested that the school needed to do more to watch or police these students. Significantly, the hip hop clothing and language styles that many Hmong American youth adopted were associated with urban youth of color. Thus, bad Americanization seemed to be code for things associated with blackness. On the other hand, good American ways were associated with white, middle-class culture.

UHS educators who advanced the cultural deficit (i.e., "at risk") perspective seemed to believe that the students' problems lay outside the school. According to these educators many Hmong students simply lack the appropriate support for education within the home. Mr. Dixon, for example, asserted that it was nearly impossible for schools to help students from "dysfunctional families."

SL: Is there anything schools can do in that situation?

MR. DIXON: I thought about that. I thought about that. . . . The idealistic answer is that schools should reach out to some of these families and kids. But how do you, you know, actually reach? You know, effectively do that? Is it the job of the school to do that? At some level, you have to hold the students accountable and to hold the family accountable at some level. I know that there are families that want to do the right thing, but [do] not know how to do that. I think that support staff can help them do that. But I think that it has to be initiated by the families.

Mr. Dixon was struggling with how to help at risk Hmong American, African American, and Latino students, but because he saw the problem coming from the families he concluded that the school could only wait for the families to initiate change. Similarly, in identifying early marriage as the central barrier to education for Hmong girls Mrs. Smith and others have located the problem within the Hmong culture and therefore outside of the school. Although early marriage does present impediments for some Hmong American girls, educators who focused on cultural deficiencies rarely considered what the schools might do to better serve girls who marry early at their parents' insistence or by choice (Lee, 2001a).

Aihwa Ong (2000) has argued that nonwhite immigrants undergo a process of ideological whitening or blackening:

> Non-white immigrants in the First World are simultaneously, though unevenly, subjected to two processes of normalization; an ideological whitening or blackening that reflects dominant racial oppositions and an assessment of cultural competence based on human capital and consumer power in the minority subjects. (p. 262)

Ong argues that low-income Asian immigrants, particularly Hmong, Cambodian, and Laotians, have been ideologically blackened. They have been cast as economic failures and social deviants. UHS educators who describe Hmong Americans in terms of cultural deficiency are engaging in an ideological blackening of Hmong American students.

At UHS, the cultural difference and cultural deficiency perspectives were both used to relieve the school from the responsibility of serving and/or recognizing the specific needs of Hmong American students. In both discourses, whiteness/middle classness remained the unspoken yet pervasive norm against which others were judged. Hmong American students were seen either as culturally different or culturally deficient when compared to the white norm. Thus, Hmong Americans were cast as the other. Whiteness was also associated with being American (in a good way), and Hmong American students were implicitly classified as foreign (i.e., un-American) or they were seen as falling into bad patterns of Americanization, which were associated with urban youth of color.

HIDING AND RESISTING: HMONG STUDENTS' RESPONSES TO THE CULTURE OF WHITENESS

Based on their experiences at UHS, particularly their relationships with teachers, Hmong American students have developed a sense of themselves as a racially and culturally marginalized group. Specifically, Hmong American students have learned that whites sit at the top of the racial hierarchy, and whiteness sets the standards against which groups of color are judged. The power and position of whites is largely confirmed by popular culture where Hmong American students also get information about America. As at UHS, whiteness is pervasive as the unnamed norm and whiteness and Americanness are collapsed in popular culture (Fiske, 1994; Nakayama, 1994).

Perhaps the most insidious influence of the culture of whiteness was that it led Hmong American students at UHS to internalize the implicit message that whites are the only "real" Americans. For example, Hmong American students reserved the term *American* for white students and referred to all other students by their race or ethnicity. Second-generation Hmong American students referred to themselves as "Americanized" Hmong but did not refer to themselves simply as "Americans." When I asked Hmong American students to describe "Americans," they described white people, often stereotypic blue eyed and blond haired. Furthermore, when they spoke about "American culture," they typically described the culture generally associated with the white, middle-class people they saw on TV.

Hmong American students perceived that Hmong culture played a role in marking them as foreign and un-American. In an effort to distance themselves from the foreigner image, second-generation students attempted to emphasize their "Americanized" identities. Most distanced themselves from Hmong American students who were recent immigrants. In fact, second-generation students commonly referred to the newcomers as FOBs (Fresh Off the Boat). Second-generation students commonly mocked recent Hmong immigrant students for being "old fashioned" and for wearing "out of date 1980s style clothes." Although second-generation students adopted an "American" style, they did not adopt the white, middle-class style. Instead, most second-generation students adopted a hip hop style associated with urban youth of color and were consequently described by UHS educators as becoming Americanized in a bad way. Hmong American students were well aware that their clothes were read in racialized terms. For example, they commonly referred to their hip hop style as "ghetto." In doing so, they revealed the fact that they equate poverty with blackness. Hmong American students' adoption of hip hop style reveals the fact that they identify themselves as sharing a raced and classed position with African Americans, a position that stands in opposition to white, middle-class Americans.

Hmong American students' embrace of hip hop culture was partly influenced by popular culture. During my fieldwork, the movie *Romeo Must Die*, starring Jet Li, martial artist and star of multiple action movies, and Aaliyah, the African American hip hop artist, was playing in theaters. A modern day retelling of Romeo and Juliet, *Romeo Must Die* focused on two families, one Chinese American and one African American, fighting for control of the waterfront. Li, dressed in hip hop clothing, portrayed the Romeo character as a charismatic, oppositional hero who regularly defeated his enemies with amazing martial arts acrobatics. Jet Li was one of the Hmong American students' favorite celebrities. While Hmong American girls were generally critical of Hmong American boys for being "too short" and presumably not masculine enough, they asserted that Jet Li was "cuter than most Asian guys." For Hmong American boys, hip hop style appeared to be a way to emulate celebrities such as Jet Li and to simultaneously assert their masculinity (Lee, 2004).

In order to appear less foreign and to avoid the judgment of non-Hmong students and staff, Hmong American students hid aspects of their culture that they assumed would be viewed negatively by the dominant society (e.g., funeral rituals, marital status). In fact, two of my informants hid their married status from me for months until they felt I could be trusted. Similarly, in her ethnographic research on Hmong immigrants in Wisconsin, Koltyk (1998) found, "As the Hmong have learned that aspects of their culture seem primitive or offensive to many Americans, they have become reluctant to talk to outsiders about them" (p. 14).

Although hiding aspects of their culture served to protect Hmong American students from the gaze of outsiders, it also had a negative impact on their academic experiences. Students who did not trust their teachers to treat their identities with respect were less likely to approach teachers for academic assistance (Lee, 2001a). In my observations of classes, I found that Hmong American students were typically quiet during class discussions. Many teachers assumed that these students were simply shy or not yet comfortable with English (i.e., culturally different). Many of these students, however, were members of the second generation and were fluent in English. I learned that Hmong American students had come to expect that their non-Hmong classmates or teachers would not value their ideas. For example, one student explained that she never spoke in class: "I'd rather just listen. I don't really have much to say. The American kids have had a lot of really interesting experiences. Lots of them have been to Europe and stuff." This same student was bilingual and had lived in Hmong American communities in California and Wisconsin. Despite these varied cultural experiences, she did not feel empowered to speak in class.

In conversations with second-generation Hmong American students I learned that most did not trust their teachers. Many complained that teachers failed to respect Hmong culture and failed to demonstrate that they cared about Hmong students. Students' distrust of teachers was related to their general distrust of whites. One student remarked:

> For me, . . . I feel like some white people neglect me. I mean as much as I try to be nice to them, give them respect, they don't give it back to me. Why should I even bother with them? Because I feel like I really don't need people like that. . . . I mean, if you're not Asian like me you don't understand where I'm coming from either.

Although most second-generation Hmong American students were critical of whites and somewhat distrustful of white authority, I did find some evidence that Hmong American youth also idealized whites. Based on what they saw on TV, many Hmong American students had come to idealize the white family. They assumed that white parents were more supportive of their children than Hmong parents. In the normal "American" (read: white) TV family, the parents are supportive of their children and communicate with them openly (Pyke, 2000). One Hmong American student described her image of the white family like this:

> When I think of the mainstream I think of a white family I guess. As both parents working . . . have really good jobs and maybe one kid or two kids, three at the most. And the kids are doing house chores and everything; they like have good grades, and even when the girl grows up, the woman, the mom has a good job like a doctor or something.

This student and other Hmong American students envied their white peers for having more successful and more supportive (read: better) parents. Girls, in particular, assumed that white families offered girls greater gender equality (Lee & Vaught, 2003). The idealization of white families serves to exacerbate intergenerational conflict in Hmong American families.

Although most second-generation Hmong American youth adopted a hip hop style, some were also trying to emulate white standards of beauty. A few Hmong American girls, for example, lightened their hair and wore blue or green contact lenses in what appeared to be an effort to look less Asian. Other Hmong American girls aspired to a standard of extreme thinness associated with white, middle-class gender aesthetic and epitomized by stars such as Gwyneth Paltrow and Jennifer Anniston. One girl, for example, asserted that she wanted to lose enough weight to wear a size 0. These girls were also the ones who were most critical of Hmong American boys because they were "too short" (Lee, 2004). Short stature, for men, was not in keeping with popular culture norms of the male hero as hegemonically masculine (read: tall and white) (Espiritu, 2000).

UNVEILING THE CULTURE OF WHITENESS AND (RE)CONSTRUCTING AMERICA

At UHS the culture of whiteness/middle classness implicitly equated whiteness with real "Americanness" even in the face of very real evidence to the contrary. Whiteness was simultaneously normalized and rendered invisible (and thus above criticism), and culture was understood to be something located solely within the nonwhite other. As the children of immigrants of color, Hmong Americans found themselves cast as the other within this framework. Hmong American students were seen either as culturally different (i.e., foreign) or culturally deficient (i.e., not like whites). Both characterizations served to reflect and preserve the normative nature of whiteness and maintain the existing racial hierarchy. Located as outsiders, many Hmong American students were academically and socially marginalized at the school.

Public schools have the opportunity to (re)construct definitions of "America" and "Americans" to reflect the reality and diversity of the U.S. schools. In particular, schools need to challenge the association between whiteness and authentic Americanness. In order to challenge the idea that whites are the only true Americans schools need to commit to teaching the *full* and *complete* history of the United States, that is, the history of Asian Americans and other nonwhite Americans as an *integral* part of U.S. history, not simply as ethnic window dressing. In an increasingly diverse society it is imperative that schools teach all students that there are multiple ways of "being American."

To do this requires that schools understand and explore whiteness not as a norm against which all other cultures are measured but as a creation, a constructed culture that has occupied a position of privilege in the racial hierarchy. Schools also need to help students become critical consumers of popular culture. Furthermore, schools can work to dislocate the normalization of whiteness that positions culture solely within the other by helping all students see the dominant white, middle-class culture through the eyes of outsiders. Likewise, educators need structured opportunities to critically examine the dominant culture in order to make the familiar strange (Erickson, 1987).

NINE

In the Bad or Good of Girlhood

Social Class, Schooling, and White Femininities

Lyn Mikel Brown

Accounts of working-class life are told by tension and ambiguity, out on the borderlands. The story . . . cannot be absorbed into the central one: it is both its disruption and its essential counterpoint: this is a drama of class.

—Carolyn Kay Steedman, 1987, p. 22

THIS CHAPTER OFFERS a critical analysis of class and gender, as lived by tension and ambiguity through the lives of two groups of white girls, one working class, one middle class.[1] I explicate the performances and knowledges produced and resisted by these differently positioned girls as they disrupt social constructions of gender, class, and race and invent spaces and possibilities for themselves.

My initial intent in listening to these girls was to counter what anthropologist Michelle di Leonardo calls the "feminist metonymic fallacy: to portray white middle class women's [and girls'] experiences as the whole of women's history" and experience (Di Leonardo, 1991). I also wanted to redress the relentless overpsychologizing of girls—that is, to contest my own training as a developmental psychologist—that has served to render invisible the social and material conditions of girls' lives, even as I hoped to undermine the psychological sameness attributed to the working class. And I wanted to contribute to broader attempts to mark out differences within whiteness, to understand how the construction of whiteness varies across lines of class.[2]

THE GIRLS

The 19 girls in this study are, or were at the time of this study, 11–14 year olds. Thirteen of these girls, the working-class group, lived on farms, in trailers, and "in the woods," in and around a small rural town in south central Maine. Mansfield, with a population of about 900, is spread over a wide expanse of farm and woodland, which also includes a nucleus of houses, a few combination grocery store–gas stations, a bait and tackle shop, a post office, two small wood mills, a volunteer fire department, and a K–8 elementary school. "Although there are a few people in town who 'have money,'" my collaborator, teacher assistant, and Mansfield resident, Diane Starr explains, "most scratch out a living and support their families" with low-paying or part-time jobs. "This," she adds, "puts everyone more or less on equal economic footing."

Most of the Mansfield girls are from working-class families, although a few move in and out of poverty, depending on seasonal job opportunities, such as wreath making or fruit picking. Some of the girls' fathers work part-time or full-time in the woods cutting trees for the local mills; others drive trucks or haul gravel or wood; one is a self-employed mechanic; another is unemployed because of a physical disability. More than half of the girls' mothers work part-time; one as an LPN, another at the wood mill, and others in local stores or as waitresses.

The middle-class group was comprised of 6 girls from Acadia, a midsized city (by Maine standards) with a population of roughly 18,000. Unlike Mansfield, there are fairly clear distinctions and divisions between upper-, middle-, working-class, and poor sections of Acadia. Reflecting the community, Acadia Junior High also has clear class divisions based on individual wealth, parents' education, and family social standing. Popularity, with a few exceptions for star athletes, falls to those on the higher end of the economic spectrum. Of the "three major cliques," the 6 Acadia girls in this group identify explicitly with the "middle class," a term that evokes some, but not all, of the qualities and characteristics of the middle class in society at large.

The Acadia girls do not experience material want; structurally and socially they are firmly grounded in the privileges of white, middle-, and in some cases, upper-middle-class culture. Their fathers and mothers are by and large professionals; most have four-year college degrees; many have attended graduate school. A few are teachers; one is a doctor; one an engineer, one a lawyer, and one a state representative. In each family both parents work, although in some cases the girls' mothers have returned to part- or full-time employment as their children have grown.

These were all outspoken girls who agreed to be interviewed and, over the course of a school year, to meet weekly for videotaped sessions to explore their views on what so often lies on the border or off the map of white adolescent girls' public discussion and focused attention: their strong feelings, particularly of anger and outrage, their critical opinions about the ways things go in their schools, their local definitions of femininity and its tensions with societal ideals of girls and women.

MANSFIELD

In listening to and watching the Mansfield girls, it became immediately clear that their experiences and future imaginings were filtered through the reality of their material locations. Their expressions of longing and desire gave rise not only to anxiety, self-doubt, and self-deprecation, but also to anger, frustration, defensiveness, hope, and determined resistance. Even as they longed for money and success, as they did often, they anticipated lives of hard work, supported by friends and family members; they expected, against their most fervent hopes, that they would always be concerned about having enough. Such realities affected the relationships they sought and the kind of people they imagined themselves to be: outspoken, direct, strong, loving, invulnerable to pain and hurt, ready to defend themselves and loved ones in their care against unfairness and cruelty.

Viewed through the lens of idealized femininity, such imaginings are disruptive, if not incomprehensible. In her book, *Daddy's Girl,* Valerie Walkerdine argues that "the little working class girl presents, especially to education, an image which threatens the safety of the discourse of the innocent and natural child. She is too precocious, too sexual . . . she is deeply threatening to a civilizing process understood in terms of the production and achievement of natural rationality, nurturant femininity" (Walkerdine, 1997, p. 78). In her description of a young working-class girl in relationship with her father, Walkerdine explores such a girl threat in the making: "She is his baby, but also his tomboy, his fighter. Such a combination of baby girl and fighter do not go down well at school and [her] strategies are noticeably unsuccessful with her teacher" (Walkerdine, 1997, p. 174). The Mansfield girls, too, were "noticeably unsuccessful." Their propensity to fight verbally, and physically when necessary, to speak the unspeakable, to be nurturing and also tough and self-protecting, threatened to disrupt the boundaries of appropriate femininity proselytized—though not always modeled—in their school.

And yet the Mansfield girls insist on bringing their loud, direct selves to school. In doing so, they engaged in a daily public struggle with their teachers over the interpretation of reality and the contours of legitimate knowledge. Their refusal to be contained or disciplined, reveals, as it did in Wendy Luttrell's study of white, working-class women, an implicit critique of schooling that ignored "the exigencies of poor and working-class families" by rewarding "'good girl' behavior and traditional middle-class femininity" and denying "the reality and legitimacy of working-class femininity, an image of women as hardworking, responsible caregivers" (Luttrell, 1993, pp. 524–25). Because they tend to speak their minds, they unwittingly disrupt tacit boundaries between public and private speech; their laughter, playfulness, and anger disturbed the "bourgeois class biases" that determined proper behavior and that shaped and informed, to quote bell hooks, "pedagogical process (as well as social etiquette) in the classroom" (hooks, 1994, p. 178). Their physical aggressiveness contested the well-mannered "good girl" most teachers imagine and hope to meet each day in school.

The struggle between the Mansfield girls and their women teachers is complex. The teachers seemed unpredictable and irrational, in part because the girls come to school with different conceptions of the relationships among gender, knowledge, and power and because the signs and codes of the culture of power had never been clearly stated or explained to them (Delpit, 1988). The girls were at odds with the school culture, and they were, at various moments, angry, sad, defensive, confused, entertained, and energized by this fact. Since there was little opportunity to express their anger, frustration, and hurt in ways that would be heard and understood, they protected themselves and engaged their teachers by playing into this miscommunication—searching out those issues or behaviors that "get to" their teachers, taking bets on when a teacher will have "had enough" or simply, as eleven-year-old Cheyenne said, "bugging the crap out of them."

But there was more to the Mansfield girls' resistance. Cheyenne pointed to a deeper struggle when she observed that "people don't listen because they don't like us." The girls knew that their presence in the school was disruptive. Their teachers' reactions—their anger, overattention to rules, excessive interest in the way the girls spoke and presented themselves—reinforced the girls' sense of being different and hence inadequate. In response, the girls defensively professed their hatred of their teachers, but also they professed their own stupidity. They were positioned and perceived, and also experienced themselves, in ways that signaled their failure. Just as Foucault argues, "a piece of work is not good; it is in the good"; so too, these working-class girls were not bad; they were in the bad. Within the particular configuration of power/knowledge in their school, these girls were often positioned as improper, excessive, disturbing, stupid.

Diane Starr and I understood that our reasons for working with these girls were not to "help" them, describe them, speak for or about them but to understand as best we could where they were coming from and to activate their white, working-class identities as "perverse identities"—that is, to encourage them to speak out of their social locations as white, working-class girls and to willfully refuse to do what the culture of the center expects or desires of them (Zimmerman, 1991). The emphasis for us was on "will"—on conscious, deliberate agency. Our hope was to facilitate what we saw as an emerging class consciousness so that these girls could interrupt and claim themselves apart from their teachers' perceptions of them and their expected place within their school.

In their initial group sessions the girls read the white, middle-class culture of their school as reality and themselves, in turn, as excess, marginal, disturbing, improper. Their group conversations became a time for individual girls to vent their anger and confusion against a background chorus of support and validation. While particular girls "had each others backs," primarily the girls' response to their teachers was fragmented, held together by feelings of displacement and outrage. In time, however, they began to locate common threads, look beyond the individual, and tell stories that were "telling" stories of their teachers' ignorance, abuse of power, and mistreatment.

One such story, told first by eleven-year-old Cheyenne, begins as part of a group diatribe about unfairness and irrational behavior on the part of teachers. Over the course of the year, however, the story is picked up by the other girls, repeated, and retold, until simple reference to "the coat" evokes familiar feelings about their teachers and carries the disparate threads of their emerging collective critique:

CHEYENNE: Yesterday, Miss Davis came in from recess and was really mad and nobody knew why. And she goes to [Donna], she goes, "Take off your coat." And she wouldn't take off her coat. . . . Because she didn't feel comfortable taking it off, and she said, "Go out in the hall," and then half an hour later she went out in the hall with Donna, and before she did that she was walking around and everybody would ask her for something and she'd start screaming at 'em.

DIANE: Did she say why?

PATTI: Maybe she had PMS!

CHEYENNE: Wait! No. Anyways, they were out in the hall, and she asked Donna why she wouldn't take off her coat and she goes, "Because I don't feel comfortable taking it off."

DONNA: No. I said I didn't want to.

CHEYENNE: Oh, because she didn't want to. And she goes, "I want you to write me" . . . two pages on why she wouldn't take off her coat.

DONNA: No, two pages why she should let me wear my jacket.

RACHEL: Oh, because she always wears *her* jacket. *[some of the girls start to talk]* Listen! She's like, at the end of last year, she goes, "Okay when it's winter time I'm going to have my window open and you guys are going to have to live with it." So, okay, we're wearing our coats. *She* can wear her coat when she's cold, but we can't. We get in trouble for it.

CHEYENNE: And then after that she says, "Go down to the office. I don't want your kind here."

DIANE: To you?

CHEYENNE: No, to Donna because she wouldn't take off her coat. And it's not fair because she can keep her coat on whenever she wants—

RACHEL: She thinks she can say whatever she wants.

DONNA: I wrote a two page letter, and I told her . . . that if I didn't want to take off my coat that I didn't have to and that she shouldn't make me do anything that I didn't want to do . . . and that she said that I'm going through a stage where I don't like my body.

DIANE: That's what she said?

SUSAN: *[laughing, squeals in a high feminine voice]* "I don't like my body!"

CHEYENNE: I don't like it when teachers say something, and they don't know what's going on though, and they say something mean to you. They butt in and say, "Well, I know what's wrong with you," and think they know what is going on.

This particular incident encapsulated what was off or wrong between the girls and their women teachers. Whether or not Cheyenne is quoting Miss Davis accurately, the girls generally felt that their teachers "don't want [their] kind here." In fact, it would seem, from this and other incidents the girls recounted, that their teachers did not understand who "their kind" were. Miss Davis' explanation for Donna's resistance—that she was going through a stage where she does not like her body—echoed the voluminous literature on white, middle-class adolescent girls' struggles with body image and alerted the girls to the kind of girl their teachers did want or expect. They were stunned and incredulous when they first heard about the remark. They hooted with laughter. Susan poked fun at the very idea that this would be Donna's reason for resisting Miss Davis' no coats rule. Cheyenne called the teacher's comment "mean" and was angered by her presumptuousness. Donna, who refused to write the letter Miss Davis asked for—flatly choosing to defend her actions rather than to submit to what appears to be a supercilious demand for explanation—concluded that Miss Davis "just wanted something to bitch about." But ultimately it came down to the outrageous fact that "they think they know us, and they don't."

Although from the teacher's point of view, the girls' anger, in some cases born of family stress, in some cases the result of unfairnesses experienced at school, must feel hostile and threatening and the girls out of control and unreachable at times, what these girls seem to want, what they long for and seem unable to attain, is genuine communication with their women teachers. They speak fondly of those rare occasions when they felt "closer" to a teacher, when "it feels more like she's a person," when a teacher shows "she really cares about us," or when teachers "know how I'm feeling."

The girls make a clear distinction between such closeness and care and the intrusion, the false assumptions, about which they complain so often. The intrusions are overlays of interpretation, projections of meaning not grounded in relationship—interpreting a coat in class as a psychological act of resistance (self-loathing) rather than a political act (resistance to unfairness or a statement about invisibility or a desire to escape). As such, they serve as reminders to the girls that they are not what their teachers know, value, and expect in a girl and that, in their attempts to be the girl others want, they so obviously fall short. And such voice-overs are reminders that their teachers who do not "really know" them nonetheless have the power to interpret their lives and the meaning of their actions. These reminders create barriers to the possibility of meaningful, rational action. What makes the working-class girls' stories of their interactions with their teachers so compelling is thus not only their angry refusal to be contained by dominant constructions of femininity, but also their vulnerability in the face of such barriers to relationship.

For the most part the Mansfield girls' wishes fall on defensive, or perhaps frustrated, ears. What these girls believe are their attempts to be heard and understood, to be respected and taken seriously, to respond to unfairness, unpredictability, and lack of understanding on the part of their teachers, many of their teachers seem to experience as disruption, lack of attention and effort, and impulsive, childish behavior. Without someone to assist them in negotiating this gap, these girls are disqualified both from relationships with their teachers and from the culture of their school—a culture supported even by those women teachers with working-class roots. As a result the girls and their teachers unwittingly contribute to perceptions of the girls as rebellious or "stupid" and therefore marginal students and risk that they will remain outside the system, disconnected, and therefore ineffective.[3]

ACADIA

Although in a very different way, the Acadia girls too struggle with the contradictory voices telling them what it means to be a good or proper girl. Their material privilege invites expectations and fantasies of success constructed in the familiar, accessible terms of white middle-class America: voices of unfettered entitlement and radical individualism press them to go forth, to embrace competition, to leave others behind. But acceptance, protection, and security, they also understand, is assured for those girls who attain and maintain the dominant feminine ideal—for those who are perfectly kind and nice, who are accommodating, who do not call attention to themselves or make waves. Their teachers' preference for the popular girls and boys complicates this picture, too, by reinforcing the importance of wealth, appearance, and physical beauty, as well as the power of personal, "emotional or even erotically tinged" relationships between teachers and their favorite students (Luttrell, 1993, p. 538). While the Acadia girls say they refuse to be the kinds of girls who are the "teacher's pets"—preoccupied with appearance, feigning compliance and dependence, presenting false selves to fit in with the popular group or to please their teachers—they long for the attention, recognition, and power the popular girls gain by such performances.[4]

Deciphering and negotiating such contradictory constructions of femininity and possibility is difficult. Aware both of what they have to lose and what they hope to gain, the Acadia girls play it safe, holding in or holding back their strong feelings and opinions. In so doing, ironically, they bury the very qualities that would move them to act on their own behalf and prove them to be unique, creative, deep, special—that is, the very qualities they insist they "really" have, the qualities they will, in fact, need in order to be taken seriously.

The Acadia girls are thus more likely than the Mansfield girls to move their feelings and thoughts out of the public arena of school and into the active underground.[5] They hone the fine art of indirect speech, cultivate public smiles, and practice signs of rapt attention—their bodies bent forward in anticipation, their eyes wide open, heads nodding[6]—even while, behind the scenes and between the lines, they imperceptibly catch each others' eyes, make faces of disgust, or surreptitiously kick a bothersome boy. They express their anger and resistance toward unfair school practices and social conventions quietly and creatively—seeking out adults who will listen, providing wrong answers to the popular kids, developing witty, but obtuse, comebacks to sexist remarks, reappropriating derogatory terms, and speaking condescendingly or in carefully encoded language—and then they attend our group sessions filled up with frustration or return home, where they say they can be themselves.

And yet, in spite of the middle-class girls' struggles against and expressed resistance to the regulation and control of their strong feelings and expressions, they and their teachers share a common understanding and language. Educated their entire lives in the "cultural capital"[7] of idealized femininity and white, middle-class values, they understand the rules and codes of the culture of power (Delpit, 1988, p. 24). They share an "oral style" with their teachers. They know well, for example, what their teachers' indirect questions or suggestions imply; they understand that "veiled commands are commands nonetheless" (Delpit, 1988, p. 34). And they know well, as bell hooks explains, that "silence and obedience to authority" are "most rewarded"; that "loudness, anger, emotional outbursts, and even something as seemingly innocent as unrestrained laughter" are "deemed unacceptable, vulgar disruptions of classroom social order," are, indeed, "associated with being a member of the lower classes" (hooks, 1994, p. 179). In school they actively participate in the policing of too loud, inappropriately direct voices, of less than subtle demeanors and actions, even as they react negatively to the demands such constraints place on them and the invisibility they assure.

The constant attention the Acadia girls give to "those" kids who "think they are the higher point of life" speaks volumes about their ambivalence and the level of anxiety they feel about their own social class position in their school. Even though they describe the hurtful and embarrassing things the popular kids do to them and allude to their propensity at times to protect their more vulnerable classmates, and as much as they resent the popular groups' power and intimidation tactics, they are quick to distinguish themselves or their friends from "the lower life" or "the scrubs." "Scrub," Lydia explains, refers to "like your hands need to be scrubbed. Or, Kirstin adds, "Like scrub my garbage dump." It implies, twelve-year-old Jane says, that "you come from a garbage dump. Well not from a garbage dump," she says, revealing her reticence to appear too mean. "Well, garbage dumps aren't always bad, but . . . You know, you have to come from really bad homes, whose father are, are . . . gone, and their mothers offer them pot, and stuff like that."

The Acadia girls question the social hierarchy of their school, but they also reluctantly accept it and at times participate in it and perpetuate it. They make commonly accepted associations between social class and morality and between social class and personal choice: kids from otherwise "good" families choose to align themselves with the "troublemakers"; being unpopular is justified by poverty rooted in families in which fathers leave and parents offer their kids drugs.

The line the Acadia girls draw between good girls and bad reflects, to a large degree, familiar dichotomies that have long regulated white, middle-class feminine behavior: nice girls are kind, caring; they listen; they do not hurt others, get in trouble, or cause scenes; they do not express anger openly or say what they want directly; they do not brag or call attention to themselves. Bad girls, however, are sexual, express their desires, dress provocatively, speak too often and too loudly, and express their anger directly; they call attention to themselves, they are thus "out of control" and "obnoxious." The Acadia girls police the borders of these divisions through their dress and behavior, their talk of other girls, and their teasing of each other.

What confuses and outrages the Acadia girls is that the popular girls do not play by these rules; they do not acknowledge or respect these boundaries, and they not only get away with it, but flourish. Such popular girls are not "bad" per se, at least not in ways people, particularly adults, seem to see or care much about, but from the Acadia girls' perspective, they are often covertly mean, "whiny," and "conceited." While not necessarily sexually experienced, some dress in short shorts and tight tops and therefore call attention to themselves; they change their personalities when they are around boys; they react instead of act, always metaphorically testing the winds of popular opinion; they are shape-shifters, chameleons. Rather than good, as the Acadia girls see themselves, they are bad girls in the good. The Acadia girls cannot understand how such "fake" people carrying on in apparently fraudulent relationships can

curry so much favor and maintain their "high" position. They watch in amaze-
ment and dismay as these girls who "talk about people behind their backs,"
who if "they don't like you they'll cast you out," command the attention of the
teachers, other girls, and especially boys.

The Acadia girls struggle with what Paulo Friere calls an "existential
duality"—caught between their contempt for the powerful group and their
passionate attraction toward it. In either case, oriented above, looking to the
"higher" kids for meaning, the girls risk being "submerged" in an "order" that
serves the interests of the popular, and thus the girls risk losing sight of their
own collective and political power (Friere, 1970/1992, p. 48). Within this
order the girls fight for recognition, struggle to be seen and understood,
against those "who have, like, power and think it's their thought," and who
treat the "middle group" as though "we have no feelings." The anxiety that
accompanies such dehumanization and the risk that acting on behalf of
those who are lower in the order may devalue one's own social currency
works to reify the hierarchy, casting the unpopular kids as either hapless victims or deserving troublemakers. In this manner the Acadia girls both struggle against and participate in the regulation of the deeply classed culture of
their school.

EDUCATING THE RESISTANCE

Class differences clearly inform the girls' expectations of and identifications
with their teachers. While the middle-class girls said they wanted a teacher
who will be herself, hold to her beliefs and convictions, the working-class girls
said they were looking for someone who can put her beliefs on hold and create space, through humor, play, and fun, for new understandings and possibilities. Both groups of girls desired their teachers' loyalty and, conversely, had a
sharp eye for betrayal.

But the Mansfield and Acadia girls were also "hungry for an us" (Fine &
Macpherson, 1995), and their group sessions point to the transformative
potential of girls' interactions with each other. While the dynamics of the
group sessions were mediated by class and culture, both the Mansfield and the
Acadia girls found in their group a sense of home—"a safe space, where one
can weave whole cloth from the fragments of social critique and sweet
dreams" (Pastor, McCormick & Fine, 1996).

From the very beginning of the study, the Mansfield girls conveyed the
importance of their friendships and the group to their psychological survival.
Their strong, supportive relationships helped to minimize the hurtful and
oppressive features of both home and school.[8] The group gave them an opportunity and forum to articulate their feelings and thoughts and also an emerging sense of their collective power to act on their own behalf.

Movement toward collective, constructive action depended on the girls listening closely to each other, trusting each other. Learning about each others' feelings and thoughts over the course of the year increased their solidarity and support of each other. Their exterior toughness, protective invulnerability, and defensive teasing yielded to a wider range of emotions and more open attempts to understand and identify with each others' feelings. The girls learned they had different, more complicated, more subtle feelings than they knew or expected. They became more reflective about their treatment of others, more sensitive to others' feelings, more considered in their behavior.

As the Mansfield girls became more aware of each others' feelings, more vulnerable in the presence of others, their solidarity and support of each other increased. As they became more articulate and open about the reasons they felt treated badly, they began to consider the possibility of collective action. With Diane's encouragement and explication of "the culture of power" they began to formulate resistance strategies, focusing their attention on rules they felt were unjust or redressing grievances they had identified over the course of the year. In two cases, the coat incident and girls' unequal access to the basketball court, they took their cases before the school governing board and were able to affect school policy. They could wear their coats; they had the court every other recess.

Perhaps sensing both the possibilities and the dangers of such action, the Mansfield girls came to define themselves as an "oppositional culture" within their school (Ogbu, 1989). Although their opposition was not grounded fully in a coherent, conscious "cultural frame of reference," they began to experience and voice the power of their collectivity. This sense of groupness took shape, not only as a result of their increased support of one another but also as a result of their successful political action.

The Acadia girls began their group sessions not assuming that they were all alike but believing the intensity of their feelings around invisibility, their struggles with pressures to be perfect, and their anger at the popular boys and girls were experiences unique to them. Although the girls knew each other, some quite well when the group began, and although they shared a common identification as the "smart," "regular" girls, they too were surprised at what their meetings revealed. Jane, for example, was amazed when she discovered that the other girls "thought like I did on a lot of things . . . think the same things I do on a lot of issues." The Acadia girls' early discussions of their personal writings and diaries seem to attest to the extent of their emotional separation from each other, particularly with respect to anger and sadness.

Over the course of the year, these girls began to appreciate both the similarity of their experiences and concerns and the shared intensity of their feelings. They spoke of the pressures they felt to move their academic capabilities, as well as their social critique and strong feelings, underground in order to escape others' judgments, to avoid embarrassment and rejection. Their group became a safe place to express their anger and complain, as they did frequently and vociferously, about the power of the popular kids and their frustration about the frequent disregard for the rules of meritocracy. And their discussions spilled over into their nightly phone conversations and sleepovers, creating other homes and safe spaces for their social critique. Increasingly the sessions became a place to let go of what had been held in, to be outrageous and silly. The girls found support, encouragement, and shared resistance in the group meetings, as well as an opportunity to experiment with responses to the popular boys' behavior, to create "cool" ways to distinguish themselves from the popular girls, to disagree and argue, to complain about their siblings and friends, to test their developing theories of life and politics. In these moments they imagined different possibilities, played with forms of resistance, developed a shared language and an acceptable group image of themselves as witty, deep, and smart. The active underground thus offered a brief respite from judgment, a shared vision, creative alternatives, and new, more subtle and effective responses to their situations.

These middle-class girls did not, however, openly challenge the culture of the school or publicly dispute those others who held the power to constrain their expressions and movements, nor did they successfully confront the tension between expectations of conventional femininity and dominant notions of success. As the year progressed, the girls began to struggle with the felt contradiction between maintaining loyalty to each other and allegiance to the ideology of individualism and meritocracy they and their school so embraced. The relationships among the girls, initially a source of genuine pleasure, voice, and underground resistance, became a liability as the girls struggled for recognition and visibility, to prove themselves to each other and to their school. Within such a competitive system, they could not afford the risk that group loyalty would silence their individual voices and hold them back. By the end of the school year, the Acadia girls were struggling to support one another and maintain a sense of collective critique of the school structure and social scene.

The struggles of the Acadia and Mansfield girls highlight not only the importance of class for understanding their subjectivities but also the intimate, layered relationships among class, femininity, culture, and race. Listening to these middle- and working-class girls, it becomes impossible, for example, to conflate whiteness with material privilege, or white femininity with indirectness and passivity or a desire to please others. Through their conversations and performances these girls disrupt the metonymic fallacy and, often unwittingly, specify the particular "locations, discourses, and material relations to which the term 'whiteness' applies" (Frankenberg, 1993, p. 6). As a result, they vividly remind us of how little we talk about or reflect on the various cultural configurations and classed identities of white girls.

More specifically, the working-class girls, in their difference from the mainstream, point to a construction of whiteness derived from their particular cultural identity, material disadvantage, and racial privilege. The voices of these girls carry the self-protective anger and moral defiance of a group living off the map of material wealth and privilege. Yet theirs is a position backed by the privileged history of the white race in the United States. Perhaps because the benefits of this privilege are out of their reach, the working-class girls and their families feel and express a sense of anxiety and frustration (see Stevenson & Ellsworth, 1993; Weis, 1990). Such anxiety and frustration may contribute to the family violence and abuse some of the girls describe, as well as to their willingness, at times, to protect and understand their abusers (see Brown, 1998).

The middle-class girls reveal a childhood and adolescence in which race and class privilege are givens. Even their anxieties about their class position underscore this fact, since they reflect not self-examination or cultural critique but a need to justify the prevailing concerns of the middle-class in the United States: that no one is listening to their needs, that they are taken advantage of, "pooped" on, squeezed out by the poor on the one side and the rich on the other. Not surprisingly then, color and poverty are conflated and encoded in the Acadia girls' discourse, most obviously in their descriptions of the poor as lazy, deceitful, and fertile. This is so even though, in their experience, the poor are white. As with the white women Ruth Frankenberg interviewed, racism emerges not as "an ideology or political orientation chosen or rejected at will" but "as a system of material relationships with a set of ideas linked to and embedded in those material relations" (Frankenberg, 1993, p. 70). As seventh graders, these girls are actively negotiating their identities, speaking in and through the voices most familiar and, for the moment, most persuasive to them.

These girls, both middle- and working-class, thus offer us strategies for educating the resistance, even as they warn us of the roadblocks we might expect to encounter in our attempts to do so. The Acadia girls point to the transformative power of language, especially for those educated into the culture of power, and thus comfortable enough to play with, to reinterpret, transform, or reappropriate the meanings of hurtful, unjust, or divisive words and actions.[9] They underscore the importance of the active underground as a safe house for the resistance (Gilligan, 1991)—a place for girls to know each other, to explore the pressures to disconnect from themselves and other girls, and to examine critically the social and educational scene. But these girls also speak to the compelling attraction of the culture of individualism and its distrust of relationship and to the pressures they feel to conform to idealized notions of femininity that will assure their safety and protection. Encouraging white, middle-class girls at the edge of adolescence to stay with the reality of their experiences, to stay in touch with one another, and to bring their critique into the public world—just as these dominant voices intensify—is an enormous challenge.

The Mansfield girls point to the personal and political power of experience, directly expressed and held in relationship with other girls and with
women who remain in their presence during the long, difficult process of
breaking through layers of invulnerability and toughness. The girls' relationship with Diane Starr suggests the importance of women who will listen with
"open hearts and minds"; who will allow the experiences of girls who are different from them to "edge themselves into [their] consciousness" (Delpit,
1995, pp. 46–47). Their relationship with Diane made room for strong feelings and opinions, out of which came their social critique and a useful explication and interrogation of the expectations and norms of the culture of
power. Without this explication the girls would not and could not have acted
effectively in their school.

Conclusion

"Where the notion of 'proper' operates, it is always and only improperly
installed as the effect of a compulsory system," Judith Butler argues (Butler,
1991, p. 21). Femininity is voiced and performed throughout girls' lives, but
at early adolescence, the conventional gender/sex system becomes more regulated and controlled. How this is done and how girls respond to such attempts
at socialization depends on how they are positioned vis-à-vis the dominant
culture, as well as on the nature of their relationships with one another and
with the adults in their lives.

In many ways, these adolescent girls, both working and middle class,
interrupt our too often unexamined notions of idealized femininity. While the
Acadia girls "appear" to capitulate to or appropriate white, middle-class ideals
of feminine behavior, beneath the surface they are frustrated, annoyed, and
angry with the lack of recognition and the invisibility such conventions
demand. They say what they know, what they feel and want, if only in the pri-
vacy of their interviews and focus groups. They are aware of the pressure and
rewards of performing or impersonating idealized femininity. Their anxiety
about public expressions of anger and perceived unfairness make it easier for
them to adopt a radically individualized approach to schooling that keeps
their competitive desires safely out of sight, which also works to undermine
their potentially effective coalition.

The Mansfield girls are more likely to vocalize and live their anger in full
view of their teachers, administrators, and classmates. And yet their outrage at
and distrust of authorities, the confusing, often contradictory messages they
receive about appropriate behavior, and their justified belief that they will not
be heard or taken seriously land them "in the bad." This same outrage supports a shared vision and, with the support of an adult who "gets them," the
power to organize.

In spite of the Mansfield girls' expressed hostility and frustration, there are numerous signs that their teachers actually do care and are trying to listen. During the year teachers notified the authorities about one girl's abuse and raised concerns about another's physical and emotional well-being; school policies *were* changed in response to the girls' complaints, and even though Miss Davis may have misinterpreted Donna's refusal to take off her coat, she seemed to try to engage Donna in a dialogue she thought was important for her student. The problem, in fact, seems not to be that the teachers do not care, but that there are subtle, unexamined class and cultural divides preventing shared understanding between the girls and their teachers.

For both the Acadia and Mansfield girls, anger is a source of knowledge and motivation. As different as these girls seem, their expressions of anger signify an opening. As a sign of self-respect, a signal that something is wrong in their worlds, their anger focuses our attention away from the psychological and toward the political. Such a shift is critical if we are to foster an education for liberation.

Offering girls safe spaces for real conversation and social critique means fully appreciating the ways schools position girls in the good or bad and developing creative, age-relevant ways to educate girls about the culture of power. In my current work, I have attempted to create groups that cross class and race lines. While such groups struggle a good bit initially, in time they begin to name their experiences and imagine different realities than the limited ones offered them in school and society. This process holds the potential for deepening our and their understanding of the complicated intersections of gender, race, and class. Should we pay close attention we may well find ourselves participating in a different kind of conversation with girls, open to new meanings, offering creative pathways, and developing alternative realities.

TEN

The Culture of Black Femininity and School Success

Carla O'Connor, R. L'Heureux Lewis, and Jennifer Mueller

Now my grandfather was a provider for his family, and he taught his sons to be providers. But they [grandmother and grandfather] also taught their girls to stand up. So there was never any question that I was going to work, or that I was waiting for someone to rescue me. That was not part of my upbringing. People didn't get rescued. You did what you had to do in order to do what you had to do.

—Theresa Renier, 46 years old, December, 1997

She was out there finger popping and trying to get through this world. And the world was trying to pull her down and tear her apart. And they didn't know what they were up against. She just kept on coming back for more. And smashing hands and "Here I am, still. Skin a cat another way. Get that skin off that cat."

—Sidney Ellwood, 60 years old, speaking about herself, December, 1997

SIDNEY ELLWOOD AND THERESA RENIER, like the other 17 women featured in this chapter, are black women of lower social class origins who became first-generation college graduates. Like the other women, Ellwood and Renier

163

vividly recalled how being black, being female, and being poor or working class had circumscribed their educational opportunity and threatened their chances of going to and completing college. But Ellwood, Renier, and the other women also discussed how living life on the margins also facilitated their ability to succeed in school. It was from these margins that they were often provided the impetus, orientations, and dispositions necessary for persevering through school. It was also there that they cultivated strategies necessary for negotiating or confronting those barriers that promised to limit their educational attainment and subsequent life chances.

Herein, we show how living life at the intersections of race and gender developed these women's sensibilities that they would not be "rescued." Rather, they would have to do what they had to do to smash those hands that promised to pull them down, tear them apart, and circumscribe their educational outcomes. We reveal how black womanhood or, more precisely, cultural conventions of black femininity, enabled these women to "keep coming back" academically to eventually become the first (or among the first) in their families to receive a college and, in many cases, a graduate school degree.

In this chapter, cultural conventions of femininity signify culturally inscribed presumptions about how women should look, how they should behave, and for what roles they should assume or hope. In the case of the women featured in this text, we specifically focus on how gender socialization and sex role expectations were articulated within the black community to affect the actions and imaginations of these women in ways that had a positive impact on their experience with school.

THE CULTURE OF BLACK FEMININITY AND SCHOOL EXPERIENCES

Researchers who study conventions of black femininity repeatedly document the finding that black people raise their girls to be assertive and independent (Lewis, 1975; Slevin & Winegrove, 1998). Additionally, black families socialize their girls not only to take the roles of wife and mother, but to assume the role of worker. The heightened attention to developing voice, independence, and the worker identity has been linked to black men's historic marginalization in the workforce relative to white men. Black families necessarily had to raise their daughters in ways that would facilitate their girls' ability to assume partial, if not full, responsibility for the financial survival of their families upon becoming women (Lewis, 1975; Ward, 1996).

On the one hand, researchers have argued that this orientation toward voice and independence is a positive adaptation. Unlike white women—particularly upper/middle-class, white women—black women are not necessarily expected to silence their experiences, thoughts, and desires in relations with others. Researchers have subsequently suggested that these differential expectations might explain why black girls generally have higher self-esteem than their white and Latina counterparts and why they are able to maintain this esteem throughout adolescence (AAUW, 1991). Fordham (1993) also showed how this orientation toward voice enables the "loud black girl" to "retrieve a safe cultural space" for herself in school—one in which she is not rendered invisible. Instead, she can creatively subvert the expectations that she be female (rather than male) in a black (and not a white) sense. Finally, Holland and Eisenhart (1990) showed that as a consequence of how black femininity is articulated, black women, compared to their white counterparts, were less preoccupied with romance and were less likely to be manipulated by men. Researchers, however, associate these same expressions of black women's agency with negative educational outcomes.

The same voice and power that are said to protect women against the loss of esteem and the loss of a culturally specific gendered self are also said to place them at academic risk when they produce psychological isolation and are realized in conflict with school officials (Fordham, 1993; Taylor, Gilligan, & Sullivan, 1995). In the case of Fordham's (1993) work, she identified a high-achieving African American female who used her voice to affirm her existence. This expression of voice "propel[led] this young woman to the margins of 'good behavior'" but never "actually forc[ed] her into the realm of 'bad behavior.'" Fordham, however, maintained that most "loud black girls" are not as strategic in their use of voice, and such "loudness" eventually "mutilates the academic achievement of large numbers of female African American students" (p. 5). Researchers also find that it is often the most assertive low-income and minority girls who leave or are pushed out of school (Fine, 1991; Fine & Zane, 1991). Those more likely to stay in school mute their own voices and express high conformity and limited political awareness.

In a similarly contradictory fashion, Holland and Eisenhart (1990) showed that black women focused less of their attention on men and were less manipulated by them. However, this independence did not translate into strong and consistent efforts in school. Having determined that grades of "C" would be sufficient for completing college, the black women were more likely than the white women to accept this grade. Holland and Eisenhart attributed this less than competitive performance to the black women's recognition that blacks were not equitably rewarded for their efforts in school. In the case of this text, there was nothing about the culture of black femininity that mitigated the negative effects associated with the perception of a limited opportunity structure. The culture of black femininity may have been cast in agentic terms, but such agency did not translate into competitive academic performance.

In sum, when reporting on cultures of femininity, researchers have most often emphasized the reproductive rather than the liberatory nature of these cultures. Having identified the liberatory "potential" of these cultures, this work rarely demonstrated how this potential was articulated in the lives of women to facilitate rather than impede their life chances. What work has been done on the liberatory possibilities and practices of black womanhood has been generally conducted outside of the field of education. This work emphasizes how the culture of black femininity informs the general resilience of black women—especially their ability to maintain their mental health, affirm their identities, and nurture their families (e.g., Collins, 2000; hooks, 1992). Little work examines how this culture is specifically articulated in school to generate academic success. We are therefore left with little indication that there is anything in black women's cultural tool kit that makes them able to work against those aforementioned race- and school-based phenomena that promise to constrain their educational and subsequent life chances. In light of this gap in the literature, this chapter focuses on how particular elements of the culture of black femininity informs black women's educational success rather than their academic vulnerability.

In reporting on the liberatory potential and practices associated with the culture of black femininity, this chapter recognizes that conventions of femininity are not static phenomena. Rather, these conventions change over time in response to shifting social and economic opportunities.[1] Importantly, then, our 19 women are distributed across 3 age cohorts that will be elaborated upon below. This cohort distribution affords us the opportunity to show how cultural conventions of black femininity were differently articulated across time to affect the women's experience with school success. In total then, this chapter will not only discuss the liberatory potential and practices of the culture of black femininity in relation to how well and how far these women went in school but also will show that elements of this culture were differentially reflected over time and thus differentially taken up (or not) by the women to facilitate their educational success. Before discussing the findings of this investigation, we will briefly report on how we documented the voices and experiences of the women in this study.

DOCUMENTING THE WOMEN'S VOICES AND EXPERIENCES

The data for this chapter derive from a larger investigation of the life histories of 19 black women who were first-generation college graduates and grew up in low-income and working-class households.[2] The women were born and then first attended a postsecondary institution within the following age cohorts. Cohort I (the precivil rights era cohort) includes those women who were born between 1926 and 1931 and first attended a postsecondary school before the 1950s. Cohort II (the postcivil rights era cohort) includes those women who born between 1946 and 1955 and first attended a postsecondary school during the mid-1960s to mid-1970s. Cohort III (the post

Reagan era cohort) represents those women who were born between 1966 and 1970 and first attended a postsecondary school after 1984.[3] All of the respondents were first-generation college graduates, and in all but two cases they were the first in their families to receive a baccalaureate degree. In every case, they were the first females in their immediate families to earn this degree. All of the respondents also attended what I will refer to as "Midwest University" (MU).[4]

We captured the women's life stories via in-depth individual interviews that were audiotaped and transcribed verbatim.[5] For the purposes of this chapter, data analysis was directed toward answering the following questions: (1) What gender-related narratives were communicated in these women's life stories? (2) How did these gender-related narratives reveal constraints to and/or opportunities for educational achievement and mobility? (3) What were the processes by which the women developed, maintained, and exercised commitment to school to attain high levels of education given the representation of gender-based constraints and opportunities that were particular to their space and time? More specifically, we focused on how the women articulated the ways that gender (including how it may have intersected with race and/or social class) operated in their "everyday," as well as within the greater social context in which they grew up. Some of this data was generated in response to questions like the following:

- Did anyone ever talk to you about what it was like to be a woman in general and a black woman in particular?
- Have you experienced or felt any hostility from others because you were female?
- Were there times when you may have benefited from being a woman?
- What were the most significant events affecting the lives of women when you were growing up? How do you think these events affected your life in particular?
- When did you begin dating?
- What messages did you receive about dating or about boys?

The women also volunteered information about how their physical appearance; their experiences as daughters, mothers, and wives; and their being female in school or work affected their life chances and trajectories. Often they would introduce gender-related issues in light of talking about how they experienced other social identities (i.e., racial and social class).

Beginning with within-case analyses, we analyzed each case to identify any data that was relevant to gender. We identified interview excerpts in which the respondents (1) answered a question that either imposed gender as a social category or introduced gender-related issues (e.g., dating), or (2) volunteered information about how their own gender or that of others factored into the experiences they had, were privy to, or about which they were informed. We also attended to the sex of the actors in the respondents' narratives in order to assess whether males and females operated differently in the women's lived experiences and, therefore, provided the women with implicit messages about gender roles, expectations, and experiences. We also examined the women's life stories in an effort to determine whether aspects of the women's narratives appeared consistent with or contradictory to previous research findings about the culture of femininity in general and black femininity in particular. Across-case analyses were subsequently conducted within and then across the three age cohorts in order to interpret any shifts in the content or representation of these gender-based narratives across the age cohorts.

FROM WHENCE THEY CAME

Before reporting on how these 19 women lived and responded to their experiences with how black women should look, the characteristics women should possess, and the roles women should assume, we will offer some basic background information about them. At the time in which the women shared their life stories, they were employed in or retired from a wide variety of professions that signaled their evident upward mobility in light of their lower social class origins. In our efforts to document those origins, we learned that for the most part these women grew up in homes that were solidly working class. With few exceptions, they grew up in two-parent households. And with only one breadwinner in the home, their families in most cases (even when extremely large) generated the financial resources necessary to avoid public or even charitable assistance. Most of the women additionally reported that for much of their childhood their family owned their home (though for the oldest cohort the homes were in most cases built rather than bought by their parents or guardians). In the majority of the cases, such homeownership coincided with the upward mobility of the family. That is, more than half of the women indicated that over time (particularly in relation to buying a first or a larger house) their families moved to "better," safer, and more economically stable communities.

Most of the women also grew up with fairly well educated caretakers. Although none of their primary caretakers was a graduate of a four-year college, seven of the women had at least one parent or guardian who had received some postsecondary school training, and thirteen had at least one caretaker who had graduated from high school.

Growing up in a financially stable household with two parents who are more, rather than less, educated has long been interpreted as protecting youth against failure in school (see Masten, 1994 for a review). Life in economically viable communities is also positively correlated with higher educational achievements and attainment (e.g. Crane, 1991; Benard, 1991). Consequently, with regards to socioeconomic indices, this sample of women, when taken as a whole, experienced advantages (if only relative) when it came to doing well in school. These socioeconomic advantages did not, however, protect these women against those risks that were specifically tied to them being women, and black women in particular. The women's life stories, among other things, revealed how racism and cultural conventions (both dominant and culturally specific) surrounding how (black) women should look, how they should act, and the roles they should assume and hope for circumscribed their "everyday" experiences and threatened their life chances. But their life stories also revealed that they often drew strength specifically from the culture of black femininity. This culture not only developed their voice and independence but also extended their imaginations regarding life's possibilities. We show how through the coupling of this power and imagination the women came to resist those race- and gender-based expectations and barriers that constrained their access to, progression through, and equitable treatment in school.

THE CULTURE OF BLACK FEMININITY: DEVELOPING VOICE, INDEPENDENCE, AND POSSIBILITY

Across the age cohorts the women discussed the messages they received within the community with regards to how black women should look, how they should behave, and for what roles they should assume or hope. In many instances, these messages seemed orientated toward circumscribing these women's bodies and, to a lesser degree, their life chances. And as might be expected, Cohort I was most apt to discuss how these conventions were directed toward such circumscription. Only in this cohort did women report that it was not only schooling agents but also their own family members who sought to suppress their educational ambitions precisely because they were women. The first, Sidney Ellwood, explained that her father had "slapped [her] face" when he learned that she had applied and had been admitted to Midwest University. Given his own sexism that was articulated via religious dogma, he had determined that women should not go to college because it would make them "worldly" and would cultivate rather than suppress their "evil power." The second, Dee Hawk, remembered that her own mother did not see any point in her pursuing higher education, as she imagined that Hawk would only end up getting married.

Across the age cohorts, the women's stories also revealed that physical indices of femininity required women to be light in complexion, have fine and long hair, and be "thick" (neither fat nor skinny) in body. However, these physical requirements of femininity were more salient in the experiences of Cohort

I. Although darker women, skinny women, women who were more round than thick, and women with short hair revealed that they received less if not negative attention from men and were less welcomed into popular or middle-class circles, the oldest cohort (Cohort I) most often referenced how these physical "requirements" impacted their social interactions. The youngest cohort (Cohort III) made the least reference to the influence of these requirements. While these findings are consistent with other accounts of how skin color and hair length, in particular, operated in the black community over time (e.g., Russell, 1992), these women's life stories suggest that these physical requirements of beauty had important educational effects. This was particularly revealed in the case of Cohort I members who, in the absence of school-sanctioned support for their educational ambitions, had to rely heavily on informal social networks to access information and encouragement for their college attendance. Their stories revealed that their physical appearance determined whether they would be welcomed into more elite social circles that had accordant access to knowledge and resources upon which they could draw to facilitate their educational mobility.[6]

With regards to how the women's lives were otherwise circumscribed, they reported (without evident distinctions between the cohorts) that while growing up, restrictions were placed upon their bodies. Sometimes these restrictions were articulated via their inability to move as freely about public space as compared to their brothers and other male counterparts. For example, Leona Holmes recounted that she would often question why her brother experienced a degree of freedom that was not accorded her. She would ask her mother, "And how come he does that?" Her mother would respond, "He's the oldest." Leona further explained, "But, you know, he was the boy. The oldest but a boy again, you know. He's out in the street running wild with my uncle, cause they were like a couple of years apart. No street running for me." Later she added, "He was older than me—yes—but I never reached an age where I could do what he did."

At other times, the women found that these bodily restrictions were a function of how "etiquette" prescribed how, where, when, and with whom they could or could not use or move their bodies. Sometimes indices of etiquette referred to dating etiquette or if and when they could begin dating and in accordance with what rules. The women indicated that compared to the males in their family, they encountered severe or at least more severe dating rules and regulations. Otherwise, etiquette lessons focused on defining the women's physical comportment. For example, when Tia Richardson was asked whether anyone had spoken with her about what it was like to be a woman, in general, and a black woman, in particular, she responded:

> I know definitely etiquette-wise, for lack of a better word, you know. And that came from my mother, my grandparents, extended family. You know, ladies don't do that. How you sit. How you dressed. How you talked. I mean, the whole kind of etiquette side.

In the case of Cohorts II and III as well as for most members of Cohort I, these restrictions on the body did not coincide with familial efforts consciously directed at restricting the women's imaginations of life's possibilities. Thus, in the same breath that Richardson (above) reports on the restrictions she received about being a woman "etiquette-wise," she stressed that no such restrictions were imposed upon her ambitions. In the absence of our prompting and without her skipping a beat, Richardson continued, "Career-wise I was never told that women can't do anything. I was never told that. Never, you know. What do you want to do? [was how I was approached] I was *never* discouraged" (original emphasis).

Repeatedly, the women conveyed that they received communications that they should not be constrained in their ambitions *because* they were women. Sometimes these communications were conveyed in light of what was not said, as when Tia reported that she was "never told that women can't do anything." Other times, these communications were modeled on the bodies of other women. Sometimes this modeling was reflected in the actions of seemingly ordinary women pursuing more routine activities. For example, when we asked Desiree Strong whether anyone had ever taught her what it meant to be a woman, in general, or a black woman, in particular, she responded:

> Well, first of all, my mother . . . taught me in her own way that *you could do anything*. My mother didn't start driving till I think she was in her 40s. . . . Got tired of waiting on my father to teach her how to drive. Saved her little change, bought her own car, took driving lessons, was driving. (Original emphasis)

The actions of Desiree's mother conveyed how women could define their power independent of men through more mundane efforts. In other instances, the participants of this study referenced black women who had accomplished seemingly extraordinary acts and were mavericks of a place or a time. For example, when Doreen Kingsley was asked to discuss persons who stood out in her life, she discussed three of the extraordinary women she knew and how each of them provided a model of black womanhood that was distinct from the one afforded by her mother. She spoke of Mrs. Blaine who was "so active out in the community . . . and . . . was always very politically involved [when her own] mother wasn't." She "remember[ed] [her] good friend's mother . . . who became Supreme Basmith for [a black sorority]. She also recalled a good friend of her mother, Dr. Rachel Jefferson, who helped "build the women's clubhouse . . . on the corner of Forest and Bradford . . . [and who] met with presidents . . . and with governors." Kingsley explained that she saw these three women "as women . . . that had done good things." Additionally, they were "models"—"get out and do kind of models."

While Kingsley's recollections spoke to those mavericks whose lives had extended the notion of what black women could do, other mavericks conveyed that in the pursuit of these extraordinary acts, there were things that black women did not *have* to do. Candace Weber-Smith recalled the aunt who she "modeled [herself] after." She explained that at the same time that her aunt was the only woman she knew who had financial power, she had acquired this power in the midst of bucking conventions of feminine beauty:

> I remember my aunt was overweight. . . . [And] I remember other aunts commenting negatively. [Among other things, they would say] she needs to wear more jewelry. My aunt didn't care anything about that. She just was who she was and did not need an external confirmation, affirmation, validation. And I just watched her in awe, move things. And so, for some people, they found her abrasive. I saw her, of course, as no-nonsense and powerful. But I know others had difficulty with her authority and her power. . . . I watched her. I knew there was a correlation between money and power. And I saw so few females who could, if they wanted to, do something, reach in their pocket and pull out their own money. . . . But I watched my aunt, and there was no other female I knew who had financial power.

Sometimes the women reported that they came to understand the voice and power of black women outside of those women who were personally known to them. This was especially the case for the members of Cohort II, five of whom discussed how Angela Davis, in particular, signaled what they were capable of as black women. An exchange with Renee Kirkland illustrates how publicly available maverick figures were able to extend the imaginations of some of the participants.

In Kirkland's effort to explain the significant events that affected her life, she began by discussing "the life of Martin Luther King, the death of Martin Luther King, the life of Malcolm X, the death of Malcolm X, Rosa Parks, the whole civil rights movement . . . all the people that were very active in that." She continued to explain that these persons and events made her "aware of the challenges, that faced [her] as an African American . . . made [her] more aware of the past . . . where [she] c[a]me from . . . what situation [she] was in at that point and time." Additionally, she became aware of "the different roads that led . . . into the future [and] also, the many choices that [she] faced [and] the different roles [she] could have taken. Having followed up by asking her whether there were any figures who made her especially aware of the roles she could have taken, she responded:

> For me, I would have to say Angela Davis, cause she was a *strooong* black woman and . . . I am aware of the fact that the civil rights movement was mostly a male-dominated movement and . . . although not to . . . take anything away from it but . . . there was not a real strong role that African American women played in that. Martin Luther King's wife, she was kind of . . .

docile, you know, in the background. But Angela Davis, I think, made an impact on me about strong black women. . . . The potential that we . . . have, and I think . . . I got a lot of my strength from . . . just watching . . . and learning more about Angela Davis—knowing that women can be strong, *just* as strong, too. (Original emphasis)

The stories recounted above demonstrate the multiple ways in which women in this study came to know and/or emulate the voice and power of black women. Candace's aunt taught her, if only indirectly, that black women not only can wield financial power but also can move things and benefit from a no-nonsense stance. Desiree's mother showed her that women need not wait on a man but can act efficaciously in their "everyday" efforts to pursue their own interests. Angela Davis and the extraordinary women in Kingsley's life provided evidence of black women's political will and agency. These different representations of black women's voice and power were weaved throughout the participants' life stories. Importantly, when the women further reported on their familiarity with black women's voice and power and the processes by which they became acculturated to these expressions of womanhood, they often discussed how family members often established an explicit link between these expressions and the receipt of higher education. For example, Leona Holmes' mother told her, "Honey, get your degree so that you don't have to be tied down to no Negro. . . . You can always take care of yourself." Tia Richardson explained that her parents wanted her sister and her "to be able to go to college so that we could, you know, provide for ourselves and, you know, be self-sufficient so where we would have to necessarily rely on someone else to provide . . . for us." Nora Bentley explained that her father provided her with the most "predominate" message regarding dating or the role that romantic relationships should play in her life. His message was, "Get a degree. Don't depend upon any man."

Nearly to a person, the members of Cohort III indicated that they received explicit exhortations that they needed to get an education so that they could enact their agency by being independent of men. In contrast, most of the women in Cohort I did not recall their family members encouraging them to pursue an education in order to ensure their power in relationships with men. In two instances, in fact, members of Cohort I found that family members sought to constrain their educational ambitions. The life stories that Cohort I members told indicated that they were, nevertheless, able to develop a sense of black feminine agency via maverick female figures who were intimately involved in their lives. These figures were grandmothers, aunts, family friends, mothers, and neighbors who transcended traditional notions of womanhood because they were financially independent, highly educated, physically strong, unusually courageous, or sexually powerful. In the case of Cohort II, their life stories indicated that they came to understand the social, political, and/or economic efficacy they could and should wield as black women in light of publicly available maverick figures such as Angela Davis, as well as their intimate ties with black women who had demonstrated their agency in sometimes routine and otherwise extraordinary acts. Many of the Cohort II members, like the members of Cohort III, also experienced the same verbal exhortation to go far in school in order to ensure their domestic efficacy and independence.

COPING WITH CONSTRAINTS

Having been socialized toward voice and power as a consequence of explicit exhortation, as well as via intimate and publicly available models of black women's individual, economic, social, and political agency, it is not surprising to learn that the women in this study described themselves as "pushy," "strong," "loud," "aggressive," "assertive," "demanding," "determined." Having asked one participant, L'Nette Farnsworth, why she used one of the adjectives above to describe herself (in her case, she was explaining why she would describe herself as strong), we were not surprised to receive the following response:

> I feel that I can take a stand even though I am female. . . . I don't have to succumb to certain issues because, you know, men are supposed to be the superior sex and, you know, wear the pants in the family. . . . I'm not afraid to speak up for what I believe, and . . . if I feel that someone is stepping on my toes or because I am a woman or whatever, . . . I'm not afraid to challenge someone as it relates to being a woman.

While some have suggested that such voice and power are likely to put black women at academic risk (e.g., Taylor, Gilligan, & Sullivan, 1995; Orenstein, 1994; Fine & Zane, 1991), Cohort III members (along with some members of Cohort II) explained that it was this very socialization that explained, in part, their pursuit of and persistence in higher education. Members of Cohort III indicated that much of their motivation to go far in school was fostered in light of the explicit exhortation that they achieve high levels of education in order to wield their power in relationship with or independent of men.[7] Sometimes they would hold onto these exhortations when they encountered educational obstacles. Cyrillene James remembers feeling out of place at Midwest University. She recalled sometimes feeling overwhelmed by the academic demands and the inhospitable racial climate. She, however, indicated that when "the thought of quitting crossed [her] mind, [her] mother's voice would ring in [her] ears—Baby you don't want to *have to* depend on a man" (original emphasis).

In contrast to Cohort III, Cohorts I and II specifically indicated how they actually employed their voice and power in their effort to have others respond to, support, or not hinder their own school-related pursuits.[8] Thus, when Ellwood's father slapped her face for applying to and being admitted to Midwest University, she stated that she "drew strength" from her grandmother whom she "quietly emulated." She explained:

> [I did] not [emulate] my pious grandmother but my worldly grandmother. I just didn't tell anybody, you know. . . . 'Cause she wouldn't take any stuff from anybody. . . . She was raunchy. She was downright nasty. . . . 'Cause she would have a wicked little grin and laugh at men. . . . And she told us about puntang. I always cracked up . . . because that was do it and do it right, you know. So grandma was a worldly lady. She worked. . . . I'm not sure what she did. But she was like the beginning of women's lib. She became what she wanted to, and if she got tired of the man, she said, "Get out!" And she said, "I didn't marry 'em. And I divorced them meant, 'I divorce you, turn and go out the door.'"

In a follow-up interview, Ellwood explained, "I looked to her [her worldly grandmother], and I knew I could and would defy my father." Most of the women in the study did not, however, find that it was their family members who sought to constrain their educational ambitions. In most instances, they discussed how schooling agents, teachers, and professors sought to circumscribe their educational experiences and outcomes. In these instances, they again drew upon their socialization toward voice and power. Sometimes they invoked these orientations to claim a space for themselves and to protest the discrimination they experienced in white-dominated schools. For example, Karen Washington recalled that there was only one high school in her community, and the blacks had to "cross the tracks to go there." She continued:

> I wanted to get out there and jump around like the rest of those people—with all the whites. And my grandmother said, "Well go ahead and try." So I tried . . . and they allowed me to [become a cheerleader]. But when we would go into places like Pelham, which is a suburb, it's like an enclave—white folks for sure enough serious—like Klan territory, they would not allow me to cheer. . . . Now I rode with them on the bus, but they made me sit on the bench. But, you know, I went. I never said I'm not going because I can't cheer. *I went and sat there as a symbol of what you all don't want.* [There had not been a black] on the debating . . . I got on the debating team, I'd shoot, girl. I was smart. I could talk. There was no reason why I couldn't get on there. *Anything I wanted to do, my grandmother never told me I could not do it. Even at that time, I pushed.* (Authors' emphasis)

In this excerpt, Washington revealed that her grandmother did not bind her imagination regarding what she could do as a black woman. So she would push. She pushed her way into school spaces that had been previously all white. In these spaces, she then used her voice to her advantage (i.e., on the debate team) and expressed her strength via silent and symbolic protest against evident inequities (being denied the opportunity to cheer at those away games that were played in racially hostile communities).

In other instances the women reported that their very willingness to express their voice and power in conflict with teachers or professors sometimes reaped them better academic outcomes. For example, Weber-Smith first discussed how she successfully challenged a high school teacher who graded her down on a writing assignment because she found the content unacceptable:

> I had a writing class where a teacher gave me a B, and I argued, for lack of a better word, with her, and she changed my grade to an A. The reason why I argued . . . it was a creative writing thing, and I had written that I was the inside of a bullet . . . in a black revolutionary's gun pointed at the head of a white person. . . . I had no shame, I didn't care, I was radical. I did not care. . . . She bad enough to teach on the east side of [Mid City]. But anyway so I write this paper, and I remember describing the smell of gunpowder because I'm inside the bullet. She wrote back and said that . . . the paper was good, but I should have used a term [that reflected the] accurate smell of gunpowder. . . . And I told her I didn't know what that word meant. I never heard it before. . . . We went back and forth. She changed it to an A. . . . [She was] an excellent teacher, but she didn't like the content . . . the nerve, to mark me down for that. . . . I knew that she could get me on sentence structure, or I hadn't developed my point, something, but not on one word— Oh no! I don't think so, uh uh, uh uh! So that was it.

Weber-Smith subsequently explained that she sometimes had to get "a bit feisty" with her professors in college "so that they too would give [her her] due."

Leona Holmes similarly reported on how she too became "bold" with her college instructors in her effort to receive better, if not equitable, academic treatment. In her effort to account for her boldness, Holmes began by reporting that her professors "arbitrarily would give you a grade, and then they wouldn't write anything on your paper." She added that they were subsequently hostile to her inquiries about the grade she received. In her words, "And then you would go and question them and then that's when they would just like . . . cut you down, 'Are you questioning me?' 'Yes.' 'No, you don't question me. You have no right to question me. It's a C. It's not worth anything more. . . . It's not even worth the paper.'" Having experienced such treatment "one time after another," Holmes initially began saying, "God, I'm not meant to be here." "But then [she] took a look at . . . the mess [her white peers] were turning in, and they got B+, A." It was then that "she realized the professors were just out" [t]here to do a number on [her]." She, therefore, became "really bold" and would

> BAM BAM BAM . . . knock on that door, "Excuse me professor, can I talk to you?" *[both laugh]* . . . I just got really bold with it 'cause I realized, hey, I'm going to flunk out or they just going to put me out, or they going to flunk me out anyway 'cause they could. . . . So I figured, hey, let's go out with a bang. So I just became very . . . what do they say? Brazen or whatever.

It is evident from her inclusion in this study that Holmes never flunked out of Midwest University. Additionally, she reported that her brazen efforts to have teachers account for their evaluations of her work sometimes led to her receiving a more favorable assessment of her performance on a given assignment.

Sometimes the women reported that they waged conflict not only to receive more favorable educational outcomes but also to affirm nondominant perspectives that had been marginalized in their schools. These perspectives, in some instances, affirmed the humanity and experience of African Americans. For example, Renee Kirkland reported on her conflict with one of her teachers in Midwest's nursing program. She explained:

> [I was] supposed to write like a little thesis for [a nursing] class—something to deal with cultural differences, and my paper was on African Americans and how Midwest University does not adequately address the cultural differences of the patients that they serve, and that's not meeting their needs. . . . I focused on . . . [how] they don't teach about differences in hair. They don't teach about their skin, dotta, dotta, da. I remember her giving me a "D." And that was a good paper. So I remember meeting with her, and she just went off on me. You people, you know, you have to learn to do what the Jewish people did. You have to learn to assimilate into society. And I . . . said, "Look, you have blue eyes. You have white skin, you can assimilate." I said, "How the hell am I going to assimilate?" And I said, "Besides what does that have to do with my paper?" But basically she felt that African Americans— we were just making trouble. That the Jews, they had their troubles, but they're okay now and they're doing well, and we're not. And we need to take a lesson from them. So she was just gonna pound on me. So . . . she wanted me to redo my paper. I went and talked to . . . one of the deans and, you know, she gave me a passing grade, but it was . . . begrudgingly.

In short, it was Kirkland's willingness to make "trouble" that allowed her to receive a higher grade (if not the grade she deserved) while forwarding black cultural frames and experiences that had been silenced in the academy. Like Weber-Smith and Holmes, Kirkland's assertive stance with her teachers proved to be an asset rather than a liability.[9]

Summary and Conclusion

These women's stories require us to reassess previous research, which suggests that black women's socialization toward voice and power is likely to put them at risk for school failure. Though little research has been conducted on this topic, what work is available suggests that when black girls express their voice and power in school, they are placed at an academic disadvantage. They experience psychological isolation, find themselves in conflict with school officials, and are more likely to be "pushed" out of school. The findings of this study, however, require us to generate a more complicated picture regarding how the culture of black femininity can shape the educational experiences and outcomes of black girls. More precisely, the findings reported herein reveal how the culture of black femininity can be productive in relation to schooling.

The life stories featured in this chapter show how the culture of black femininity impacted black women's ability to imagine that black women in general, and they in particular, could act efficaciously despite gender-based barriers that operate in the "everyday" and in society at large. Just as important, these stories convey how this culture (articulated via exhortation or feminine models) informed the cognitive and behavioral processes by which the women actually resisted those constraints that threatened their academic success and persistence. Researchers have otherwise provided evidence that success within and outside of school is in part a function of how individuals begin to imagine and then act upon life's possibilities despite constraint (O'Connor, 1997; Etter-Lewis, 1993; Young, 1999).

The women in Cohorts II and III indicated that, in part, their positive valuation of education, their college aspirations, and their persistence through school were fostered by their family members' efforts in socializing them to become self-sufficient (i.e., independent of men). Additionally, the women were able to invoke their voice and power in ways that enabled them to resist those efforts, cultures, and practices directed at circumscribing their educational experiences and outcomes. In most instances, these women experienced such circumscription in academic settings and at the hands of schooling agents. However, they would draw on black feminine agency to protest inequitable treatment and to claim school spaces that had been previously denied to blacks. Often the women's protests and their willingness to be in conflict with school officials produced (more) positive educational outcomes. Conflict in these instances was productive. In the absence of engaging in conflict, these women would have been further marginalized in academic settings. Additionally, they would have resigned themselves to inequitable grading practices and lower grades.

Although these findings reveal the productive character of the women's socialization towards black feminine agency, we must be mindful of evidence that the voice and power of black women is at best suppressed and often negatively sanctioned in schools. What is at stake when schools and educators seek to suppress, sanction, or push out those traits that are central to cultivation of worldviews and strategies that can expand black people's life chances? If we have any chance of working toward a more just society, schools and educators must take up the challenge to explore how they might build upon, rather than work against, the socially productive nature of black femininity.

ELEVEN

Speech and Silence

An Analysis of the
Cultural Practice of Talking[1]

Heejung S. Kim and Hazel Rose Markus

DIVERSITY—in gender, race, culture, social class, and sexuality—is increasingly the fact of life and at the same time, an important goal of schools in the United States. Many schools devote their resources to increase and accommodate diversity as they recognize the political and pedagogical virtue of diversity. Yet, diversity in classrooms does not always function well, as is the case with understanding how to accommodate diversity beyond representing different faces and experiences in the classroom. This chapter addresses an example of the challenges of diversity frequently found in classrooms in the United States.

In ethnically and racially diverse classrooms in the United States, teachers often note the silence of East Asian students. A newspaper article entitled "Some Students Must Learn to Question" (Lubman, 1998) describes this commonly perceived problem. The article claims that East Asian and East Asian American students do not participate verbally in class as much as instructors want them to, and this relative lack of verbal participation is a concern for educators. The problem, in the eyes of some faculty and administrators, is that East Asian students' reluctance to speak up in class is a hurdle for them to become "independent thinkers" who can express themselves.

Speech, verbal expression, and debate occupy vitally important places in much of Western and particularly European American education as valued practices in themselves and also as tools to enhance thinking. The widely observed silence of many East Asian students, including many East Asian students who have grown up in America, is a problem for educators who, obviously, want to teach their students the "right" things in the "right" way and would like students to gain the most from their classroom experiences. With nothing but good intentions, American teachers drawing on their own implicit models of intelligence and education urge these students to participate more, to contribute more, and to talk more.

Yet is talking always good, and does it necessarily promote better thinking? Is the fact that many East Asian students are quiet in the classroom setting a problem that needs to be fixed? In this chapter, we will step back a bit and consider various perspectives and some research on the purpose, function, and practices of talking in a variety of sociocultural contexts. Further, we will suggest that educators, supervisors, and managers engaged in systems that value and encourage talking might want to acknowledge and reflect on the fact that in other cultural systems, good thinking and good performance can be associated with verbal reserve.

Humans talk. Being able to use language distinguishes humans from other living creatures, and the ability to talk is the unique and universal nature of human animals. Talking is undeniably one of the most important forms of communication, one of the best avenues to thinking, and one of the most common forms of expression. Yet, talking is not an automatic response to the sound of another voice or to the internal pressure of an unexpressed thought. Talking, like many seemingly mundane social acts, is a culturally saturated activity. The ways in which people talk are socially shaped and shared and entail the incorporation of culture-specific models (Bruner, 1996; D'Andrade, 1990, 1995; Fiske, Kitayama, Markus, & Nisbett, 1998; Quinn & Holland, 1987; Shore, 1996; Shweder, 1991). These cultural models are bundles of ideas and practices, many of them tacit, about why to talk, how to talk, when to talk, whom to talk to, and toward what end. Striking variation in these cultural models exists among Americans, variation that is associated with socially significant categories such as ethnic group, region of the country, social class, and gender. Such variation poses significant challenges to the effective functioning of diverse groups in schools and workplaces.

Talking is a perfect example of a human action that cannot be understood without regard to particular and intertwined sets of local cultural, historical, and institutional representations and practices. In the course of tracing the meaning of talking in a given cultural context, one finds an intricate knot of meanings and practices, all of which recruit and implicate each other. In some cultural traditions, talking is powerfully associated with notions of individuality, freedom, equality, democracy, reason, intelligence, and honesty. In yet other cultural traditions, the act of talking is intricately bound with notions of relationship, hierarchy, status, face, and empathy and also with conceptions of immaturity and carelessness. In the following sections of the chapter, we will compare two divergent perspectives on talking and examine their implications. More specifically, and more practically, it will become apparent why it is not always a simple matter for "nontalkers" to become "talkers" and why this solution to the "problem" is only one of several that might be endorsed.

CULTURAL MEANINGS AND
PSYCHOLOGICAL CONSEQUENCES OF TALKING

Cultural contexts vary in their prevalent models of talking and silence and how they are woven into the practice of everyday life. How people make sense of each other's habits of talking depends on these models that include the reasons for speaking and the value of speaking. As Austin (1962) has established, utterances have various functions besides conveying information, and these functions depend on the context. Even a cursory review of the literature on the practices of talking and not talking reveals a surprising diversity of views and underscores the necessity of understanding the meanings of talking and silence that are common in a given sociocultural context.

As talking makes up an important part of the social lives of people, it always implicates the self and the other. The meaning of talking should be affected by the concept of the 'self,' because the act of talking involves projecting one's own thoughts and ideas into the world. The meaning of talking should also be affected by the concept of the 'relationship,' because talking functions as a tool of connecting and maintaining connectedness among people. Thus, to the extent that the concepts of the self and of relationship vary from one society to another, what the act of talking means should also differ across cultures.

TALKING, THE SELF, AND SOCIAL RELATIONSHIPS

A cultural analysis takes into account the core cultural ideas, the social representations, and the background understandings relevant to talking, as well as those practices and institutions within which talking takes place. One of the most important tacit understandings within this net of ideas and practices is what it means to a "good" or "proper" person (Markus & Kitayama, 1991; Markus, Mullally, & Kitayama, 1997). In many cultural contexts of the United States, the individual is understood and practiced as a separate or distinct entity whose behavior is determined by some amalgam of internal attributes. The cultural model of the independent person is one of the most prevalent models in North America. This model of a person holds (1) that the person is a stable, autonomous, "free" entity; (2) that he or she possesses a set of characteristic, identifying, and self-defining attributes—preferences, motives, goals, attitudes, beliefs, and abilities—that are the primary forces that enable, guide, or constrain behavior; (3) that individuals take action that is oriented toward the expression of their opinions and beliefs, the realization of their rights, and the achievement of their goals; and (4) that the individual often regards relationships as competing with personal needs and considers the expectations of others and obligations to others as interfering with personal goals (for full discussion of these and other cultural commitments of individualism, see Fiske, et al., 1998). In many middle-class cultural contexts, talking is an act that defines and affirms the American self because it is one of the ways in which internal attributes can be most directly and clearly expressed.

In these cultural contexts, speaking one's mind is often synonymous with being a person. Thinking and talking have been Western preoccupations at least since the time of the ancient Greeks (Nakamura, 1964/1985; Nisbett, Peng, Choi, & Norenzayan, 2001). Of course not everyone communicates their thoughts easily, and even within the U.S. cultural context, there is tremendous individual, group, and regional variation. For instance, women in the United States who generally pay more attention to relational aspects of themselves and are less concerned about asserting independence are also less verbally expressive in public settings than men. Yet along with the freedom to choose one's government and one's religion, the right to speak one's mind, should one so desire, is protected as an absolute birthright. Speech is part and parcel of America's democratic traditions, and speakers have a responsibility to exercise their rights to communicate what is on their mind. In American contexts, talking becomes interwoven with speaking the truth, with the meanings and practices of freedom, with individual rights, and with expression and personhood. It becomes cemented as a foundational and uncontested good.

There are, however, other models of a person, and with different models, the act of talking takes on different meanings. In many cultural contexts, the person is commonly understood not as an independent entity but primarily a relational entity. In models of the self that are prevalent in many East Asian contexts including China, Japan, Korea, and South Asia, the relationship has a type of moral primacy, and the person is viewed as connected with others (Triandis, 1989; Markus & Kitayama, 1991; Shweder & Bourne, 1984). These cultural models of the person place greater stress than individualist models on social and relational concepts such as 'empathy,' 'reciprocity,' 'belongingness,' 'kinship,' 'hierarchy,' 'loyalty,' 'honor,' 'respect,' 'politeness,' and 'social obligation.' Typically in these contexts, social relationships, roles, norms, and group solidarity are more fundamental to social behavior than self-expression. This model of the person holds the idea that a person is (1) a flexible, connected entity who is bound to others; (2) participates in a set of relationships, groups, and institutions that are the primary forces that enable, guide, or constrain actions; (3) conforms to the relational norms and responds to group goals by seeking consensus and compromise; and (4) often regards personal beliefs and needs as secondary to norms and relationships (Fiske, et al., 1998). Interdependent models of the person have powerful consequences for the analysis and practice of talking and silence. When others and relations with others are focal, words are perhaps more easily constructed as weapons and their potentially harmful consequences more evident. It is likely, for example, that in places and situations where it is important to view the self as primarily independent, the expressive function of talking will be more salient, whereas in the cultural contexts where it is important to construct the self as interdependent, the relational function of talking will be emphasized.

In communication practices in East Asian cultural contexts, for example, instead of assuming that the speaker has the responsibility to speak directly and to convey what is on one's mind, the major responsibility is placed on the listener who should be as empathic as possible, precisely so that the speaker does not have to communicate ideas and opinions too explicitly (Gudykunst, Gao, & Franklyn-Stokes, 1996). Listening and not hastily talking are highly valued as ways of demonstrating sympathy and trying to understand what others are feeling. When these types of ideas about talking prevail, words are less likely to be taken at face value, and meaning is to be inferred rather than conveyed. While straight talking is a good way to convey one's meanings in many Western contexts, it is indirectness that is a powerful theme of East Asian life (Gudykunst, et al., 1996; Hall, 1976), and silence facilitates this indirectness.

When silence is appreciated and valued with this perspective on talking, other forms of communication become important. The Japanese term *ishin denshin*, for example, marks the culturally significant idea of "an immediate communication between two minds which does not need words" (Morsbach, 1987, p. 202). And the closer individuals are assumed to be, the more they are thought to rely on nonverbal communication that relies on inferences from cues of gesture and tone (Clancy, 1986). Yan (1987) in characterizing Chinese communication says that communication is viewed as a process in which people first try to understand others, then try in turn to be understood by them. Gao, Ting-Toomey, and Gudykunst (1996) claim that in China, only a privileged few are believed to be skillful in talking and that, as a consequence, talking is not a primary path to self-identity or achieving an individual goal.

Some analyses of East Asian communication processes argue that because of the central importance of maintaining harmonious relations and honoring the hierarchy, the processes of face saving and face negotiating are explicitly recognized in some situations to be more important than honest or truthful negotiation (e.g., Gao, et al., 1996). Being open, straightforward, or assertive in public East Asian situations rarely has any of the positive connotations of honesty, power, confidence, or competence they have in many American contexts. Instead actions of this type can threaten the cohesion of relationships and can even signal the bad character of the individuals involved (Tseng, 1973). What appears as passivity or critical lack of assertiveness from an American view point carries with it in many East Asian contexts a whole palette of highly positive associations including intelligence, flexibility, managing face, cooperativeness, power, and maturity (Gao, et al., 1996; Giles, Coupland, & Wiemann, 1992).

In an initial explanation of these hypothesized differences in the cultural meanings of talking, a survey (Kim & Markus, 2002) that included the open-ended question, "Why do you think the ability to speak is important/unimportant?" was administered to comparable college student samples from a Korean cultural context, where the self is represented to be more interdependent, and to an American cultural context where the self is represented to be more independent.

Participants overall generated a fairly similar list of responses in that the majority of both groups of participants thought the ability to speak is important because it "allows us to communicate" and "allows us to express." There were, however, large cross-cultural differences in which of these two responses was emphasized, and even larger differences in how participants focused on subtle aspect of these responses.

Fifty-two percent of Korean participants, and 62 percent of American participants thought that the ability to speak is important because of communication. Similarly, 48 percent of Korean participants and 42 percent of American participants thought that the ability to speak is important because of expression. However, these groups differed a great deal in what they thought was the content of expression or communication. The majority of Korean participants (61 percent) indicated that it is important to speak because of expression or communication with *others* (e.g., "to communicate in order to maintain and improve relationships with other people," "communications to influence and convince other people," "to let my thoughts to be communicated to others and to learn about other people's thoughts"), whereas only 25 percent of American participants mentioned *others* in their response. Moreover, Korean participants also listed more relational responses more often than their American counterparts. Korean participants thought it was important to speak because it helps us "to understand other people (21% vs. 4%)," "to ease relationships (14% vs. 0%)" or "to cooperate with others (7% vs. 0%)."

In contrast, the majority (51 percent) of American participants thought the communication or the expression functions are important because they convey personal ideas, thoughts, and feelings (e.g., "Language serves to give us signifiers for our abstract ideas. It is a tool and can be used by nearly anybody to express thoughts, ideas, and values," "a medium of thought. It is a way to express ideas and feelings within the mind" and "We can express our innermost ideas and desires in a way that is unique to our species"), whereas only 21 percent of Korean participants mentioned such themes. In addition, American participants (8 percent) also mentioned "help learning" significantly more than Korean participants did (0 percent). American participants (19 percent) responded, "to express oneself" somewhat more than Korean participants (9 percent) did, although the difference was not significant.

The results supported the idea that people engaged in cultural contexts or situations where the focus is primarily on the individual may invoke different models of talking. They may view the purpose of talking as the expression of one's ideas and thoughts. However, people engaging in cultural contexts or situations where the emphasis is more on the person as relational or interdependent may tend to see the purpose of talking as connecting the self with others.

Talking and Intelligence

Is talking a sign of intelligence or a sign of ignorance? The answer to this question depends on how one defines an intelligent thinking. As with the meanings of talking, the models of intelligent thinking also vary across cultures. For example, in Western cultural traditions, intelligent thinking is very often defined as a linear and analytical reasoning relying on formal logic and explicit rules (Markus, et al., 1996; Nisbett, et al., 2001). In contrast, in East Asian cultural traditions, intelligent thinking very often involves a holistic thinking attending to relations among objects, as well as relational thinking in which listening and talking another's viewpoint are emphasized (Azuma, 1994).

One cultural difference in what the act of talking means in relation to intelligence might exist in what kind of inference people from different cultural contexts make about a person from both the content and the context of the person's talking. How well a person can reason as reflected in the content of a speech can often give good clues about how intelligent the speaker is. At the same time, how thoughtful and sensitive the person is about social surroundings as reflected in the context in which the speaker is engaged in talking can also give good hints about how intelligent the speaker is. Sometimes, the clues about the person gathered from both sources are compatible, but other times, these different sources can give out incompatible information about the person. When this incompatibility occurs, there seems to be cross-cultural difference in which source is taken as the more important one over the other in making inference about the speaker's intelligence. People in U.S. cultural contexts often evaluate those who are quick and effusive in their verbal responses more favorably than those who are quieter. For example, Swann and Rentfrow (2001) found that those who score higher on the BLIRT (the Brief Loquaciousness and Interpersonal Responsiveness Test)—who are verbally quick and responsive—are also rated as more intelligent and interesting than are those who are not as verbally responsive. Swann and Rentfrow (2001) also show that European American students have the general tendency to score higher on the BLIRT than East Asian American students. While these researchers did not look at any cultural differences in links between talking and intelligence, it seems plausible that the evaluation of a person's intelligence based on verbal responsiveness would differ as well cross-culturally.

Moreover, according to the classification proposed by Hall (1976) regarding language use, some cultures, such as American, tend to focus more on the *content* of a speech (called "low-context" culture). Other cultures, such as East Asian, tend to focus more on the *context* of the speech, such as who the speaker is and the particular setting of the speech (called "high-context" culture). Thus to appear intelligent in a low-context culture, a person should talk more and better than others, while in a more high-context culture, the appearance of intelligence is contingent on talking more cautiously and paying attention to the relation between oneself and others to appear "intelligent."

CULTURAL PRACTICES OF TALKING

Cultural meanings and social representations about talking are embodied in common social practices, and through the practices, the collective beliefs are implicitly transmitted to people in the cultural contexts where the beliefs are commonly shared (Bruner, 1990). In social interactions and institutions, such as parenting and education practices, and interactions in work places, there are core beliefs that guide which behaviors should be encouraged and which behaviors should be discouraged in order to maintain the integrity of the society. These principal beliefs and sentiments are products of collective consciousness (Moscovici, 1993). Moreover, to the extent that there are differences in beliefs from one community to another, there will be differences in the social practices that implicate these beliefs. Thus, the divergent cultural beliefs about talking should also be reflected in divergent social practices and interactions where talking is either encouraged or discouraged.

Talking in Parenting

The purpose of parental and formal education is to cultivate beliefs, skills, and feelings in order to support particular cultural ways of understanding the world (Bruner, 1996). If a given cultural context emphasizes talking as a positive act, and people believe that talking means assertiveness and intelligence, parents and teachers will encourage their children to practice their verbal skills to foster them to be expressive and articulate. In contrast, if a cultural context emphasizes silence and listening, and people think that silence means thoughtfulness and being considerate, parents and teachers will discourage their children from talking too much to make them be serene and attentive to others.

There is a growing body of empirical evidence to support the idea that cultural patterns in parenting style and educational practices related to talking are generally consistent with cultural meanings of talking. Through interactions between children and parents, children learn how to do basic things, such as how to eat, how to sleep and how to talk. Caudhill and Weinstein (1969) showed that Japanese middle-class mothers speak much less frequently to their young children than their American counterparts do. Also, Chinese preschool teachers see quietness as a means of control, rather than passivity, and appreciate silence more than American teachers (Tobin, Wu, & Davidson, 1989). Comparisons of narratives by Minami and McCabe (1995) between Japanese and North American children showed that Japanese mothers asked their children to further describe their comments less compared to American mothers. As a consequence of the less emphasized verbal interactions in East Asian cultural contexts than in European American cultural contexts, East Asian children are not as verbally active as their European American counterparts even as early as seven months of age (Kagan, Kearsley, & Zelazo, 1978; Minami, 1994).

Talking in Education

Differences in cultural patterns of talking are also evident in more formal education. For example, many Western cultural contexts are grounded in Socratic traditions, and thus the private and public questioning of widely accepted knowledge and generating of one's own ideas are highly valued (Tweed & Lehman, 2002). European and American educational practices regarding speech reflect the idea that discussion and verbal activities will facilitate the achievement of these goals. Training for discussion is thought to be beneficial for developing students' social skills, logical thinking, confidence, and even citizenship (Backlund, 1990; Thonssen & Gilkinson, 1955). Consequently, verbal participation in class is an integral aspect of education in middle-class American cultural contexts, and in higher education, verbal participation often constitutes part of the students' grade.

    In contrast, in East Asian cultural contexts, verbal participation of students during learning is often not very important. Class is intended to be a time and place to listen to what a teacher has to say, and good students are supposed to listen and absorb the essential knowledge (Tweed & Lehman, 2002). Often, verbal participation of a student in class is frowned upon by both instructors and other students as it can disrupt the flow of the teaching and "waste" others' learning time by one's idiosyncratic point of view. The culturally good student is one who shows good listening, who takes in what the teacher says, and who does not voice one's own opinions too hastily. If something is not clear, the student should listen more attentively, and the assumption is that it will become clear. The idea is that students are in class to hear what the expert, the teacher, has to say. In most East Asian cultural contexts, very little importance is attached to speaking skills, and instead the curriculum emphasizes listening skills, writing skills, and reading skills (Gao, et al., 1996). As expressed by a Japanese graduate student, "Before I can ask a question I have to ask myself, (1) does this question need to be asked? and (2) am I the right person to ask it?" The presumption here is that if someone more senior has not asked such a question there is probably no need to ask it.

Because of this difference in teaching and learning styles in East Asian cultural contexts, students from East Asian cultural contexts who are being educated in an American education system are thought to be somewhat "problematic," in spite of their generally successful performance in school (e.g., Lubman, 1998). How these students construe being a good student is apparently different from how American education expects a good student to be, and without engaging in the culturally important aspect of education, talking, East Asian students are sometimes seen as passive and incapable of thinking for themselves, rather than as thoughtful and mature. Thus, these students are frequently expected to alter their actions to conform to the American cultural ideal. This expectation of assimilation often exists without the recognition that what these students have to do is not as simple as "just talking more" but actually changing a dense network of cultural values and beliefs about how to be a good person.

Talking in Workplaces

The positive meaning of talking in America continues to be reinforced in work settings. In middle-class American workplaces, both bosses and employees are advised to directly communicate what is on one's mind. In addition to being direct and explicit, American speakers are schooled to be redundant, especially in formal presentations. ("Tell them what you are going to say; tell them; and then tell them what you said.") In sharp contrast, in many East Asian cultural contexts, the best communication is that which is contained, reserved, implicit, and indirect (Gao, et al., 1996). It is crucial not to spell out everything and to leave a sufficient amount unspoken so that the listeners can infer. Listening, however, should be active and done with full attentiveness. Leaving things unsaid makes possible "free advance and retreat" (Gao, et al., 1996) and is the key to flexibility and harmonious interpersonal relations.

Many Americans complain that when doing business with their East Asian counterparts, it is difficult to know their intentions and goals because they are not expressed directly. Yet in the workplace, many Asians consider talk less important than other forms of communication. In one study of Chinese managers, for example, oral communication skills were seen as least important for prospective employees (Hildenbrandt, 1988). Compared to American settings, feedback, challenging, questioning, and interrupting others are reduced or absent in managerial meetings (Lindsay & Dempsey, 1985). Being assertive and outgoing are considered to be among the most positive and essential features to be a leader or to succeed in American business contexts (Peters, 1987). In many work settings, being vocal is a trait necessary to leadership and thus is an important factor in both hiring and promotion decisions. Expressing one's ideas is listed in many American business books as a key trait.

Thus, even titles of many American business advice books, such as *Talk Your Way to Success* (Wilder, 1986), *Talk Your Way to the Top* (Flaherty, 1999), *Everything You Need to Know to Talk Your Way to Success* (Kaplan, 1995), or *I Wish I Said That: How to Talk Your Way out of Trouble and into Success* (McCallister, 1994) emphasize the importance of talking in business success. One book suggests, "Don't be afraid of the sound of your own voice, show off your expertise, offer your insight" (White, 1995, p. 156).

This public advice is indeed taken in actual business practices. For example, in an incident that happened to an acquaintance of one of the authors, a job applicant for a position to be a fashion designer was not hired after an interview with the potential employer, and the explanation given by the interviewer was that the applicant appeared to be too shy. While the applicant, who is Korean American, thought she was being appropriate and respectful in the situation, the interviewer thought the applicant was shy and passive. Hence, the cultural misunderstanding of the meaning of talking cost the applicant a job.

Another striking aspect of the incident was that even for the jobs for which verbal skill is not an essential ability, employers still want people who are outgoing and assertive. Being able to express one's thoughts is not only a matter of ability but also a matter of personality, as an outgoing person is a "good" and likable person in American cultural contexts (Kim & Markus, 2002). As a consequence, individuals who do not share the tendency to express themselves are disadvantaged in decisions of hiring and promotion that matter in occupational success.

One of the most common complaints from Asian Americans is that they are notably absent at the higher levels of administration and managerial occupations and that despite their relatively high education, there is a clear "glass ceiling." Statistics regarding the numbers of Asian Americans in leadership indeed support this perception. One of the reasons for the glass ceiling phenomenon seems to be that Asian Americans are often seen as passive and reserved and hence lacking leadership (Takaki, 1989). In other words, the "problem" is that Asian Americans do not talk enough to make themselves stand out and to show that they can lead. In order to succeed in America, Asian Americans often need to act in a way that goes against their cultural ideals of thoughtful silence. This effort to assimilate to the American cultural value by talking more not only makes them feel uncomfortable but also might be a disturbance to the thoughtfulness that their cultural beliefs dictate.

CULTURE AND THE EFFECT OF TALKING ON THINKING

The collectively represented meanings of talking shape social practices in a given cultural context, and through these practices, also influence psychology of individuals who participate in the cultural context. The cultural practices foster certain psychological tendencies over others (Bruner, 1996; Shweder, 1991), and thus, it is more likely one will develop those psychological tendencies that are culturally reinforced than those that are not. If talking is important in a cultural context and is encouraged, talking is more likely to play an important role in the psychology of people. In contrast, if talking is unimportant and is not particularly encouraged or even discouraged, talking will play a less significant role in psychology.

Thinking often has been studied in relation to talking in psychology, as thinking and language are considered to be closely connected (e.g., Ericsson & Simon, 1993; Wierzbicka, 1992). However, the assumption behind the studies that "naturally" bind talking and thinking as related aspects of psychology may be reflecting Western cultural assumptions rather than reflecting a universal psychological reality. Cultural differences in the meanings and practices of the act of talking should lead to differences in how talking and thinking are related in psychological processes. These differences should also be reflected in how much people rely on language when they are thinking, and the effect of talking should differ for people from different cultural contexts.

Talking has been closely related to thinking in Western cultural contexts (Whorf, 1956; Wierzbicka, 1992). Thought is believed to be internalized speech (Plato as shown in Miller, 1981; Watson, 1920). Since Ancient Greek civilization, as exemplified by the Socratic method, eloquence has been highly regarded, and the skill of debate was considered one of the most important skills for a man to have (Nisbett, et al., 2001). The connection between thinking and talking is weaker in many East Asian cultural traditions. Since Ancient Chinese civilization, East Asians have believed that talking impairs higher level thinking. Using the metaphor of water for mind, East Asians believe that only in its very serene state, or contemplative state, can mind clearly reflect the truth. In these contexts, talking is considered to be a disturbance that hinders people from understanding the truth.

To examine the influence of cultural beliefs about talking and the actual effect of talking on thinking, the cultural variation of the effect of talking on thinking was examined (Kim, 2002). The research utilized the method of "think aloud" that is often used to gain access to people's thought processes in psychology. In the procedure of thinking aloud, people are instructed to vocalize their internal thinking processes as those occur. For example, as a person is working on a problem, 2 x 5 = 10, the procedure of thinking aloud would have the person say "two times five equals ten" out loud concurrently as these thoughts enter his or her mind. Obviously, this methodology is founded on the assumption that the internal thinking processes are conscious, accessible, and easily verbalized. Questioning the universality of this assumption, the research examined the effect of talking (i.e., thinking aloud) on thinking, focusing on whether talking enhances, impairs, or does not affect cognitive problem solving. In the studies, East Asian American and European American participants were asked to think aloud as they were working on a standardized reasoning test, and their performance on the test was measured as an indication of how talking affected their thinking.

One study (Kim, 2002) examined the basic issue of whether or not cultural differences in the beliefs about the effect of talking on thinking in East Asian and American cultural contexts are reflected in actual difference in cognitive performance of people from the respective cultural contexts. The results showed that while the overall performance did not differ between the two groups of participants, the impact of talking on each group's performance differed greatly. Verbalization of the thought process significantly impaired the performance of East Asian Americans, whereas the same verbalization did not affect the performance of European Americans. These results demonstrated that there are indeed psychological tendencies in how talking affects thinking that are consistent with the cultural assumptions about how talking and thinking are related.

A follow-up study (Kim, 2002) was conducted to understand the source of this cultural difference in the effect of talking on thinking. The study tested the possibility that the cultural difference in the effect of talking on thinking can be explained, at least in part, by the difference in the relative reliance on language in thinking for people from different cultural contexts. Psychological research has shown that the nature of the effect of verbalization largely depends on the type of task. Thought processes involved with a linear and analytical reasoning are found to be easy to verbalize (Ericsson & Simon, 1993; Schooler, Ohlsson, & Brooks, 1993), and talking while thinking can in fact help clarify the thought process (Hafner, 1957; Ericsson & Simon, 1993; Loftus & Bell, 1975). However, thought processes involved with insight (Schooler, et al., 1993) or holistic thinking (Penney, 1975) are found to be difficult to verbalize, and talking while thinking can hinder the thought processes (Schooler, et al., 1993; Kim, 2002). These findings suggest that different cultures that tend to differ in the most typically used mode of thinking (Nisbett, et al., 2001) probably differ in their relative use of verbal versus nonverbal thinking. A final study predicted that talking would hinder the thinking of East Asians because they are more likely to engage in nonverbal thinking but that talking would not affect the thinking of European Americans because they are more likely to engage in verbal thinking. This study tested this possibility by examining the effect of an articulatory suppression task—a task designed to suppress internal speech—in combination with the effect of thinking aloud on the thinking of people from different cultural contexts. The results showed that the degree to which people from the different cultural contexts use verbal thinking differs; European Americans were more likely to use verbal thinking, whereas East Asian Americans were less likely to use verbal thinking. In other words, talking was less likely to affect European Americans' performance because they tended to use verbal thinking that is easier to verbalize. In contrast, talking was more likely to impair East Asian Americans' performance because they tended to use more nonverbal thinking that is more difficult to verbalize.

Together the findings from these studies illustrate two broad points. First, cultural beliefs regarding the relationship between talking and thinking reflect the cultural realities in East Asian and European American contexts. The cultural beliefs not only are abstract beliefs but also are a reflection of the cultural realities. How people process information is not free or independent from the social and cultural contexts in which the processes take place and therefore can have quite divergent behavioral and social consequences. The results from this research support the idea of the social construction of even "basic" psychological processes. Second, a notable aspect of the findings is that the performance outcome of both verbal and nonverbal modes of thinking did not differ, showing that one mode of thinking is not necessarily superior to the other. However, the effect of talking on thinking differed countering the common American assumption that talking is good for thinking. Even an identical act that is thought to lead to the same experience for everyone in fact may not be experienced as the same act by different actors. The act can have different effects on individuals depending on the cultural assumptions and practices regarding the act.

The assumptions of how talking is related to thinking are culture specific. Thus, even the same task of thinking aloud, can differ dramatically depending on the cultural models that are used to make sense of it or to give it meaning. Such a task feels natural to people from cultural contexts where the assumptions about the importance and value of expressing oneself are widely shared but feels unnatural and debilitating for people engaging in cultural contexts where these assumptions are not shared. Without recognizing the important and fundamental influence of cultural meanings and practices on the shaping of psychology, it is easy to overlook the negative and unforeseen consequences that may accompany a push toward behavioral assimilation, such as the expectation of active verbal participation in class.

TALKING IN A MULTICULTURAL WORLD

As much as talking is a tool universally used for communication and expression in every culture, and language is one of the most distinctive aspects of human nature, the act of talking is also a social and cultural act, and the meanings and practices of talking are culturally diverse as any human acts. Psychological phenomena, such as the effect of talking on psychology, are often reflections of cultural values and beliefs; therefore, psychology cannot be meaningfully separated from practices or beliefs. Once society recognizes this interdependence between culture and psychology, it becomes easier to understand how closely related the issue of assimilation of psychology is to the issue of assimilation of cultural creed. The act of talking is a practice that is replete with cultural meanings. Like many other cultural practices, the practice of talking is intricately integrated with relevant cultural systems. Isolating the issue of talking from its appropriate cultural context limits a full appreciation of what talking means to people and how talking affects the minds of these individuals.

The issue of talking and Asian American students dramatizes a crucial point concerning diversity in the growing multicultural world, especially in the higher educational settings. The problem results from a clash in cultural practices. People sometimes assume that their own practices are "natural" and "good" and the practices of "others" in their schools and workplaces are somehow "unnatural" and "bad." What is typically obscured in these clashes is that the "deficient" or "unsophisticated" practices in question are often aspects of complex cultural systems that have their own histories, philosophies, institutions and ways of life. What is even less visible is that one's own practices are not natural or inevitable ones but are in fact the particular results of mainstream American cultural commitments and ways of life. Without fully recognizing the cultural meanings of the act of talking, educators may problematize a tendency of students who do not hold the mainstream cultural view, thereby stigmatizing those students as passive and uncreative. This example highlights that developing an educational setting where diversity can function positively involves incorporating diversity even with respect to pedagogical assumptions, such as the value of talking.

The implications of the cultural observations made in this chapter should not be limited to the situations of East Asian Americans. Indeed, many groups in the United States that do not epitomize the mainstream American culture, such as women, ethnic minorities, and underprivileged social classes, often do not fit the American cultural ideals. Sometimes, they do not talk as much as they should, they do not think in the way they should, and they do not act as they should, according to the American ideal. These differences are intricately related to the differences in the cultural values, practices, and worldviews of each group.

A society needs unifying assumptions and values to function as a coherent unit, and it is often necessary to inscribe or enforce one particular set of assumptions and values over others. If, however, the enforcement of these assumptions creates a systematic privileging of certain groups over others, perhaps the society should collectively raise the difficult question of whether individuals should assimilate to the existing assumptions or whether the assumptions need to be questioned and modified in order to reflect the diverse needs and realities of individuals. If educators in California are concerned that East Asian and East Asian American students do not actively participate in the academic community, they should begin to question whether talking in class is necessarily beneficial for these students and whether the students should be "encouraged" to talk more or whether they should be allowed the freedom to pursue learning in alternative ways.

In answering this question, one could assert that America is a place where the positive meaning of talking is assumed and that all students who are learning in America should learn the American way of doing things, because this is ultimately beneficial for the students in order to excel in America. Another answer might be that whereas the lesson of talking is important, the lesson of silence and listening is also valuable, and hence, American education should emphasize positives from both cultural beliefs and revise the unifying set of educational assumptions and values. Still another answer might be that American educators should provide enough freedom for students to speak up and think and to stay silent and think as they want, and this value of freedom should be the unifying assumption of America.

Whether or not to emphasize talking in the classroom is a difficult question to answer, and we are yet to figure out which answer is the right or the best answer. Yet considering the potential answers requires the realization that the act of talking is a cultural practice and that "freedom of speech" should not become a "pressure to speak." A "freedom of silence" may be no less a fundamental cultural right than is a "freedom of speech."

Educating for Change

TWELVE

Global Politics, Dissent, and Palestinian American Identities

Engaging Conflict to Reinvigorate Democratic Education

Thea Renda Abu El-Haj

IN THE FALL OF 2003, a group of Palestinian teenagers and a social studies teacher at a large urban, public school joined three Arab American colleagues and myself to form an Arab youth group. This initiative emerged in response to a pattern of stories we had been hearing from students and teachers about the chilly, antagonistic school climate that they faced in the wake of the events of September 11, 2001, and in light of the ongoing, devastating conflict between Palestinians and Israelis. Our aim in forming this group was to create a space in which Palestinian[1] youth could work collectively to share their knowledge, experiences, and stories with each other and with a broader public, using a variety of media: specifically, writing, photography, and dance. Reaction to the announcement of the formation of this Arab youth group was swift and angry. Most starkly, the teacher sponsoring the group, Anne Larson,[2] was confronted by an enraged colleague who demanded, "Why are you sponsoring the Arabs? They are the same as the Ku Klux Klan." Despite the school principal's assurances that there was no need for us to be concerned by what he described as the threats of a small group of outliers, after our fourth meeting, he called Anne into his office and told her that, due to complaints of unfairness, we could no longer convene the group at our designated time because no other student groups were allowed to met then. The only time we would be permitted to meet was after school, a time of day that, as he well knew, was impossible for the majority of our students because of work and family commitments. Students met the news with anger, but without surprise. Many students had anticipated from the start that the school would find some excuse to close down the group. Fortunately, in light of this adversity, a strong subset of this group has become even more committed to continuing this work, rearranging afterschool commitments in order to attend.

Having now lived in the United States for twenty-five years, I am quite familiar with the multiple ways that Palestinian voices in particular, and Arab voices in general, are passively neglected or actively silenced. Myriad examples come to mind. Sadly, that a high school principal would be pressured to shut down an Arab youth group comes as no surprise to me. I begin with this story, however, not simply to highlight the acts of silencing that pervade the experiences of Arab Americans. This story suggests that the perceived threat of a Palestinian youth group comes from the ways that expressions of Arab youth identities weave together inextricably culture and politics. That is, a Palestinian youth group inevitably crosses the "safe" line of multiculturalism. It is not possible for Palestinian youth to narrate their lives without raising contentious political debate. As members of a transnational community, Palestinian youth forge their identities at the crossroads of domestic and international politics. Thus, I tell this story of silencing because it raises a key question for educators committed to social justice: How can we constructively wrestle with, rather than silence and expel, dissenting political perspectives about global conflicts?

In this chapter, I explore the relationships among political conflict, education, and democracy through a qualitative study of Palestinian youth living in a large city in the United States. I explore two intersecting issues. First, I examine how Palestinian youth identities are forged, in part, at the complex intersection of domestic and international politics, with concrete, everyday consequences for how young people are positioned and position themselves within local schools and communities. As contemporary politics reconfigure the boundaries of inclusion into the American nation, certain Palestinian/Arab/Muslim identities are framed as incompatible with liberal, democratic citizenship. Second, I track some of the consequences that these exclusionary discourses have on Palestinian American (and other Arab American) students inside their schools. I show how political dialogue and dissent are being silenced (or expelled under the frame of disciplinary action) in favor of the less threatening trope of multiculturalism. Finally, I explore how Arab youth speak back in the face of silencing. The experiences of Arab youth raise challenges for all educators in all contexts who seek to engage their students in risky, contentious political dialogue—dialogue that is indispensable if we are to make imaginable a world in which peace and justice are possible.

Methods

The data for this chapter are drawn from two sources: from a qualitative study[3] of Palestinian American youth that crosses multiple educational contexts and from my role as an Arab American community advocate and activist. I draw on interviews with Palestinian American youth ages 9 through 18; interviews with teachers, parents, and community members; participant observation at an Arabic language and culture camp and a high school afterschool club; and my own participation in meetings at the school district and in the community. In this work there are no neatly carved boundaries between research and advocacy.

It was in the aftermath of September 11, 2001, that I began to draw together my professional work in the area of urban education and my personal commitment to peace and social justice in the Middle East. I reconnected with an old friend of mine who is a leader in the local Arab American community and the sponsor of a new Arab American community development organization. As tensions mounted in local schools, we began meeting with parents, principals, and the school superintendent to discuss issues that affect the Arab American community. As a result of what we were hearing, and through the organizing efforts of ACCESS—the largest Arab American social services agency in the country located in Dearborn, Michigan—the local community development organization was able to recruit two Americorps volunteers to develop programs for the community.

The Americorps program opened up the venue for engaging in action-oriented research with youth and families. Ahlam Yassin, one of the Americorps volunteers—an insider to the community—dedicated her time to working on issues involving youth and schooling. We have worked together for the past year to document youth experiences in different educational contexts (primarily in public schools and an Arab-language and culture camp) and to use the knowledge we were gaining to design new programs that support Arab youth to express their experiences through a variety of media. Building on relationships that Ahlam had within her neighborhood, we have been able to reach out to families and youth combining more traditional research methods (in-depth interviews and participant observation) with our roles as advocates (for example, for teenagers involved in disciplinary actions) and educators.

Forging Identities at the Intersection of Racialized Discourse, Global Conflict, and Transnational Communities

After September 11, kids would say stuff. "We should kill them all. They shouldn't be in this country."

—Amal, high school senior

They really do just raise them all up to be suicide bombers.
—Teacher speaking of Palestinian students to another teacher

This is the world's fight. This is civilization's fight. This is the fight
of all who believe in progress and pluralism, tolerance and freedom. . . . Every nation, in every region, now has a decision to
make. Either you are with us, or you are with the terrorists.
—President Bush's address to the
Joint Session of Congress September 20, 2001

Since the beginning of the second intifida in Palestine and with increasing
intensity in the aftermath of the September 11, 2001 attacks, racialized discourse at work in the public sphere of media and politics perniciously infuses
the local spaces within which Arab American youth identities and subjectivities are forged. In this section, I focus on how Palestinian youth identities are
fundamentally shaped with reference to contemporary American politics, as
well as within the context of a nationalist struggle against Israeli occupation.
Exploring how youth position themselves in relationship to transnational
identifications raises critical questions for democratic education.

RACIALIZED DISCOURSE AND THE PROBLEM OF CULTURE

In the first weeks of the U.S. invasion of Iraq, I received paperwork to fill out
for my new job. One familiar form gathered demographic data about gender,
citizenship, marital status, and of course, race and ethnicity. Following U.S.
federal guidelines, the form creates a series of forced choices, and the only box
that I could check to describe my race or ethnicity was white (people of European, Middle Eastern, or North African origins). This classificatory system
based on residual notions of race as a biological concept flagrantly concealed
the particular post Cold War project positioning Arabs as other within a set
of racialized discourse and practices. Federal guidelines for classifying race and
ethnicity place Arabs invisibly within the boundaries of whiteness, even as
legislative, legal, and policing practices deny many Arabs even the most basic
civil rights.

    Moreover, in the discursive realms of politics, popular media, and acade-
mia, it is the language of "culture" that continually recasts Muslims, Arabs,
and particularly Palestinians outside of the confines of "civilization," enemies
of freedom, tolerance, and pluralism. 'Culture' is a contended concept within
anthropological circles. However, in society at large it is alive and well, put to
the service of what Omi and Winant (1986/1994) term a "racial project"—an
interpretation that reorganizes and redistributes power. Public discourse in the
media and politics is replete with pronouncements that purport to explain the

"culture" of various groups of people in ways that allow us to dismiss their humanity, diversity, and agency. I offer here only one of many examples: the myriad articles and talk shows that have sought to explain the cultural roots of suicide bombers. Of significance for this historical moment is the extra burden that Islam has borne and continues to bear within this discourse of culture, a burden imposed in both popular and academic venues. For it is Islam that is posited as most culturally other, inimical to "Western" values and traditions in an essential "clash of civilizations" (see Lewis, 2002; Huntington, 1996; and for critique, Said, 2001). With one encompassing gesture, the language of culture and civilization wipes out diversity, conflicting perspectives, structural inequalities, histories of imperialism and colonialism in the name of "other" people's uniform adherence to a way of life that seems incomprehensible to "us."

For the purposes of this chapter, I want to focus for a minute on the positioning of Palestinian culture as one that "breeds" suicide bombers: one in which, for example, one pundit declared that peace was impossible until "Palestinians love their children more than they hate Jews" (Chavez, 2002). The complexity and variability of Palestinians, their society, politics, and culture are rendered invisible by a discourse that pushes them all to the margins of humanity: as people who do not even love their children. This racialized discourse inevitably pervades the daily experiences of Palestinians living in the United States. It seeps into educators' beliefs about students as exemplified by the teacher, quoted above, who took as a statement of commonplace knowledge that Palestinian parents raised their children to be suicide bombers. In a national climate set by President Bush's admonition, "Either you are with us, or you are with the terrorists," Arab youth describe frequent hostile encounters with strangers in their neighborhoods, peers, and teachers. These encounters make visible the evolving racialized boundaries of the nation, reconstructing Arabs and Muslims as dangerous, always potentially "enemies within."

For Palestinian youth and their families, public spaces have become charged and volatile territory; fear and aggression loom large. Girls frequently described the harassment to which those who wear the *hijab*[4] have been subjected while shopping and driving, screamed at by complete strangers who call them "terrorists." Haneen described the fear in her family following September 11, 2001.

> [W]e started hearing from [my mom's] friends that some of them, they took their scarves off and then some of the families get punished, killed, stuff. We worried a lot. And then I was like what am I going to do? And so I thought of death for a second. Is someone going to kill me? My mom was like we want you to take off the scarf. And I was like, no, hell no. I've been in this school for like a year, and that was a year later, and everybody saw me with the scarf and just because of 9–11, take it off? No.

Despite her decision to keep wearing the *hijab*, Haneen took measures to hide it when she went walking on the streets, covering her scarf with a hat as a precaution.

Male students often found themselves framed as dangerous and suspicious. Many describe harassment by police officers. Within their schools, they feel targeted for disciplinary action. One teacher wrote a student up for a disciplinary infraction on the charge of "being a terrorist." Gharib, a seventeen-year-old Palestinian American student, described a conversation in class in which he commented on the lax security at his high school. The next day, he was called to the dean's office and was accused of having threatened to plant a bomb in the school. On a lighter note, a Palestinian boy was sent to the principal's office ostensibly for sporting an Osama Bin Laden T-shirt. As it turned out, it was Bob Marley.

As students encounter these images, some adolescents play with the power the images afford or feel they have no choice but to resist discrimination by fighting. For example, some males wrap their shoulders, heads, and faces in the traditional scarves (kafiyyas) adopted by the *fedayeen* (guerilla fighters), and a few students claim that they are protected from harassment by cultivating dangerous, threatening images and by their willingness to fight. In turn, symbolic representations of the Palestinian nation become flashpoints for conflict as some schools banned students from wearing the kafiyyas or displaying Palestinian flags. At one high school, a Palestinian flag was burned shortly after September 11, 2001.

Some Palestinian students lay claim to other racial identities within which to hide. Lina, an outspoken, lively sixteen year old, decided to make her life simple by "tell[ing] everyone I'm Spanish." This was not an uncommon practice among Arab students who found that they could pass as Latino/a. Anne Larson, the social studies teacher who sponsored the Arab youth club, related the story of a Palestinian girl who in describing her origins, had initially written that she was from Israel. Anne had taught this girl's older sisters and knew the family came from a village in the West Bank and identified as Palestinians. Anne knew that somewhere in her schooling, this young girl had learned that it was risky to write that her family was from Palestine. Anne was able to communicate to the student that she need not fear using the word *Palestine* in her class.

At the same time, other Arab youth resist denying their national origins, working instead to educate their school communities about their cultural and religious practices in ways that emphasize the ideology of American pluralism. Serving as an ambassador for her religion, Haneen described the thrill she felt when she had the opportunity to do a public presentation about marriage and divorce in Islam. "With the senior project, I'll never forget that because I really loved it when the principal came and all the teachers came, and I should have been shaking but I wasn't. I wish the whole building, everybody knows. Here is the information." Teaching others about Muslim or Arab traditions and practices may interrupt some of the more pernicious misconceptions that frame dominant beliefs about Islam and Arabs. This is a familiar project of pluralist multiculturalism. The message conveyed is that we may do culture differently, but underneath we are all essentially the same (Erickson, 1997; McCarthy, 1993). Yet, deploying a different view of "culture" carries with it the risk of freezing rather than undermining monolithic images of Arabs and Muslims. For example, one school administrator—an administrator who had, perhaps coincidentally, heard Haneen's presentation—confidently informed me that Arab girls and women rarely speak out in public because of their culture.

Culture discourse masks more critical dialogue about race, politics, and power. The varied stances that Palestinian youth adopt all suggest the ways that their identities and subjectivities take shape within and against the contemporary public, political discourses that are defining what it means to be American, discourses that represent racial projects (Omi & Winant, 1986/1994).

Transnational Communities and Identity

At the same time, exploring Palestinian American identities makes visible the difficulty of conceptualizing national identifications as bounded by nation-states in the face of transnational global migration trends (see Suarez-Orozco, 2001). For example, I asked a nine-year-old Palestinian American, Muslim boy U.S. born and raised mostly in the United States to tell me about himself. Omar stated, "I live in Palestine." For the Palestinian American youth and adults I have interviewed Palestine plays a central role in their lives. Omar's use of the present tense to describe where he lives—in Palestine—did not indicate confusion or grammatical error. Rather, it reflected a deeply felt national consciousness and aspiration that pervades the diasporic community (Khalidi, 1997). For Omar, as for many others in his community, Palestine was not an imagined homeland but rather a place that he visited on a regular basis and had lived for an extended period of time. It is a place that he described joyfully, as he recollected the adjoining houses that circumscribed a world of extended family, a beloved uncle and cousins. Many youth who had spent time in Palestine spoke longingly of returning to live in "my country." However, even Palestinian youth who, because of the refugee status of their families, had never been to Palestine actively engaged in political action (peace demonstrations, fundraising drives) to aid in the struggle for a nation-state.

To a person, the youth I interviewed stated that they were "Palestinian" not American. Khalida was born in the United States but lived in the occupied West Bank for seven years, before returning as a teenager. Her response was typical.

I don't think of myself as both. I only think of myself as Arabian. A Palestinian actually. Most people ask me, you're a Palestinian American? I told
them no, just Palestinian. Then they start getting stupid about it. And then
how do you know English? I'm like, no, I'm American Palestinian. I just
want to be a Palestinian. Most of the reason I feel that way is because Palestinians suffered a lot. And they're still suffering actually.

Part of the explanation for this dichotomous view of Palestinian and American identities resides within the contemporary discourse about the American
nation, discussed above.[5] However, it also emerges from the experiences that
Palestinian youth and their families have had living under Israeli occupation
or as refugees. Gharib described how his strong identification as a Palestinian
emerged when as an early adolescent, he had returned for a year to his family's village in Palestine. "Before I went to my country I didn't look into [being
Palestinian] at all. I went back home and then I seen three people die in front
of me, and it was a big change." Politicized by his experiences witnessing the
shooting of peaceful demonstrators and being subject to curfews, Gharib
returned to the United States with a different sense of himself as a Palestinian and an Arab.

The data suggest that identifications are never so neatly demarcated as
the youth describe and that identities are culturally produced at the nexus of
multiple, intermingling systems (see Hall, 2002).[6] However, my point here is
that notions of citizenship and belonging that are premised on the boundaries of nation-states do not capture the experiences of youth who have dual
(or even multiple) national identifications as they live transnational lives
(Sarroub, 2001), caught at the crossroads of international political conflicts.
Being Palestinian American often involves not only hyphenated but also
fractured identities.

DISCIPLINE AND DISSENT:
THE LIMITS OF MULTICULTURAL EDUCATION

These dual (and dueling) political identifications have profound consequences
for the educational experiences of Palestinian American students in schools.
In this section of the chapter, I explore the pervasiveness with which alternative narratives about international conflicts are being silenced, rather than
engaged, within educational contexts. This silencing acts to banish the deeply
felt transnational identifications of Palestinian (and other Arab) American
youth to the margins of acceptable speech.

I begin this discussion by telling two stories that are deeply interwoven,
although they occurred in very different contexts. In the weeks prior to the
U.S. invasion of Iraq, the school district's curriculum office decided to be

proactive and send out some background materials on the Middle East for teachers and principals. The small packet that was sent to regional offices and schools included 15 pages from Georgetown University entitled, *Who Are the Arabs?* (Tamari, 1999) followed by different sets of age-appropriate materials about Iraq (detailing for example, the various players—Kofi Anan, Tariq Aziz, Colin Powell—and their positions). The local chapter of the Zionists of America—a group often denounced by mainstream Jewish organizations as a right-wing fringe group—successfully mobilized a broad coalition that importantly included other local mainstream Jewish organizations such as the Anti-Defamation League and the Jewish Federation to demand that the school district pull these background materials from schools because of the three references to Palestine and Palestinians contained in the overview essay, *Who Are the Arabs?* They objected to the use of the term *military occupation* to describe the political status of the West Bank and Gaza, and they argued that the inclusion of a poem by one of the most famous Palestinian poets describing his experience as an Arab living inside Israel, was an "incitement to violence." As a result, many schools were told to "use discretion" in distributing the materials to teachers.

The district subsequently constituted a new task force that included community partners to create materials on the Middle East. At the first task force meeting, two members of the Anti-Defamation League argued that the district should avoid all teaching about the Israeli-Palestinian conflict because as one stated, it was "too confusing for teachers to figure out," and teachers could not be expected to be knowledgeable enough to assess unrepresentative "extremist perspectives." Instead they advocated that the goals of such a task force should be to help teachers teach students to be tolerant of one another. As several of us remarked at the time, this approach effectively maintained status quo knowledge about the Middle East conflict and foreclosed critical public deliberation about a complex, multifaceted issue. Teaching tolerance without content conveniently silences subordinate perspectives on the conflict in the Middle East. This task force never met again, and no curriculum materials were developed to help educators teach about the Middle East.

At the same time that this controversy was unfolding at a district level, at a local high school, Palestinian and Jewish students were fighting. Such fights had occurred at this particular school every year for the past three years. As a result of the fights, two Palestinian teenage boys were recommended for disciplinary transfers to disciplinary schools. Although versions of events differ slightly, it is clear that at a multicultural fair earlier in the year, Palestinian students had performed a traditional folk dance—the debke—for the school. They had, however, been explicitly forbidden to display a Palestinian flag during the performance because it was perceived to be too controversial. The students were led to believe that all flags were banned at school events. At the subsequent multicultural fair at which the fight occurred, Palestinian students were confronted with a large Israeli flag at the Israel table. An argument ensued, in which, according to the disciplinary report, one Arab student said to the students staffing the table, "Fuck. That's not Israel. That's Palestine." Several days later there was another argument in which a Palestinian boy was reported to have cursed at Jewish students, "Fuck the Jewish kids." These incidents were written up as racial/ethnic harassment, a second level disciplinary offense in the school district. The students were suspended and recommended for transfers to disciplinary schools. School administrators argued that there were no underlying ethnic/racial tensions or problems and that this action was in keeping with the school's and the district's "zero tolerance for intolerance" policy.[7]

Rather than denying the embedded racial-ethnic and religious tensions, the ongoing conflicts between Jewish and Arab students might have been viewed as ripe educational opportunities to explore the different experiences and narratives of each community and in so doing, potentially lessen the prejudicial attitudes of the groups and the likelihood of continued animosity between them. However, to do so demands directly confronting, rather than avoiding, conflicting perspectives. It means we cannot limit the political perspectives in discussions to those with which we already agree. We must be willing to traverse uncomfortable territory, rather than retreat behind the gloss of a discourse on tolerance. Moreover building curriculum that can address seemingly intractable interethnic conflict depends on teachers having access to materials that support the development of a rich, deep understanding of the complexity of the historical, political, economic, and social forces at work.

These two stories are not isolated incidents. Rather they reflect a disturbing trend in educational settings of silencing critical political discussions and disciplining or expelling unpopular opinions.[8] Many Arab students reported ongoing harassment by their peers, and sometimes even their teachers, while few have experienced educational forums in their schools or classrooms that directly address issues of Middle Eastern politics, the attacks of September 11, 2001, the War on Iraq, or the racialized stereotyping and profiling of Arabs and Muslims. For example, in the fall of 2001, Khalida had just returned to the United States after a seven-year stretch living with her family in their village in the West Bank. Describing her return to the United States, she stated:

> It's been kind of hard because the same year I attended this school was the year of 9–11. And there was a lot of teasing going around. And I was called "terrorist" and they actually say it to my face. And I kind of had a lot of trouble. . . . There was some students that were very ignorant about it. And then, they'd be like, "not to be ignorant or anything" they'd be telling me up to my face, "but I think all Arabs are terrorists after 9–11." I was like you really be ignorant just saying it to my face. Actually, I had a pink [disciplinary] slip

once. I almost got suspended for having a fight about something like that. Some girl actually threatened me. That's why I didn't get suspended. She, she called me "Arabian bitch." Then she called me "Arabian whore." . . . And she got suspended for that same reason.

Khalida echoed stories we heard from many students across school contexts, stories of pervasive anger and hostility directed at them in the wake of September 11. However, she also pointed to the ways that dominant racialized discourse about Arabs, Muslims, and terror was rarely interrupted by educators, other than to discipline the conflicts that arose from these unexamined ideologies. Both the disciplinary write-up that Khalida received as a result of her argument and the suspension of her adversary failed to disrupt the positioning of Arab and Muslim youth as "enemies within." Rather, disciplinary actions served to maintain the veneer of a congenial, multicultural school community in which racial/ethnic conflict would not be tolerated, without addressing the profound social and political rifts in the national polity that fueled the recurrent conflicts between students (see Apple, 1979).

Although we heard about many individual acts of kindness toward Arab students on the part of teachers and administrators on September 11, 2001, we heard very few reports that teachers or administrators had organized productive forums for discussion and education about the attacks or about the impact of those attacks on Muslim, Arab, and South Asian communities. One student reported that no adults spoke with them about the World Trade Center attacks on the day they returned to school. "There wasn't any explanation. Actually the students just took the idea from the news that it's Arab Americans and all that. No one explained about it much. There were some teachers that were very kind, and they didn't want to hurt others' feelings, so they wouldn't talk about it." Thus, educators' silence played a contradictory role. It served to fuel conflicts between students, leaving unchallenged the dominant political and cultural discourses about Arabs and Arab Americans. However, some students interpreted this silence as an act of kindness presumably because raising the more difficult political questions might have unleashed attitudes and behaviors that teachers felt unprepared to address. Unequipped to develop a rich and nuanced curriculum that could address the historical, political, economic and social forces that led to the attacks of September 11, many teachers appear to have opted for silence in exchange for maintaining control in the classroom, a stance McNeil has called "defensive teaching" (1983). However, educators' silence about contemporary politics may have reinforced broader school climates that were hostile and harassing toward Arab students.

If silence proved a problematic stance, engaging political dialogue also served, in many instances, to perpetuate an inhospitable environment for Arab students. For some students, experiences in the immediate aftermath of

September 11 further polarized political stances. Khalida, for example, described the situation that evolved in her history class on the day that school reopened after September 11. The class conversation quickly turned from the attacks to the Palestinian-Israeli conflict. Khalida reported:

> We had half a day on 9–11. Then we came back. And we were discussing about terrorism and what we think about what happened. So I don't know exactly how, but it all came up to the issue of Palestine and Israel. My [history] teacher said kinds of things like Palestine will never be free and it's Israel. He said Palestine doesn't exist, and he's trying to stuff it in our face that there's no more Palestine. It's Israel.

In this class, talk about September 11 quickly reduced the complexity of Middle Eastern politics to an unproductive and one-sided argument about the Palestinian-Israeli conflict.

Describing the same class, Gharib recalled how the teacher would constantly try to incite Palestinian students to act out. He offered the following example.

> He just started saying all the Palestinians deserve to die. And they're all dogs. Look at them when they're running in the streets, happy, happy and going in front of a tank and getting run over. Then the Israelis laugh at them. [The Palestinians are] like the animals. And one guy he just took it to the heart. He was like, "Don't talk about them like that, alright?" And the teacher was just like, "What're you going to do? Hit me?" [The student]'s about to lose it. Then the teacher called security, and the Arabs didn't get in trouble for it because it was him that started it, and we had all the witnesses in the room.

It is tempting to dismiss the stories about this one teacher as unrepresentative or as a violation of the professional duties of an educator. Students told similar stories about some other teachers. These narratives suggest that the remedy for silencing is not at all simple. These stories indicate the critical need for educators and students to find ways to engage with complex political issues such that conflicts are not reduced to winners and losers.

Many Palestinian students registered their political dissent by resisting the routine activities that their public schools demanded as symbolic offerings to U.S. nationalism. Some students reported refusing to stand for the Pledge of Allegiance and rejecting requests that they buy U.S. flags to raise money for the families of the victims of September 11 or that they wear black in commemoration of the anniversary of the attacks. Students and one teacher also told stories of young people forced to stand for the Pledge of Allegiance against their will or disciplined for refusing to comply.[9] These everyday resistances make visible the fault lines within modern multiracial, multiethnic states in which Palestinian youth, like students from other communities of color, recognize the ongoing social inequality and exclusion that belie democratic ideals (Banks, 2004; Castles, 2004).

This sense of alienation from the U.S. polity can be heard in Khalida's description of the events in her history class in the aftermath of the World Trade Center attacks. The history teacher asked students to stand for a moment of silence in memory of the victims of the attack. When the five Arab students refused to stand, the teacher called the school police officers to remove them from class. This was not the only instance in which Arab students were disciplined for remaining seated when a moment of silence for the September 11 victims was requested. As I write, I find myself ambivalent about revealing these stories because of the risk that the Arab students' refusal to stand in silence in respect for the dead will be interpreted as insensitivity at best and support for terrorism at worst. However, it is critical to understand this refusal as a more complex political response. Here Khalida's explanation for the refusal to stand in silence is revealing. "My teacher was like standing up and giving a moment of silence. Then they [the Arab boys] all started arguing. They were like I don't see anybody giving a moment of silence to the Palestinian people that died." Deeply connected to a transnational community engaged in a struggle to establish a homeland, Palestinian youth were responding to what they perceived to be a profound indifference to the deaths of Palestinians. Palestinian students see through the veil of the political discourses of equality and respect for all, discourses that mask a hierarchical valuing of lives. If we are truly committed to work toward a more peaceful and just world, the challenge we face is how to cultivate a respect for the value of all lives lost or damaged by conflict. We must push our work for justice beyond national boundaries to a notion of global citizenship (Banks, 2004).

Instead, in the place of political discussion and debate, culture is offered as the only acceptable display of difference. Food and dance[10] are celebrated, while certain political positions and dissenting opinions (the Palestinian flag and poems by famous poets) are banished, expelled too often within the discourse of discipline. The language of "tolerance" and the practices of multiculturalism build impenetrable walls that place conflicting and dissenting perspectives outside the boundaries of the sphere of education.

FROM MULTICULTURAL TO INTERNATIONAL PERSPECTIVES

The persistent silencing of, and adversity toward, the subordinate political perspectives through which Palestinian youth view contemporary politics in the United States and the Middle East is cause for alarm. However, it is only part of the story here. Palestinian youth also actively speak out against the injustices they perceive and work diligently to offer their teachers and peers alternative evidence and new lenses for interpreting global conflicts. They are supported in these efforts by some of their teachers. I offer here a few examples of youth speaking out.

Palestinian youth described actively challenging the dominant narratives and ideologies of their teachers and peers, drawing on alternative evidence and media to make their points. For example, Gharib challenged the history teacher described above to provide evidence for his claims. Rather than retreating into silence, he constantly questioned his teacher's perspective and argued for a different view. Gharib also sought opportunities to share narratives from the Arabic media with his teachers and peers. In the first weeks of the U.S. invasion of Iraq, for example, his biology teacher allowed him to show his classmates a videotape from Arabic satellite television showing the killing of an Al-Jazeera cameraman. In addition, Gharib made active demands on school administrators to address issues of discrimination against Arabs.

> People were starting to harass us because of 9–11. "Oh you come to school thinking that's it. That's over? You bomb the towers and that's it? Get the hell out of this school you dirty animals." That would start a fight. I knew the only way something is going to be done about it, I'm going to go ahead and take action. I'm going to go and talk to somebody about it, instead of getting everybody fighting. So I was like *(ahlo)*, I told the *(arab)*[11] I'm going to go talk to the principal, and he better hear me. I went and talked to him, and I told him, "Look there's a lot of people harassing us and a lot of Arabs keep getting suspended because of fighting, and it's because they keep harassing us about 9–11 telling us we don't deserve to be in this school because we bombed the towers. And it wasn't us. It was probably—at this point we didn't know if it was Arabs." Next day in the morning, they make an announcement on the radio: "Anybody who harasses Arabs in this school will be thrown out of this school immediately and sent to a disciplinary school."

Whereas the efficacy of the principal's strategy to address discrimination and harassment is clearly questionable, my point is simply that Palestinian students are, in general, highly politicized by the nationalist struggle of their community, and many actively speak out against oppression and insist on voicing alternatives to the dominant ideological perspectives on global events.[12]

Classrooms and schools that cultivated knowledge about the world by drawing on international perspectives—what Banks (1996) has called a "ethno-national framework"—provided Palestinian students safe, productive learning environments. Nada, the only student who reported no incidents of harassment after September 11, 2001, attended a public high school focused on world affairs. Nada's school devoted three days after September 11, 2001, to ongoing discussions of what had happened and directly addressed the problems of stereotyping and discriminating against Arabs and Muslims. Nada and another girl at her school were also invited to speak to an assembly of the entire school about their cultures and religions. This response to September 11 clearly drew upon the school's ongoing commitment to address international affairs. Nada described her involvement with the school's World Affairs Council prior to September 11, 2001.

In high school I was a member of the World Affairs Club, and being the only Palestinian, everybody had questions. And at that time it was when the war had started between Israel and Palestine. And that was—for about two months that was the issue. And we actually visited the Israeli consulate, twice I think. And pretty much they sat, and they talked, and they had their side of the story. And you know I said I'm going to go because I know what they're going to say. And pretty much what they did is they sat there, and they said, "In Palestinian textbooks, they teach them to hate Jews." And my only comment towards the woman was, "All you have to do is bring me the textbook that shows children to hate somebody and then I'd just sit here and be quiet." And she said, "Well, that I can't do." And actually by the time we left, everybody said—because I had that look on my face like how dare she say that about, you know. And I had—more than one student came up to me and said, "You know I didn't believe that about the textbook." And I said I hope not, because I wasn't just going to stand there and argue back and forth with her. It's so unprofessional. And that day when we went, I actually didn't even say much. The students talked back to her. When she'd say something, they'd talk back to her and say even though I heard that in the news, I read somewhere else—I read different. And the media is biased, and I'm not going to go by what you say.

Thus, Nada felt supported by her peers who, as a result of ongoing opportunities to consider world events from multiple perspectives, were able to challenge dominant narratives about the Israeli-Palestinian conflict.

Although our data show plenty of evidence of students speaking out individually, since September 11, 2001, there has been a growing interest in creating opportunities for Arab youth to work collectively to address oppression and to work for peace and justice. The Arab youth group described at the beginning of this chapter reflected one of several local efforts to join with youth in collective, collaborative action. Despite the principal's actions, we have persisted in our efforts, finding other times that we can meet. Our first project drew on Islamic geometric patterns and mosaic forms to construct a mural on which each student designed a tile to represented her/himself. The centrality of the Palestinian flag and ideas of struggle and liberation made highly visible the inextricable link between self and national identity. Students were inspired by local Palestinian college students who, for many years, belonged to a traditional dance troupe through which they raised money for charitable causes in Palestine. As a result, students in the youth group are forming a new dance troupe to carry on this tradition, already lined up to perform at a major benefit this spring. At the same time, we are working on a photography and oral history project to document the experiences of youth, families, and the community. As I write, we are still in the early stages of our work together, and it remains to be seen where our work will carry us. However, what is clear is the need that many Palestinian youth feel for this kind of shared experience. Khalida spoke strongly to the group's role as support and educational forum.

> I want people to know not just about my experience, but other students' experiences and hopefully we can get most of them to open up and tell us about their experiences because that would be really helpful. I'm hoping after this society getting together it can be more easier. Teachers and students can understand where we're coming from. We can be a support group. So maybe it will be easier to digest if someone says something to us.

EDUCATING FOR DEMOCRACY AND DISSENT IN A GLOBAL COMMUNITY

On September 11, 2002, my daughter, Reem, came home from her friend's house puzzled. Her friend's school had required all the children to wear red, white, and blue that day. Reem had asked her friend's sister for an explanation and was told that the children were remembering the September 11 victims. What confused Reem was that her friend's sister said, "Your mom will be upset." I cannot be sure why her friend's sister thought I would be upset, although I had some sense that it involved the dichotomous positioning of American and Arab identities. However, I tried to communicate to Reem the great sadness I felt for all the victims of September 11 and my sense of the importance of moving beyond national boundaries toward an agenda for global justice. As I was muddling through an attempt to translate this sense into language that an eight year old could understand, Reem suddenly told me that if her school had asked the children to wear something special to commemorate the anniversary, she would have worn her United Nations T-shirt, which depicted flags from all over the world. "Out of the mouths of babes" comes this simple but profound vision of our shared humanity and connectedness.

What kinds of educational experiences develop students' understandings of our global interconnectedness and foster their concern for social, political, and economic justice beyond our national borders? What possibilities arise when we are challenged to reinvigorate notions of a democratic education such that it addresses global political conflicts and engages dissenting perspectives? The questions raised by the education of Palestinian or Arab American youth have profound implications for teaching in all contexts. In a world characterized by global interdependence and increasing transnational migration, educating for social justice necessitates confronting racial, economic, social, and political injustices beyond the borders of nation-states. For many Americans, the attacks of September 11, 2001, pierced through their illusion of isolation from the rest of the world. Despite this national awakening, the narratives of Palestinian youth suggest that, in many educational settings, acts of silence and silencing have maintained the insularity that shields students and teachers from confronting uncomfortable perspectives. I argue that, especially in times of conflict and war, educators need to resist the positioning of certain knowledge and perspectives outside of the boundaries of public deliberation. Rather, education for peace and justice demands that we seek to affirm our deep human interconnectedness by addressing injustices and conflicts that cross national and international boundaries (see Banks, 2004). Public education in a democracy, ideally, has a key role to play, engaging students in critical deliberation about contentious political issues (Gutmann, 1987; Reich, 2002). This deliberation is ever more critical in times of war.

THIRTEEN

Risky Business

Teaching about the
Confederate Flag Controversy
in a South Carolina High School

Dennis Carlson and Susan L. Schramm-Pate

(with Richard R. Lussier)

JAMES WEST, A SEVENTH GRADER at a Derby, Kansas, middle school, was in math class one day in 1998 when he decided to pass the time before his next class by doing some sketching rather than homework. He began drawing a flag he'd seen on the television show *The Dukes of Hazzard*, a flag that appeared in each episode on the roof of General Lee, the 1968 Dodge Charger that was one of the stars of that show. When his math teacher caught him sketching the flag, he immediately confiscated the piece of paper and sent James to the office. The boy was subsequently suspended for three days for violating the school's "racial harassment and intimidation" policy, a policy that banned students from possessing "any written material, either printed or in their own handwriting, that is racially divisive or creates ill will or hatred." The policy had been adopted in 1995 after a series of racial "disturbances" in the schools and the community. In order to ensure that such disturbances did not occur in the future any "symbolic expression" that might provoke conflict was banned from school property. West's parents filed suit against the school district, claiming that it was violating their son's first amendment right to freedom of expression. James, for his part, maintained, "I didn't even know what it meant. I don't see it as being racial."

A school official argued in defense of the policy, "You don't display a Confederate flag. You don't display a swastika. You don't write a racial slur on the front of your notebook." However, the school did acknowledge that the Confederate flag could be used in an "appropriate" context. For example, "It would be appropriate to study or draw a Confederate flag in the context of a history class." Interestingly, the president of the Wichita, Kansas chapter of the National Association for the Advancement of Colored People (NAACP) sided with the student, arguing that while children need to be informed about racism and slavery, the nonmalicious act of drawing the Confederate flag should not warrant suspension. "If you start running from history," he told reporters, "and you don't know why you're running from history, then you have tunnel vision." A federal trial judge and the 10th U.S. Circuit Court of Appeals ruled in favor of the school district. But it was a complicated decision that reemphasized the importance of understanding the specific context of usage. In this case, testimony revealed that West had previously been suspended for calling a student "blackie" and had been reminded of the harassment and intimidation policy at that time. The appeals court wrote in its decision that the school district "had reason to believe that a student's display of the Confederate flag might cause disruption and interfere with the rights of other students to be secure and let alone" (U.S. Government Information/ Resources, 2000).

Whether young James West had or had not, consciously or unconsciously, been influenced by a racist ideology of "whiteness," we cannot help but wonder how things might have turned out differently if his teacher had used the Confederate flag drawing as a context for beginning a dialogue on race and identity rather than for silencing such a dialogue. The current controversy over the flying of the Confederate flag on the state dome and state grounds in South Carolina provides another opportunity for such a difficult but necessary conversation on race in public schools. Research reported in this chapter was part of a study designed to get an idea of how the flag controversy was being handled by high school social studies teachers in the state, involving interviews with 30 teachers, all of whom were white and most of whom were male. Most of the teachers reported that they did not have the time to deal with anything other than the assigned curriculum. When pressed, most also fell back on some variation of a "risky business" defense. They felt that teaching about the Confederate flag controversy was something that could get them into trouble with administrators, parents, and/or community groups. Finally, many teachers expressed an attitude of feeling "uncomfortable" personally talking about class, race, gender, or sexual orientation. The few examples teachers provided of talking about the Confederate flag controversy were of an informal nature, with individual students between classes, in the hall, or in the cafeteria—and then only when students raised the issue. While the teachers voiced a strong commitment to preparing young people to be critical thinkers and participate in important public debates, when it got down to actually bringing the Confederate flag controversy into the curriculum and encouraging open dialogue on the controversy in their classes, most still felt it was just too risky.

Teaching about race relations and racial identity unfortunately continues to be risky business in public schools in America (Wildman & Davis, 2000), and particularly so in South Carolina and other southern states currently locked in debate and conflict over the rewriting of Southern history and the redefinition of Southern pride. Nevertheless, it is important at this crucial time that public school teachers be willing to take risks, in this case to help students understand the roots of the current controversy over the Confederate flag and rethink their own racial identities as part of an antiracist pedagogy. Furthermore, we believe there is some limited but nevertheless significant room for important conversations about race, class, gender, and sexual identity in public schools (Weis & Fine, 2003). Too often, teachers silence themselves and decide not to take risks, even when their fears are not well-founded. What we call for here is a deliberate pedagogical strategy of risk-taking, to see how much room can be carved out of the curriculum and the school day for critical conversations about identity and difference. At the same time, we suspect that teachers who are the best risk takers also make sure that they have a network of support and collaborate with others.

What follows documents one such effort at collaboration, involving the authors of this chapter and one social studies teacher (Richard R. Lussier) in a rural South Carolina high school. Throughout the fall of 2000, Richard worked with Susan in planning a unit on the Confederate flag controversy for one of his classes, as part of a school-university collaboration. Dennis was involved in helping conceptualize the unit and in telling its story. The town, with a population of 1,500, is essentially a mill town in an age in which smokestack industries founded around the turn of the 20th century are in a terminal state of decline. In 2001, the town's largest employer closed its mill, and the next biggest employer, which makes socks for Fruit of the Loom, declared bankruptcy. The increasing obsolescence of the town's industrial base, along with its isolation from major interstate highways and urban areas, meant that it was being left behind in the restructuring of the Southern economy. The reaction of many of the town's working-class, white population was to blame the town's decline on its black residents. They reminisced about the "good old days," when the town's predominantly Scottish-Irish population was able to achieve a modest level of financial security, without having to compete with blacks for scarce jobs.

In 2000, racial tensions in the school and the community became particularly tense after a number of white students, parents, and evangelical church leaders protested a celebration of Kwanzaa as part of the Winter Assembly in the high school. When the administration stood by the celebration, these

whites felt betrayed. Partially in response, a number of white students organized an informal rally at the school on Confederate's Day. The involved students were suspended. This, in turn, led to an increasingly ostentatious display
of the Confederate flag on white students' pick-up trucks and cars and the
wearing of Confederate flag T-shirts to school. School administrators
responded by banning all display of the Confederate flag on the school
grounds. At the same time, there was a growing sense among administrators,
teachers, and civil rights groups in the community that some more proactive
effort had to be made to ease racial tensions. Richard's unit was one way of
opening up a needed dialogue among blacks and whites in the school and thus
gained administrative support.

Fifteen students were enrolled in his 12th-grade civics class in the spring
of 2001—nine African Americans (four females and five males) and six whites
(two females and four males). The students, both white and black, came from
similar socioeconomic backgrounds, although white students sometimes liked
to think of themselves as coming from more "respectable" families—families
one notch above comparable black families on the socioeconomic hierarchy.
Nevertheless, all had parents who worked in mills and factories, on farms, or
in small businesses in town. What they had in common as well was a desire to
pursue a college education. While they were no more middle class than other
students, they did view themselves as wanting to get ahead. Black students in
particular had a strong sense that they needed to better themselves so that
they could better serve their communities. It was within this context, then,
that Richard began a unit of study on the Confederate flag controversy. We
turn now to examine that unit, and the issues it raised, in more detail.

GETTING TO THE "FACTS" AND THE "TRUTHS"
ABOUT THE CONFEDERATE FLAG

The unit involved a study of the "facts" of the controversy, along with the
"truths" that had been constructed around these facts—that is, how these facts
were presented, represented, and interpreted consistent with particular narratives of Southern history and racial heritage. The "text" for this study consisted of over 200 pages of photocopied articles on the flag controversy from
newspapers in South Carolina, as well as articles from various websites on the
internet, that Susan had been collecting over the past several years. A number
of these articles were then selected for students to read and analyze. They
began by laying out a time line of events related to the controversy.

Students quickly learned, to the surprise of most, that the roots of the
current controversy lead back most directly to the civil rights era. A resolution
in the state legislature in February 1962 authorized the flying of the Confederate flag atop the capital dome in Columbia—a resolution widely acknowl-

edged as an act of defiance against the civil rights movement and Northern "interference." Flying the Confederate flag symbolized, its supporters said, defense of a great "Southern heritage" that was under attack. It was not until the early 1990s that National Association for the Advancement of Colored People (NAACP) leadership in the state felt it had enough support—in government, the business community, and the public—to challenge the continued flying of the Confederate flag above the capial dome. In July 1999, after several unsuccessful efforts in support of legislation to remove the flag, the NAACP called for a national tourism boycott of the state. As the South Carolina General Assembly convened in the year 2000, 46,000 antiflag marchers surged through Columbia, where they were met with 6,000 proflag marchers, many in Confederate regalia and waving Confederate flags. On January 19, 2000, in his state of the state address, Democratic Governor Hodges called for the removal of the Confederate flag from the state capital dome. He asked both sides to "take a deep breath and talk" and immediately launched a series of meetings with business leaders to work out a "compromise." The plan they pushed through the state legislature kept the flag on the state house grounds but relocated it to a 30-foot pole behind a monument to Confederate General Wade Hampton. On July 1, 2000, 38 years after it was raised, the Confederate flag was finally lowered from the capital dome, although the boycott by the NAACP continues since the flag still flies on the capital grounds.

In asking his students to lay out these "facts" about the flag controversy, based on the reading of various newspaper and website articles, Richard wanted to demonstrate that it is not possible to merely lay out the facts in historical or contemporary social conflicts. Facts always are produced, or occur, within the context of cultural conflict, and this conflict and its players are more important than the facts as such. In studying the Confederate flag controversy, students would be studying the cultural production of meaning or "truth" by various groups—each with their own set of interests, beliefs, and projects. For example, the fact that the Confederate flag was raised above the capital dome in 1962 could not be separated from the meaning of such an act within the context of the civil rights movement. Since the civil rights era, the battle has continued to be about what the Confederate flag means, or is perceived to mean, when it is flown or worn. Furthermore, Richard suggested to the students that individuals and groups view the world and make sense of events from particular *standpoints*—informed by their position within various identity binaries of race, class, gender, sexual orientation, and so on (Collins, 2000). This means there is no "truth" about the flag controversy that is uninterested, a truth produced outside of a standpoint. Nevertheless, Richard argued, our standpoint need not determine what we believe. He hoped that students could find some "common ground," some basis for determining what was "socially just" in this case. He also said that he thought it best, when in doubt, to believe the "voice from the bottom" in systems of oppression—for they know when something is racially offensive or degrading to them. In the discussion of the Confederate flag, this meant white students would need to listen carefully to what their black classmates had to say. One white, male student complained at this point that "it's unfair to ask whites to do all the listening. Blacks have to listen too." This turned out to be an ongoing conflict in the unit on the Confederate flag. Some white students accused Richard of "not playing fairly" and of "playing favorites" in the class. They felt that their views were not treated equally to those of blacks—a perceived role reversal that is another expression of a white racial politics of resentment, of "reverse discrimination."

The next part of the unit consisted of a more detailed analysis of various standpoints in the flag controversy. *Standpoint* was defined as a position from which an individual or group constructed particular truths about the meaning of the Confederate flag. One's standpoint includes one's positioning within racial dynamics but is not limited to racial identity. Thus, it is too easy to see the controversy as merely a dispute between two oppositional standpoints that pits blacks against whites, although at times it seemed that way. With Richard's help the class identified and discussed four identifiably different standpoints on the flag controversy represented in the public media. These included: a neo-Confederacy standpoint, a "heritage, not hate" standpoint, a civil rights standpoint, and a business leaders' standpoint. The presentation and discussion of these four standpoints provided the basis for what turned out to be a very heated and often emotional dialogue in the class; and if this dialogue led to no consensus, and if it only seemed to exacerbate conflicts at times, it did offer the basis for finding some common ground as well.

The neo-Confederate standpoint represented the flag controversy in terms of a struggle to preserve a proud Southern heritage—explicitly or implicitly understood to be a white heritage. The website for *The Southern Partisan* turned out to be a particularly useful text in helping define the neo-Confederate standpoint. *The Southern Partisan* enjoys a wide distribution in South Carolina and is considered "respectable" by many politicians. Students visited the website of the magazine and analyzed its context. The first thing they noticed was that the website seemed very commercial. A magazine advertised on the website was titled *Boy Heroes of the Confederacy*. The subscription coupons show a Confederate army with the Second National Confederate flag. A full page subscription form was emblazoned with a picture of Robert E. Lee and his personal Confederate flag. Many of the articles focused on the Confederacy and remembrance activities. Among the beliefs that ran throughout neo-Confederate discourse was the belief that slaves were not treated badly in the "Old South," but rather made part of the plantation "family," taking their place in the "natural order," protected by their white masters who looked after their needs. Along with this romanticized vision of the past, neo-Confederates often implied, or explicitly stated, that they believed black people to be less intelligent than whites and thus not deserving to be "catered to." For example, Senator Arthur Ravenel of the so-called Charleston aristocracy gave a speech at a Charleston rally staged in opposition to the NAACP boycott in which he proclaimed:

> Can you believe, can you believe, can you believe that there's those who think that the General Assembly in South Carolina is going to pull its wool, knuckle under, grovel and do the bidding of that corrupt organization known as the National Association for Retarded People? (cited in Stroud, January 11, 2000, A1)

To add insult to injury, when asked to apologize, Ravenel said he wanted to apologize to retarded people for mistakenly associating them with the NAACP. Similarly, the infamous (but also popular) South Carolina restaurateur and crusading white supremist Maurice Bessinger proclaimed that "God gave slaves to whites." For whites to continue to occupy their position of superiority in the "natural order," however, they supposedly must maintain a pure blood. "You are WHITE because your ancestors believed in SEGREGATION," reads a tract distributed by a group of which Bessinger is a past president—the National Association for the Preservation of White People (Monk, October 1, 2000, B5).

Richard's white students for the most part disassociated themselves from the neo-Confederacy standpoint and acknowledged that it was linked to white racism. Neo-Confederates such as Bessinger were understood to be "bad whites," the kind of whites who gave the white race and Southern heritage a bad name. By acknowledging this, white and black students found a common ground, if an unstable one, upon which to build solidarity with black students. This common ground was unsettled, however, by the second standpoint students presented, associated with the slogan Heritage, not hate. This was a contested standpoint from the outset, in that white students viewed it as a distinct standpoint and black students all questioned whether it could be separated from the neo-Confederacy standpoint. It was represented in the popular press by comments from "the man on the street" or in stories in which reporters deliberately sought out the views of rural, small town whites. It is true that a good number of these people associated the Confederate flag with lifestyle, along with pride in a white cultural heritage, and that they went out of their way to disassociate themselves from racist whites. For these whites, the Confederate flag was an icon associated with hunting and fishing culture and the NASCAR lifestyle. Thus, a popular bumper sticker showed the Confederate flag and the NASCAR flag crossed. One popular T-shirt among white students in the school, before it was banned by the administration, expressed this general perspective. It read, "Fly me with dignity not bigotry," over a Confederate flag background. The T-shirt contained in small print the following statement:

I was not designed as a hate object, although many people look at me this way today. I was not born to represent white sheets and shaved heads. I was designed to support states rights and soldiers who wore grey.

White students who endorsed this standpoint, and most did, at least in the beginning, could not understand why black people saw only hate in the Confederate flag, when it was not their intention to hate anyone. But black students questioned whether it was possible for whites to have pride in Southern heritage, when the heritage they were defending included slavery and Jim Crow laws.

The third standpoint identified by the students was that of the NAACP and the civil rights movement, which had, after all, "begun" the controversy by announcing the boycott of the state. Richard asked white students to introduce and speak for this standpoint, in order to see if they could take the side of the other and speak from that standpoint. Specifically, white students were asked to speak for and defend the NAACP's resolution adopting economic sanctions against South Carolina (July 12, 1999). The resolution argues that the Confederate flag has come to symbolize "resistance to the battle for civil rights and equality" and that it took on such meaning when it was raised to the top of the capital dome in the 1960s. Furthermore, according to the resolution, the Confederate flag continues to be linked to "numerous modern-day groups advocating white supremacy." Then the NAACP resolution shifts to the issue of "sovereignty," the issue of who the Confederate flag speaks for when it flies above the capital dome. The NAACP questioned whether the state of South Carolina is acting like a democratic sovereign, representing the interests of all of its citizens, so long as a flag that is the symbol of discrimination and oppression continues to be used to represent the state, to say nothing of the fact that flying the flag over the capital dome implies "allegiance to a nonexistent nation." In such a context, the flag is "an affront to the sensibilities and dignity of a majority of African Americans in the state of South Carolina." The resolution ends with a call for the removal and relocation of the flag "to a place of historical rather than sovereign context." It decries the compromise of moving the flag to the front of the capital grounds on a 30-foot pole, noting that this is still a position of sovereignty, and that it is also a slap in the face to those citizens of South Carolina "who do not accept or revere the supposed heritage represented by the flag" (see South Carolina NAACP web site for the entire resolution).

By arguing from the standpoint of the NAACP, white students at least began to better understand and respect that standpoint, rather than merely dismiss it as based on ignorance or hate. As one student acknowledged, "If I were a black person, I'd probably feel that way too." White students acknowledged that the other had some legitimate points, even as they affirmed their own whiteness. The NAACP resolution, they said, represented "black people's viewpoint," and since they were not black they could hardly be expected to think accordingly. Still, they could argue black people's case, they could act as if they were black, and from that standpoint, they could at least entertain what it might feel like to be in the other's shoes.

The final standpoint students identified in popular reporting of the flag controversy was associated with the voice of big business, which played a key role in engineering the "compromise." The key phrase in the lexicon of corporate leaders was the *new South*, a phrase coded with both economic and cultural meaning. The new South was to be built on economic revival, which meant attracting more multinationals. And multinational corporations, so this argument went, like all of their employees to work together cooperatively. Business leaders were also concerned that South Carolinians welcome the new population of Mexican Americans and Asians being brought into the state to work in the mills and factories and that it not get branded as an intolerant state. These concerns were linked to a much more pragmatic concern among business leaders: the NAACP was threatening to expand the boycott to all products made in the state. It is not surprising, consequently, that BMW and Michelin, two multinational corporations with a sizable presence in South Carolina, took the lead in pressuring legislators and the governor to work out a compromise that involved removing the flag from the capital dome. The fact that the NAACP and most African Americans in the state did not accept the "compromise" meant that it was a compromise in name only. However, by asserting that a compromise or settlement had been reached, business and political leadership hoped the public (both nationally and in South Carolina) would view the dispute as effectively settled. That has proven not to be the case.

White female students in Richard's class were most supportive of the idea of finding a compromise, although no one spoke up in support of the current compromise. From their perspective, both sides deserved something, and at some point both sides needed to give a little. White male students felt that the compromise represented a form of "caving in" once more to the presumed power of the black community, another example of how white people's views do not get respected by state political leaders dependent upon the black vote and fearful of what a boycott might do economically. Black students were uniformly opposed to the compromise. They were united in their belief that no compromise would be acceptable other than removing the flag from the state grounds and all state buildings. As one black female remarked, "You can't compromise with hate." Like the broader public, Richard's students were still deeply divided as the Confederate flag unit came to an end. But they were beginning to have better-informed opinions, and they were beginning to relate their own views to those expressed by different movements and power blocs in South Carolina society.

RISKY DIALOGUE

Now that we have sketched out the general terrain of the unit on the Confederate flag controversy, we want to examine the dialogue on race that was organized around and out of that unit of study in more specificity and detail. Richard began the unit by talking about the rules of dialogue. Indeed, the first real dialogue in the class was about how to engage in democratic dialogue, one in which all voices are heard, participants treat each other with respect as much as possible and listen to each others' "truths," and truth claims are backed up as much as possible with concrete examples or evidence (Burbules 1993; Burbules & Rice, 2000). Beyond this, a democratic dialogue is directed toward some common ground about how to make society more equitable and just. Finally, he acknowledged that any dialogue on race, particularly in this high school, in this state, at this time, would call upon students to take risks, and that conflict was not to be considered necessarily bad, so long as it could be kept within the norms of democratic dialogue and keeping the conversation going.

One class session that sparked a particularly heated dialogue was organized around the reading of an editorial column in the major newspaper in the state by an African American writer. The writer sought to counter the argument of flag supporters that the civil rights movement is over and that it is inappropriate to think of this use of the flag as an issue involving civil rights. He wrote that the civil rights struggles continued in South Carolina and used as an example the fact that there are a disproportionate number of African Americans on death row in South Carolina. He concluded by questioning whether black males were not being "railroaded" into prison so that the police could claim they had solved crimes that remain unsolved. For once, the black males in the class felt empowered to speak. The article, said Greg, "spoke to what black men in this country know and have to live with every day of our lives. The brother told it like it is." Instead of responding to what Greg had to say, Samantha, one of two white females in the class who were most outspoken, spoke directly to Richard. She complained that making them read this article was another example of how everything in this class is "too gloomy and too negative," or that it is "slanted toward the black viewpoint." Pam, who often spoke up to support what her friend Samantha said, added that "everything is black in this class." Here meaning seemed to be to play on the word *black*, to refer both to black people and to "negative" or "gloomy" talk.

Richard tried to help the white students realize that what they were feeling was similar to what black students must feel like most of the time when all they get is white perspectives on the news. If nothing else, he said, white students could learn a valuable lesson about how it feels to be marginalized, if only briefly. Dianna, an African American student, agreed, saying, "In my twelve years of schooling I have learned only about white people and their history, nothing about me." Leonard, an African American male, echoed this sentiment. "White students," he said, "should have to take African American history since we have been forced to study white history all our lives." At this point, Tameka acted to calm things down with a "truth" she had learned from her grandmother: "There will always be people who disagree with it one way and talk about it in another." Her point was that people can disagree and still get along. Greg, a black student, supported this truth and added another: "The world would be much better if people would learn to be more accepting. Everybody is hurt by discrimination and hate." Richard asked if the class could at least reach some consensus on that, and in a rare moment of solidarity, class members all raised their hands. The class ended on this high note. But as a subsequent class discussion indicated, this sudden solidarity among black and white students, this desire to get beyond historic battles that have divided blacks and whites and affirm a common humanity, was to be fragile and easily broken.

Each week during the term, the class watched a videotaped segment of the PBS series *Eyes on the Prize*. Several black students regularly hum along with the chorus soundtrack that opens each episode: "If it's one thing we did right, it's the day we started to fight. Keep your eyes on the prize, hold on!" Pam usually made a deliberate show of sleeping through segments of *Eyes on the Prize*, and Samantha sat with her arms folded and with an angry expression on her face. They were a bit more responsive to the History Channel's presentation, *The Unfinished Civil War*, a video on Civil War reenactment and reenactors that also includes an extensive presentation of the Confederate flag controversy in South Carolina. After viewing the video the class read and discussed some of the press reaction to the broadcasting of the program in the state for the first time in February 2001. Some of those who participated in the reenactment were quoted as saying that they were angry with the producers because they felt they had been unfairly portrayed as a "bunch of idiotic racists" (*The State*, online, March 14, 2001, p. 2), Samantha said and Pam agreed. According to Pam,

> I don't see how the blacks can call us white people racist when they are too. They get mad when we call them the "n" word, but is it right for them to call us a "cracker" and "white trash"? The Confederate flag don't mean slavery or hate. . . . To me I can't understand why they are so down on the Ku Klux Klan when the NAACP is the same thing—Negroes Against All Caucasian People.

Here, Pam is articulating a white hegemonic standpoint theory, one whose truth claims rest on the presumption that whites and blacks are equally guilty or not guilty of racism. Dianna, an African American female, called Pam on her remark, and in doing so made an important distinction. "The Ku Klux Klan is a hate group, and the NAACP is a civil rights group that fights hate." One represents the voice of white supremacy in its most violent and oppressive form, and the other represents the voice of those who historically have been the target of the violence and oppression. As for those whites who like to dress up in Confederate uniforms and reenact Civil War battles, Dianna maintained: "They're trying to make it [the "Old South"] out to be a lot better than it was for black people. The history they were defending included slavery."

As the discussion continued, Samantha moved to resolve the conflict by suggesting that "the Confederate flag can mean many different things to different people." She was at least willing to accept the truth of what Dianna had to say, from her standpoint, and she seemed worried that Pam and Dianna were very confrontational in their attitudes to one another. From Samantha's perspective, some groups were rallying around the flag for the "wrong reasons," and the "right reason" for flying the Confederate flag on the capital grounds should be to honor the war dead and a proud Southern heritage. Pam agreed with that position, but Dianna clearly did not. In words that were very emotion-laden and angry, Dianna said: "The Confederate flag will *always* mean slavery, Jim Crow, segregation, and generations of suffering. It's the *heritage* that makes me hate it. . . . The facts aren't going to change. The ability of Southerners to own slaves was their *heritage*." Jennifer, another black student, added that "honoring ancestors who fought for secession and states' rights to allow slavery is also honoring the cause of slavery." Black students united against any compromise with a symbol of hate, and for a moment the class seemed frozen in opposing black and white groups, each ready to say again, as they had before, "I give up."

It was at this point that Chris, a white, male student who typically kept quiet, at least as much as he could, spoke up. He was a bit of an other student in his own way, a white, working-class kid who listened to rap and identified at least in some small way with hip hop culture. One reason he did not speak before, perhaps, was that he risked being considered a "race traitor" if he did not fall into lockstep with other white students, setting up whiteness against blackness. Chris said, "Samantha, I hope you don't include all of us whites when you talk about your heritage. How can we really revere our 'heritage' if heritage was hatred to begin with?" This turned out to be the first crack in the discourse of whiteness circulating in the class, and it was followed by the first open disagreement between Pam and Samantha, who before had always spoken in one voice. Pam conceded that "for African Americans, the Confederate flag will probably always be a reminder of slavery" and that some compromise might be worked out. She asked, "What more do you [black students] want us to do?" For Dianna, that "more" was complete removal of the Confederate flag from the State House grounds. Dianna said that in her view the best compromise would be place the Confederate flag in a museum to the war dead, but nowhere else. Pam was upset at this tentative and partial alliance between Samantha and Dianna and seemed more entrenched than ever in her belief in the current "compromise." She urged those who might be offended by the current placement of the flag behind the war memorial on the capital lawn to "use a different street" when they went to the capital so they could avoid seeing it.

Stan, a working-class student who identified with a hunting and fishing lifestyle, stepped up to support Pam in her defense of the flag and her implicit defense of white people. "If anyone is discriminated against here," he said, "it is the Southern white loyalists. In this school, we honor African American month and Hispanic month. Nothing is done to honor our grandfathers of the South that means so much to over half of the student body." Here we find a white politics of resentment in an almost pure form. Whites are now those being picked on, discriminated against, and otherwise not respected. Of course there is a good deal of truth to the fact that the voices of poor, rural white folks have been largely ignored in history books. But black people were hardly to blame for this. Richard tried to make students see that the voices and collective memories of both poor black and white people had been left out of the history texts and that once more they shared more than they were willing to acknowledge.

The unit came to an end without any sense of resolution but with a commitment to keep the conversation going. Black students, of necessity but also because of identification with an historic struggle for social justice, were in solidarity with one another and if they disagreed, they lived by the implicit code of never disagreeing in public, in front of whites. Generally, they felt empowered by the unit and found dialogue worthwhile. White students were less united, which was in some ways a very good sign. It meant that some white students were beginning to break away from unquestioned allegiance to the hegemonic narratives of whiteness and Southern heritage, if only tentatively. What black and white students agreed to, ultimately, was to live with each other, to treat each other with more respect, and even to interact as friends within the context of the classroom world. That was no small achievement.

CONCLUSION

The battle over the Confederate flag wages on in South Carolina, as it does elsewhere in the United States. In April 2000, the Jackson, Mississippi, City Council voted to condemn the flying of the Confederate flag in any sovereign place. In Alabama, where the Confederate flag is flown every April 26 for the state's Confederate Memorial Day, the legislature has proposed replacing the Confederate battle flag with the first national flag of the Confederacy as a compromise. Supporters hope that flag, which is similar to the American flag, will evoke less acrimony. In Georgia, where the state flag also incorporates the battle flag, protesters at the Super Bowl in 2000 demanded that the flag be brought down. Meanwhile, in Virginia, the state is taking an opposite tack, of seeking to block the use of the Confederate flag on the state's new personalized license plates. It is being sued by the Virginia Sons of the Confederacy. One lesson to be learned from all of this is that symbolic battles, such as those over the Confederate flag, count. They provide an important means for surfacing, in this case, the unhealed, still gaping, wounds of white racism in America and for reflecting upon the meaning of history, heritage, and identity. Symbolic battles also, to the extent that they are brought within the context of a democratic dialogue and public debate, can open up possibilities for rethinking the world and reconstructing the self in relation to various others.

This leads us to another lesson we would draw from this study, that dialogue counts, and that more room needs to be reserved for dialogue in public schools and classrooms, at least if we look to the schools as primary sites for the democratic reconstruction of culture (Dimitriadis & Carlson, 2003; Carlson, 2002). Dialogue begins with a critical, deconstructive reading of various cultural "texts." The objective is to demystify these cultural texts, to reveal how they either support or contest structured systems of social and economic inequality. This is similar to the kind of dialogue advocated by Paulo Freire (1970) in his "pedagogy of the oppressed," by Henry Giroux (1993), and other advocates of what is often called "critical pedagogy" in the academe. Critical pedagogy orients dialogue toward the critique of systems and structures of domination and toward forms of truth production informed by commitments to social justice and equity. However, as poststructural feminists such as Elizabeth Ellsworth (1989) remind us, the "oppressed" is not a unified category, and it is not always easy to say what constitutes social justice in a given situation. Attempts to use dialogue to impose a consensus upon a group may even be used to silence opposition and erase difference. Dialogue will not necessarily lead us to consensus on what is true or what is just. Dialogue is not some abstract space where we leave positionality, power, and body behind and engage with an "unclouded" intellect, as if that were ever possible. All of this suggests that progressive teachers and educators need to walk a fine line. On the one hand, they need to affirm the importance of certain transcendent values (equity, social justice, and human freedom, for example); and they need to actively take a stand against racism, sexism, homophobia, classism, and other forms of domination. On the other hand, progressive teachers need to resist a doctrinaire "politically correct" form of pedagogical authority, the kind that insists everyone agree on one set of truths. That, we believe, only fosters more resistance and resentment.

Some would argue that the kind of dialogue opened up by this unit on the Confederate flag controversy only succeeded in troubling waters that are better left still, picked at racial scabs that are best left untouched, so they can heal. We have argued, instead, that it incumbent upon those who are committed to the ideals of multiculturalism, social justice, and diversity to trouble waters and pick at cultural scabs. Such teachers take risks. They leave the safe harbors of what is "comfortable" and predictable in nondialogic teaching and enter into the messiness of standpoint theory and multiple and contradictory truths that do not come together in some unifying synthesis. If democratic dialogue does not lead to any idealized consensus on the truth, any final or complete resolution of conflicts, it does offer a chance to move the conflict to new levels, the chance for students to develop new forms of self-awareness and self-reflexivity, no longer taking their own cherished beliefs as "only natural." Dialogue also offers the hope that people can better understand and perhaps even empathize with the perspective of the other and thus gain an appreciation for different points of view, along with a willingness to live with disagreement. Conversely, the active stifling of such dialogue is a form of running from history that blocks democratic change.

Another lesson we would draw from the case study is that teachers have some limited but nevertheless significant room in public schools to teach against the grain. Progressive teachers need to take advantage of what limited space there is in public school systems for a pedagogy that critically engages young people in the study of racism, classism, homophobia, sexism, ablism, and other forms of cultural domination and oppression, and they need to work to carve out more such space. We realize, at the same time, that this is risky business. Richard was willing to take risks only because the unit on the Confederate flag controversy was developed as part of a collaborate project with the university and only because school administrators supported it as one small effort at opening a dialogue on race among students. Our point here is that teachers are likely to be more effective in carving out significant space in schools for "subversive" teaching when they work with others and when they frame their project in ways that address the interests of administrators and other power brokers in the school and the community.

Within these constraints, progressive-minded teachers need to rekindle a politics of political and pedagogical possibility, aimed at turning more and more public schools and classrooms, along with other sites in the public, into "safe spaces," places in which young people feel safe to express their beliefs and feelings in dialogue with others. Young people marginalized by class, race, gender, sexual identity, and other markers of difference need their own safe spaces to build solidarity and self-awareness. But young people also need educational safe spaces to come together across racial and other differences to find some common democratic ground, to affirm some common democratic commitments, if nothing more than a commitment to making space for difference. We cannot, as Weis and Fine (2000, 2003) remind us, afford to romanticize safe spaces in schools, classrooms, and other sites in the public as ever "innocent," "uncontaminated," or 'free." They are, at best, spaces in which privilege can be questioned even as it continues to shape discourse and in which identity can be affirmed even as it is troubled and reconstructed.

FOURTEEN

Popular Culture, Pedagogy, and Urban Youth

Beyond Silenced Voices

Greg Dimitriadis

THE FIRST EDITION of *Beyond Silenced Voices* (1993) forwarded several groundbreaking arguments about contemporary public schooling and youth. In particular, the editors and authors argued that schools typically "silence" marginalized youth, eliding the "words, critiques, dreams, and fantasies of those who have dwelt historically on the margins" (p. 2). Collectively, the editors and authors looked to bring this heterogeneous complexity to the forefront of discussion. For Fine and Weis and colleagues, this complexity was a starting point for asking "what might be" if schools were to fulfill their promise as democratic public spheres, a starting point for what William Pinar (2004) calls a "complicated conversation" about curriculum.

In many respects, the processes that Fine and Weis highlighted over 10 years ago—what they called "the structuring of silence"—has only become increasingly pronounced, with the emergence of high-stakes testing and other market-driven imperatives. More and more, standardized test scores are the currency in which and through which schools are deemed "effective" or "ineffective." Disconnected from the lived realities of teachers and students, these tests are largely driving day-to-day life in our public schools. *Accountability* has become the watchword for policing what education can mean for youth in state-funded institutions. The tragedy here, of course, is that affluent students can often attend private schools, where student-centered learning is often enabled by material privilege. As always, those most marginalized are under constant surveillance, are continually silenced.

As schools are becoming increasingly routinized, I believe, young people are turning toward alternative kinds of curricula (e.g., popular culture) and alternative kinds of institutions (e.g., community centers). More and more, these are the sites where young people choose to "homestead," choose to stake out meaningful spaces for themselves in and against often hostile sets of social, cultural, and material circumstances. Fine, Weis, Centrie, and Roberts write:

> Young men and women are 'homesteading'—finding unsuspecting places within their geographic locations, their public institutions, and their spiritual lives to sculpt real and imaginary corners for peace, solace, communion, personal and collective identity work. These are spaces of deep, sustained community-based educative work, outside the borders of formal schooling. (Fine, Weis, Centrie, & Roberts, 2000, p. 132)

These sites exist largely independently from traditional school settings, challenging those of us in education to decenter our own assumptions about what "education" means for youth today. These are the sites where young people choose their own educative texts and work with them in specific and often counterintuitive ways—making ethnography critical to understanding these "silenced voices."

Decentering our research agenda, I argue, has important implications for thinking about questions of "difference." Finding the spaces where young people live their lives allows us to engage with questions of race, class, and gender, outside of often managerial discourse of difference imported into school settings. Race, in particular, is being lived today in ways that exceed the explanatory mechanisms of popular notions of multiculturalism. As Cameron McCarthy has most powerfully argued, racial hybridity and changeability is an evolved social fact, and race is lived out in very different ways in different contexts depending on a whole host of social, cultural, and material variables. He highlights the idea that

> the intersection of race, class and gender in the institutional setting of the school is systematically contradictory or nonsynchronous and can lead to the augmentation or diminution of the effectivity of race, or for that matter, any other of these variables operating in the school environment. The concept of nonsynchrony summarizes the vast differences in interests, needs, desires and identity that separate different minority groups from each other and from majority whites in educational settings. (1990, pp. 9–10)

Indeed, looking beyond what he and Warren Crichlow call "the limitations of . . . calcified position[s]" (p. xxi), looking toward "change, contradiction, variability, and revision within historically specific and determinate contexts" (1993, p. xv) poses new sets of questions for educators, educators who can no longer predict a priori what kinds of students will be invested in what kinds of curricula and why, educators who have to be more humble and creative in thinking through profoundly complex questions of curricula construction today.

Understanding this kind of contingency and complexity poses very daunting questions and challenges for contemporary curricula theorists, those who would attempt to inform public educational discourse and policy in tangible ways. Jabari Mahiri (1998) provides an excellent example of the difficulties of reading race in simple ways off of teachers and texts in his book *Shooting for Excellence*. Here, he documents the paradoxical failures of a black teacher, Ms. Jackson, to teach black students "ethnic" literature. As he so tellingly argues, "the nature of classroom discourse and culture are tied to the meanings enacted by a particular teacher and class"—in ways that can radically circumscribe how these texts are picked up and used (p. 100). Particularly important here is the role of popular culture, the ways it is drawn on, the ways it is ignored or elided. As Mahiri argues, the most successful teachers he worked with were those able to scaffold their lessons with the affectively charged popular texts in which young people were so invested. Black popular culture took on a particular kind of salience here, with both white and black teens gravitating toward these texts in ways that challenged simple notions of cultural property and ownership. The complexity of these popular cultural resources, the paradoxical ways in which they were used by young people in negotiating new and emergent identities, offered a profound challenge to which the best teachers were able to rise.

Gauging from this example as well as others (e.g., Heath & McLaughlin, 1995; McCarthy, et al., 1999; Yon, 2000), the demand for sustained research and reflection on race, popular culture, and curriculum is great. Recent work on popular culture and education has looked at how young people have utilized these texts in use, practice and performance (Buckingham, 1993, 1996, 1998; Buckingham & Sefton-Green, 1995; Tobin, 2000). David Buckingham and Julian Sefton-Green, for example, have treated media literacy as a kind of symbolic social action. Their work has explored how young people mobilize popular texts as discursive resources in particular and meaningful ways, using them to negotiate senses of self and community. In *Cultural Studies Goes to School* (1995), the authors offer several case studies of young people using the media to create personally relevant texts—from magazines to photographs to popular music—as they author their lives, so to speak. "In adopting 'critical' positions in discourse, in staking out their tastes and identities, and in intervening directly in popular cultural forms, these writers are actively defining themselves in relation to wider social, cultural, and ideological forces" (p. 82). This is a less defensive approach than are many current "media literacy" approaches. In fact, Buckingham (1998) has noted that this kind of work often invites problematic kinds of pleasures from students. Even these—perhaps especially these—must be understood if we are to engage with the lives of young people in authentic ways.

Julian Sefton-Green (1998, 1999) extends this work, focusing on the relationships among popular media culture, the arts, and the Internet. In *Young People, Creativity, and New Technologies* (1999), Sefton-Green gathers recent theoretical and empirical work "to describe the opportunities digital technologies offer for communicating, disseminating and making culture as well as acting as a vehicle for personal and collective self-expression" (p. 1). Among other topics, contributors discuss multimedia memoirs, self-produced CD-Roms, on-line school scrap books, and personal web pages. These new and creative uses of information technologies are part of a broader redefinition of youth culture that has implications for all manner of educational practice, from the classroom to the dance floor (Sefton-Green, 1998).

More recently scholars in education have moved toward less prefigured, ethnographic approaches that look at the ways young people construct identities through popular culture and their implications for school life (Dimitriadis, 2001; Dolby, 2001; Yon, 2000). For example, Nadine Dolby and Daniel Yon have developed similar ethnographic projects in the field of education, though both have looked to settings outside the United States. Dolby (2001), in a particularly fascinating study, looks at how young people at a high school in South Africa (Fernwood High) negotiate ideas about race in the aftermath of apartheid. Here, music and fashion became ways to carve out ideas about being "white," "black," and "coloured," at a moment when a priori racial categories are called into question. These popular symbols circulated and were ascribed different meanings at different times. "Rave music," for example, "is understood specifically as 'white' music. A coloured student who listens to rave would be ostracized by her or his classmates, and seen as a threat to 'coloured' identity" (2000, p. 206). In sum, she argues, "'Race' at Fernwood reinvents itself (as it does constantly) as a site of identification that takes its meaning, in large part, from affect and affective investments. Students are invested in the emotions of desire that surround consumptive practices, particularly the practices of global youth culture" (p. 203).

Yon, in turn, looked at a multiethnic high school in Toronto (Maple Heights), focusing on the ways in which young people negotiate their day-to-day identities. Yon offers portraits of different young people and the creation of complicated identities through their investments in popular culture. He writes, "Many of the signs and symbols of the popular cultures of these youth, like dress codes and musical tastes, are racialized. This means that the signifiers of race can also change with the changing signs of culture and identity, and what it means to be a certain race is different from one context to the next" (2000, p. 71). He offers several examples of young people constructing notions of self through popular culture. These include a Canadian-born black youth, a white youth who identifies with black culture, and a black immigrant from the Caribbean, all of whom use popular culture to negotiate and stake out particular senses of self.

In sum, these authors make it clear that we cannot understand young people's identities in predictable ways. More and more we must ask ourselves what kinds of curricula—broadly defined—young people draw on to understand, explain, and live through the world around them. This is messy terrain, one that exceeds a priori notions about identity often privileged by educators. As these authors make clear, the multiple uses to which popular culture is put challenge and belie easy notions of "cultural identification." Young people in the United States and around the world are elaborating complex kinds of social and cultural identifications through music such as hip hop and techno in ways that challenge predictive notions about texts, practices, and identities. "The global context of popular culture," Dolby writes, is critical for "the marking of racialized borders, and for their subsequent displacement and rearrangement" (2001, p. 9). Such attention to popular culture, I argue, offers educators a more ecumenical and open-ended disposition toward understanding and thinking through student identity. Such attention looks past the conscribed treatment of difference, often privileged in dominant approaches to multiculturalism.

THE STUDY

My own work has looked at how young people construct notions of self, history, and place through their uses of hip hop texts, focusing on how these young people use these texts in concert with—and in counterdistinction to—school texts (Dimitriadis, 2001, 2003). For example, I looked at the ways in which two teenagers constructed notions of a Southern tradition through their use of Southern rap texts; how young people constructed notions of history through viewing the film *Panther* (1995), a film they connected to hip hop culture more broadly; and how young people constructed powerful senses of self through talk about the life and death of icon Tupac Shakur. All are examples of popular culture's reach and power. "We see popular culture," I wrote, "more and more, providing the narratives that young people are drawing on to deal with the issues and the concerns most pressing in their lives." These investments, I showed, "played out in often unpredictable ways" (2001, p. 120). I would like to highlight here the role of popular culture in the understanding and actualization of history and historical knowledge.

The site for this study was a local community center (or "club") in a small Midwest city where I developed and ran a weekly program devoted to discussing African American vernacular culture generally and hip hop or rap music specifically. I maintained the program and its curriculum for two and a half years. This program was offered as one of a handful of programs at a center that serves over 300 economically marginalized African American children in the community. In this program, we discussed popular texts and figures—most often related to hip hop or rap music—in open-ended and nondirected ways. I typically brought in a number of prompts for discussion (e.g., copies of song lyrics) and gauged what my participants were most enthusiastic about discussing. I then chose a new prompt when discussion seemed to wane. I usually began by asking them to interpret or explain the meanings of these texts, though these discussions almost always led us towards key events in their daily lives. The participants ranged in age from 10 to 17 and eventually met in two separate groups (ages 10–12 and 13–17). These focus groups on average consisted of 3 to 10 participants who attended many but not all sessions. The younger group typically attracted larger numbers, and the older groups typically attracted fewer. The younger groups typically attracted more boys than girls, and the gender balance was more even in the older group.

The majority of this study was conducted by way of focus groups. As George Kamberelis and I have recently argued, focus groups allow for a unique democratization of the research process, decentering the role and importance of the interviewer, allowing for more explicitly dialogic and heterogeneous interactions (Dimitriadis and Kamberelis, in press). Focus groups are key sites where the pedagogical and the political converge, allowing researchers to—at least potentially—transform qualitative inquiry practices. In many respects, I led and directed these focus groups, choosing texts and questions for group discussion. But I was only able to sustain these groups through participant interest and involvement. I had to continually calibrate the group dynamics, ever reworking my initial research plans, agendas, and goals. As I will demonstrate below, the group would typically "take over" sessions as they did when we discussed the film *Panther*, choosing to move forward with one plan and eliding another. In fact, the suggestion to show *Panther* came from a group member.

Focus group work was thus key for exploring the "voices" of young people in all their multiple manifestations. Focus groups allowed for the proliferation of multiple meanings and perspectives, including my own, as well as interanimation between and among them. More specifically, the focus group format allowed me (in part) to move away from the dyadic interview context and its (often) common-sense assumptions about student voice. Here, voice is often assumed to be embedded in young people's "deep selves," able to be simply elicited and expressed through talk. In the focus-group context, the interaction itself—in all its multiple complexities and tensions—was the "unit of analysis." Decentering my authority allowed for the more complex voices of youth to emerge in ways that were both unpredictable and (at times) somewhat stereotypic. Moving "beyond silenced voices" was a tricky endeavor, one ever negotiated in the group context.

I begin now with a look at how young people spoke about history as it was taught in school—perhaps the most important "official site" in their lives. This discussion will offset and highlight the ways these young people reacted to the popular film *Panther*.

HISTORY IN SCHOOL

The participants in this study spoke in almost wholly negative ways about how "history"—traditionally conceived—was taught in schools. Most young people noted that the life and work of Martin Luther King Jr. was stressed too exclusively and that black history was only relegated to one month of the year—the shortest month. This antipathy to the ways black history was taught in school was expressed often and in many ways. For example, one young person stressed that the Black Panthers and Malcolm X were ignored in school in favor of King, "We talking about Martin Luther King but not Malcolm X. . . . Everybody know about Martin Luther King Jr." Another teen noted that all they talk about in school is "Dr. Martin Luther King famous speech, *I Had a Dream*. We learned that back in second grade. Why you still teaching us that? Why don't you teach us something else, that's more important?" This teen also commented, "They won't teach you about nothing that Martin Luther King did except that yes, he was a famous black African American." He continued: "In a school district, they'll take one month and learn a little bit about African American history. All the famous people . . . the same thing over and over and over every single year."

It seems then as if individual icons who are explicitly nonviolent were stressed first and foremost in school settings. As one young person said, teachers talk about "people that was famous, that's all . . . they talk about Bill Cosby . . . um . . . mostly she always be talking about Martin Luther King Jr. and Robert Clemente . . . not the one's that's violent." As mentioned above, the life of Martin Luther King Jr. has come to stand for nonviolence itself and is often stressed to the exclusion of other figures, indexing black history completely. The construction of King as supremely emblematic of "blackness" itself, in addition, often rubs up against and can contradict, at least in part, more local notions of what counts as black. For example, this same young person commented that rapper Snoop Doggy Dogg was "problack" in the video "Gangster Party" "'cause he, it was like, he did all that kind of black stuff. He was drinking, riding in the cars, sagging, all that stuff." Sagging is a way of wearing one's pants low and is often associated with prisoners and gang members. It is surely not a symbol of passive resistance or of nonviolence.

In addition to disliking how black history was taught, many young people resented how other groups were taught in contrast. For example, many young people said that they did not like the way they were forced to focus on the Jewish Holocaust. One teen was not allowed to take a test on the Holocaust: "My grandmom won't let me take the, um, the Holocaust test. . . . She just thought they [the Nazis] were some crazy white people. . . . We making, um, a Holocaust museum, I can't participate in that. She won't let me do it . . . 'cause she said if they can teach that, they can teach us something about Africa too, and they really, they don't. . . . During black history we don't do nothing." Another teen reiterated about this museum, "They made us go through it and a whole bunch of people didn't want to, but if we didn't go through it, then we got in trouble." As Cameron McCarthy and I have argued (2001), "resentment" is about forging identity through erasing the other. Because their own histories were not attended to, it seemed, these young people appeared to mobilize such modes of resentment toward other groups.

Thus, young people spoke both about the exclusive focus on King and how he was taught, including in relation to events and figures key for other groups. Many indicated, following the above, that King was merely inserted into an already existing, uninspiring curriculum, his presence strictly "pro forma," to satisfy the demands of Black History Month. Nothing as participatory or as engaging as building and physically going through a museum was stressed. If anything, this use of King during Black History Month seemed to evoke deep feelings of anxiety, especially vis-à-vis their teacher's exclusive stress on King's philosophy of nonviolence. Their responses echo and underscore the work of many critical theorists of curriculum who stress the ways that multicultural education serves to reproduce a liberal-pluralist model of education, the ways such icons are uncritically added on as a footnote to history (Beyer & Apple, 1998).

However, while many young people expressed dissatisfaction with the almost exclusive stress on King in schools as well as how he is taught, they also had a deep respect for the man. As ex-black Panther Kathleen Cleaver (1998) noted recently, the popular appropriation of King to index an ideally nonviolent and passive black population often belies the respect and admiration many feel for him in other more locally validated settings. Indeed, during Black History Month, the club where this research was conducted held a speech-making competition/celebration, and young people were given the opportunity to deliver speeches about black history and culture. I was in charge of much of the event and photocopied a range of speeches and poems, including those of Huey Newton, Malcolm X, Langston Hughes, and King. The young people, however, gravitated almost exclusively and with much enthusiasm to the speeches of King. Even the young person referred to above, the one who talked about how everyone knows about Martin Luther King Jr. immediately went for the King speeches. This same young person, on the day of the competition, brought in a number of photos of his family's trip to the site of King's assassination. These included photographs of the jacket King was wearing when he was shot as well as photos of the hotel. He displayed these pictures proudly and suggested passing them to the assembled crowd. This young person also brought in a sheet of paper with the words of the speech "I Have a Dream" printed out, decorated on a blue background. Apparently, this text hung on a wall in his home. Indeed, many young people have similar photos and plaques in their homes, with lithographs of King as well as printed text from his speeches. These texts are plainly very important to many of these young people and their families.

These young people, therefore, challenge us to move beyond questions of curricular "representation" toward questions of curricular "performance"—for example, how key historical figures are picked up, used, and mobilized by whom and for what purposes. This is an important distinction. Contemporary discussions about the curriculum have largely been motivated by what Dwight Conquergood (1998) calls a "textual" bias, one that assumes that we can think about representation out of context. Rather, following the above, we need to think about curriculum as a performed relationship. Here, to echo Norman Denzin, "context replaces text, verbs replace nouns, structures become processes. The emphasis is on change, contingency, locality, motion, improvisation, struggle, situationally specific practices and articulations, the performance of con/texts" (Denzin, 2003, p. 16). More than anything, these young people challenge us to think about history in all its radically particularity and contingency, in all its performativity.

As noted, the main methodological tool for my research was weekly discussion groups around rap music. During these focus groups, I attempted to make links between rap and other historical texts and events. For example, over the course of a few sessions, I showed the film *Malcolm X* and attempted to generate discussion about his life in comparison with the life of King. Though the links with rap seemed self-evident to me, during one discussion a young person asked, "What does this have to do with rap?" Another young person answered, "Well, right now, we're talking about Black History Month." When I asked if rap had anything to do with Black History Month, the students all answered "no." One commented, "At first we was talking about rap, about Tupac and Biggie." I then asked about another film we had seen, *Rosewood,* a film about an all-black community in the South in the twenties that was destroyed by white racists. *Rosewood,* they said, has something to do with rap—more than *Malcolm X,* which, one noted, was about a "black leader" and as such seemed more "schoollike" than "raplike" (thus echoing the earlier discussion).

Young people expressed more or less interest for the historical films I introduced, including *Malcolm X, Rosewood,* and *Panther.* The level of enthusiasm seemed to unfold roughly in that fashion, with *Panther* garnering, by far, the most enthusiasm, and *Malcolm X,* the least. As I will demonstrate, young people made more intertextual links with this film and the other popular media forms in which they are invested. This accounts in large measure, I argue, for the enthusiasm afforded the film.

I first decided to show clips of *Panther* to my discussion group after one young person expressed an interest in the film (again, these focus groups allowed for such negotiation between myself and these youth). However, the overwhelming consensus among the group was that I should show the whole film. I then devoted a series of sessions to the film, with discussion afterward. The group's enthusiasm was unabated. At their request, I then showed an episode of the PBS documentary *Eyes on the Prize* that discussed the Panthers, to considerably less enthusiasm as I will note.

Panther and the Local Construction of Racial Consciousness

The group reaction to the film *Panther* can be delineated as follows. First, the participants all made intertextual links between this film and other films that featured the same actors; second, they made connections between the Panthers and their own informal cliques; third, they drew together, as a group, around the most violent scenes, especially those featuring guns; fourth, and in turn, they tended to carry out their own agendas (such as talking and teasing each other) during scenes that featured talking; and finally, they focused, thematically, on the film's antipolice subtext, making connections with their own lives and experiences. These viewing practices helped form the contours around which these young people processed this historical text and claimed it as their own.

From the very first session devoted to *Panther*, young people identified characters and actors as "playing in" other films of the new black cinema such as *Friday* (1995), *Jason's Lyric* (1994), and *Menace II Society* (1993). When such actors appeared on the screen, they became the focus of much spirited group discussion. For example, the main antagonist in *Panther* is a local drug dealer who teams up with the police to help quell the group. This actor, A. J. Johnson, was featured as a "hype" or crack addict named Ezel in the film *Friday*, a comedy featuring rapper Ice Cube. *Friday* is about a seemingly typical day in the life of two teens in a Los Angeles "ghetto." It was a highly successful film, and many young people considered it one of their favorites. Whenever A. J. Johnson appeared on the screen, young people made comments such as "There goes Ezel!" and routinely referred to "Ezel" when discussing the film.

Filmmakers have plainly capitalized on young people and their knowledge of these artists and their different roles. For example, A. J. Johnson played a comedic role in the film *Friday*. While his role was, on one level, very different in *Panther*, he had certain comedic dimensions to his character toward which these young people gravitated. He played a fast-talking, funny, and wily character. When he was shot in the ear at the end, many young people laughed at Johnson's reaction. In contrast, Bokeem Woodbine plays more physically imposing characters, in *Panther* as well as in other films. These actors, in large measure, are typecast, in ways that allowed these young people to connect them to other films and to predict how different films might unfold.

In addition to making links between films, these youth also used *Panther* to talk about their own social positioning relative to their social networks. During the very first session devoted to the film, the youth began to claim characters. For example, when the character of Huey Newton appeared, one young person commented, "There go me!" to which another responded, "That's me right there! I already called it!" Seemingly, there was a kind of exclusivity to claiming roles here, as only one person could claim each of the available characters. Again, these young people used the positioning of characters in the film to inform their own positioning relative to the group. The film, quite clearly, afforded particular roles as indicated by comments such as, "I'm the black dude!" and "That's my man!"

Interestingly, these comments were often made by young people who already had a degree of social capital relative to the group and others at the club. Indeed, these were also often highly competitive individuals who made (successful) concerted efforts to position themselves as valued in other locally validated activities. One homologous activity here was sports. Nearly all the youth who claimed these roles during these sessions were active in sports and often got similarly worked up during competition, whether in Ping-Pong, basketball, or pool. These same young people who competed for "claiming" Huey Newton also taunted each other during Ping-Pong games (e.g., "You're sorry! Get off my table!") or against other clubs when competing at sports such as basketball ("We're gonna smoke that team!"). Interestingly, those who did not claim characters during our film-viewing sessions tended to be non-competitive in sports and not so antagonistically vocal during activities such as Ping-Pong.

For the youth at the center, the social positioning in the film also implicated their own particular social networks or cliques. Indeed, in this same discussion group, the talk turned to some of the fights that group members got into and the ways in which they stood up for each other. At one point, they talked about a young man, Jalin, and how he had been picking on a group member's sister. Another member of the group commented, "All us right here [in the group], gonna jump on Jalin." Sensing an opportunity to interrogate the kinds of conflicts in which these young people engaged, I asked why they stuck up for each other. One responded, interestingly, "'Cause we help each other. We the Black Panthers." Thus the kind of positioning and community represented in *Panther* was deeply implicated for these youth in their own cliques. Importantly, this kind of positioning often valorized violence as opposed to other kinds of responses (talking to the police, teachers, or family, etc.). This is a theme echoed and underscored throughout their viewing practices and its contours.

These informal cliques also had homologies in other popular cultural forms. Indeed, after the young person above said, "We the Black Panthers," another said "We NWO." At the end of this focus group, members called out in excitement, "World Championship Black Panthers!" and "Black Panthers for Life!" These are references to professional wrestling, including the famous chant of NWO (New World Order, a group of wrestlers)—"NWO for Life." Professional wrestling is marked today by groups of wrestlers who form formal groups that are very similar to the self-proclaimed cliques that young people form (both are linked to broader conversationalizing discourses, as noted elsewhere [Kamberelis & Dimitriadis, 1999]). These young people thus appropriated the relationships in the film to comment on their own social networks in ways that connect them to other popular cultural texts. These links, however, seemed odd relative to more traditional black cultural practices, speaking, as they do, to the particular coarticulation of discourses that mark so much popular culture today (Bakhtin [1986] proves helpful here). For example, one could hardly imagine an older person making similar comments about Martin Luther King Jr. in relation to wrestling. One might find chants like "Student Nonviolent Coordinating Committee for Life!" or even "Nation of Islam for Life!" profoundly odd.

It is important to note that these group processes were at work in the actual viewing practices of these young people, in what they conspired to focus on, and where they were disruptive. Most important, these youth tended to engage in off-task activities during narration and quiet dialogue and focus on the film during highly violent or action-filled scenes. These were routinely called "the good parts" and were met with collective focus. Indeed, staying focused on a particular text is a group process and can either facilitate or disrupt the group's resonance with a particular text. For example, there was an intense focus on the last scene in which the Panthers had a gun fight with "Ezel" and his bodyguard Tiny. My young viewers commented, "There go Ezel!" and, during the shooting, "Ezel killing everybody!" to which another young person commented, " 'Cause he got that buff dude named Tiny!" During this scene, "Ezel" got his ear shot off, and this elicited a great deal of laughter. This audience focused carefully on these scenes. There was no effort to disrupt the group process with individual agendas as there was during other scenes. While it is entirely possible that young people, viewing the film by themselves, would also be distracted during scenes that did not feature heavy action, I did, nonetheless, see this group dynamic at work here. The violent scenes very much informed the collective responses to the film, including the kinds of messages they gleaned about the Panthers and how they were connected to a range of popular media forms.

It is significant, then, that these youth tended to look away, talk, or tease each other during scenes that featured heavy talking. These were the "boring parts," during which talk turned to other subjects or there was just general disinterest. This empirical observation is crucial, as many of these scenes established the subtext that the government was complicit in the influx of drugs into black communities as a way to placate the radicalism elicited by the Panthers. Much of the focus on Judge being a double agent was lost, and in later discussion, many expressed confusion about what his role was exactly. The scenes that developed this theme were marked by heavy talking and were, again, all but ignored. Thus, the dialogue that these young people collectively established with each other during the film helped influence the kinds of meanings they took from it and were able to mobilize as a result. By and large, highly stylized violence and conflict were privileged here.

Yet it would be a mistake to assume that the group response to *Panther* was apolitical. This stress on conflict and highly stylized violence was linked in the film to an antipolice community empowerment agenda that was very much a part of the Panther's program as well. Indeed, one of the most dramatic scenes in the film featured Huey Newton confronting the police with a group of Panthers. During this scene, the Panthers come upon a black man being beaten by the police. The Panthers take out their guns—then legally, because they are in plain view—and challenge the police on the abuse. Newton calls them "pigs" and says that he has the right to observe them carrying out their duties from a "reasonable distance." At one point, an officer asks Newton if his gun is loaded. He clicks his gun, putting the shell in the chamber and says, "Now it is!"

Nearly all the young people said that this was their favorite scene. As one member put it, "I liked when he called him 'pig'!" As another young person put it: "I like the part when . . . that man, Huey Newton, start talking to the police and then they start backing down. . . . The police knew that was their right and they couldn't do nothing about it." Still another commented: "I like the part when the cops said, 'Is that gun . . . automatic loaded?' He said 'It wasn't but now it is.'" The young people clearly felt a sense of power during this scene, noting that the police, for a change, were scared of African Americans. The Panthers clearly empowered the community here and gave people the courage to stand up for themselves. Indeed, during this scene, a crowd assembles to watch the Panthers; the police tell them to leave, but Newton says they have the right to stay. As one young person said, "Them other people was scared of the police, but then they told them, not to, uh, they don't have to go nowhere."

Many of these viewers expressed satisfaction when watching this scene. As numerous authors have noted, there is a long history of anger toward police in black neighborhoods (Fine & Weis, 1998). This city is no exception, and many young people have commented that the police exercise their power in arbitrary ways and treat black people differently than they do whites. As one adolescent put it, people get "bullied around by the police and stuff," adding that the police will often speed through his neighborhood past stop signs and red lights.

Similarly, when I asked young people if there were any organizations around that reminded them of the Panthers, most of them responded, "Gangs." The connection seems logical, one enabled by the kinds of messages taken from the film, including the antipolice sentiment, the liberal use of guns, and the more general use of highly stylized violence. There are also important historical connections here as well, as the Panthers were very successful recruiting members of street gangs in the sixties and were even negotiating with the Blackstone Rangers in Chicago to merge the groups. When I commented to an older teen that some of the younger kids were making this connection, he noted: "I kinda see where they coming from . . . 'cause . . . they see the guns . . . and they see most gang members with guns, so therefore it put them in the mind of gangs. And then they got like a little clique and everything like the gang's got."

Panther, in addition, resonated with young people in ways that more traditional documentarylike work did not. For example, we watched the *Eyes on the Prize* television episode that dealt with the Panthers, and it was not very well received. The episode relied on many traditional documentary conventions, including stock footage and long interviews with key figures. There was, of course, no action or violence.

Interestingly, when I asked what they thought about the TV show in comparison to the film *Panther*, one young person commented, paradoxically, that the film was more "realistic" than the documentary, noting that it had more "action." A teen made a similar connection in another context, noting that she liked films such as *Menace* more than television news because such films are more emotionally charged and feature clearer use of narrative:

> The news don't got good stuff in it every day—not saying good stuff like they be killing each other . . . it's the way they portray it. It's the way the message get across. On the news . . . it don't give a lot of details. It just give like the basic outline of what happened, what went on, who died, stuff like that. And then, in the movies, they go to why they got killed, and who killed them, how many times they shot 'em. Then they go when they do it again. Stuff like that.

Narrative conjured up the "real" for these young people, a point underscored by much research in the affective dimensions of language (Besiner, 1990). Similarly, another teen commented that he preferred *Panther* over *Eyes on the Prize* because it was in color. Another noted: "One thing I liked about the movie, you know how Huey was always, he had went to law school, and he was like 'I am 12 [to] 28 feet from you, man, so I can have the right to take my, to have my weapons with me.' . . . He snapped." The drama of this scene was thus favored over and above the more conventional pedagogical narrative of the documentary.

MAKING IT REAL: *PANTHER* AND THE
KU KLUX KLAN IN THIS CITY

In summary, while *Panther* allowed young people to learn something about the Panthers, they did so in specific and highly circumscribed ways, allowing certain meanings while disallowing others. These meaning-making practices had very real consequences for these youth, as evidenced by the ways in which they were able to deal with a proposed march by the Ku Klux Klan (KKK) in town.

During the fall of 1997, the Klan proposed a series of rallies through the state, one of which was to take place in this city. Though the rally never materialized, it raised many concerns and questions nonetheless. In particular, many young people were terrified by the prospect of the Klan coming to town. Many thought they would be targeted with violence. As I noted in the larger project (2001), many young people have complex family histories in the South, and many spoke of Southern racism, particularly as realized in the Klan's violence. A number of younger people felt, in turn, that the Klan was going to come and burn down their homes or attack them physically.

The unit director, Johnny, commented to me one day that "the Klan got these kids scared" and also noted that many parents are not doing a good job "educating" their children about the Klan and letting them know that they are not a real threat. When one young person expressed fear about burning crosses, Johnny commented that the cross is a "symbol" the group uses, just like the Gangster Disciples gang uses a six-point star. Johnny, as director, also made efforts to educate young people about the group and tried to dissipate some of their fears by noting that they had the "right" to march, and even to call black people "niggers" but not to physically assault them. He said he would not be out protesting but would only respond if they came to his neighborhood. Clearly, he sought to demystify the Klan's presence, most especially by invoking the discourse of rights.

This was a familiar discourse for these young people, one that they encountered in school and one they reproduced in their everyday talk. When asked about black history, young people, mirroring the schoollike discourse evoked earlier, tended to stress iconic figures (e.g., King, Harriet Tubman, Rosa Parks, and Frederick Douglass) and "rights." When asked about important events in black history, for example, young people would cite the historical fact of separate schools and water fountains. However, as I will note, the discourse was not mobilized by these young people to deal with this emotionally charged event.

Indeed, the Klan seemed a source of real terror, and many even claimed to have actually seen Klan members in town (though I am doubtful about this). One teen's remarks:

They already here. They was chasing people. They almost got shot up. It was
out at the park. . . . Remember that park we went to last, for the summer pic-
nic? They was down there chasing people. . . . We was driving by, all you see
is people in white sheets.

This knowledge about the Klan was mediated by both popular culture and
interpersonal relationships. For example, young people spoke about the
miniseries *Roots* as well as the movies *Malcolm X* and *Rosewood*, both of
which feature hooded Klansmen, and *Higher Learning* (1995), which features
skinheads (who many felt are essentially the same as the Klan). Many young
people also spoke of their relatives who told them stories about the Klan,
especially in the South where, as many young people noted, the group is still
very active. One stated that his grandfather's friend was killed by the Klan.
These stories became affectively invested—made more real—by way of the
films noted above.

Interestingly, some young people spoke of watching and discussing such
films and TV shows with their relatives. For example, one young person said,
"My grandmom that live upstairs, she got like a *Roots* thing . . . with all the
movies." Another teen said, "My grandmom I asked her . . . I asked her, did
she know about Klan. She was like, 'Yeah,' she said . . . sometime she seen
them on TV." In fact, our discussions prompted others, like this young person,
to further investigate the Klan on their own.

In addition, the racism that the Klan symbolizes was often given a
veneer of invisibility or secrecy by my participants, much as racism seems to
function today. One person commented, "Some places you might see some
white people and then they try to be your friend and then next thing you
know, they be like, 'I'm a Ku Klux Klan.'" Another said, "They ride cars, then
try to act normal, but at night, they just come out." Another commented that
his grandfather, who had some trouble with the Klan, told him to be careful
and that you do not always know who is in the Klan and who is not. In large
measure, for these young people the Klan came to embody racism as a whole,
constituting an ever-present and invisible fear, made real and given voice by
way of this particular event as well as through popular cultural forms and
social networks.

We must now ask how young people dealt with the proposed Klan rally
in town, how they made sense of this event. In large measure, many of these
youth drew on the kinds of highly stylized images of violence and myths of
invulnerability as those realized in the film *Panther*. Young people commented
that they would deal with the Klan in individual ways and with violent force.
During an initial discussion, one young person said, "They come on Johnson
Street, I'm going to war, bring like 40 guns." Another said, "I'm gonna have
knives here, I'ma have guns here, guns here. . . . I'm gonna look like Robocop."
Robocop, a film and TV character who is half-man half-machine/human

arsenal, is violent in the extreme. This same person, interestingly enough, commented: "We need the Panthers! We need some Black Panthers! Really, I need some Black Panthers by my house." Thus, young people indexed the kinds of invulnerability discussed earlier—an invulnerability linked to film, wrestling, Robocop, and, of course, the Black Panthers. While they drew on historical constructs to deal with the march, they were highly circumscribed constructs connected with popular culture.

Yet, while these participants resonated with the violent ganglike aspects of the Panthers, they evidenced a reflective critique of this approach as well. Indeed, we had a very interesting discussion about how the Panthers would deal with the Klan as opposed to how gangs would deal with them, which brought this critique to the forefront. In fact, when I first asked the group what they thought the best response to the Klan would be, many commented that gangs were going to provide the community with protection. There was some talk about how these groups were already planning a response—notably, Black P-Stone (interestingly, the latter-day manifestation of the Blackstone Rangers who were initially going to merge with the Panthers). However, some commented that gangs might not be strategic enough in their response, substituting a wholly violent response for a more measured approach. One said: "Panthers, they handle it a different way. The gangs, they'll just go get guns. . . . Panthers they'll just call a white person a pig or something. 'You pig!' Like they did in the movie." Of course, this young person was referring to the scene, discussed earlier, in which the Panthers confronted the police, who were, for this young person, implicitly connected with the Klan. Another commented that gangs would get high and do a drive-by on the Klan and possibly kill innocent people or one of their "own people." Over all, these young people sought a highly physical response to the Klan but also seemed to be self-conscious about the limits of such an approach. Highlighting youth's perspectives here was key, a point underscored by other recent work on youth and violence (Daiute & Fine, 2003; Mahiri & Conner, 2003).

Thus, the youth at the center were able to use this film to critically examine the Klan's presence as well as what the best response to them might be. Their proposed response was both complex and very different from the response seemingly favored by Johnny, the unit director—education about their right to march while acknowledging the fact that the Klan could not physically attack anyone. The discourse of rights as wholly implicated in traditional notions of schooling was not mobilized here at all. These young people seemed to foreground a physical response mediated by popular culture, though they were critical about its limits. We see a kind of group consciousness emerging here for these young people, one that is enabling and constraining as well as highly situated by and in popular cultural forms.

Conclusions

The group response to the Klan was very much linked to the kinds of popular histories the youth in this study found most compelling. The kinds of historical knowledge offered in school, as noted, did not resonate with these young people as clearly as it might have and was not made use of in this crisis. This kind of knowledge, as noted, tended to be driven by a discourse of icons and rights. Rather, the popular filmic representation of the Black Panthers was mobilized, implicated, as it was, in other popular texts including hip hop culture, film, action heroes, and wrestling. As such, these young people made the kinds of unpredictable links enabled by a black popular culture shot through with multiple coarticulated discourses (Bakhtin, 1986). To echo Della Pollock (1998), these young people "made history go," using popular texts to make history relevant in the here and now and thus transforming history from a noun to a verb.

Yet, I do not want to valorize uncritically what young people were able to "do" with this text. Plainly, an important political subtext was lost as these young people gravitated toward the kinds of knowledges and images that resonated in other popular cultural forms. Moreover, these knowledges and images tended to have distinctly and perhaps stereotypically masculine overtones: recall, the violent and action-filled parts were typically marked as "the best parts." On one level, this reflects the fact that the groups tended to attract more adolescent males than females. On another, it reflects the patriarchal girding of much popular culture (Neal, 2002) as well as some currents of the "Black Power" movement that rose to prominence in the 1960s (Brown, 1993).

Understanding young people's specific investments in these texts, therefore, is not a last step for educators. Rather, it is a first step, a moment to pause and reflect upon the complexity of the dynamics that engulf young people today as they navigate their way through an increasingly complex and unpredictable world. There are plainly roles for adults in traditional school settings, roles honestly and openly engaging the specific contours and dynamics of young people's lives. Such dynamics exceed the explanatory frameworks offered in multiculturalism and take us to the terrain of everyday struggle, a terrain that does not privilege nostalgia and transcendence but the very real and the very immediate. This kind of (I hope) humble, partial, and contingent reflection might allow educators and teachers some break, some crack, some fissure, in our thinking about race and curricula today, in an increasingly routinized and professionalized field, one that would be quite content to banish such reflection *tout court*.

FIFTEEN

The Alchemy of Integrated Spaces

Youth Participation in Research Collectives of Difference

Mariá Elena Torre

IT IS LATE TUESDAY AFTERNOON, 5:30 to be exact, half an hour beyond the paid hours we all agreed to, yet no one looks that anxious to leave. Welcome to the Institute for Arts and Social Justice. In the summer of 2003, researchers at the Graduate Center of the City University of New York brought together a diverse group of young people from 13 to 21—community elders, social scientists, spoken word artists, dancers, choreographers, and a video crew—to collectively pour through data collected from over 9,000 students in high schools across the nation by the Educational Opportunity Gap Project (Fine & Burns, 2003); to learn about the legal, social, and political history of segregation and integration of public schools; and to create *Echoes*, a performance of poetry and movement to contribute to the commemoratory conversation of the 50th anniversary of *Brown versus Board of Education* of Topeka, Kansas. Together we sit as a radically diverse group, intentionally integrated in our efforts to actively respond to the chilling *re*segregation trends within public schools across the nation (Orfield & Lee, 2004). Our bodies have shifted from sitting face forward giving full attention to invited speakers into a loose circle. Some of us are in chairs, others are on the carpeted floor of the dance studio where we have spent the better part of the day. The conversation holding our attention is about the Harvey Milk school, an independent public school for gay, lesbian, bisexual, and transgender youth that recently received money to expand into a full-fledged high school:

> IRALMA: I can understand where they're coming from, but I totally, totally disagree with it. Because I feel like the only way you're gonna learn about our society is if you're around different people. You can't be around the same kind of people and expect to learn about everything and anything. You know what I'm saying? Like you can't be in a school with the same people and expect to have whole different varieties of opinions. . . .
>
> AMIR: Yeah, but when you break someone's spirit, not always will they be able to be strong and be able to get through things. You can really cripple someone like that. I know that being in my school, my grades didn't go up until I started getting into my history, and I actually found, you know, about what made me great. You know what I mean? And I had to go out of school to get that. So we should be integrated, but there's nothing wrong with going somewhere that will teach you about yourself, because you need to get a sense of self-worth.
>
> IRALMA: But if you learn along with someone who's white, then you can educate them about your history, about what makes you great and then they'll appreciate you a lot more. . . .
>
> AMIR: Me and my friends we're in this organization, Messengers of Black Cultural Awareness, that we all put together ourselves, with that purpose. But we all had to go back and get these things on our own, you know, and learn about ourselves, and now we're bringing it to the table, and we're still learning with other people. But at the same time, like I said, I had to go to the black bookstores and talk to black people about our history. You know what I mean? With my own people, and then I can go back out there and share with everyone.
>
> ANNIQUE: I come from a historically black college, basically all black, and I think that can make you stronger, too. I don't think that there's a right or wrong in this situation. I mean, the diversity at Howard is crazy. I mean, first off you have black people from all over the diaspora. You have them from all over the world. So you're gonna have different opinions regardless, 'cause we're all different.
>
> JOANNA: Really if you're talking about learning about yourself, I think that one of the reasons we're so dependent on one another, like as humans, is because we need to learn about the people around us to learn about ourselves. Like, that's necessary. . . . I need to see myself through your eyes and like . . . I don't know, it's just this back and forth thing. I need to learn about you to make myself a better person. I mean, in any

context . . . diversity of thought is just as important as diversity in terms of ethnicity. I mean no matter where you are you are going to be absorbing so much knowledge about the people around you and about yourself.

STEPPING BACK: THE EDUCATIONAL OPPORTUNITY GAP RESEARCH PROJECT

The above conversation took place during the *Echoes* Institute, the fourth in a series of "research camps" and the most recent effort of the Educational Opportunity Gap research project. The two-year project was designed to build a multigenerational, multiple district, urban-suburban database on youth and elders, tracing the history of struggle for desegregation and social science evidence of contemporary educational opportunities and inequities analyzed by race, ethnicity, and class (see Fine, et al., 2004). Over 100 youth from urban and suburban high schools in New York and New Jersey joined researchers from the Graduate Center of the City University of New York in a participatory action research design to study youth perspectives on achievement/opportunity gaps. Students participated in a series of research camps, each held for two days at a time (except for the week-long Institute), in community and university settings, where they were immersed in methods training and learned about interviews, focus groups, survey design, and participant observation, as well as the history of the *Brown* decision, civil rights movements, and struggles for educational justice. Some received high school credits (when a course on participatory research was offered in their schools), and 42 ultimately received college credit for their research work.

Across the research camps we designed a survey, translated it into Spanish, French Creole and Braille and distributed it to 9th and 12th graders in 13 urban and suburban districts. Together, we analyzed the qualitative and quantitative data from 9,174 surveys, 24 focus groups, and 32 individual interviews with youth. Teams of youth and adult researchers crossvisited four urban and suburban schools to document structures, opportunities, and social relations layered through a lens of race/ethnicity.[1] This chapter draws on data collected during the final research camp, from participant observation, pre- and postinterviews with the 13 youth involved in the *Echoes* Institute, and participants' writings.

In the following pages, we will enter into the collaboratively "constructed site" (Weis & Fine, 2000) of the *Echoes* Institute and analyze the experiences of three of its participants, raising for discussion questions of silence and collective voice in integrated spaces, the benefits and necessities of contact across difference (at *and between* the levels of individual, collective, and "space"), and what it means both theoretically and practically to create diverse democratic spaces of inquiry.

As Sonia Sanchez (2003) reminds us, "Integration is not just putting bodies next to each other." We must think seriously about what happens in such spaces. What are the contexts, conditions, and consequences of contact? In 1954, months before the United States Supreme Court decided that separate was not equal in the case of *Brown versus the Board of Education,* Gordon Allport published the ground-breaking text *The Nature of Prejudice,* formalizing for the first time the situational conditions necessary for improving intergroup relations. Inspiring generations of research on intergroup contact, Allport outlined four critical conditions: equal group status within the situation; the presence of a common goal; intergroup cooperation; and the support of authorities, laws, or customs. Allport's original hypothesis was concerned about *when* intergroup contact would lead to positive changes in attitude and behavior and said little, if anything, about the processes—the *how* and *why*—that bring about or sustain the change (Pettigrew, 1998; Fine, Weis & Powell, 1997).

In the years since, researchers have built on the four conditions, demonstrating, for example, that intergroup cooperation is more successful when it is free from competition (Aronson & Patnoe, 1997; Sherif, 1966) and that equal group status is not simply achieved—if desegregated spaces are to thrive, further conditions must be met, including "a sense of community; a commitment to creative analysis of difference, power, and privilege; and an enduring investment in democratic practice" (Fine, Weis & Powell, 1997, p. 249). The collaborative work of the *Echoes* Institute fundamentally embraced the learning of contact theorists from Allport to the present and provides an opportunity to look inside an extended moment of intergroup contact, paying specific attention to process and power.

THEORIZING AN EDUCATIONAL SETTING AS A CONTACT ZONE

The *Echoes* Institute brought an intentionally diverse group of young people together—by gender, race, ethnicity, class, sexuality, (dis)ability, "track"; by experiences with racism, sexism, homophobia, school administrators, social service agencies, "the law"; by (dis)comfort with their bodies, dance, poetry, groups; and so on. Youth interested in writing, performing, and/or social justice were recruited for the project from youth groups and public schools in the greater New York metropolitan area, including northern New Jersey.[2] In doing so, we consciously created what might be called, in the words of Mary Louise Pratt, a "contact zone," a messy social space where differently situated people "meet, clash, and grapple with each other" across their varying relationships to power (Pratt, 1992, p. 4). Conceptualizing our collaborative as a contact zone, both theoretically and methodologically, allows for a more textured analysis across power and difference. More specifically, it creates an opening for an analysis that lingers in the "space between," not only in the borderlands

(Anzaldua, 1987) between differences but also within a constructed space of "difference"; not only in the multiple intersections within the individual but also in the collective; not only in the multiplicity of the collective but also in the collaboratively constructed space itself. Following in the theoretical tradition of Michelle Fine and Lois Weis with conceptual support from Mary Louise Pratt, this chapter asks, Under what conditions can we create zones of contact that move us *Beyond Silenced Voices* and into *Extraordinary Conversations?* And once created, how do differently situated young people experience and negotiate these spaces?

STRUCTURING AN INTEGRATED SETTING
FOR DEMOCRACY AND RADICAL INCLUSIVITY

In conceiving the *Echoes* Institute as a contact zone, an attempt was made to construct a "democratic space of radical inclusivity," a space where

- each participant is understood to be a carrier of knowledge and history,
- everyone holds a sincere commitment to creating change for educational justice,
- power relationships are explicitly addressed within the collaborative,
- disagreements and disjunctures are excavated rather than smoothed over, and
- there is a collective expectation that both individuals and the group are "under construction."

Most significantly, we were organized as a group of adults and youth, intentionally diverse, interested in exploring (not papering over) questions of power and difference, refusing assimilation and consensus, committed to a common goal of understanding, researching, and ultimately performing the legacy of the *Brown* decision.

With this as our foundation, we then designed a week that braided knowledge building, writing and social movements, and dance movement. Youth participated in workshops on the history of *Brown,* civil rights law, the activism of the Young Lords party, and the Opportunity Gap research, all of which provided the group with a common language and knowledge from which to draw, enabling youth to more equally participate. The racial/ethnic and class diversity of our workshop facilitators matched the diversity of our group, and their professional status was recognized, not to reify hierarchy, but to add to the collective potential power of the group. We designed our times together so that youth were learning and creating with resource-filled people dedicated to the collaborative process and the outcomes of the project. We hoped and anticipated that this would reinforce the importance and seriousness in the work, that upon seeing that their efforts had the potential to make a large impact, youth researchers might take risks they may have not otherwise taken.

Analysis

For the purpose of this chapter, I draw on three data sources—participant observation in the camps and institute, individual interviews pre- and post-institute with 13 youth members, and their written drafts of poetry/spoken word. To address the theoretical concerns of *Beyond Silenced Voices*, I have selected material that speaks to the power of integrated educational settings, and analyzed for the following:

- how youth interrogate their *positions* within schools and the larger society (race, ethnicity, class, privilege, and positions of social marginality);
- how youth talk about *silence and speaking out* against injustice;
- how youth find *individual and cultural identities of meaning* within integrated settings; and
- how youth conceptualize *responsibility for social change*, given the evidence of overwhelming injustice within public education.

WELCOME TO THE INSTITUTE: AN INTEGRATED SPACE
FOR EDUCATION, DEMOCRACY, AND CRITICAL INQUIRY

The opening dialogue is an excerpt of what became known as the Harvey Milk conversation, one of the pivotal discussions that took place within the *Echoes* Institute, where participants began to situate themselves, for the first time, in relation to a more complicated understanding of integration. Simple understandings of "we should all be one, together" matured into layered analyses of how "coming together" can be emotionally, physically, and even intellectually costly for some students marked "different" by race/ethnicity, sexuality, and so on, when they are without structural support. The way the conversation unfolded—the engaged and supportive body language, the level of listening and respect demonstrated during potentially tense and difficult moments—made a huge impact on the participants, one that was referred to repeatedly. "The conversation was so thought provoking," Joanna, a white young woman who attends a large, tracked, desegregated, wealthy inner-ring suburban high school, later described it, adding, "We started out facing forward because we were listening to [the presentation] . . . but then we morphed into a circle . . . sharing our different opinions. . . . We didn't really ever come up with a conclusion, but we didn't even need a conclusion." Individual and collective identities shift with bodies and ideas.

The youth participants uniformly described the institute as the most diverse group in terms of race and ethnicity with which they had ever worked. As Tahani, a Palestinian American young woman who attends an integrated small school in Brooklyn, put it, "So many different minds, so many different points of view ... just having so many different people, so many ways of thinking ... it was intense." While we specifically worked to bring together youth with a wide variety of life experiences, we did not realize how unique such a space would be. The postinstitute interviews revealed that the uniqueness of the space was not simply in the level of diversity but also in the way the space was structured. Participants felt a profound level of respect and commitment, in the way their opinions and experiences were equally discussed with those of the workshop presenters, through working side by side with respected artists who shared their desire for social justice and in knowing that their efforts would be presented before local and national audiences. All of these structures translated into a space where youth demonstrated a tremendous dedication to working through a diverse, challenging set of ideas individually and collectively. This dedication was reflected in near perfect attendance, even with several youth working long hours after their 9–5 day at the institute. It should be noted that after the institute, one young person stopped participating, as he was struggling to meet life responsibilities. All of the other youth have remained with the project, some with free and open schedules, others juggling the rehearsals amid afterschool jobs and serving as family translators.

FOR WHOM IS SILENCE A CHOICE?
RELATIONSHIPS TO POWER, THE SILENCE OF PRIVILEGE,
AND THE VULNERABILITY OF PARTICIPATION

Reflecting on the Harvey Milk and other conversations, Elinor, a white young woman who attended a large, tracked, desegregated suburban high school (80 percent white, 18 percent Latino, with most of the whites middle and upper middle class, and the Latinos split between working class and middle class; the school is located in a wealthy, largely white, and elite county) recalled the strong opinions that were aired, describing the conversation as "constructive arguing," and she noted that the level of respect allowed people to build on each other's opinions. Elinor remained silent during the conversation, not feeling comfortable with what she perceived as either side of a binary argument. She said, "I ended up writing about that in a poem, because there were like two distinct sides on it ... school of thought A and school of thought B. ... So I made [laughs] myself a third category in the poem." Elinor went on to elaborate, "My school's integrated, but there's a lot of self-segregation, which, I mean, I don't know, is that unfortunate? Is that the best way for people to handle it?"

Elinor, with the rest of us, came to learn that one of the consequences of contact is that low-power groups often need segregated spaces within larger integrated ones. This was not an easy lesson for some in the institute, particularly the white youth, and some of the white educators, in understanding the simultaneous need for separation and integration. Over time, Elinor came to respect and understand individuals' needs to feel the support of people like them. However, with the same breath, she worries about people feeling "pressured" to only hang out within their own groups. Embedded in her concern is a search for self: if everyone stays within their group, where do those who want to live in the borderlands sit? In carving out a third category, she seeks her own meaningful role, in this case as an ally in the struggle for integration and against racism (Tatum, 1994).

For Elinor, working with the *Echoes* collaborative provided an opportunity to use parts of her identity not often exercised and to think through her relationship to power, the silence of privilege, and the vulnerability of participation. This process was facilitated by regular group conversations, check-ins, poetry read-arounds, and group feedback sessions, in all of which everyone (from youth participants to workshop presenters) had the opportunity to comment and contribute ideas. The layering of these activities across the writing, movement, and research components allowed youth to participate differently in different moments, highlighting alternate parts of their identities as they desired.

> Well, being around a group of people that's like a completely fresh start, like there wasn't . . . I don't know, I didn't feel like I was the kind of quiet sarcastic girl, you know, which comes out more in school. . . . *[laughs]* In the beginning [of the institute], the things I wrote were kind of like humorous, or like they were *[laughs]* surrealist. I guess they were a little more like, safe, but they were also more prosy. . . . And then as the week went on, [I began] writing more in the style of poetry and then writing about choosing to be silent, which was so personal and which is like something that I know a lot of my friends say about me, and I've never been able to defend that much to them. Well, because we don't really talk about it. But I know they think of me as quiet, or as, not necessarily quiet, but not really sharing like really intimate things with them. And to be able to talk about that, and then think about my own school and tracking, was really personal, too. And I don't have too many spaces where I'm really honest about things that are difficult or painful.

She continued this line of inquiry in an early version of one of her poems, where she questions what it means to be silent, examining the power silence can hold when it is chosen. An excerpt of her poem reads:

It doesn't feel good to be silent
Except for when it does.
Can't I be my own best friend?
To keep thoughts and beliefs inside,
Sometimes means more power to me.

I was given two ears and one tongue
Can't I listen more than I speak?
Where is the harm in that?
The "lent" in silent means that I'm
Giving that space back.
To be quiet in public earned me
The title Self-Righteous Ice Queen.

I'm not frozen.
Nothing is as warm as self.

Elinor later joined this poem with another written by Natasha, an African
American young woman who attended an integrated small school in New
York City. Initially grouped together by one of the poet educators because
their individual poems used similar language, Elinor and Natasha used the
writing sessions to make sense of their different experiences and understandings of silence. Each understand silence to be potentially powerful and use the
knowledge embedded in their difference, as well as their writings and relevant
data from the Opportunity Gap study, to ask questions of each other's positions. What is the difference between *being* silenced and *choosing* silence?
When is silence personally powerful for one's own development, and when
does it result in complicity or an absolution of social responsibility? When a
high-powered person chooses silence, is that an active way of providing space
for others to speak? The final version of their collaborative poem ends with:

42% of white American teenagers in public schools speak up
when they hear racist comments. (E)
    Bold (N)
        Decisive (N)
            Be fierce (N)
                Be confident (N)
                    Be honest (both)

But what kind of schools do we have
where 58% of white students don't speak out against hatred? (E)
Being quiet is a strong choice (N)
    —except when it isn't. (E)

Working collaboratively with and through questions of position and privilege (topics she had not considered much before), Elinor analyzes, challenges, and refines her thinking on silence. This was a crucial educational moment—and important for readers to note—about when and how well-resourced students might critically consider the larger arrangements in which they/we sit (see Burns, 2004). At first Elinor looks for safety and comfort in her silence, finding a form of protection in her privilege. This comfort shifts to a more complicated *dis*comfort, however, as she recognizes it is privilege, *her* privilege, that affords this shelter. She carries this dilemma with her throughout her work with the group. It informs both her participation and creation, just as her participation and creation help her clarify her thoughts on the issue. This example illustrates the developmental importance of allowing differences of thoughts and positions to remain "unsolved" and "unfixed" by the group.

THE IRONIES OF FINDING "SELF" WITHIN A DIVERSE COLLECTIVE: CLAIMING/REWRITING ONE'S HISTORY IN AND ALONGSIDE A DIVERSE COLLECTIVE

Amir, an African American young man from a large, tracked high school in a middle-class suburban neighborhood (51 percent African American, 48 percent white, and "a few in between," a school that is heavily tracked for core subject areas so that individual classes are very imbalanced with respect to race/ethnicity), came to the institute after working as a youth researcher with the Educational Opportunity Gap project. As a member of the research team at his high school, he met on an average of twice a month, with myself, another graduate student, and eight of his peers, to research the ways policies such as tracking and discipline were creating different and unequal experiences for students in the school based on race, ethnicity and class. In all the time we met, he kept his "classification" (special education) private. He spoke about being in some level two classes (courses at his school are tracked in four levels, four being the highest) but never mentioned his experiences in special education classes. It was not until he participated in the institute that he "came out" in the Harvey Milk conversation, disclosing for the first time that he was "classified" as "special ed." Sharing his story of educational marginalization, Amir bridged between his experiences in special education and those of gay male students in his own school, who formed their own group in order to support each other through the harassment they face from other students. He spoke of the need for "safe spaces" where individuals can be nurtured while they grow into their intellectual and emotional skins.

I'm not saying that people should be separate, but I do think if you're around people, like if you're ridiculed for something, and get put down for it, [its better to] put yourself around people just like you, [because] they understand exactly where you're coming from. So you can build each other up.

On the final day of the institute Amir brought in a poem that directly addressed his personal experiences, as well as the larger injustice committed against students who are given a "classification." An excerpt from his poem reads:

The classification caused me to break into tears. It was my frustration. My reaction to teachers speaking down to me saying I was classified and it was all my fault.

Had me truly believing that inferiority was my classification. 'Cause I still didn't know, and the pain WAS DEEP. The pain—OH GOD! THE PAIN! The ridicule, the constant taunting, laughing when they passed me by.

Told me that community college should be my goal.

It wasn't until Ms. Cooper came and rescued me with her history class.

Showed me the importance of my history and told me the secrets my ancestors held.

She told me about the Malcolm Xs and the Huey Newtons.

She told me to speak out because this is the story of many and none of them are speaking.

And the silence is just as painful.

With a profound understanding of the scope of the injustice and a sense of responsibility to others in similar situations, Amir decided to use the *Echoes* Institute to speak out.

I was thinking on the way over [to the institute] one day, this thing is dedicated to getting people out of problems. . . . And I thought about how much it hurt me one day when I [realized] how they were—they were honestly segregating special education kids from the rest of the school. Like there was a constant effort to do so. It wasn't . . . that blatant, but that's exactly what they were trying to do. And the pain I felt that day . . . [my friend] Anthony had to calm me down, because I was really angry. It actually brought me to tears. So I'm like, why wouldn't I bring something like that, to the *[Echoes]* group? I felt that I grew close enough to them to tell everyone. . . . Because it's a really dangerous thing. That's why I said [in my poem] that the silence is just as painful, because like no one, honestly, *no one's* speaking about it. And that's what's killing us. And so I wasn't just talking on behalf of me; I was talking on behalf of everybody in it.

In a postinstitute interview, Amir further explained why he chose to expose his personal struggles at the institute rather than before.

> I just saw it as an opportunity, you know? . . . [I]f I get it out here [at the institute], it'll go directly where I want it to go. To the people who are doing it. . . . [I]f I didn't use this [opportunity], it would be foolish of me, it would be stupid, and I couldn't call myself any type of activist or whatever you want to label me.

Amir understands the space of the institute as a supportive collective committed to educational justice (including his personal political agenda) and to working across and through power differences. Amir taught us that an integrated space *cannot* insist on assimilation and that segregation within may be essential to the sustenance of integrated settings. In this instance, Amir recognized that as a member of this collective he can capitalize on the power networks of the higher powered members—the graduate students and faculty that have greater access to foundations, policy makers, and publishers. The diversity of the power relationships within the group enabled Amir to further his political concerns beyond his individual means. Seeing this level of possibility, Amir pushed himself past what was comfortable and took a personal risk within the collective.

> Things in special education, like anything that makes you feel uncomfortable, that makes you feel like you're less . . . has power over you. [It] makes you scared to talk about it, and it's powerful. What I was doing in the poem was reducing what special education was to me. The fact that I could tell somebody I was in it showed that I was actually overcoming it, not just talking about it. Yeah, you know, [it's] like kind of like when someone's really scary, you don't even want to say their name. But once you keep saying their name . . . it shows that you're not really afraid. I felt uncomfortable reading [my poem]. . . . And I still kind of do, whenever I read it. Because it still has a little power over me.

In revealing such a personal struggle and making himself so vulnerable to the group, Amir's risk allows for a poignant moment of learning for other participants. The exchange thus repositions him from a student in need of special tutors to an educator in his own right.

MOVING FROM COMFORT/DENIAL TO CONTACT/RECOGNIZING PRIVILEGE AND ONE'S RESPONSIBILITY TO JUSTICE

In the beginning of the *Echoes* Institute, Joanna, who described herself as "feeling totally comfortable and totally allowed to be myself in every situation" still felt, like many of the participants, a little unsure about her writing. "On Tuesday morning when we had our first read-around, I felt like my piece kind of stuck out as like a kind of la-la fluffy piece. . . . Everyone else's poems were so powerful and kind of hard, like with sharp edges. That night I remember being like so frustrated that I couldn't get any hard edges out of myself to put on paper." However after one of the read-arounds, when one of the spoken word mentors pointed out the value in Joanna's point of view, she began to see her contribution to the whole. "That was like the moment where I realized that I can't doubt my own contribution to the project, because I was contributing a lot and so was everyone else. That all of us together made up the whole thing, not just any person, or any one writing."

On the last day of the institute, a reading of the youth spoken word was held at the Nuyorican Poets Café. Joanna's family came to the performance and later took her out for a celebratory dinner. Part of the ensuing family conversation was a challenge, echoing Amir's concerns, that sometimes integration is implemented on the backs of particular populations. In recalling the discussion, Joanna resists this argument:

> I can't think of it that way, because that's not . . . a constructive way to look at it. It's not like, I'm not . . . we're not sacrificing a certain group of people by keeping ourselves integrated. . . . It's not like minorities are outside looking in or inside looking out at this whole fight for social justice, because we're—what I learned this week, even though I'm not black, or I'm not a minority, racism is still my problem, because it's affecting me. And so it's affecting everybody. So how could it be a sacrifice of just one group of people if we're all in the same situation? . . . [T]hat's the only way we can do this. . . . It really is a together movement.

Refusing a language of sacrifice, she continues, learning from Amir about the importance for people who have been marginalized to "hold on . . . or live in, your amazing culture, and, like Amir did, be so proud of your history, or start a club to find more about your history." But she questions that effort when it takes place in separate spaces. "Removing yourself from like . . . I don't know, I just don't think that's forward thinking, or moving as we need to get to where we want to go."

While Joanna talks about an understanding of one's history and culture as something valuable, there is a sense of this knowledge as something "extra" to pursue, like an extracurricular "club." Amir talks about this knowledge as life sustaining, describing his learning about his history and culture as an essential part of his education. However, for Joanna to share a similar articulation, she would have to sit with what it might mean practically—on emotional, physical, and academic levels—to attend a school that at best ignores, and at worst derogates, her history and culture. While she comes to recognize that racism and inequality negatively impact her even though she is not a person of color, and therefore the struggle to end segregating school policies is hers as well, she slips into a position that shies away from how these policies differentially impact students, based on their race/ethnicity, gender, class, sexuality, and so on.

In the opening conversation, Joanna talks about creating a sense of self through learning about others. She later adds another layer, asking how to understand oneself not only in relation to others but also to injustice. Locating herself within the struggle for social justice was central for Joanna throughout the institute. It is, in part, what informs her resistance to anything but a "together movement." If individuals choose to separate themselves, even for vital reasons, where does that leave the integrated space for which she is fighting? Where does that leave white students from well-resourced communities, like her?

> [I came to the institute] being really accepting of everyone else, and then coming out [at the end], I felt like *I* was really accepted. . . . [T]hrough the week I thought, wow, I'm really lucky that these people are as open as I'm being, because I technically was, like me coming from where I am from, and being [a] white person, could have been . . . strange.

A critical shift for Joanna came when she moved from understanding herself as working for justice *for* others to working *with* others for justice. In an interview, she stated that working with "the most diverse group in terms of ethnicity and 'diversity of thought'" made her "more of a genuine person." For the first time, she had the opportunity to work, fully supported, through complex thinking about integration, privilege, and social movements and to begin to articulate her role and responsibility to the larger struggle for educational equity.

> [W]hen you're all fighting for the same thing, having such different experiences and such different world views, and you're all coming together to work for the same goal. . . . [I]t just adds . . . so many different levels. [You] ask more questions and come up with more solutions when you're coming from different experiences.

The Promise of Racially Inclusive Educational Spaces for Intellectual and Social Development

With the institute and the creation of *Echoes*, we witnessed the enormous potential of democratic spaces of radical inclusivity. Employing and building on Allport's original four conditions, and paying strict attention to power and process, a space was produced that set the stage for young people to come together across difference with adults, artists, and academics; to actively interrogate and engage power relationships; and to collaboratively work through diverse ideas and experiences of educational (in)equities with the aim of creating a performance of art and social justice for the anniversary of *Brown versus Board of Education*. We saw that when the cooperatively strived for "common goal" is a matter of justice and equality, a profound level of respect and commitment is engendered among the group, which then translates into high levels of individual and collective engagement—critical listening, learning, imagining, and creating. And when differences and power are explored, rather than ignored, individual identities can flourish alongside collective identities.

As witnessed in Elinor, Amir, and Joanna, youth pushed beyond that which felt comfortable, inhabiting parts of their selves different than those used in their everyday lives. In engaging in this more individualized activity of identity play, youth in turn set off actions and reactions within the collaborative, challenging others to push their own "selves," evoking new thinking on both the individual and the collective levels. Youth were able to try out new political positions, for example, and, in doing so, prompt others to clarify their own thoughts on the topic as they worked their ideas through, positioning and repositioning themselves. The interactive and improvisational dimensions of the space not only served to collaboratively create new subjectivities ("I'll never be the same after this experience") but also to produce new knowledge that each subject, as a situated individual, would not likely come to on her or his own. This new knowledge was then woven into the larger political agenda of the collective, broadening the depth of the inquiry and expanding the breath of the *Echoes* performance. Within the institute, an infectious energy was witnessed, the kind that accompanies the experience of having one's ideas, creativity, and capacity not only taken seriously, but respectfully challenged, stimulated, and encouraged. Beyond working within a movement with a deep sense of purpose, the youth were working as leaders and inventors. Over the course of *Echoes* rehearsals after the institute was over, we heard youth yearn for the creation of similar spaces in their lives, where constructive power negotiations, trust, and the struggle for social justice are given places where their selves, passion, and ideas can continue to grow.

While the *Echoes* Institute took place outside of schools, the promise of such spaces should inspire our continued efforts to dismantle segregating policies and maintain the precious few integrated spaces remaining in public schools. At a time when integrated schools are in jeopardy (Orfield, 2001; Frakenberg & Lee, 2002), the experiences of these youth underscore the necessity of these schools for realizing the democratic promises of public education for *all students*—for youth of privilege and poverty, of European, Asian/Pacific Island, African, Central/South American, and mixed decent. The loss of these schools, the withdrawal from desegregation decrees that

Orfield and Lee detail, is not simply a matter of a retreat to segregationist politics and educational inequity, but a loss of academic and intellectual growth for us all.

The youth in the institute demonstrate well the possibilities within radically inclusive spaces for intellectual and social development. The development of new ways of thinking and being in the world; of new subjectivities, subjectivities that having experienced the intoxicating intellectual, social, and political potential of such spaces desire more. Whether or not Elinor, Amir, and Joanna continue to collaborate, they will bring their new ideas, understandings of self, others, and the promise of diverse collectives into whatever they do next. They are part of a growing community of researchers, artists, and activists that has expectations of a world that understands the profound importance of equal opportunities and resources for all people. Emily, a young Latina, who started her first year of college after the institute, eloquently describes how she realized that she was now part of such a community, during the last writing assignment of the institute:

> [E]veryone was really quiet and everyone was really thinking. I thought it was so cool to sit and hear the scratching of other pens and pencils besides my own. I thought that my pen was the only one moving to the rhythm of social justice. But now it's defiantly apparent that other pens and pencils are listening to the same beat.

Notes

CHAPTER 1

Some of the information in this section is based on Orfield & Lee, 2004.

1. For a full discussion of the consequences of segregation, see table 6.

2. Our definition of the regions is as follows: *South:* Alabama, Arkansas, Florida, Georgia, Louisiana, Mississippi, North Carolina, South Carolina, Tennessee, Texas, and Virginia; *Border:* Delaware, Kentucky, Maryland, Missouri, Oklahoma, and West Virginia; *Northeast:* Connecticut, Maine, Massachusetts, New Hampshire, New Jersey, New York, Pennsylvania, Rhode Island, and Vermont; *Midwest:* Illinois, Indiana, Iowa, Kansas, Michigan, Minnesota, Nebraska, North Dakota, Ohio, South Dakota, and Wisconsin; *West:* Arizona, California, Colorado, Montana, Nevada, New Mexico, Oregon, Utah, Washington, and Wyoming. Note: Hawaii and Alaska, which have very distinctive populations, are treated separately, and the District of Columbia is treated as a city rather than a state.

3. For the rest of the chapter, the term *segregation* is used to describe the degree to which students of different racial groups attend separate schools.

4. Although the Census instituted multiracial categories in 2000, school statistics to this point use mutually exclusive categories as reported from the school level

5. Central cities in the NECMA are cities that categorized as central cities of a Metropolitan Statistical Area or a Consolidated Metropolitan Statistical Area.

6. Central cities that lie within Route 495 are considered inner satellite cities; those that lie without, outer satellite cities.

7. U.S. Department of Commerce, Bureau of the Census.

8. The Sunbelt includes the southern states, California, Arizona, Colorado, and Nevada.

9. Los Angeles, whose school district, the nation's second largest, was the first major city to abandon its busing plan after a state referendum, Proposition 1, was enacted in 1981, after busing opponents promised that the proposition would bring back whites. The system has less than one tenth white students.

10. These numbers include the schools in reservations reported by the Bureau of Indian Affairs where all students are tribal members.

11. Balfanz and Legters found that cities with high dropout rates also had high poverty rates. See Balfanz & Legters, 2001. See also Schofield, 1995; Natriello, McDill, & Pallas, 1990.

12. In Georgia, Freeman, Scafidi, and Sjoqist found that teachers who transferred moved to schools with higher student achievement and fewer minority and poor students. See Freeman, Scafidi, & Sjoqust, 2002; Anyon, 1997; Dawkins & Braddock, 1994.

13. See Eaton, 2001. In this study, Eaton documents the experiences of scores of Boston students who had access to the white suburban public schools and the powerful impact this has had in their adult lives. See also Wells & Crain, 1994.

14. *The Impact of Racial and Ethnic Diversity on Educational Outcomes: Cambridge, MA School District,* Civil Rights Project, Harvard University, January 2002.

15. In *Milliken v. Bradley,* 418 U.S. 717 (1974), the Supreme Court ruled against desegregation across city-suburban lines, exempting majority white suburbs from the desegregation effort outside the South.

16. Because Native Americans are not present in the Boston metropolitan area in enough numbers for an accurate portrayal of the demographic changes, they are not included in the analysis and discussion.

17. 1989 was the earliest year in which enrollment data disaggregated by race and by grade was available.

18. For the most part, the suburbs are small and predominantly white. The 20 largest suburbs are still more than 80 percent white and except for Newton, enroll less than 10,000 students. Framingham, Quincy, Brookline, Revere, and Salem are suburbs where at least 30 percent of the student body is nonwhite.

19. Stuart found that to in order to achieve racial and ethnic integration, more than half of the minority homebuyers would have had to have purchased a home in a different city from 1993 through 1998.

20. Throughout the study, we use the term *intensely segregated white* for schools where at least 90 percent of the student body is white.

21. The problem is compounded by the fact that about half of Boston's white students attend private schools so that the white share of enrollment (14 percent) is smaller than their proportion of the under-18 population of 25 percent (Logan, 2003).

22. Throughout the study, we use the term *intensely segregated minority* for those schools where at least 90 percent of the student body is minority.

23. The overenrollment of white students in private schools in metropolitan areas such as Boston also contributes to the segregation of minority students in the public schools (Logan, 2003; Reardon & Yun, 2002).

24. Poverty levels are measured by the percentage of students on free and reduced lunch.

25. See discussion on poverty rates and segregation levels, above.

26. Predominantly white schools are schools where at least 90 percent of the students are white. See Frankenberg, Lee & Orfield, 2003.

27. See Table 9 in Frankenberg, Lee & Orfield, 2003.

28. For the purposes of this study, low-minority and low-poverty schools are schools with less than 10 percent minority students and where less than 10 percent of the students are on free and reduced lunch.

29. The federal desegregation aid program, the Emergency School Aid Act, was enacted in 1972 and signed by President Richard Nixon. For a legislative history of the act see Orfield, 1975, pp. 173–88. The program survived until 1981, when it was eliminated in the first major legislation of President Ronald Reagan's administration, the Omnibus Budget Reconciliation Act.

CHAPTER 2

The research reported in this chapter was supported with a generous grant from the Ford Foundation. For such support we are extremely grateful, but note that the views expressed herein are not necessarily those of anyone other than the authors. This chapter summarizes findings from a longer research report on the education pipeline study, which can be found, along with the data files used in the study, at the National Board on Educational Testing and Public Policy website at www.bc.edu/nbetpp.

1. See our full report *The Education Pipeline in the United States, 1970–2000* (Haney, et al., 2004) and in Miao (forthcoming). Alternative methods for calculating graduation rates are explored and discussed in detail. Based on these comparisons we have concluded that the simple Grade 8 to graduation and Grade 9 to graduation approaches afford straightforward and consistent ways of examining changes in the education pipeline and yield results consistent with more complex methods.

2. This discussion is based on National Vital Statistics Reports Volume 50, No. 15, September 16, 2002 Death: Final Report for 2000. Available at http://www.cdc.gov/nchs/products/pubs/pubd/nvsr/50/50-16.htm#currentpro.

3. NCES, Digest of Education Statistics 2002, Table 59, p. 71.

4. http://www.hslda.org/research/faq.asp#1, accessed November 14, 2003.

5. A transcript of the *60 Minutes II* broadcast "Texas Miracle" is available at http://www.cbsnews.com/sections/60II/main3475.shtml. Last retrieved January 11, 2004.

6. Haney (2001) discusses recent evidence indicating that in terms of employment opportunities, recipients of GED high school "equivalency" diplomas are more like high school dropouts than like high school graduates.

CHAPTER 3

1. The research team was led by Jeannie Oakes and Amy Stuart Wells. Research associates included Robert Cooper, Amanda Datnow, Diane Hirshberg, Karen Ray, Irene Serna, Estella Williams, and Susan S. Yonezawa.

2. We analyzed our data in two main ways. First we used the interview and observation data to construct a case report documenting the reform elements and development for each school site. We used these case reports to glean common themes across the 10 sites. We then returned to individual interviews and observations to pursue further themes that were salient across sites and recode the data for these salient themes.

3. Habitus is a continuously evolving construct that is nondeterministic but also cumulative, bearing the weight of one's previous experiences and interactions (Harker, 1984).

4. *False authenticity* is a term coined by bell hooks to describe the efforts of some black women to "essentialize" black identity and measure a person's "blackness" by the actions and racial associations he or she maintains. This effort is criticized by hooks for its unrealistic expectations given that many black women must engage in white communities to further their work and critically interrogate white racism in multiple contexts.

CHAPTER 4

Support for the research in this chapter came from the Spencer Foundation and the Rockefeller Foundation.

1. All names, of both schools and students, are pseudonyms.

2. The students in this study, therefore, sit at the intersection of race and class, a not-unusual situation in this country, where race too often overpredicts class. In this chapter, I do not attempt to separate out these "variables" but instead to understand the structural effects of sitting at this junction. (For more on this, see MacLeod, 1995.)

3. This is particularly noteworthy given research on SES and college application: Carnevale and Rose (2003) found an inverse relationship between the percentage of students receiving free lunch at a school and the percentage who take college entrance exams and, similarly, a study conducted by MPR Associates for the Education Department in 1997 (using data from the NELS-88) suggest that across the country, many needy students who are qualified for college do not bother to take college entrance exams or fill out applications (Burd, 2002).

4. Median annual earnings for workers aged 25 and over. U.S. Bureau of the Census. March 2001.

5. Particularly, Title IV of the act established three kinds of student assistance: direct "Educational Opportunity Grants" (EOG) to the neediest students, federally guaranteed loans to a range of students, and work-study aid (Mumpers, 1996, p. 78).

6. While college prices have risen astronomically, the size of the average grant has dropped by more than $400 between 1975 and 1993, and the size of the maximum grant (awarded to the most needy students) has declined by almost one third since 1970 (Mumpers, 1996, p. 57).

7. Data from 1975 from Mortenson (1990b). Data from 1988 and 2001 from L. Gladieux, "Low Income Students and the Affordability of Higher Education," in R. Kalenberg, ed., *America's Untapped Resource: Low Income Students in Higher Education* (New York: Century Foundation). While Mortenson states that in 1988, only 30 percent of student aid was made up of grants, Gladieux uses a higher figure, based on data from "Trends in Student Aid 2001," the College Board. I have chosen to use Gladieux's figures here because his data is more recent. Also, these columns do not add up to 100 percent, because of various other federal programs that account for some percentage of aid, such as veterans benefits.

8. Greg Forester, a researcher at the Manhattan Institute, recently commented, "Lack of financial resources is not preventing a substantial number of students from going to college. I'm not disputing that there are barriers to going to college, but they're not financial" (Cavanagh, 2004).

9. For a further discussion of the importance of students' "choice contexts" and the effects of these contexts on students' perceptions of their educational opportunities, see M. Paulsen and E. St. John (2002) "Social Class and College Costs: Examining the Nexus Between College Choice and Persistence," *The Journal of Higher Education, 73*(2).

10. Campaigne & Hossler, 1998, p. 89.

11. Winter, 2003.

12. Mumpers calculates, "The student who borrows the maximum Stafford loan amount for each of his or her four years of college will have borrowed $18,000 when they graduate. When the loan is finally paid off, he or she will have repaid more than $27,000" (1996, p. 131).

13. As reported in a study by the National Center for Public Policy and Higher Education.

14. From the U.S. Census Bureau Current Population Survey (March, 2000). *Income in 1999 by Educational Attainment for People 18 Years Old and Over, by Age, Sex, Race, and Hispanic Origin* (Table 8).

15. Likewise, Kern (2000) estimates that the labor market requires only 27 percent of workers to have 16 or more years of education, another 26 percent to have 8 to 10 years plus additional on-the-job training, and the rest to have less education.

16. Saquina did eventually make it up to Wheaton to visit for the day, but, alone on a tour during exam week, with no one there to welcome her, it was not what she had been expecting. Here was college, finally, her college, only it resembled no *Friends* episode she had ever seen.

17. Mark Dudzic and Adolph Reed Jr. make the same suggestion in "Free Higher Ed!" *The Nation,* February 23, 2004.

18. The College Opportunity and Career Help (COACH) program in Boston, founded by economist Thomas Kane, is an interesting example of a community-based program that specifically helps students with financial aid.

19. See McDonough (1997) for more on the impact of intensive college preparation programs, in private Catholic schools, that have great success in getting low-income students to college.

CHAPTER 5

This chapter is based on a talk that the author gave at the University of Texas at Austin on February 25, 1998. The presentation was sponsored by the Center for Mexican American Studies and the Department of Curriculum and Instruction. It originally appeared as Angela Valenzuela, "Subtractive Schooling: U.S.–Mexican Youth and the Politics of Caring," *Reflexiones 1998: New Directions in Mexican American Studies* (Austin: Center for Mexican American Studies, University of Texas).

1. All names used herein are pseudonyms.

2. I use the term *Mexican,* a common self-referent, to refer to all persons of Mexican heritage when no distinction based on nativity or heritage is necessary.

3. My extensive observations of Seguín's CTE program have led me to conclude that the acquisition of work skills is compatible with students' college-going aspirations because it reinforces the academic curriculum. The CTE program is effective because the teachers enjoy higher salaries, small class sizes, access to career counselors, and, in the higher level courses, the ability to select their students.

4. I administered a questionnaire to all 3,000 students in November 1992. It included questions about students' family background, English and Spanish language ability, generational status, school climate, teacher caring, and academic achievement. With a 75 percent response rate, a sample of 2,281 students for analysis resulted.

5. My study adopts a conventional generational schema. First-generation students were, along with their parents, born in Mexico. Second-generation students were born in the United States but had parents born in Mexico. Students were classified as third generation if they and their parents were born in the United States. I use the self-referent *Mexican American* and the term *U.S.-born* to refer to second- and third-generation persons. (Fourth-generation youth [i.e., those whose parents and grandparents were born in the United States] were combined with third-generation youth because of their resemblance in both the quantitative and qualitative analyses.)

6. The comparable figures for Mexicans in California and the nation are 11.1 and 10.4 years of schooling completed and dropout rates of 39 and 48 percent, respectively. Mexicans from Texas are thus faring even more poorly than their underachieving counterparts nationwide (Chapa 1988).

7. The Texas Bilingual Education Code (Sec. 29.051 State Policy) rejects bilingualism as a goal: "English is the basic language of this state. Public schools are responsible for providing a full opportunity for all students to become competent in speaking, reading, writing, and comprehending the English language."

CHAPTER 6

Editor's Note: George W. Smith died of AIDS in November 1994. I, Dorothy E. Smith, have completed and edited this version of an unfinished chapter from a number of versions he left. I have not always been clear which he saw as his most complete, particularly as his energies faded in the last months of his life. I have been helped in the decisions I made by friends who have read and commented on various of my own versions. My deep appreciations go to Gary Kinsman, Liza McCoy, Eric Mykhalovskiy, and Lorna Weir. Steven Seidman's comments were also very helpful. This work is taken from: G. W. Smith (1998). The ideology of "fag": The school experience of gay students. *The Sociological Quarterly, 39*(2).

CHAPTER 8

1. I use the term *America* to refer to the United States because it is the term used by my informants.

2. Because the school district lumped all students of Asian descent into one category it was not possible to obtain an exact count of Hmong American students.

CHAPTER 9

1. See Brown, 1998, for a full explication of this analysis and the girls' relational and social contexts.

2. Fine, Weis, Powell, & Wong, 1997; Wray & Newitz, 1997. Although I did not directly ask about race—and because all the girls are white, and whiteness is the unmarked norm, they do not offer their views about race spontaneously—I look to the girls' class-related struggles with identity, their relationship to power and privilege, their constructions of otherness, and their views of the normal and acceptable to reveal their cultural and racial positioning.

3. Here I draw from Paul Willis' (1977/1981) analysis of working-class boys' school experiences in Britain for this interpretation. While there are a great many differences between these girls and his "lads," I find most helpful Willis' emphasis on the cultural tension between school ideology and the boys' lives and his exploration of the processes by which the boys' active opposition to school authorities serves to reproduce their working-class standing.

4. While here I draw here on Wendy Luttrell's (1993) perceptive analysis of the meaning of teacher's pets for working-class, white and black women recalling their school experiences, it is interesting to note that such distinctions are made by the middle-class and not the working-class girls.

5. See Brown & Gilligan, 1992, for a description of this move and its consequences.

6. As I have shown, the Mansfield girls also practice such gestures and voices, but they do so more playfully; perfecting such personas is serious business for the Acadia girls—a way to assure their protection and secure their place in white, middle-class culture.

7. "Cultural capital," a phrase made popular by French sociologist Pierre Bourdieu (1984) and used by critical or resistance theorists in education, "refers to the general cultural background, knowledge, disposition, and skills that are passed on from one generation to another. Cultural capital represents ways of talking, acting, and socializing, as well as language practices, values, and styles of dress and behavior" (McLaren, 1989, pp. 197–98).

8. Angela McRobbie (1991) also reports that friendships and supportive networks provide such a role for working-class girls in Britain.

9. Donna Eder, 1995, makes this point in her book, *School Talk*.

CHAPTER 10

The research for this chapter was supported by grants from the Spencer Foundation, the National Science Foundation/American Sociological Association Fund for the Advancement of the Discipline, and the University of Michigan Institute for Research on Women and Gender.

1. In the same way that the culture of femininity is not consistent across racial and social class groups, the culture of femininity, even when culturally specific, is not consistent across historical time. To take one case example, there is evidence that since the 1960s, political and labor market shifts have enabled women to increasingly emphasize their worker over their care-taking identities (Weis, 1988). Weis specifically showed that the girls in her study "were not living to get married and none of them placed home/family relationship before wage-labor work" (p. 195). Rather, they were "attempting to control the conditions of their own lives in a way that previous generations of women did not" (Weis, p. 197). Weis eventually shows that this change is fundamentally contradictory because the girls desire secretarial and clerical jobs that "do not usually pay enough to allow women to exist outside the bounds of marriage though their wage labor orientation is directed towards the possibility of this end." Despite this contradiction, her work confirmed that the culture of femininity was not a static phenomenon.

2. The findings of this larger investigation have been otherwise documented in O'Connor (2002).

3. The cohorts were determined a priori to reflect often-recognized shifts in America's opportunity structure. Focused expressly on the experiences of African Americans in the North, Cohort I, the precivil rights era cohort, signals a period in which the economic, political, and educational disenfranchisement of African Americans not only was unabashedly practiced in the North but also had increased from the previous generation as a consequence of the white hostility and hysteria that arose in response to the Great Migration (Morris, 1984; Browning, Marshall, & Tabb, 1990). Compared to the previous generation, then, students experienced more blatant racial hostility and exclusion in northern schools, which in turn diminished the

already narrow possibility that they would attend college (Spear, 1967; Grossman, 1989; Marks, 1989; Lemann, 1991; Massey & Denton, 1993; Mirel, 1993; Donato, 1999; Walker, 2000).

Cohort II, the postcivil rights era cohort, signals the expansion of opportunity, including educational opportunity, for African Americans and other marginalized populations. As a consequence of political activism and other social movements, African Americans during this period increasingly received legal protections against overt discrimination both within and outside of schools (e.g., via the *Brown v. Board of Education* decisions, the Civil Rights Act, the Voting Rights Act). Other legislative and social initiatives created institutionalized mechanisms for redressing the historical marginalization of those who were female and poor, with many of these initiatives being targeted toward increasing educational opportunity (e.g., the passage of Title IX; the development and/or expansion of Head Start, Job Corps, and adult education programs; the institutionalization of affirmative action via federal policy and private initiatives; the generation of need-based government grants, low-interest loans, and work study for attending college) (Browning, Marshall, & Tabb, 1990; Morris, 1984; Nettles, 1988; Lemann, 1991). In accordance with this expansion in educational opportunity there was a concomitant rise in the educational attainment of African Americans, particularly African American women.

Cohort III, the post-Reagan era cohort, subsequently marks the rising tide of systematic efforts to roll back the gains of the civil rights era. In this era, we have witnessed the retrenchment of social programs, "the attack on the welfare state" (Block, Cloward, Ehrenreich, & Piven, 1987), the legal and public assault against race-based affirmative action (Bowen & Bock, 1998), the "quiet reversal of Brown v. Board of Education" (Orfield & Eaton, 1996), and a drop in need-blind admissions policies. The members of this cohort who resided in urban contexts also faced the economic brunt of deindustrialization, white flight, and the outmigration of industry to the west, sunbelt, and overseas (Wilson, 1987; Farley, Danziger, & Holzer, 2000). Northern urban schools consequently suffered under a shrinking property tax base (Kozol, 1991) and a concomitant and growing emphasis on comprehensive education programs that watered down the academic offerings for what was now in many instances a predominantly minority student body. See O'Connor (2002) for a discussion of how women's enrollment and achievement in school coincided with these eras.

4. The Alumni Association (BAA) at Midwest University served as my conduit to project participants who came of age in each of the aforementioned age cohorts. More specifically, BAA's mailing list constituted my sample of prospective respondents, and, on my behalf, the BAA office mailed letters requesting participation in the study to women members of BAA who graduated from MU during the specified age cohorts. Of the 31 women who responded to the mailing and met my criteria for inclusion in the study (i.e., they had graduated from college and were first-generation college graduates), 5 indicated that they were unwilling to participate in the study. We were able to schedule interviews with 23 (5 in Cohort I, 9 in Cohort II, and 9 in Cohort III) of these 26 women (7 in Cohort I, 9 in Cohort II, and 10 in Cohort III).

In one instance, we began but were unable to complete our interview with the respondent due to the hectic nature of her family and professional life. In two instances, the respondents did not allow us to tape-record the interview and the hand-recorded data was not comparable in content and depth to the tape-recorded data. In one instance, the interview could not be transcribed because the audiotape of the interview was highly inaudible due to difficulties that arose with the recording equipment. The 19 women featured in this chapter, therefore, represent those respondents with whom interviews were completed, tape-recorded, and transcribed (5 in Cohort I, 7 in Cohort II, 7 in Cohort III).

5. An initial interview was conducted with each respondent. This first interview captured the women's identities as students and their experiences with education. We were especially interested in examining how these identities and experiences were shaped by (1) the role and functioning of family members and adult significant others (including teachers); (2) peer relationships and other social networks; (3) the neighborhood contexts in which they grew up; (4) the primary and secondary schools they attended; (5) the role of institutions outside of the family and school (e.g. church, community organizations); (6) the process by which they came to access and graduate from college; (7) critical events, whether personal, social, or historical, that demarcated turning points and/or opportunities; and (8) how race, class, and gender operated in their "everyday" as well as within the greater social context.

After each initial interview was completed, transcribed, and reviewed, a second (and in some instances a third follow-up) interview was conducted in order to have the respondent clarify and elaborate upon issues raised in the initial interview. These follow-up interviews also provided an opportunity for the respondents to offer any additional insights into their life history that might be relevant for understanding their educational achievement and attainment.

Each respondent was interviewed in a location that was most convenient for her. In most instances, interviews were conducted in the respondent's home. However, some respondents opted to have the interview conducted at their workplace. There were also individual cases in which interviews were conducted in the respondent's motor vehicle, the interviewer's home, and an office on a local college campus. Initial interviews ranged from 1 hour to 3.5 hours in length with a mean of 1.5 hours. Follow-up interviews ranged from 20 minutes to 1.5 hours in length with a mean of 45 minutes. There were a total of four interviewers, all of whom were African American women (including the principle investigator). In most instances, the same interviewer conducted both the initial and follow-up interview(s). However, due to shifts in personnel, there were three instances in which the respondent was interviewed by two different individuals.

6. For an empirical elaboration of how the physical requirements of femininity informed the development of social capital, which could be activated to facilitate knowledge of the college admissions process, see O'Connor (2002).

7. One member of Cohort I did indicate that her mother and aunts had encouraged her to keep her funds "separate" from those of the man in her life. She did not, however, report that they had associated the accrual of these funds with acquiring high levels of education.

8. See O'Connor (2002) for a discussion of how Cohort III employed their voice and power through their participation in political activities aimed at improving the campus racial climate. These efforts did not, however, have a direct impact on their individual educational experiences and personal educational outcomes.

9. See O'Connor (2002) for a discussion of how this orientation toward conflict was also articulated in social protest.

CHAPTER 11

1. For a fuller discussion, please see Kim & Markus, 2002.

CHAPTER 12

1. Although this group was formed as an Arab American youth alliance, the Arab population in the school is majority Palestinian, and it is these youth who have, to date, gravitated to the meetings.

2. All names and identifying features of individuals and schools have been changed to protect the confidentiality of those involved in this study. Students chose their own pseudonyms.

3. This research was supported by a National Academy of Education/ Spencer Foundation Postdoctoral Fellowship.

4. A *hijab* is the scarf with which some Muslim girls and women cover their hair.

5. Ladson-Billings (2004) notes the ways that notions of citizenship for African American youth are mediated through their cultural identities. Palestinian American citizenship identities can be viewed as similarly negotiated.

6. In her study of British Sikh youth, Hall makes the interesting point that the young people describe themselves as caught between two distinct cultures, even as they produce new "cultural orientations and identifications" (2002, p. 11).

7. Parents and students from the community, however, were quite clear in labeling this and a reported 11 other recent disciplinary transfers of Arab students as blatant acts of racism. One of the consequences of not categorizing Arabs as a racial/ethnic minority is that the district does not collect disciplinary data in a way that would make it possible to track discriminatory practices against Arab students.

8. At the recent annual meetings of the American Educational Research Association (AERA), a participant from New Mexico told a chilling story of several teachers who were suspended from their jobs for addressing the war on Iraq in their curriculum. This was one of several reports from across the nation of punitive measures taken against educators who were teaching for peace and justice.

9. It is important to remember that this push for displays of patriotism is also deeply affecting teachers. One of the teachers in this study—a member of a pacifist religious group that refuses to take any oaths—was warned by her principal that her

colleagues were complaining that she was undermining their efforts to make students stand for the pledge. This teacher also reported having to attend a mandatory faculty in-service workshop and luncheon sponsored by the U.S. Army to inform teachers about how they might help recruit students for military service.

10. This research makes visible the ways that food and dance are not simple cultural markers but also offer terrain for political conflict. Palestinian students danced not just to represent their culture but as a symbol of the nation. Further, part of the conflict with the students at the Israel table during the multicultural fair was over food. Palestinian students took issue with presenting hummous and falafel as Israeli, not Arab, cuisine.

11. "Ahlo" literally means family. Gharib used the Arabic word for Arabs *(arab)*.

12. It is also true that contemporary politics in the United States embodied in the U.S. Patriot Act, detentions and deportations make speaking out riskier terrain. This fear is especially felt by adults, more aware of the ramifications for their families and communities.

CHAPTER 14

An earlier version of this chapter appeared in *Theory & Research in Social Education, 28*(1), 38–62.

CHAPTER 15

1. Youth researchers took up (and published) research studies of finance inequity, tracking, community-based organizing for quality education, and the unprecedented success of the small schools movement. See http://www.thebrooklynrail.org/poetry/fall02/moneyfornothing.html; http://www.rethinkingschools.org/archive/18_01/ineq181.shtml.

2. Out if the 13 that applied, all but 1 were accepted. Three young women applied from the same school. In our attempt to create as diverse a group as possible, we decided not to have more than 2 students from the same school.

References

Adelman, C. (2002). The relationship between urbanicity and educational outcomes. In W. Tierney & L. Hagedorn (Eds.), *Increasing access to college: Extending possibilities to all students*. Albany, NY: State University of New York Press.

Allport, G. W. (1954). *The nature of prejudice*. New York: Addison-Wesley.

Alpfelbaum, E. (1979). Relations of domination and movements for liberation: An analysis of power between groups. In W. G. Austin & S. Worchel (Eds.), *The social psychology of intergroup relations*. Belmont, CA: Wadsworth.

American Association of University Women & Greenberg Lake the Analysis Group. (1991). *Shortchanging girls, shortchanging America. A nationwide poll to assess self esteem, educational experiences, interest in math and science, and career aspirations of girls and boys ages 9–15*. Washington, D.C.: American Association of University Women.

Anyon, J. (1997). *Ghetto schooling: A political economy of urban educational reform*. New York: Teachers College.

Anzaldúa, G. (1987). *Borderlands/La frontera: The New Meztiza*. San Francisco: Aunte Lute.

Apple, M. (1979). *Ideology and curriculum*. London: Routledge & Kegan Paul.

Apple, M. (2001). *Educating the "right" way: Markets, standards, God, and inequality*. New York: RoutledgeFalmer.

Aronson, E., & Patnoe, S. (1997). *The jigsaw classroom*. New York: Longman.

Associated Press. (2003, September 10). *Are Texas schools nudging out low performing students?* Available on-line at http://www.khou.com/news/local/education/stories/khou030905_mh_dropouts.77b521f2.html [Retrieved September 16, 2003].

Au, K., & Jordan, C. (1981). Teaching reading to Hawaiian children: Finding a culturally appropriate solution. In H. Trueba, G. Guthrie, & K. Au (Eds.), *Culture in the bilingual classroom: Studies in classroom ethnography* (pp. 139–152). Rowley, MA: Newberry House.

Austin, J. L. (1962). *How to think with words*. Oxford: Oxford University Press.

Ayres, L. P. (1909). *Laggards in our schools: A study of retardation and elimination in city school systems*. New York: Charities Publication Committee.

Azuma, H. (1994). *Japanese discipline and education*. Tokyo: Tokyo University Press.

Backlund, P. (1990). Oral activities in the English classroom. In S. Hynds & D. Rubin (Eds.), *Perspectives on talk and learning*. Urbana, IL: National Council of Teachers of English.

Bainbridge, W. L. (2003, April 16). Texas model for school achievement doesn't hold up. *Columbus Dispatch*.

Bakhtin, M. M. (1981). *The dialogic imagination: Four essays* (Edited by M. Holquist). Austin, TX: University of Texas Press.

Bakhtin, M. M. (1986). *Speech genres and other late essays* (V. W. McGee, Trans.). Austin, TX: University of Texas Press.

Balfanz, R., & Letgers, N. (2001, January 13). *How many central city high schools have a severe dropout problem, where are they located and who attends them?* Paper presented at the "Dropout Research: Accurate Counts and Positive Interventions" Conference Sponsored by Achieve and the Harvard Civil Rights Project, Cambridge, MA.

Banks, J. A. (1997). *Teaching strategies for ethnic studies* (6th ed.). Boston, MA: Allyn & Bacon.

Banks, J. A. (2004). Introduction: Democratic citizenship education in multicultural societies. In J. A. Banks (Ed.), *Diversity and citizenship education: Global perspectives* (pp. 3–15). San Francisco, CA: Jossey-Bass.

Barr, R., & Dreeben, R. (1983). *How schools work*. Chicago, IL: University of Chicago Press.

Baudrillard, J. (1983). *Simulations*. New York: Semiotext(e).

Bauman, K. J. (2002, May 16). Home schooling in the United States: Trends and characteristics. *Education Policy Analysis Archives, 10*(26). Available on-line at http://epaa.asu.edu/epaa/v10n26.html [Retrieved November 12, 2003].

Beatty, J. (1994, May). Who speaks for the middle class. *The Atlantic Monthly*, 65–78.

Benard, B. (1991). *Fostering resiliency in kids: Protective factors in the family, school, and community*. Portland, OR: Northwest Regional Educational Laboratory.

Bennett, W. (1994). *The book of virtues*. New York: Simon & Schuster.

Besiner, N. (1990). *Narratives in popular culture, media, and everyday life*. Thousand Oaks, CA: Sage.

Beyer, L., & Apple, M. (Eds.) (1998). *The curriculum: Problems, politics, and possibilities*. Albany: State University of New York Press.

Bhabha, H. (1994). *The location of culture*. New York: Routledge.

Bielick, S., Chandler, K., & Broughman, S. P. (2001). *Homeschooling in the United States: 1999* (NCES 2001–033). Washington, DC: National Center for Education Statistics.

Block, F. L., Cloward, R. A., Ehrenreich, B., & Piven, F. F. (1987). *The mean season: The attack on the welfare state*. New York: Pantheon Books.

Bourdieu, P. (1984). *Distinction: A social critique of the judgment of taste*. Cambridge: Harvard University Press.

Bowen, W. G., & Bok, D. C. (1998). *The shape of the river: Long-term consequences of considering race in college and university admissions*. Princeton, NJ: Princeton University Press.

Braddock, J. H., & McPartland, J. (1989). Social-psychological processes that perpetuate racial segregation: The relationship between school and employment segregation. *Journal of Black Studies, 19*(3), 267–289.

Braddock, J. H., & Slavin, R. (1993). Why ability grouping must end: Achieving excellence and equity in American education. *Journal of Intergroup Relations, 20*(1), 51–64.

Brint, S., & Karabel, J. (1989). *The diverted dream: Community colleges and the promise of educational opportunity in America, 1900–1985*. New York: Oxford University Press.

Brown, E. (1993). *A taste of power: A black woman's story*. New York: Anchor Books.

Brown, L. M. (1998). *Raising their voices: The politics of girls' anger*. Cambridge, MA: Harvard University Press.

Brown, L. M., & Gilligan, C. (1992). *Meeting at the crossroads: Women's psychology and girls' development*. Cambridge, MA: Harvard University Press.

Browning, R. P., Marshall, D. R., & Tabb, D. H. (1990). *Racial politics in American cities*. New York: Longman.

Bruner, J. S. (1990). *Acts of Meaning*. Cambridge, MA: Harvard University Press.

Bruner, J. S. (1996). *The Culture of Education*. Cambridge, MA: Harvard University Press.

Buchanan, P. (1992). We stand with President Bush. In C-Span Transcripts (Eds.), *1992 Republican National Convention* (pp. 6–9). Lincolnshire, IL: Tape Writer.

Buckingham, D. (1993). *Children talking television: The making of television literacy*. London: Falmer.

Buckingham, D. (1996). *Moving images: Understanding children's emotional responses to television*. Manchester: Manchester University Press.

Buckingham, D. (Ed.). (1998). *Teaching popular culture: Beyond radical pedagogy*. London: University College of London.

Buckingham, D., & Sefton-Green, J. (1995). *Cultural studies goes to school: Reading and teaching popular media*. London: Taylor & Francis.

Burbules, N. (1993). *Dialogue in teaching: Theory and practice*. New York: Teachers College.

Burbules, N., & Rice, S. (2000). Dialogue across differences: Continuing the conversation. In M. Duarte & S. Smith (Eds.), *Foundational perpectives in multicultural education* (pp. 247–274). New York: Longman.

Burd, S. (2002, January 25). Rift grows over what keeps low-income students out of college. *Chronicle of Higher Education*.

Buriel, R. (1984). Integration with traditional Mexican-American culture and sociocultural adjustment. In J. L. Martínez, Jr., & R. Mendoza (Eds.), *Chicano Psychology* (2nd ed.). Orlando, FL: Academic.

Buriel, R., & Cardoza, D. (1988). Sociocultural correlates of achievement among three generations of Mexican American high school seniors. *American Educational Research Journal, 25,* 177–192.

Burns, A. (2004). The racing of capability and culpability in desegregated schools: Discourses of merit and responsibility. In M. Fine, L. Weis, L. Pruitt, & A. Burns (Eds.), *Off white: Readings in race, power and privilege.* New York: Routledge.

Burowoy, M. (1991). *Ethnography Unbound: Power and Resistance in the Modern Metropolis.* Berkeley, CA: University of California Press.

Butler, J. (1991). Imitation and gender insubordination. In D. Fuss (Ed.), *Inside/out: Lesbian theories, gay theories.* New York: Routledge.

Callahan, R. E. (1962). *Education and the cult of efficiency.* Chicago, IL: University of Chicago Press.

Campaigne, D., & Hossler, D. (1998). How do loans affect the educational decisions of students? Access, aspirations, college choice and persistence. In R. Fossey & M. Bateman (Eds.), *Condemning students to debt: College loans and public policy.* New York: Teachers College.

Campbell, R. (1987). Securing the middle ground: Reporter Formulas in 60 Minutes. *Critical Studies in Mass Communication, 4*(4), 325–350.

Carlson, D. (2002). *Leaving safe harbors: Toward a new progressivism in American education and public life.* New York: RoutledgeFalmer.

Carnevale, A., & Rose, S. (2003). Socioeconomic status, race/ethnicity, and selective college admissions. In R. Kahlenberg (Ed.), *America's untapped resource: Low-income students in higher education.* New York: Century Foundation.

Carter, M. (1979). You are involved. *Poems of resistance* (p. 44). George Town, Guyana: Guyana Printers.

Castles, S. (2004). Migration, citizenship, and education. In J. A. Banks (Ed.), *Diversity and citizenship education: Global perspectives* (pp. 17–48). San Francisco, CA: Jossey-Bass.

Caudhill, W., & Weinstein, H. (1969). Maternal care and infant behavior in Japan and America. *Psychiatry, 32,* 12–43.

Cavanagh, S. (2002, September 11). Merit grants bloom even as budgets wither. *Education Week.*

Cavanagh, S. (2004, January 21). Barriers to college: Lack of preparation vs. financial need. *Education Week.*

Chapa, J. (1988). The question of Mexican American assimilation: Socioeconomic parity or underclass formation? *Public Affairs Comment, 35*(1), 1–14.

Chavez, L. (1991). *Out of the barrio: Toward a new politics of Hispanic assimilation.* New York: Basic Books.

Chavez, L. (2002, July 1). *Jewish World Review.*

Clancy, P. M. (1986). The acquisition of communicative styles in Japanese. In B. B. Schieffelin & E. Ochs (Eds.), *Language socialization across cultures.* Cambridge, England: Cambridge University Press.

Cleaver, K. (1998). Three ways that Martin Luther King changed my life. *Black Renaissance, 2*(1), 51–62.

Clotfelter, C. T. (1999, November). Public school segregation in metropolitan areas. *Land Economics, 75,* 487–504.

Cole, J., & Omari, S. (2003). Race, class, and the dilemmas of upward mobility for African Americans. *Journal of Social Issues, 59*(4).

Coleman, J. S. (1988). Social capital in the creation of human capital. *American Journal of Sociology, 94,* 95–120.

Coleman, J. S. (1990). *Foundations of social theory.* Cambridge, MA: Harvard University Press.

The College Board. (2003). *Trends in student aid, 2002.* www.collegeboard.com.

The College Board. (2003, January). *Challenging times, clear choices: An action agenda for college access and success.* National Dialogue on Student Financial Aid. www.collegeboard.com.

Collier, V. P. (1995). Acquiring a second language for school. *Directions in Language and Education, 1*(4), 2–14.

Collins, P. H. (2000). *Black feminist thought: Knowledge, consciousness, and the politics of empowerment.* New York: Routledge.

Comer, J. (1976). The oppositional child: Is the black child at a greater risk? In E. J. Anthony & D. G. Gilpin (Eds.), *Three clinical faces of childhood.* New York: Spectrum.

Cone, J. K. (1990). Literature, geography, and the untracked English class. *English Journal, 79*(8), 60–67.

Conquergood, D. (1998). Beyond the text: Toward a performative cultural politics. In S. Dailey (Ed.), *The future of performance studies: Visions and revisions* (pp. 25–36). Washington, DC: National Communication Association (NCA).

Cooper, R. (1996). *The politics of change: Racial tension and conflict on school campuses: Strategies to improve intergroup relations.* Paper presented at the annual meeting of the American Educational Research Association, New York, NY.

Crane, J. (1991). Effects of neighborhoods on dropping out of school and teenage childbearing. In C. Jencks & P. E. Peterson (Eds.), *The urban underclass* (pp. 299–320). Washington, DC: Brookings Institution.

Crowley, J. E., & Shapiro, D. (1982). Aspirations and expectations of youth in the U.S. *Youth and Society, 13,* 391–422.

Cummins, J. (1981). The role of primary language development in promoting educational success for language minority students. In California State Department of Education (Ed.), *Schooling and language minority students: A theoretical framework.* Los Angeles, CA: Evaluation, Dissemination, and Assessment Center, California State University.

Cummins, J. (1986). Empowering minority students: A framework for intervention. *Harvard Educational Review, 56,* 18–36.

Cusick, T. (1987). Sexism and early parenting: Cause and effect? *Peabody Journal of Education, 64*(4), 113–131.

Daiute, C., & Fine, M. (2003). Youth perspectives on violence and injustice. *Journal of Social Issues, 59*(1), 1–14.

D'Andrade, R. (1990). Some propositions about the relations between culture and human cognition. In J. W. Stigler, R. A. Shweder, & G. Herdt (Eds.), *Cultural psychology: Essays on comparative human development.* New York: Cambridge University Press.

Darder, A. (1991). *Culture and power in the classroom: A critical foundation for bicultural education.* New York: Bergin & Garvey.

Darder, A. (1995). Buscando America. In C. E. Sleeter & P. L. McLaren (Eds.), *Multicultural education, critical pedagogy, and the politics of difference.* Albany, NY: State University of New York Press.

Darling-Hammond, L., & Wise, A. E. (1985). Beyond standardization: State standards and school improvement. *Elementary School Journal, 85,* 315–336.

Datnow, A., & Cooper, R. (1997). Peer networks of African American students in independent schools: Affirming academic success and racial identity. *Journal of Negro Education, 66*(1), 56–72.

David, M. E. (1993). *Parents, gender, and education reform.* Oxford: Polity.

Davies, L. (1983). Gender, resistance, and power. In S. Walker & L. Barton (Eds.), *Gender, class, and education* (pp. 39–52). Sussex, England: Falmer.

Davis, M. (1992, June 1). Urban America sees its future: In L.A. burning all illusions. *Nation, 254*(21), 743–746.

Dawkins, M. P., & Braddock, J. H. (1994). The continuing significance of desegregation: School racial composition and African American inclusion in American society. *Journal of Negro Education, 63*(3), 394–405.

DeBlase, G. L. (2003). Missing stories, missing lives: Urban girls (re)constructing race and gender in the literacy classroom. *Urban Education, 38,* 279–329.

Debold, E. (1996). *Knowing bodies: Gender identity, cognitive development and embodiment in early childhood and early adolescence.* Unpublished doctoral dissertation, Harvard University.

Delpit, L. (1988). The silenced dialogue: Power and pedagogy in educating other people's children. *Harvard Educational Review, 58,* 280–298.

Delpit, L. (1995). *Other people's children: Cultural conflict in the classroom.* New York: New Press.

Denzin, N. (2003). *Performance ethnography: Critical pedagogy and the politics of culture.* Thousand Oakes, CA: Sage.

Devault, M. (1990). Talking and listening from women's standpoint: Feminist strategies for interviewing and analysis. *Social Problems, 37,* 96–116.

Di Leonardo, M. (1991). Contingencies of value in feminist anthropology. In J. Hartman & E. Messer-Davidow (Eds.), *(En)gendering knowledge: Feminists in academe.* Knoxville, TN: University of Tennessee Press.

Dimitriadis, G. (2001). *Performing identity/performing culture: Hip hop as text, pedagogy, and lived practice.* New York: Lang.

Dimitriadis, G. (2003). *Friendship, cliques, and gangs: Young black men coming of age in urban America.* New York: Teachers College.

Dimitriadis, G., & Carlson, D. (Eds.). (2003). *Promises to keep: Cultural studies, democratic education, and public life.* New York: RoutledgeFalmer.

Dimitriadis, G., & Kamberelis, G. (in press). Focus groups: Strategic articulations of pedagogy, politics, and inquiry. In N. Denzin & Y. Lincoln (Eds.), *Handbook of qualitative research* (3rd ed.). Thousand Oaks: Sage.

Dimitriadis, G., & McCarthy, C. (2001). *Reading and teaching the postcolonial: From Baldwin to Basquiat and beyond.* New York: Teachers College.

Dolby, N. (2000). Changing selves: Multicultural education and the challenge of new identities. *Teachers College Record, 102*(5), 898–912.

Dolby, N. (2001). *Constructing race: Youth, identity, and popular culture in South Africa.* Albany, NY: State University of New York Press.

Donato, R. (1999). Hispano education and the implications of autonomy: Four school systems in southern Colorado, 1920, 1963. *Harvard Educational Review, 69*(2), 117–149.

Dornbusch, S. M. (1994, February 12). *Off the track.* Presidential address to the society for research on adolescence, San Diego, CA.

Dougherty, K. (1994). *The contradictory college: The conflicting origins, impacts and futures of the community college.* Albany, NY: State University of New York Press.

Duffy, J., Warren, K., & Walsh, M. (2002). Classroom interactions: Gender of teacher, gender of student, and classroom subject. *Sex Roles, 45,* 579–593.

Dumais, S. A. (2002). Cultural capital, gender, and school success: The role of habitus. *Sociology of Education, 75,* 44–68.

Duneier, M. (1999). *Sidewalk.* New York: Farrar, Strauss, & Giroux.

Dunn, T. (1993). The new enclosures: Racism in the normalized community. In R. Gooding-Williams (Ed.), *Reading Rodney King* (pp. 178–195). New York: Routledge.

Dyer, R. (1993). *The matter of images: Essays on representations.* New York: Routledge.

Eaton, S. E. (2001). *The other Boston busing story.* New Haven: Yale University Press.

Eckert, P. (1989). *Jocks and burnouts: Social categories and identity in the high school.* New York: Teachers College.

Eder, D. (1995). *School talk: Gender and adolescent culture.* New Brunswick, NJ: Rutgers University Press.

Eliot, T. S. (1964). The love song of J. Alfred Prufrock. In T. S. Eliot (Ed.), *Selected poems* (pp. 11–16). New York: Harcourt Brace Jovanovich.

Ellis, C. (1993). *The rage of the privileged class: Why are middle class blacks angry? Why should America care?* New York: HarperCollins.

Ellsworth, E. (1989). Why doesn't this feel empowering: Working through the repressive myths of critical pedagogy." *Harvard Educational Review, 59,* 297–324.

Erickson, F. (1987). Transformation and school success: The politics and culture of educational achievement. *Anthropology and Education Quarterly, 18*(4), 336–355.

Erickson, F., & Mohatt, G. (1982). Cultural organization of participant structure in two classrooms of Indian students. In G. Spindler (Ed.), *Doing the ethnography of schooling: Educational anthropology in action* (pp. 132–175). New York: Holt, Rinehart, & Winston.

Ericsson, K. A., & Simon, H. A. (1993). *Protocol analysis: Verbal reports as data.* Cambridge: MIT Press.

Espiritu, Y. (1992). *Asian American panethnicity: Bridging institutions and identities.* Philadelphia, PA: Temple University Press.

Espiritu, Y. (2000). *Asian American women and men: Labor, laws, and love.* Walnut Creek, CA: Altamira.

Etter-Lewis, G. (1993). *My soul is my own: Oral narratives of African American women in the professions.* New York: Routledge.

Farley, C. J. (1994, December 19). Patriot games. *Time Magazine,* pp. 48–49.

Farley, R., Danziger, S., & Holzer, H. J. (2000). *Detroit divided.* New York: Russell Sage Foundation.

Fedarko, K. (1993, August 23). Holidays in hell. *Time Magazine,* pp. 50–51.

Ferguson, A. A. (2000). *Bad boys: Public schools in the making of black masculinity.* Ann Arbor, MI: University of Michigan Press.

Fine, M. (1991). *Framing dropouts: Notes on the politics of an urban public high school.* Albany, NY: State University of New York Press.

Fine, M., Bloom, J. L., Burns, A., Chajet, L., Guishard, M., & Torre, M. E. (2004, in press). Dear Zora: A letter to Zora Neal Hurston fifty years after *Brown. Teachers College Record.*

Fine, M., & Burns, A. (2003). Class notes: Toward a critical psychology of class and schooling. *Journal of Social Issues, 59*(4).

Fine, M., & Macpherson, P. (1995). Hungry for an us. *Feminism and Psychology, 5*(2), 181–200.

Fine, M., & Weis, L. (1993). *Beyond silenced voices: Class, race, and gender in United States schools.* Albany, NY: State University of New York Press.

Fine, M., & Weis, L. (1998). *The unknown city: Lives of poor and working-class young adults.* Boston, MA: Beacon.

Fine, M., Weis, L., Centrie, C., & Roberts, R. (2000). Educating beyond the borders of schooling. *Anthropology & Education Quarterly, 31*(2), 131–151.

Fine, M., Weis, L., & Powell, L. (1997). Communities of difference: A critical look at desegregated spaces created for and by youth. *Harvard Educational Review, 67*(2), 247–284.

Fine, M., Weis, L., Powell, L. & Wong, M. (Eds.) (1997). *Off white: Readings on race, power, and society.* New York: Routledge.

Fine, M., & Zane, N. (1991). Bein' wrapped too tight: When low-income women drop out of high school. *Women's Studies Quarterly, 1 & 2,* 77–99.

Fiske, A., Kitayama, S., Markus, H. R., & Nisbett, R. E. (1998). The cultural matrix of social psychology. In D. T. Gilbert, S. T. Fiske, & G. Lindzey (Eds.), *Handbook of social psychology.* New York: McGraw-Hill.

Fiske, J. (1994). *Media matters: Everyday culture and political change.* Minneapolis: University of Minnesota Press.

Flaherty, T. S. (1999). *Talk your way to the top.* New York: Putnam.

Flores, W. V., & Benmayor, R. (1997). *Latino cultural citizenship: Claiming identity, space, and rights.* Boston, MA: Beacon.

Fordham, S. (1993). Those loud black girls: (Black) women, silence and gender passing in the academy. *Anthropology and Education Quarterly, 24*, 3–32.

Fordham, S. (1996). *Blacked out: Dilemmas of race, identity, and success at Capital High.* Chicago, IL: University of Chicago Press.

Fordham, S., & Ogbu, J. U. (1986). Black students' school success: Coping with the burden of acting white. *Urban Review, 18*(3), 176–206.

Fossey, R. (1998). The dizzying growth of the federal student loan program: When will vertigo set in? In R. Fossey & M. Bateman (Eds.), *Condemning students to debt: College loans and public policy.* New York: Teachers College.

Foster, H. (1983). *The anti-aesthetic.* Seattle, WA: Bay.

Foucault, M. (1980). *Power/knowledge: Selected interviews and other writings, 1972–1977* (Colin Gordon [Ed.]; Gordon, et al., Trans.). New York: Pantheon.

Frankenberg, E., & Lee, C. (2002). *Race in American public schools: Rapidly resegregating school districts.* Cambridge, MA: Civil Rights Project.

Frankenberg, E., & Lee, C. (2003). *Charter schools and race: A lost opportunity for integrated education.* Cambridge, MA: Civil Rights Project.

Frankenberg, E., Lee, C., & Orfield, G. (2003). *A multiracial society with segregated schools: Are we losing the dream?* Cambridge, MA: Civil Rights Project.

Frankenberg, R. (1993). *White women, race matters: The social construction of whiteness.* Minneapolis: University of Minnesota Press.

Freeman, C., Scafidi, B., & Sjoquist, D. L. (2002). *Racial segregation in Georgia public schools, 1994–2001: Trends, causes, and impact on teacher quality.* Paper presented at the Resegregation of Southern Schools Conference, University of North Carolina at Chapel Hill.

Freeman, K. (1999, March). The race factor in African Americans' college choice. *Urban Education, 34*(1).

Fregoso, R. L. (1993). *The bronze screen: Chicana and Chicano film culture.* Minneapolis, MN: University of Minnesota Press.

Freire, P. (1970). *Pedagogy of the oppressed.* New York: Seabury.

Freire, P. (1970/1992). *Pedagogy of the oppressed.* New York: Continuum.

Gamoran, A. (1986). Instructional and institutional effects of ability grouping. *Sociology of Education, 59*(4), 185–198.

Gamoran, A. (1992). Access to excellence: Assignment to honors English classes in the transition from middle to high school. *Educational evaluation and policy analysis, 14*(3), 185–204.

Gao, G., Ting-Toomey, S., & Gudykunst, W. B. (1996). Chinese communication processes. In M. H. Bond (Ed.), *Handbook of Chinese psychology.* Hong Kong: Oxford University Press.

Gardiner, M. (1992). *The dialogics of critique: M. M. Bakhtin and the theory of ideology.* New York: Routledge.

Garet, M. S., & DeLany, B. (1988, April). Students, courses, and stratification. *Sociology of Education, 61*, 61–77.

Garfinkel, H. (1967). *Studies in ethnomethodology.* Englewood Cliffs, NJ: Prentice Hall.

Gaskell, J. (1985). Course enrollment in the high school: The perspective of working class females. *Sociology of Education, 58,* 48–59.

Gates, D. (1993, March 29). White-male paranoia. *Newsweek,* pp. 48–53.

Gerbner, G. (1970). Cultural indicators: The case of violence in television drama. *Annals of the American Association of Political and Social Science, 338,* 69–81.

Gibson, M. A. (1988). *Accommodation without assimilation: Sikh immigrants in an American high school.* Ithaca, NY: Cornell University Press.

Gibson, M. A. (1993). The school performance of immigrant minorities: A comparative view. In E. Jacob & C. Jordan (Eds.), *Minority education: Anthropological perspectives.* Norwood, NJ: Ablex Publishing.

Giles, H., Coupland, N., & Wiemann, J. M. (1992). "Talk is cheap . . . but my word is my bond": Beliefs about talk. In K. Bolton & H. Kwok (Eds.), *Sociolinguistics today: Eastern and Western perspectives.* London: Routledge.

Gilligan, C. (1991). Joining the resistance: Psychology, politics, girls, and women. *Michigan Quarterly Review, 29,* 501–536.

Giroux, H. A. (1988). *Schooling and the struggle for public life: Critical pedagogy in the modern age.* Minneapolis, MN: University of Minnesota Press.

Giroux, H. A. (1993). *Border crossings.* New York: Routledge.

Gladden, R. (1998). The small school movement: A review of the literature. In M. Fine & J. Somerville (Eds.), *Small schools, big imaginations.* Chicago, IL: Cross City Campaign for Urban School Reform.

Goffman, E. (1977). *Asylums: Essays on the social situation of mental patients and other inmates.* Garden City, NY: Anchor.

Goldstein, B. (1985). *Schooling for cultural transitions: Hmong girls and boys in American high schools.* Unpublished doctoral dissertation, University of Wisconsin-Madison.

Good, T., & Brophy, J. (1987). *Looking in classrooms* (4th ed.). New York: Harper & Row.

Gordon, M. M. (1964). *Assimilation and American life: The role of race, religion and national origins.* New York: Oxford University Press.

Gotbaum, B. (2002, November 21). *Pushing out at-risk students: An analysis of high school discharge figures.* Report by the Public Advocate for the City of New York and Advocates for Children, New York, NY. Available on-line at http://www.advocatesforchildren.org [Retrieved April 5, 2003].

Gottdiener, M. (1985). *The social production of urban space.* Austin, TX: University of Texas Press.

Granovetter, M. S. (1973). The strength of weak ties. *American Journal of Sociology, 78*(6), 1360–1380.

Granovetter, M. S. (1983). The strength of weak ties: A network theory revisited. In R. Collins (Ed.), *Sociological theory* (Vol. I). San Francisco: Jossey-Bass.

Greene, J. P., & Forster, G. (2003, September 17). *Public high school graduation and college readiness rates in the United States.* (Working paper No. 3). New York: The

Manhattan Institute. Available on-line at http://www.manhattan-institute.org/ ewp_03_embargoed.pdf [Retrieved September 15, 2003].

Greenhouse, C. J., & Greenwood, D. (1998). Introduction: The ethnography of democracy and difference. In C. J. Greenhouse (Ed.), *Democracy and ethnography: Constituting identities in multicultural states* (pp. 1–26). Albany, NY: State University of New York Press.

Grossberg, L. (1992). *We got to get out of this place.* New York. Routledge.

Grossman, J. R. (1989). *Land of hope: Chicago, black Southerners, and the great migration.* Chicago, IL: University of Chicago Press.

Grubb, W. N. (1999, June). *The economic benefits of sub-baccalaureate education: Results from national studies.* Community College Research Center [CCRC Brief No. 2].

Gudykunst, W. B., Gao, G., & Franklyn-Stokes, A. (1996). Self-monitoring and concern for social appropriateness in China and England. In J. Pandey, D. Sinha, and D. P. S. Bhawuk (Eds.), *Asian contributions to cross-cultural psychology.* New Delhi: Sage.

Gutek, G. L. (1993). *American education in a global society: Internationalizing teacher education.* White Plains, NY: Longman.

Gutierrez, K., Rymes, B., & Larson, J. (1995). Script, counterscript, and underlife in the classroom: James Brown versus *Brown v. Board of Education. Harvard Educational Review, 65*(3), 445–471.

Gutmann, A. (1987). *Democratic education.* Princeton: Princeton University Press.

Hafner, A. J. (1957). Influence of verbalization on problem solving. *Psychological Reports, 3,* 360.

Hall, E. T. (1976). *Beyond culture.* New York: Doubleday.

Hall, K. (2002). *Lives in translation: Sikh youth as British citizens.* Philadelphia, PA: University of Pennsylvania Press.

Hallinan, M. T., & Sorenson, A. B. (1985). Ability grouping and student friendships. *American Educational Research Journal, 22*(4), 485–499.

Hallinan, M. T., & Williams, R. A. (1989). Interracial friendships choices in secondary schools. *American Sociological Review, 54,* 67–78.

Haney, W. (2000, August 19). The myth of the Texas miracle in education. *Education Policy Analysis Archives, 8*(41). Available on-line at http://epaa.asu.edu/epaa/ v8n41/. [A printed version of this monograph is distributed by the Harvard Education Publishing group.]

Haney, W. (2001, January 13). *Revisiting the myth of the Texas miracle in education: Lessons about dropout research and dropout prevention.* Paper prepared for the Dropout Research: Accurate Counts and Positive Interventions Conference Sponsored by Achieve and the Harvard Civil Rights Project, Cambridge, MA. Available on-line at http://www.civilrightsproject.harvard.edu/research/dropouts/ call_dropoutpapers.php.

Haney, W., & Madaus, G. (1978). Making sense of the minimum competency testing movement. *Harvard Educational Review, 48*(4), 462–484.

Haney, W., Madaus, G., Abrams, L., Wheelock, A., Miao, J., & Gruia, I. M. (2004). *The education pipeline in the U.S. 1970–2000.* Chestnut Hill, MA: National Board on Educational Testing and Public Policy (http://www.bc.edu/nbetpp).

Harker, R. (1984). On reproduction, habitus, and education. *British Journal of Sociology of Education, 5*(2), 117–127.

Harlow, C. W. (2003, January). (Revised 2003, April 15). *Education and correctional populations.* Bureau of Justice Statistics Special report. Washington, DC: U.S. Department of Justice Statistics, Office of Justice Programs.

Harrison, P. R. (1993). Bourdieu and the possibility of a postmodern sociology. *Thesis Eleven, 35,* 36–50.

Hartocallis, A. (2001, June 30). Math test needed for high school graduation had confusing errors, state officials say. *New York Times,* p. B2.

Hauser, R. M., & Anderson, D. K. (1991). Post–high school plans and aspirations of black and white high school seniors: 1976–86. *Sociology of Education, 64*(4), 263–277.

Hawley, W., & Jackson, A. W. (1995). *Toward a common destiny: Improving race and ethnic relations in America.* San Francisco, CA: Jossey-Bass

Haycock, K., & Huang, S. (2001). Youth at the crossroads: Facing high school and beyond. Thinking K–16. *Education Trust, 5*(1).

Haymes, S. N. (1995). *Race, culture, and the city: A pedagogy for black urban struggle.* New York: State University of New York Press.

Heath, S. (1983). *Ways with words: Language, life and communication in communities and classrooms.* Cambridge: Cambridge University Press.

Heath, S. B., & McLaughlin, M. (Eds.). (1993). *Identity and inner-city youth: Beyond ethnicity and gender.* New York: Teachers College.

Henke, R., Kaufman, P., & Broughman, S. (2000). *Issues related to estimating the home-schooled population in the United States with household survey data* (NCES 2000–311). Washington, DC: National Center for Education Statistics.

Henriques, D., & Steinberg, J. (2001, May 20). Right answer, wrong score: Test flaws take toll. *New York Times,* p. 1. Available on-line at http://www.nytimes.com/2001/05/20/business/20EXAM.html.

Hess, R., & Shipman, V. (1965). Early experience and the socialization of cognitive modes in children. *Child Development, 36*(4), 869–876.

Heubert, J., & Hauser, R. (Eds.). (1999). *High stakes: Testing for tracking, promotion, and graduation.* A Report of the National Research Council. Washington, DC: National Academy Press.

Hildenbrandt, H. W. (1988). A Chinese managerial view of business communication. *Management Communication Quarterly, 2,* 217–234.

Hill-Collins, P. (1991). *Black feminist thought: Knowledge, consciousness, and the politics of empowerment.* New York: Routledge.

Hirschkop, K., & David Shepherd, D. (Eds.). (1989). *Bakhtin and cultural theory.* Manchester, UK: Manchester University Press.

Hochschild, J. (1995). *Facing up to the American dream: Race, class and the soul of the nation.* Princeton, NJ: Princeton University Press.

Holland, D. C., & Eisenhart, M. A. (1990). *Educated in romance: Women, achievement, and college culture.* Chicago, IL: University of Chicago Press.

Home School Legal Defense Association. Available on-line at http://www.hslda.org/research/faq.asp#1 [Retrieved November 14, 2003].

Honora, D. (2002). The relationship of gender and achievement to future outlook among African American adolescents. *Adolesence, 37,* 301–316.

hooks, b. (1990). *Yearning: Race, gender, and cultural politics.* Boston, MA: South End.

hooks, b. (1992). *Black looks.* Boston, MA: South End.

hooks, b. (1994). *Teaching to transgress.* New York: Routledge.

hooks, b. (2000). *Where we stand: Class matters.* New York: Routledge.

Huckfeldt, R. R. (1983). Social contexts, social networks, and urban neighborhoods: Environmental constraints on friendship choice. *American Journal of Sociology, 89*(3), 651–669.

Huntington, S. (1996). *The clash of civilizations and the remaking of the world.* New York: Simon & Schuster.

Hurtado, A., & Stewart, A. (1997). Through the looking glass: Studying whiteness for feminist methods. In M. Fine, L. Weis, L. Powell, & L. M. Wong (Eds.), *White out: Readings on race, power and society* (pp. 297–311). New York: Routledge.

Jackson, G. (1975). The research evidence on the effects of grade retention. *Review of Educational Research, 45*(4), 613–635.

James, C. L. R. (1978). *Mariners, renegades, and castaways: The story of Herman Melville and the world we live in.* Detroit, MI: Bewick/ed.

James, C. L. R. (1993). *American civilization.* Oxford: Blackwell.

Jameson, F. (1984, July–August). Postmodernism, or, the cultural logic of late capitalism. *New Left Review, 146,* 59–82.

Kagan, J., Kearsley, R. B., & Zelazo, P. R. (1977, February 1). The effects of infant day care on psychological development. *Evaluation Quarterly, 1,* 109–142.

Kamberelis, G., & Dimitriadis, G. (1999). "Talkin' Tupac: Speech genres and the mediation of cultural knowledge." In C. McCarthy, G. Hudak, S. Miklaucic, P. Saukko (Eds.), *Sound identities: Popular music and the cultural politics of education* (pp. 119–150). New York: Peter Lang.

Kane, T. (1999). *The price of admission: Rethinking how Americans pay for college.* Washington DC: Brookings Institution.

Kaplan, B. (1995). *Everything you need to know to talk your way to success.* New York: Prentice Hall Trade.

Karen, D. (1991). The politics of class, race and gender: Access to higher education in the United States, 1960–1986. *American Journal of Education, 99*(2).

Keith, M., & Pile, S. (1993). The politics of place . . . In M. Keith & S. Pile (Eds.), *Place and the politics of identity* (pp. 1–21). London: Routledge.

Kenny, L. (2000). *Daughters of suburbia: Growing up white, middle class and female.* New Brunswick, NJ: Rutgers University Press.

Kern, C. (2000, July). College choice influences: Urban high school students respond. *Community College Journal of Research and Practice, 24*(6).

Khalidi, R. (1997). *Palestinian identity: The construction of modern national consciousness.* New York: Columbia University Press.

Khayatt, D. (1994). Surviving school as lesbian students. *Gender and Education, 6*(1), 47–61.

Khayatt, D. (1995). Compulsory heterosexuality: Schools and lesbian students. In M. Campbell & A. Manicom (Eds.), *Knowledge, experience and ruling relations: Studies in the social organization of knowledge* (pp. 149–163). Toronto: University of Toronto Press.

Kim, H. S. (2002). We talk, therefore we think? A cultural analysis of the effect of talking on thinking. *Journal of Personality and Social Psychology, 83*(4), 828–842.

Kim, H. S., & Markus, H. R. (2002). Freedom of speech and freedom of silence: An analysis of talking as a cultural practice. In R. Shweder, M. Minow, & H. R. Markus (Eds.), *Engaging cultural differences: The multicultural challenge in liberal democracies.* New York: Russell-Sage Foundation.

King, J. J., & Berkowitz, R. (2002). A life history analysis of women aged 15–44. *Sociology of Education, 75,* 211–230.

Kluger, R. (1994). *Simple justice.* New York: Notable Trials Library.

Koltyk, J. (1998). *New pioneers in the heartland: Hmong life in Wisconsin.* Boston, MA: Allyn & Bacon.

Kozol, J. (1991). *Savage inequalities: Children in America's schools.* New York: Crown.

Kreitzer, A., Madaus, G., & Haney, W. (1989). Competency testing and dropouts. In L. Weis & H. Petrie (Eds), *Dropouts from school: Issues, dilemmas and solutions* (pp. 129–152). Albany, NY: State University of New York Press.

Kroll, J. (1991, June 10). Spiking a fever. *Newsweek,* pp. 44–47.

Kuhn, A., & Wolpe, A. (1978). *Feminism and materialism: Women and modes of production.* London; Boston: Routledge & Kegan Paul.

Lacan, J. (1977). *The mirror stage as formative of the function of the I. Ecrits* (A. Sheridan, Trans.) (pp. 1–7). New York: Norton.

Ladson-Billings, G. (1994). *Dreamkeepers: Successful teachers of African American children.* San Francisco, CA: Jossey-Bass.

Ladson-Billings, G. (2004). Culture versus citizenship: The challenge of racialized citizenship in the United States. In J. A. Banks (Ed.), *Diversity and citizenship education: Global perspectives* (pp. 99–126). San Francisco, CA: Jossey-Bass.

Lafer, G. (2002). *The job training charade.* Ithaca, NY: Cornell University Press.

Lareau, A. (1989). *Home advantage: Social class and parental intervention in elementary education.* London; New York: Falmer.

Lasch, C. (1991). *The true and only heaven: Progress and its critics.* New York: Norton.

Lavin, D., & Hyllegard, D. (1996). *Changing the odds: Open admissions and the life chances of the disadvantaged.* New Haven: Yale University Press.

Lee, S. J. (1996). *Unraveling the "model minority" stereotype: Listening to Asian American youth.* New York: Teachers College.

Lee, S. J. (2001a). Transforming and exploring the landscape of gender and sexuality: Hmong American teenaged girls. *Race, Gender & Class, 8*(2), 35–46.

Lee, S. J. (2001b). More than "model minorities" or "delinquents": A look at Hmong American high school students. *Harvard Educational Review, 71*(3), 505–528.

Lee, S. J. (2004). Hmong American masculinities: Creating new identities in the United States. In N. Way & J. Chu (Eds.), *Adolescent boys: Exploring diverse cultures of boyhood.* New York: New York University Press.

Lee, S. J., & Vaught, S. (2003). "You can never be too rich or too thin": Popular and consumer culture and the Americanization of Asian American girls and young women. *Journal of Negro Education, 72*(4).

Lei, J. (2001). *Claims to belonging and difference: Cultural citizenship and identity construction in schools.* Unpublished Doctoral Dissertation, Department of Educational Policy Studies, University of Wisconsin–Madison.

Lemann, N. (1991). *The promised land: The great black migration and how it changed America.* New York: Knopf.

Lewis, B. (2002). *What went wrong? Western impact and Middle Eastern response.* Oxford: Oxford University Press.

Lewis, D. K. (1975). The black family: Socialization and sex roles. *Phylon, 36,* 221–238.

Lewis, O. (1966). The culture of poverty. *Scientific American, 215,* 19–25.

Lieberman, P. (1992, June 18). 52% of riot arrests were Latino, study says. *L.A. Times,* p. B3.

Lightfoot, S. L. (1983). *The good high school: Portraits of character and culture.* New York: Basic Books.

Lin, N. (1990). Social resources and instrumental action. In R. Brieger (Ed.), *Social mobility and social structure* (pp. 247–271). Cambridge: Cambridge University Press.

Lindsay, C. P., & Dempsey, B. L. (1985). Experiences in training Chinese business people to use U.S. management techniques. *Journal of Applied Behavioral Science, 21*(1), 65–78.

Lindsay, P. (1984). High school size, participation in activities, and young adult social participation: Some enduring effects of schooling. *Educational Evaluation and Policy Analysis, 8*(1).

Linn, R. L. (2000). Assessments and accountability. *Educational Researcher, 29,* 4–15.

Linn, R. L., Baker, E. L., & Betebenner, D. W. (2002). Accountability systems: Implications of requirements of the No Child Left Behind Act of 2001. *Educational Researcher, 31*(6), 3–16.

Loftus, G. R., & Bell, S. M. (1975). Two types of information in picture memory. *Journal of Experimental Psychology: Human Learning and Memory, 1*(2), 103–113.

Logan, J. (2001, April 3). *Ethnic diversity grows, neighborhood integration lags.* Presented at National Press Club.

Logan, J. (2003). *Segregation in neighborhoods and schools: Impacts on minority children in the Boston region.* Albany, NY: Lewis Mumford Center.

Lowe, L. (1996). *Immigrant acts: On Asian American cultural politics.* Durham: Duke University Press.

Loza, P. (2003, March). A system at risk: College outreach programs and the educational neglect of underachieving Latino high school students. *The Urban Review, 35*(1).

Lubman, S. (1998, February 23). Some students must learn to question. *San Jose Mercury News*, pp. 1A, 12A.

Ludwig, J. (2001). Comment on "A diagnostic analysis of black-white GPA disparities in Shaker Heights, Ohio" by Ronald Ferguson. In D. Ravitch (Ed.), *Brookings papers on education policy, 2001*. Washington, D.C.: Brookings Institution.

Luttrell, W. (1993). "The teachers, they all had their pets": Concepts of gender, knowledge, and power. *Signs, 18*(3), 505–546.

Macías, J. (1990). Scholastic antecedents of immigrant students: Schooling in a Mexican immigrant-sending community. *Anthropology and Education Quarterly, 21*, 291–318.

Macías, J. (1992). The social nature of instruction in a Mexican school: Implications for U.S. classroom practice. *The Journal of Educational Issues of Language Minority Students, 10*, 13–25.

MacLeod, J. (1987). *Ain't no makin it*. Boulder, CO: Westview.

MacLeod, J. (1995). *Ain't no makin it: Aspirations and attainment in a low-income neighborhood* (2nd ed.). Boulder, CO: Westview.

Madaus, G. (1990, December 6). *Testing as a social technology*. Boisi Lecture in Education and Public Policy. Chestnut Hill, MA: Boston College.

Madaus, G., & Greaney, V. (1985). The Irish experience in competency testing. *American Journal of Education, 93*(2), 268–294.

Mahiri, J. (1998). *Shooting for excellence: African American and youth culture in new century schools*. Urbana, IL: National Counsel of Teachers of Education.

Mahiri, J., & Conner, E. (2003). Black youth violence has a bad rap. *Journal of Social Issues, 59*(1), 121–140.

Marini, M. (1984). Women's educational attainment and the timing of entry into parenthood. *American Sociological Review, 49*, 491–511.

Marks, C. (1989). *Farewell—we're good and gone: The great black migration*. Bloomington, IN: Indiana University Press.

Markus, H. R., & Kitayama, S. (1991). Culture and the self: Implications for cognition, emotion, and motivation. *Psychological Review, 98*(2), 224–253.

Markus, H. R., Kitayama, S., & Heiman, R. J. (1996). Culture and "basic" psychological principles. In E. Tory Higgins & A. W. Kruglanski (Eds.), *Social psychology: Handbook of basic principles*. New York: Guilford.

Markus, H. R., Mullally, P. R., & Kitayama, S. (1997). Selfways: Diversity in modes of cultural participation. In U. Neisser & D. Jopling (Eds.), *Conceptual self in context: Culture, experience, self-understanding*. Cambridge: Cambridge University Press.

Marx, K., & Engels, F. (1932/1976). *The German ideology*. Moscow: Progress.

Massey, D. S., & Denton, N. A. (1988). The dimensions of racial segregation. *Social Forces, 67*, 281–315.

Massey, D. S., & Denton, N. A. (1993). *American apartheid: Segregation and the making of the underclass*. Cambridge, MA; London: Harvard University Press.

Matute-Bianchi, M. E. (1991). Situational ethnicity and patterns of school performance among immigrant and nonimmigrant Mexican-descent students. In M. A. Gibson & J. U. Ogbu (Eds.), *Minority status and schooling: A comparative study of immigrant and involuntary minorities.* New York: Garland.

McArdle, N. (2003). *Race, place, and opportunity: Racial change and segregation in the Boston metropolitan area: 1990–2000.* Cambridge, MA: Civil Rights Project.

McCallister, L. (1994). *I wish I'd said that: How to talk your way out of trouble and into success.* Chichester, NY: Wiley & Sons.

McCarthy, C. (1990). *Race and curriculum.* London: Falmer.

McCarthy, C. (1993a). Beyond the poverty of theory in race relations: Nonsynchrony and social difference in education. In L. Weis & M. Fine (Eds.), *Beyond silenced voices: Class, race, and gender in United States schools.* New York: State University of New York Press.

McCarthy, C. (1993b). Multicultural approaches to racial inequality in the United States. In L. Castenell, Jr. & W. F. Pinar (Eds.), *Understanding curriculum as racial text: Representations of identity and difference in education* (pp. 225–246). Albany, NY: State University of New York Press.

McCarthy, C., & Crichlow, W. (1993). *Race, identity, and representation in education.* New York: Routledge.

McDonough, P. (1997). *Choosing colleges: How social class and schools structure opportunity.* Albany, NY: State University of New York Press.

McLaren, P. (1989). *Life in schools.* White Plains, NY: Longman.

McNeil, L. M. (1983). Defensive teaching and classroom control. In M. W. Apple & L. Weis (Eds.), *Ideology and practice in schooling* (pp.114–142). Philadelphia, PA: Temple University Press.

McPherson, M., & Schapiro, M. (1991). *Keeping college affordable: Government and educational opportunity.* Washington, DC: The Brookings Institute.

McQuillan, P. J. (1998). *Educational opportunity in an urban American high school: A cultural analysis.* Albany, NY: State University of New York Press.

McRobbie, A. (1978). *Jackie: Ideology of adolescent femininity.* Birmingham, AL: University of Birmingham.

McRobbie, A. (1991). *Feminism and youth culture.* Boston, MA: Unwin Hyman.

Mehan, H., Hubbard, L., & Villanueva, I. (1994). Forming academic identities: Accommodation without assimilation among involuntary minorities. *Anthropology and Education Quarterly, 25*(2), 91–117.

Mehan, H., Villanueva, I., Hubbard, L., & Lintz, A. (1996). *Constructing school success: The consequences of untracking low-achieving students.* New York: Cambridge University Press.

Mejía, D. (1983). The development of Mexican American children. In G. J. Powell (Ed.), *The psychosocial development of minority group children.* New York: Brunner/Mazel.

Melville, H. (1851). *Moby Dick: Or the white whale.* New York. Harper.

Mercer, K. (1992). "1968": Periodizing postmodern politics and identity. In L. Grossberg, C. Nelson, & P. Treichler (Eds.), *Cultural Studies* (pp. 424–449). New York: Routledge.

Metz, M. (1978). *Classrooms and corridors: The crisis of authority in desegregated secondary schools*. Berkeley, CA: University of California Press.

Miao, J. (forthcoming). *High school graduation rate: Alternative methods and implications*. Doctoral dissertation. Lynch School of Education, Boston College.

Mickelson, R. (1990). The attitude achievement paradox among black adolescents. *Sociology of Education, 63*, 44–61.

Mickelson, R. A. (1989). Why does Jane read and write so well? The anomaly of women's achievement. *Sociology of Education, 62*, 47–63.

Miller, G. A. (1981). *Language and speech*. San Francisco, CA: Freeman.

Minami, M. (1994). English and Japanese: A cross-cultural comparison of parental styles of narrative elicitation. *Issues in Applied Linguistics, 5*, 383–407.

Minami, M., & McCabe, A. (1995). Rice balls and bear hunts: Japanese and North American family narrative patterns. *Journal of Child Language, 22*(2), 423–445.

Mirel, J. (1993). *The rise and fall of an urban school system: Detroit, 1907–81*. Ann Arbor, MI: University of Michigan.

Mishier, E. G. (1986). *Research interviewing: Context and narrative*. Cambridge, MA: Harvard University Press.

Monk, J. (2000, October 1). God, barbecue, slavery mix at Maurice's. *The State*, pp. B1, B5.

Morgan, S. (1993, March). Coastal disturbances. *Mirabella*, p. 46.

Morris, A. D. (1984). *The origins of the civil rights movement: Black communities organizing for change*. New York; London: Free Press; Collier Macmillan.

Morrison, T. (1990). The site of memory. In R. Fergusson, M. Gever, T. T. Minh-ha, & C. West (Eds.), *Out there: Marginalization and contemporary cultures*. New York: Museum of Contemporary Art.

Morsbach, H. (1987). The importance of silence and stillness in Japanese nonverbal communication: A cross-cultural approach. In F. Poyatos (Ed.), *Cross-cultural perspectives in nonverbal communication*. New York: Goettingen, Hogrefe, & Huber.

Mortenson, T. (1990a, February). *The impact of increased loan utilization among low family income students*. ACT Student Financial Aid Research Report Series.

Mortenson, T. (1990b, May). *The reallocation of financial aid from poor to middle income and affluent students 1978 to 1990*. ACT Student Financial Aid Research Report Series.

Moscovici, S. (1993). *The invention of society* (W. D. Halls, Trans.). Cambridge, MA: Blackwell.

Mumpers, M. (1996). *Removing college price barriers: What government has done and why it hasn't worked*. Albany, NY: State University of New York Press.

Nakamura, H. (1964/1985). *Ways of thinking of Eastern peoples*. Honolulu, HI: University of Hawaii Press.

National Commission on Excellence in Education. (1983a). *A nation at risk*. Washington, DC: U.S. Government Printing Office.

National Commission on Excellence in Education. (1983b). *Meeting the challenge: Recent efforts to improve education across the nation*. Washington, DC: U.S. Government Printing Office.

Natriello, G., McDill, E. L., & Pallas, A. M. (1990). *Schooling disadvantaged children: Racing against catastrophe.* New York: Teachers College.

NCAN Bulletin. (2003, July 15). National College Access Network.

Neal, M. (2002). *Soul babies: Black popular culture and the post soul aesthetic.* New York: Routledge.

Needham, J. (1962). *Science and civilization in China, physics and physical technology.* Cambridge: Cambridge University Press.

Nettles, M. (1988). *Toward black undergraduate student equality in American higher education.* New York: Greenwood.

Newman, K. (1999). *No shame in my game: The working poor in the inner city.* New York: Vintage Books.

Newmann, F. M. (1981). Reducing student alienation in high schools: Implications of theory. *Harvard Educational Review, 51*(4), 546–564.

Nietzsche, F. (1967). *On the genealogy of morals* (W. Kaufman, Trans.). New York: Vintage.

Nisbett, R. E., Peng, K., Choi, I., & Norenzayan, A. (2001). Culture and systems of thought: Holistic vs. analytic cognition. *Psychological Review, 108*(2), 291–310.

Noddings, N. (1984). *Caring: A feminine approach to ethics and moral education.* Berkeley, CA: University of California Press.

Noddings, N. (1992). *The challenge to care in schools: An alternative approach to education.* New York: Teachers College.

Nora, A., & Horvath, F. (1989, May). Financial assistance: Minority enrollment and persistence. *Education and Urban Society, 21*(3).

O'Connor, C. (1997). Dispositions toward (collective) struggle and educational resilience in the inner city: A case analysis of six African American high school students. *American Educational Research Journal, 34*(4), 593–629.

O'Connor, C. (2002). Black women beating the odds from one generation to the next: How the changing dynamics of constraint and opportunity affect the process of educational resilience. *American Educational Research Journal, 39*(4), 855–903.

O'Connor, C., Lewis, A., & Mueller, J. (forthcoming). Researching African Americans' educational experiences: Theoretical and practical considerations. In J. Jackson & C. Caldwell (Eds.), *Research methodology in American communities.* Oakland, CA: Sage.

O'Connor, C., Lewis, M., & Mueller, J. (in press). *Researching African American educational experiences—Theoretical and practical considerations.*

O'Day, J. A., & Smith, M. S. (1993). School reform and equal opportunity: An introduction to the education symposium. *Stanford Law and Policy Review, 4,* 15–20.

Oakes, J. (1985). *Keeping track: How schools structure inequality.* New Haven, CT: Yale University Press.

Oakes, J. (1996, July). *Mathematics and detracking in U.S. senior high schools: Technical, normative, and political dimensions.* Paper presented at the International Conference in Mathematics Education, Seville, Spain.

Oakes, J., Gamoran, A., & Page, R. (1992). Curriculum differentiation: Opportunities, consequences, and meanings. In P. Jackson (Ed.), *Handbook of Research on Curriculum*. New York: Macmillan.

Oakes, J., & Guiton, G. (1995). Matchmaking: The dynamics of high school tracking decisions. *American Educational Research Journal, 32,* 3–33.

Oakes, J., & Wells, A. S. (1996). Potential pitfalls of systemic reform: Early lessons from research on detracking. *Sociology of Education, extra issue,* 135–143.

Oakes, J., Wells, A. S., & Associates (1997a). *Beyond the technicalities of school reform: Policy lessons from detracking schools.* Los Angeles, CA: University of California, Los Angeles.

Oakes, J., Wells, A. S., Datnow, A., & Jones, M. (1997b). Detracking: The social construction of ability, cultural politics, and resistance to reform. *Teachers College Record, 98*(3), 482–510.

Ogbu. J. (1978). *Minority education and caste: The American system in cross-cultural perspective.* New York: Academic.

Ogbu, J. (1988). Cultural diversity and human development. In D. Slaughter (Ed.), *New directions in child development: Vol. 42 black children and poverty: A developmental perspective* (pp. 11–28). San Francisco, CA: Jossey-Bass.

Ogbu, J. (1989). The individual in collective adaptation: A framework for focusing on academic underperformance and dropping out among involuntary minorities. In L. Weis, E. Farrar, & H. G. Petrie (Eds.), *Dropouts from school: Issues, dilemmas, and solutions.* Albany, NY: State University of New York Press.

Ogbu, J. (1991). Immigrant and involuntary minorities in comparative perspective. In M. A. Gibson & J. U. Ogbu (Eds.), *Minority status and schooling: A comparative study of immigrant and involuntary minorities.* New York: Garland.

Olsen, L. (1997). *Made in America: Immigrant students in our public schools.* New York: New Press.

Omi, M., & Winant, H. (1986). *Racial formation in the United States.* New York: Routledge.

Omi, M., & Winant, H. (1986/1994). *Racial formation in the United States: From the 1960s to the 1990s.* New York: Routledge.

Ong, A. (2000). Cultural citizenship as subject making: Immigrants negotiate racial and cultural boundaries in the United States. In R. Torres, L. Miron, & J. Inda (Eds.), *Race, identity and citizenship: A reader.* Malden, MA: Blackwell.

Orel, S. (2003). Left behind in Birmingham: 522 pushed out students. In R. C. Lent & G. Pipkin (Eds.), *Silent no more: Voices of courage in American schools* (pp. 1–14). Portsmouth, NH: Heinemann.

Orenstein, P. (1994). *Schoolgirls: Young women, self-esteem, and the confidence gap.* New York: Anchor Books.

Orfield, G. (1975). *Congressional power: Congress and social change.* New York: Harcourt Brace Jovanovich.

Orfield, G. (2001). *Schools more separate: Consequences of a decade of resegregation.* Cambridge, MA: Civil Rights Project, Harvard University.

Orfield, G., Bachmeier, M., James, D., & Eitle, T. (1997). *Deepening segregation in American public schools*. Cambridge, MA: Harvard Project on School Desegregation.

Orfield, G., & Eaton, S. (1996). *Dismantling desegregation*. New York: New Press.

Orfield, G., Eaton, S. E., & Harvard Project on School Desegregation. (1996). *Dismantling desegregation: The quiet reversal of* Brown v. Board of Education. New York: New Press, Distributed by Norton.

Orfield, G., & Lee, C. (2004). *Brown at 50: King's dream or Plessy's nightmare?* Cambridge, MA: Civil Rights Project, Harvard University.

Ostrove, J., & Cole, E. (2003). Privileging class: Toward a critical psychology of social class in the context of education. *Journal of Social Issues, 59*(4).

Paget, M. A. (1983). Experience and knowledge . . . *Human Studies, 6*, 67–70.

Paley, V. G. (1995). *Kwanzaa and me: A teacher's story*. Cambridge, MA: Harvard University Press.

Parenti, M. (1992). *Make believe media: The politics of entertainment*. New York: St. Martin's.

Pastor, J., McCormick, J., & Fine, M. (1996). Makin' homes: An urban girl thing. In B. Leadbeater and N. Way (Eds.), *Urban girls: Resisting stereotypes, creating identities*. New York: New York University Press.

Penney, C. G. (1975). Modality effects in short-term verbal memory. *Psychological Bulletin, 82*(1), 68–84.

Perna, L. (1998, April). *Differences in the decision to attend college among blacks, Hispanics and whites*. Paper presented at American Educational Research Association (AERA) meeting.

Peshkin, A. (1991). *The color of strangers the color of friends: The play of ethnicity in school and community*. Chicago, IL: University of Chicago Press.

Peters, R. (1987). *Practical intelligence: Working smarter in business and everyday life*. New York: Harper & Row.

Pettigrew, T. F. (1998). Intergroup contact theory. *Annual Review of Psychology, 49*, 65–85.

Pettit, B., & Western, B. (2002). *Inequality in lifetime risks of imprisonment*. Available on-line at http://www.princeton.edu/~wstern [Retrieved January 28, 2003].

Philips, S. (1982). *The invisible culture: Communication in classroom and community on the Warm Springs Indian Reservation*. New York: Longman.

Pinar, W. (2004). *What is curriculum theory?* Mahwah: LEA Associates.

Piven, F. F., & Cloward, R. A. (1982). *The new class war: Reagan's attack on the welfare state and its consequences*. New York: Pantheon Books.

Pollock, D. (Ed.). (1998). *Exceptional spaces: Essays in performance and history*. Chapel Hill, NC: University of North Carolina Press.

Portes, A. (1995). Children of immigrants: Segmented assimilation and its determinants. In A. Portes (Ed.), *The economic sociology of immigration: Essays on networks, ethnicity, and entrepreneurship*. New York: Russell Sage Foundation.

Portes, A., & Zhou, M. (1993). The new second generation: Segmented assimilation and its variants. *Annals of the American Academy of Political and Social Sciences, 530*, 74–96.

Portes, A., & Zhou, M. (1994). Should immigrants assimilate? *Public Interest, 116,* 18–33.

Postman, N. (1986). *Amusing ourselves to death.* New York: Penguin.

Prairie Research Associates Inc. (1989). *The Gay and Lesbian Youth Services Network survey of gay youth and professionals who work with youth.* Winnipeg, Manitoba: Unpublished Report.

Pratt, M. L. (1992). *Imperial eyes: Travel writing and transculturation.* New York: Routledge.

President's Commission on Higher Education. (1947). Volume 1, p. 36.

Putnam, R. D. (1993). The prosperous community: Social capital and public life. *American Prospect, 13* (spring), 35–42.

Putnam, R. D. (1995). Bowling alone: America's declining social capital. *Journal of Democracy, 6*(1), 65–78.

Quinn, N., & Holland, D. C. (1987). Introduction. In D. C. Holland & N. Quinn (Eds.), *Language and thought.* New York: Cambridge University Press.

Rapple, B. (1994). Payment by results: An example of assessment in elementary education from nineteenth century Britain. *Education Policy Analysis Archives, 2*(1). Available on-line at http://epaa.asu.edu/epaa/v2n1 [Retrieved September 21, 2003].

Reardon, S., & Yun, J. (2002). *Private school racial enrollments and segregation.* Cambridge, MA: Civil Rights Project.

Reed, A. (1992). The urban underclass as myth and symbol: The poverty of the discourse about the discourse on poverty. *Radical America 24*(1), 21–40.

Reese, L., Balzano, S., Gallimore, R., & Goldenberg, C. (1991, November). *The concept of* educación: *Latino family values and American schooling.* Paper presented at the Annual Meeting of the American Anthropological Association, Chicago, IL.

Reich, R. (2002). *Bridging liberalism and multiculturalism in American education.* Chicago, IL: University of Chicago Press.

Rhoades, K., & Madaus, G. (2003, May). *Errors in standardized tests: A systemic problem.* Report of the National Board on Educational Testing and Public Policy. Chestnut Hill, MA: Boston College Center for the Study of Testing. Available on-line at http://www.bc.edu/research/nbetpp/reports.html#monographs

Rodriguez, N. P., & Nuñez, R. T. (1986). An exploration of factors that contribute to differentiation between Chicanos and indocumentados. In H. Browning & R. de la Garza (Eds.), *Mexican immigrants and Mexican Americans: An evolving relation.* Austin, TX: CMAS Publications, Center for Mexican American Studies, University of Texas at Austin.

Rofes, E. (1989). Opening up the classroom closet: Responding to the educational needs of gay and lesbian youth. *Harvard Educational Review, 59*(4), 444–453.

Rosenbaum, J. (2001). *Beyond college for all: Career paths for the forgotten half.* New York: Russell Sage Foundation.

Ross, J. A., McKeiver, S., & Hogaboam-Gray, A. (1997). Fluctuations in teacher efficacy during implementation of destreaming. *Canadian Journal of Education, 22*(3), 283–296.

Rothstein, R. (2002, January 24–25). *Out of balance: Our understanding of how schools affect society and how society affects schools.* Traditions of Scholarship in Education Conference.

Rudner, L. (1999). Scholastic achievement and demographic characteristics of home school students in 1998. *Education Policy Analysis Archives, 10*(26). Available on-line at http://epaa.asu.edu/epaa/v10n26.html [Retrieved November 12, 2003].

Rumbaut, R. G. (1994). The crucible within: Ethnic identity, self-esteem, and segmented assimilation among children of immigrants. *International Migration Review, 28,* 748–794.

Rumbaut, R. G., & Ima, K. (1988). *The adaptation of Southeast Asian refugee youth: A comparative study.* Washington, DC: Office of Refugee Resettlement.

Rury, J. (1997). The political economy of urban education. In M. Apple (Ed.), *Review of Educational Research, Vol. 22* (pp. 49–110). Washington, DC: American Educational Research Association.

Russell, M., & Haney, W. (2000, March 28). Bridging the gap between technology and testing. *Education Policy Analysis Archives, 8*(41). Available on-line at http://epaa. asu.edu/epaa/v8n41/

Russell, K. (1992). *The color complex: The politics of skin color among African Americans.* New York: Harcourt Brace Jovanovich.

Russell, M., & Plati, T. (2001). Effects of computer versus paper administration of a state-mandated writing assessment. *Teachers College Record On-line.* Available at http://www.tcrecord.org/Content.asp?ContentID=10709.

Sacks, H., Schegloff, E. A., & Jefferson, G. S. (1974). A simplest systematics for the organization of turn-taking for conversation. *Language, 50,* 696–735.

Sadker, M., & Sadker, D. (1994). *Failing at fairness: How our schools cheat girls.* New York: Touchstone.

Said, E. (2001). The clash of ignorance. *The Nation, 273*(12), 11–13.

San Miguel, G. (1987). *"Let all of them take heed": Mexican Americans and the campaign for educational equality in Texas, 1910–1981.* Austin, TX: University of Texas Press.

Sanchez, S. (2003). *Interview for echoes: The legacy of* Brown v. Board of Education, *fifty years later.* New York: City University of New York Graduate Center.

Sares, T. (1992, April 20–24). *School size effects on educational attainment and ability.* Paper presented at the annual meeting of the American Educational Research Association, San Francisco, CA.

Sarroub, L. K. (2001). The sojourner experience of Yemeni American high school students: An ethnographic portrait. *Harvard Educational Review, 71*(3), 390–415.

Schofield, J. W. (1995). Review of research on school desegregation's impact on elementary and secondary school students. In J. A. Banks & C. A. M. Banks (Eds.), *Handbook of Research on Multicultural Education.* New York: Simon & Schuster Macmillan.

Schooler, J. W., Ohlsson, S., & Brooks, K. (1993). Thoughts beyond words: When language overshadows insight. *Journal of Experimental Psychology: General, 122*(2), 166–183.

Sefton-Green, J. (Ed.). (1998). *Digital diversions: Youth culture in the age of multimedia.* New York: Routledge.

Sefton-Green, J. (Ed.). (1999). *Young people, creativity and new technologies.* New York: Routledge.

Sennett, R., & Cobb, J. (1972). *The hidden injuries of class.* New York: Vintage Books.

Shepard, L. (2002, January 24–25). *The contest between large-scale accountability testing and assessment in the service of learning.* Paper prepared at the Spencer Foundation's 30th Anniversary Conference, "Traditions of Scholarship in Education," Chicago, IL.

Shepard, L. A., & Smith, M. L. (1989). *Flunking grades: Research and policies on retention.* New York: Falmer.

Sherif, M. (1966). *In common predicament.* Boston, MA: Houghton Mifflin.

Shore, B. (1996). *Culture in mind.* New York: Oxford University Press.

Shweder, R. A. (1991). *Thinking through cultures: Expeditions in cultural psychology.* Cambridge, MA: Harvard University Press.

Shweder, R. A. (1995). Cultural psychology: What is it? In N. R. Goldberger & J. B. Veroff (Eds.), *Cultural and psychology reader.* New York: New York University Press.

Shweder, R. A., & Bourne, E. J. (1984). Does the concept of person vary cross-culturally? In R. A. Shweder & R. A. LeVine (Eds.), *Culture theory: Essays on mind, self, and emotion.* Cambridge: Cambridge University Press.

Simon, P. (2003, October 31). A GI bill for today. *Chronicle of Higher Education.*

Skutnabb-Kangas, T., & Cummins, J. (1988). *Minority education: From shame to struggle.* Clevedon, Canada: Multilingual Matters 40.

Slavin, R. (1987). Ability grouping and student achievement in elementary schools: A best evidence synthesis. *Review of Educational Research, 57*(3), 293–336.

Slevin, K. F., & Wingrove, C. R. (1998). *From stumbling blocks to stepping stones: The life experiences of fifty professional African American women.* New York: New York University Press.

Smith, D. E. (1987). *The everyday world as problematic: A feminist sociology.* Boston, MA: Northeastern University Press.

Smith, D. E. (1990). *The conceptual practices of power: A feminist sociology of knowledge.* Boston, MA: Northeastern University Press.

Smolowe, J. (1993, August 23). Danger in the safety zone. *Time Magazine*, pp. 29–32.

Solomon, R. (1990). Nietzsche, postmodernism, and resentment: A genealogical hypothesis. In C. Koelb (Ed.), *Nietzsche as postmodernist: Essays pro and con* (pp. 267–294). Albany, NY: State University of New York Press.

Spear, A. H. (1967). *Black Chicago: The making of a Negro ghetto, 1890–1920.* Chicago, IL: University of Chicago Press.

Stage, F., & Hossler, D. (1988). *Differences in family influences on college attendance plans for male and female ninth graders.* Paper presented at the Association for the Study of Higher Education (ASHE) Annual Meeting.

Stanton-Salazar, R. (1997). A social capital framework for understanding the socialization of ethnic minority children and youths. *Harvard Educational Review, 67,* 1–39.

Stanton-Salazar, R. D., & Dornbusch, S. M. (1995). Social capital and the reproduction of inequality: Information networks among Mexican-origin high school students. *Sociology of Education, 68,* 116–135.

Steedman, C. K. (1987). *Landscape for a good woman.* New Brunswick, NJ: Rutgers University Press.

Steinberg, L., Brown, B. B., & Dornbusch, S. M. (1996). *Beyond the classroom: Why school reform has failed and what parents need to do.* New York: Simon & Schuster.

Stevenson, R., & Ellsworth, J. (1993). Dropouts and the silencing of critical voices. In L. Weis & M. Fine (Eds.), *Beyond silenced voices: Class, race, and gender in United States schools.* Albany, NY: State University of New York Press.

Strauss, A., & Corbin, J. (1998). Grounded theory and methodology: An overview. In N. Denzin, & Y. Lincoln (Eds.), *The landscape of qualitative research: Theories and issues.* Thousand Oaks, CA: Sage.

Stroud, J. (2000, January 11). As legislators return, S.C. senator's "insult" hardens flag debate. *The State,* pp. A1, A10.

Stuart, G. (2000). *Segregation in the Boston metropolitan area at the end of the twentieth century.* Cambridge, MA: Civil Rights Project, Harvard University.

Suárez-Orozco, C., & Suárez-Orozco, M. M. (1997). *Transformations: Immigration, family life and achievement motivation among Latino adolescents.* Stanford, CA: Stanford University Press.

Suárez-Orozco, M. M. (1991). Hispanic immigrant adaptation to schooling. In M. A. Gibson & J. U. Ogbu (Eds.), *Minority status and schooling: A comparative study of immigrant and involuntary minorities.* New York: Garland.

Suárez-Orozco, M. M. (2001). Globalization, immigration, and education: The research agenda. *Harvard Educational Review, 71*(3), 345–365.

Swann, W. B., Jr., & Rentfrow, P. J. (2001). Blirtatiousness: Cognitive, behavioral, and physiological consequences of rapid responding. *Journal of Personality and Social Psychology, 81*(6), 1160–1175.

Swanson, C. B., & Chaplin, D. (2003, February 25). *Counting high school graduates when graduates count: Measuring graduation rates under the high stakes of NCLB.* Washington, DC: Education Policy Center, Urban Institute.

Swidler, A. (1986). Culture in action: Symbols and strategies. *American Sociological Review, 51,* 273–286.

The Syracuse Constitution (1993, August 2). A menace to society, p. 5.

Takaki, R. (1989). *Strangers from a different shore: A history of Asian Americans.* New York: Penguin Books.

Tamari, S. (1999). *Who are the Arabs?* Washington, DC: Georgetown University, Center for Contemporary Arab Studies.

Tatum, B. D. (1994). Teaching white students about racism: The search for white allies and the restoration of hope. *Teachers College Record, 95*(4), 462–476.

Taylor, J. M., Gilligan, C., & Sullivan, A. M. (1995). *Between voice and silence: Women and girls, race and relationship.* Cambridge, MA: Harvard University Press.

Thonssen, L., & Gilkinson, H. (1955). Speech. *Review of Educational Research, 25,* 139–153.

Tierney, W., & Hagedorn, L. (2002). Introduction. Cultural capital and the struggle for educational equity. In W. Tierney & L. Hagedorn (Eds.), *Increasing access to college: Extending possibilities for all students.* Albany, NY: State University of New York Press.

Tobin, J. (2000). *"Good guys don't wear hats": Children's talk about the media.* New York: Teachers College.

Tobin, J. J., Wu, D. Y. H., & Davidson, D. H. (1989). *Preschool in three cultures: Japan, China and the United States.* New Haven, CT: Yale University Press.

Triandis, H. C. (1989). The self and social behavior in differing cultural contexts. *Psychological Review, 96*(3), 506–520.

Tseng, W. (1973). The concept of personality in confucian thought. *Psychiatry: Journal for the study of interpersonal processes, 36*(2), 191–202.

Tuan, M. (1998). *Forever foreigner of honorary whites? The Asian ethnic experience today.* New Brunswick, NJ: Rutgers University Press.

Tweed, R. G., & Lehman, D. R. (2002). Learning considered within a cultural context. *American Psychologist, 52*(2), 89–99.

U.S. Bureau of the Census. (2001, March). *PCES annual demographic survey, March supplement.* Available on-line at http://ferret.bls.census.gov/macro/032001/perin/new03_001.htm.

U.S. Census Bureau Current Population Survey. (2000, March). *Income in 1999 by educational attainment for people 18 years old and over, by age, sex, race, and Hispanic origin* (Table 8).

U.S. Department of Commerce (1950). *Statistical abstract of the United States 1950, No. 72.* Washington DC: United States Government Printing Office.

U.S. Department of Commerce (1950). *Statistical abstract of the United States 1950, No. 82.* Washington DC: United States Government Printing Office.

U.S. Department of Commerce (1970). *Statistical abstract of the United States 1970, 91st edition.* Washington DC: United States Government Printing Office.

U.S. Department of Commerce (1980). *Statistical abstract of the United States 1980, 101st edition.* Washington DC: United States Government Printing Office.

U.S. Department of Labor, Bureau of Labor Statistics. (2000, October). The outlook for college graduates, 1998–2008. In U.S. Department of Education (Ed.), *Getting ready pays off!*

U.S. Government Information/Resources. (2000, October 9). *Supreme Court tosses Confederate flag sketch appeal.* Available on-line at http://usgovinfo.about.com/library.

Useem, E. L. (1992). Middle schools and math groups: Parents' involvement in children's placement. *Sociology of Education, 65,* 263–279.

Valenzuela, A. (1993). Liberal gender role attitudes and academic achievement among Mexican-origin adolescents in two Houston inner-city Catholic schools. *Hispanic Journal of Behavioral Sciences, 15,* 310–323.

Valenzuela, A. (1997). Mexican American youth and the politics of caring. In E. Long (Ed.), *From sociology to cultural studies: Sociology of culture annual series, vol. 2*. London: Blackwell.

Valenzuela, A. (1999). *Subtractive schooling: U.S.-Mexican youth and the politics of caring*. Albany, NY: State University of New York Press.

Valenzuela, A., & Dornbusch, S. M. (1994). Familism and social capital in the academic achievement of Mexican-origin and Anglo high school adolescents. *Social Science Quarterly, 75*(1), 18–36.

Valli, L. (1986). *Becoming clerical workers*. London; Boston, MA: Routledge & Kegan Paul.

Vigil, J. D., & Long, J. M. (1981). Unidirectional or nativist acculturation: Chicano paths to school achievement. *Human Organization, 40*, 273–277.

Walker, V. S. (2000). Valued segregated schools for African American children in the South, 1935–1969: A review of common themes and characteristics. *Review of Educational Research, 70*(3), 253–285.

Walker-Moffat, W. (1995). *The other side of the Asian American success story*. San Francisco, CA: Jossey-Bass.

Walkerdine, V. (1997). *Daddy's girl*. Cambridge, MA: Harvard University Press.

Walkerdine, V., Lucey, H., & Melody, J. (2001). *Growing up girl: Psychosocial explorations of gender and class*. New York: New York University Press.

Ward, J. V. (1996). Raising resisters: The role of truth telling in the psychological development of African American girls. In B. J. Ross Leadbeater and N. Way (Eds.), *Urban girls: Resisting stereotypes, creating identities*. New York: New York University Press.

Warren, J. R. (2003, August). *State-level high school graduation rates in the 1990s: Concepts, measures and trends*. Paper prepared for presentation at the annual meetings of the American Sociological Association, Atlanta, GA.

Watney, S. (1991). School's out. In D. Fuss (Ed.), *Inside/out: Lesbian theories, gay theories* (pp. 387–404). New York: Routledge.

Watson, J. B. (1920). Is thinking merely the action of language mechanisms? *British Journal of Psychology, 11*(11), 87–104.

Weatherford, M. S. (1982). Interpersonal networks and political behavior. *American Journal of Political Science, 26*(1), 117–143.

Weber, M. (1978). Class, status, party. In G. Roth & C. Wittich (Eds.), *Economy and society, Vol. 2* (pp. 927–939). Berkeley, CA: University of California Press.

Weiler, J. D. (2000). *Codes and contradictions*. Albany, NY: State University of New York Press.

Weis, L. (1988). *Class, race, and gender in American education*. Albany, NY: State University of New York Press.

Weis, L. (1990). *Working class without work: High school students in a deindustrialized economy*. New York: Routledge.

Weis, L., & Fine, M. (Eds.). (2000). *Construction sites: Excavating race, class, and gender among urban youth*. New York: Teachers College Press.

Weis, L., & Fine, M. (2003). Extraordinary conversations in public schools. In G. Dimitriadis & D. Carlson (Eds.), *Promises to keep: Cultural studies, democratic education, and public life* (pp. 95–124). New York: RoutledgeFalmer.

Weis, L., & Fine, M. (2004). *Working method: Research and social (in)justice.* New York: Routledge.

Wells, A. S., & Crain, R. L. (1994). Perpetuation theory and the long-term effects of school desegregation. *Review of Educational Research, 64,* 531–555.

Wells, A. S., & Serna, I. (1996). The politics of culture: Understanding local political resistance to detracking in racially mixed schools. *Harvard Educational Review, 66*(1), 93–118.

Wheelock, A. (1992). *Crossing the tracks: How "untracking" can save America's schools.* New York: New Press.

Wheelock, A., Bebell, D., & Haney W. (2000, November). What can student drawings tell us about high-stakes testing in Massachusetts. *Teachers College Record On-line.* Available at http://www.tcrecord.org/Content.asp?ContentID=10634

The White House. (2001). *No child left behind.* Washington, DC: White House.

White, K. (1995). *Why good girls don't get ahead, but gutsy girls do.* New York: Warner Books.

Whorf, B. L. (1956). *Language, thought, and reality: Selected writings.* Cambridge, MA: Technology Press of Massachusetts Institute of Technology.

Wierzbicka, A. (1992). Talking about emotions: Semantics, culture, and cognition. *Cognition & Emotion, 6*(3/4), 285–319.

Wilder, L. (1986). *Talk your way to success: Wilder method for effective business communication.* NY: Simon & Schuster.

Wildman, S., & Davis, A. (2000). Language and silence: Making systems of privilege visible. In M. Adams, W. Blumenfeld, R. Castaneda, H. Hackman, M. Peters, & X. Zuniga (Eds.), *Readings for diversity and social justice* (pp. 50–60). New York: Routledge.

Williams, D. (1994). Society, spatiality, and innercity disinvestment in a large U.S. city. *International Journal of Urban and Regional Research, 17,* 578–594.

Williams, R. (1974). *Television, technology and cultural form.* New York: Schocken Books.

Willis, P. (1977). *Learning to labor: How working class kids get working class jobs.* New York: Columbia University Press.

Wilson, W. J. (1987). *The truly disadvantaged: The inner city, the underclass, and public policy.* Chicago, IL: University of Chicago Press.

Winter, G. (2003, January 28). College loans rise, swamping graduates' dreams. *New York Times.*

Winter, G., & Medina, J. (2003, March 10). More students line up at financial aid office. *New York Times.*

Wood, J. (1993, August). John Singleton and the impossible greenback of the assimilated black artist. *Esquire,* pp. 59–108.

Wray, M., & Newitz, A. (Eds.) (1997). *White trash: Race and class in America.* New York: Routledge.

Wright, J. (Ed.). (2002). *The New York Times Almanac.* New York: Penguin.

Yan, J. J. (1987). On establishing the field of Chinese communication [in Chinese]. *Xing Wen Xue Kan, 10,* 50–53.

Yeo, F. L. (1997). *Inner-city schools, multiculturalism, and teacher education: A professional journey.* New York: Garland.

Yon, D. (2000). *Elusive culture: Schooling, race, and identity in global times.* Albany, NY: State University of New York Press.

Yonezawa, S. (1997). *Making decisions about students' lives: An interactive study of secondary school students' course placement decision-making.* Unpublished doctoral dissertation, University of California, Los Angeles.

Young, A. (1999, July 17). The (non) accumulation of capital: Explicating the relationship of structure and agency in the lives of poor black men. *Sociological Theory, 2,* 201–227.

Young, B. A., & Smith, T. M. (1997). The social context of education. *The condition of education,* 97–991.

Young, I. M. (2000). *Inclusion and democracy.* Oxford: Oxford University Press.

Zimmerman, B. (1991). Seeing, reading, knowing: The lesbian appropriation of literature. In J. Hartman & E. Messer-Davidow (Eds.), *(En)gendering knowledge: Feminists in academe.* Knoxville, TN: University of Tennessee Press.

Contributors

Lisa Abrams is a research associate for the Center for the Study of Testing, Evaluation, and Educational Policy in the Lynch School of Education at Boston College. She has coauthored several journal articles on the impact of high-stakes testing policies on teachers, students, and classroom practice. Her areas of expertise include test-based accountability, high-stakes testing, special education, and grade retention.

Thea Renda Abu El-Haj is an assistant professor in the Graduate School of Education at Rutgers University, New Brunswick. Her recent publications include "Practicing for Equity from the Standpoint of the Particular: Exploring the work of one Urban Teacher Network" in *Teachers College Record* and "Challenging the Inevitability of Difference: Young Women and Discourses about Gender Equity in the Classroom" in *Curriculum Inquiry*.

Janice L. Bloom is a doctoral student in urban education at the Graduate Center of the City University of New York. She taught in New York City public high schools for seven years and continues to lead professional development and teacher research workshops for small school educators. She is the author of "Betrayal: Accountability from the Bottom" in *Voices in Urban Education: Rethinking Accountability* (with M. Fine & L. Chajet).

Lyn Mikel Brown is associate professor of education and women's, gender, and sexuality studies at Colby College and cocreator of the nonprofit Hardy Girls Healthy Women. She is the author of *Meeting at the Crossroads: Women's Psychology and Girls' Development* (with C. Gilligan), *Raising Their Voices: The Politics of Girls' Anger*, and *Girlfighting: Betrayal and Rejection Among Girls*.

Dennis Carlson is a professor of curriculum and cultural studies at Miami University, in the Department of Educational Leadership. His recent books include *Leaving Safe Harbors: Toward a New Progressivism in Education and Public Life* and *Promises to Keep: Cultural Studies, Democratic Education, and Public Life* (with G. Dimitriadis).

Greg Dimitriadis is Associate Professor in the Department of Educational Leadership and Policy at the University at Buffalo, the State University of New York. He is the author of *Performing Identity/Performing Culture: Hip Hop as Text, Pedagogy, and Lived Practice* and *Friendship, Cliques, and Gangs: Young Black Men Coming of Age in Urban America*.

Ileana M. Gruia is a research assistant for the Center on the Study of Testing Evaluation and Educational Policy and a graduate student in the Educational Research, Measurement, and Evaluation program at Boston College. Her current research focuses on grade retention and drop-out rates.

Walter Haney is professor of education at Boston College and senior research associate in the Center for the Study of Testing, Evaluation, and Educational Policy. He has published widely on testing and assessment issues in scholarly journals such as the *Harvard Educational Review, Review of Educational Research,* and *Review of Research in Education* and in wide-audience periodicals such as *Educational Leadership, Phi Delta Kappan,* the *Chronicle of Higher Education,* and the *Washington Post*.

Heejung S. Kim is assistant professor of psychology at the University of California, Santa Barbara. She has written "Choice and Self-expression: A Cultural Analysis of Variety Seeking" (with A. Drolet) and "We Talk, Therefore We Think? A Cultural Analysis of the Effect of Talking on Thinking," both in *Journal of Personality and Social Psychology*.

Chungmei Lee is a research associate at the Civil Rights Project. Most recently, Ms. Lee authored *Racial Segregation and Educational Outcomes in Metropolitan Boston* (2004) and coauthored, *Brown at 50: King's Dream or Plessy's Nightmare* (2004) and *A Multiracial Society with Segregated Schools: Are We Losing the Dream?* (2003), published by the Civil Rights Project.

Stacey J. Lee is professor of educational policy studies at University of Wisconsin-Madison. She is the author of *Unraveling the Model Minority Stereotype: Listening to Asian American Youth,* and she is currently completing a book on Hmong-American high school students.

R. L'Heureux Lewis is a graduate student instructor in the Department of Sociology at the University of Michigan and a research associate in educational studies.

Richard R. Lussier recently completed an Ed.D. in curriculum studies from the University of South Carolina under the direction of Susan L. Schramm-Pate. He is certified in secondary French, Spanish, and social studies and will begin teaching in the fall of 2004 in the area of advanced-placement French at Ridgeview High School in Columbia, South Carolina.

George Madaus is currently the Boisi Professor of Education and Public Policy at Boston College. He was named as the recipient of the 2003 E. F. Lindquist award, presented by AERA and ACT to a distinguished research scientist for "Significant contributions to the field of educational measurement," and he is the former executive director of the National Commission on Testing and Public Policy.

Hazel Rose Markus is a professor of psychology at Stanford University, and she currently serves as the director of Stanford's Research Center for Comparative Studies in Race and Ethnicity. Her most recent coedited volume is entitled *Engaging Cultural Differences: The Multicultural Challenge in Liberal Democracies,* and she is the author of papers on the influence of sociocultural contexts on self, competence, choice, and well-being.

Cameron McCarthy, associate professor of communications in the Institute of Communications Research, teaches cultural studies and curriculum theory at the University of Illinois of Urbana-Champaign. He is the author of *Race and Curriculum,* and the editor of *Multicultural Curriculum: New Directions for Social Theory, Practice and Policy* (with R. Mahalingam) and *Sound Identities: Popular Music and the Cultural Politics of Education.*

Jing Miao is a doctoral candidate in the Educational Research, Measurement, and Evaluation program at the Lynch School of Education at Boston College. She currently holds the Boisi Fellowship in Education and Public Policy. Her current research interests include high school drop-out rates, grade retention, and high-stakes testing.

Jennifer Mueller is a graduate student instructor in the School of Education at the University of Michigan. She is a doctoral student in educational studies.

Carla O'Connor is assistant professor in the University of Michigan School of Education where she teaches urban education, social psychology, and sociology of education. Her most recent publications include "Beating the Odds from One Generation to the Next," in *American Educational Research Journal,* and "Making Sense of the Complexity of Social Identity in Relation to Achievement," in *Sociology of Education.*

Gary Orfield is professor of education and social policy at Harvard University and director of the Harvard Civil Rights Project. He has written and edited a number a books and many articles on issues of school desegregation, including *Dismantling Desegregation* (with S. Eaton) and has participated in several dozen class action civil rights lawsuits.

Susan L. Schramm-Pate is associate professor of curriculum studies in the Department of Educational Leadership and Polices at the University of South Carolina. Her books include *Transforming the Curriculum: Thinking Outside* *the Box* and *A Separate Sisterhood: Women Who Shaped Southern Educational Reform in the Progressive Era* (with K. Reynolds).

Dorothy Smith is a professor of sociology and equity studies in education at the Ontario Institute for Studies in Education of the University of Toronto. She is involved in the Research Network on New Approaches to Lifelong Learning. Her most current book is *Writing the Social: Critique, Theory, and Investigations.* She prepared George W. Smith's chapter for publication.

George W. Smith has written across the fields of sociology, median studies, and law. His publications include *Media Frames: How Accounts Are Produced and Read, Policing the Gay Community: An Inquiry into Textually-mediated Social Relations,* and *Political Activist as Ethnographer.* He died of AIDS in November 1994.

Mariá Elena Torre is a doctoral candidate in the Social Personality Psychology program at the Graduate Center of the City University of New York. She is a coauthor of *Echoes of Brown: Youth Documenting* and *Performing the Legacy of* Brown v. Board of Education and *Changing Minds: The Impact of College on a Maximum Security Prison.* She teaches in the education studies department at Eugene Lang College.

Angela Valenzuela is associate professor in the Department of Curriculum and Instruction and the Center for Mexican American Studies at the University of Texas at Austin. She is the author of *Subtractive Schooling: U.S. Mexican Youth and the Politics of Caring* and the editor of *Leaving Children Behind: How Texas-Style Accountability Fails Latino Youth.*

Amy Stuart Wells is a professor of educational policy at Columbia University, Teachers College, in the Department of Sociology and Education. She is a sociologist of education whose research and writing has focused on race and educational policies. She is the author of *Stepping over the Color Line: African American Students in White Suburban Schools* and editor of *Multiple Meanings of Charter School Reform: Lessons from Ten California School Districts* (with R. Crain). She has written prolifically on charter schools, including *Defining Democracy in the Neoliberal Age: Charter School Reform and Educational Consumption.*

Anne Wheelock is a senior research associate at the Center for Educational Testing, Evaluation, and Educational Policy in the Lynch School of Education at Boston College. She is author of *Crossing the Tracks: How "Detracking" Can Save America's Schools* and *Safe to Be Smart: Building a Culture for Standards-Based Reform in the Middle Grades.*

Susan S. Yonezawa is a project research scientist at the University of California, San Diego's Center for Research in Educational Equity, Assessment, and

Teaching Excellence (CREATE) and a high school English teacher in the San Diego Unified School District. She has published articles in *American Educational Research Journal, Educational Researcher,* and *Educational Leadership,* and she has a chapter in *The International Handbook of Student Experience in Elementary and Secondary School.*

Index

Aaliyah, 142
Abrams, L., xii, 21–45
Abu El-Haj, T., xiii, 199–215
Adelman, C., 66
Advisory Committee on Student
  Financial Aid, 79
Advocates for Children, 41, 42
Affect: politics of, 122–125; in race rela-
  tions, 122
Affirmative action, 19, 64
Alabama: attrition rates, 25*tab*; domes-
  tic/foreign migration in, 35*tab*; grad-
  uation rates in, 30, 32*tab*; student
  exclusion from testing in, 41, 42
Alaska: attrition rates, 25*tab*;
  domestic/foreign migration in, 35*tab*;
  graduation rates in, 32*tab*
Alienation: paranoiac, 128, 129
Allport, G., 254
Anyon, J., 60
Anzaldua, G., 255
Apartheid, 236
Apple, M., 64, 70, 209
Arab-Americans. *See* Students,
  Palestinian-American
Arizona: domestic/foreign migration in,
  35*tab*; graduation rates in, 30, 32*tab*
Arkansas: domestic/foreign migration in,
  35*tab*; grade 9 bulge in schools, 29;
  graduation rates in, 32*tab*

Assimilation: as nonneutral process, 87
Attrition: education reform and, 39–43;
  increases in, 23, 24*fig*, 25; national,
  24*fig*; reform and, 39
Au, K., 137
Austin, J., 183
Ayres, L., 21
Azuma, H., 187

Backlund, P., 189
Bakhtin, M., 95
Banks, J., 211, 212, 215
Barr, R., 54
Basic Education Opportunity Grants, 69
Baudrillard, J., 118, 123
Bauman, K., 37
Beatty, J., 121, 122, 123
Benard, B., 169
Bennett, William, 124
Bentley, Nora, 173
Berry, Halle, 128
Besiner, N., 246
Bessinger, Maurice, 223
Beyer, L., 240
Bhabha, H., 120
Biculturalism, 88, 89–91
Bielick, S., 37
Bilingualism, 88, 89–91, 272*n*7
Black Panthers, 239, 244, 249
Blackstone Rangers, 249

Bloom, J., xii, 63–81
Bogart, H., 120
Boston (MA) area: demographics of,
    12–15; desegregation and, 3–20;
    fragmentation in school systems,
    14–15; levels of segregation in,
    15–16; school enrollment in, 12,
    12*tab*, *13*; slow rate of growth in
    enrollment in, 13; uneven distribu-
    tion of students in, 13, 14*tab*
Bourdieu, P., 53, 135
Boyz 'N the Hood (film), 125, 126
Braddock, J., 11, 56
Brint, S., 66
Brown, L., xiii, 147–161
Brown v. Board of Education (1954), 3,
    254, 255
Bruner, J., 188, 192
Buchanan, Pat, 124
Buckingham, D., 235
Buendia, E., 117–131
Burawoy, M., 66
Burd, S., 64, 79
Burns, A., 260
Bush, George H.W., 80
Bush, George W., 21
Butler, J., 160

California: attrition rates, 23;
    domestic/foreign migration in, 35*tab*;
    grade 9 bulge in schools, 29; gradua-
    tion rates in, 32*tab*
Callahan, R., 88
Campaigne, D., 73
Campbell, R., 117
Capital: cultural, 54, 135, 154; human,
    86; social, 83, 91
Caring: importance in education, 91–94
Carlson, D., xiii–xiv, 217–231
Carnevale, A., 64, 73, 80
Carter, M., 131
Caudhill, W., 189
Cavanagh, S., 79

Chapa, J., 85
Chaplin, C., 119
Chavez, L., 203
Civil rights, 172; history, xiv; movement,
    63
Clancy, P., 185
Class: bias, 150; as code for whiteness,
    135; conflict, 124; consciousness,
    150; decisions on course creation
    and, 51; differences, 123; experienc-
    ing, 73; femininity and, 147–161;
    gender and, 147–161; hidden injuries
    of, 72; material conditions of
    inequality and, 73; middle, 123, 124,
    128, 135, 139, 144–145, 147–161;
    morality and, 155; significance over
    race, 135; social, 51, 64, 71, 139, 155;
    social construction of, 147; social
    order and, 88; in society, 123; struc-
    tures, 123; tracking and, 50; working,
    53, 123, 127, 147–161
Classrooms: design, xi; detracked, 48;
    heterogeneous, 48
Cleaver, Kathleen, 240
Clemente, Roberto, 239
Clinton, Bill, 21, 127
Clotfelter, C., 4
Coalition of Essential Schools, 65
Coleman, J., 83, 86
College. *See also* Education, higher:
    access to, 63–81; computing worth of
    risk of, 74–76; costs of application,
    72–73; demands of financial assis-
    tance reporting, 78, 79; difficulty in
    applying to, 70–73; financial barriers
    to, 63; as first in family to attend, 67;
    low-income students and, 63; mis-
    leading information on financial aid,
    67–73; rising tuition costs, 74; unfa-
    miliarity with, 67–69
College Opportunity and Career Help
    program, 271*n18*
Collins, 166, 221

Colorado: domestic/foreign migration in, 35*tab*; graduation rates in, 32*tab*

Comer, J., 56

Commission on Higher Education, 69

Cone, J., 49

Conflict: class, 124; desegregation and, 3; global, xiii, 201–202; misread as discipline problem, xiii–xiv; social, 124

Connecticut: domestic/foreign migration in, 35*tab*; graduation rates in, 30, 32*tab*

Conquergood, D., 241

Cooper, R., 56

Cosby, Bill, 239

Crane, J., 169

Crichlow, W., 234

Crowley, J., 52

Cultural: assimilation, 195; assumptions, 192; beliefs, 192, 194; capital, 54, 135, 154; deficiency, 138, 140, 141, 144; deprivation, 138; differences, 135, 137, 144, 192; diversity, 55–59; identification, 237; identity, 89–91, 159; inferiority, 139; institutions, 124; inversion, 92; norms, 49; politics, 123; relativism, 138; "texts," 230; tolerance, 135; traditions, 182, 192

Culture: adversarial, 87; of black femininity, xiii, 163–179; effect of talking on thinking and, 192–194; embodied in the other, 138; gang, 129; global youth, 236; high-context/low-context, 188; hip hop, 142; home, 137; of individualism, 159; interdependence with psychology, 195; language of, 202; middle-class, 139; minority, 139; oppositional, 92, 157; original, 88; peer, 56, 85, 91; popular, xii, 117–131, 233–250; of poverty, 138; of power, 150, 154, 157; school, xii, 52, 135, 137, 150; tracked, 52; of violence, 128; wars, 124; of whiteness, 134–137, 136, 138, 144–145

Curriculum: alternative, 234; equitable access to, 48; Eurocentric, 135; for youth to understand world around them, 237

Daiute, C., 249

D'Andrade, R., 182

Datnow, A., 56, 57

David, M., 54

David, S., 117–131

Davis, Angela, 172, 173, 174

Davis, M., 126

Davis, Ossie, 128

Delaware: attrition rates, 25*tab*; domestic/foreign migration in, 35*tab*; grade 9 bulge in schools, 29; graduation rates in, 30, 32*tab*

Delpit, L., 150, 154, 160

Denzin, N., 241

Desegregation: by community size, 11–12; consequences of, 19; dismantling, xii; Dowell decision and, 3; exemptions from, 268*n15*; opposition to, 7; patterns of, 4

Detracking: burden placed on students by, 49; choice-based, 47–61; choosing respect and, 49, 55–59; defining, 48–49; discrimination and, 56; favored by high-track students, 54; hidden prerequisites and, 51–52; as inequitable reform, 59; institutional barriers and, 49, 50–52; political nature of, 49; screening in, 52; selective flexibility in, 51; tracked aspirations and, 49, 52–55; uneven information given concerning, 50–51

DeVault, M., 96

Di Leonardo, M., 147

Dimitriadis, G., xiv, 230, 233–250

Disclosure (film), 119, 130

Discrimination: detracking and, 56; reverse, 222

Dissent, xii–xiii

Diversity: accommodation of, 181; cultural, 55–59; ethnic, 181; racial, 181; talking and, 195; teacher attitudes on, 135

Dolby, N., 236

Dornbusch, S., 48

Dougherty, K., 66

Douglas, Michael, 119, 128, 130

Dropout rates: poverty and, 268n11; in segregated schools, 9

Duneier, M., 64

Dyer, R., 136

Echoes performance, 251, 253

Eckert, P., 56, 136

Education: accountability in, 70, 233; attitudes toward, 76; for change, xi, xiii–xiv; constriction of high school pipeline and, 39–43; for democracy and dissent, 214–215; economizing in, 70; for employment, 70; importance of caring to, 91–94; importance of speech in, 181; income and, xii; marginalization in, 260; on meaning of Confederate Flag issue, 217–231; multicultural, 206–211; narrowed access to, xii; parental levels, 85; quality of systems of, 21–45; race relations in, 217–231; reflection of lived experiences in, 57–58; reform, 39–43; restructuring of opportunities for, xii; retreat from commitment to equal opportunity in, 79; settings as zones of contact, 254–255; students definitions of, 83; talking in, 189–190; tertiary, xii; unequal outcomes in, 70; verbal participation as integral aspect of, 189

Education, higher: access to, 63, 64; average earnings from, 75; costs of loans for, 73–74; erosion of financial assistance for, 64; financial aid, 69–70, 70tab; financial barriers to,

63–81; importance for economic self-sufficiency, 63, 66; social class and, 64; student desire for, 66–69; subsidized, 64; unsubsidized loans for, 70

Educational Opportunity Gap Project, 251–266

Educational Opportunity Grants, 270n5

Educational Opportunity Programs, 74

Eliot, T.S., 119

Ellsworth, E., 230

Ellwood, S., 163, 164, 169, 175

Emergency School Aid Act (1972), 269n29

Enrollment: grade 9 bulge and, 26–45, 29fig; national data, 27fig; private school, 36–37; variation in attrition rates and, 23

Erickson, F., 137, 145, 204

Ericsson, K., 192, 193

Espiritu, Y., 144

Etter-Lewis, G., 178

Evaluation: of educational systems, 21

Exclusion: structuring, xi, xii

Eyes on the Prize (television), 242, 246

FAFSA. See Free Application for Federal Student Aid

Falling Down (film), 119, 128, 129, 130

Farley, C., 121

Farnsworth, L., 174

Femininity: black, xiii, 163–179; cultural conventions of, 164; school success among black girls and, 163–179; social class and, 147–161

Film. See Media

Fine, M., xi–xiv, 52, 58, 60, 64, 73, 85, 156, 174, 219, 233, 234, 244, 251, 253, 254, 255

Fiske, A., 182, 184

Flag, Confederate, xiii–xiv, 217–231; "facts" and "truths" about, 220–225; finding common grounds in debate over, 222–225; risks of examining dialogue in conflict over, 226–229; symbolism of used as means of discussing discrimination, 226–229

Florida: attrition rates, 25*tab*; domestic/foreign migration in, 35*tab*; grade 9 bulge in schools, 29; graduation rates in, 30, 32*tab*

Fordham, S., 56, 57, 86, 92, 165

Fossey, R., 63, 70, 74

Foucault, M., 150

Frankenberg, E., 4, 15, 265

Frankenberg, R., 158, 159

Franklin, Aretha, 129

Free Application for Federal Student Aid, 71

Freeman, C., 4, 75

Fregoso, R., 126

Freire, P., 156, 230

Friday (film), 242

Gamoran, A., 48, 54, 56

Gangs, 129, 139, 246

Gao, G., 185, 190

Garet, M., 51

Gates, D., 130

Gender: class and, 147–161; equality, 144; relations, 99, 107–109; social construction of, 147; social order and, 88; student aspirations and, 52

Georgia: attrition rates, 23, 25*tab*; domestic/foreign migration in, 35*tab*; grade 9 bulge in schools, 29; graduation rates in, 30, 32*tab*

Gerbner, G., 120

Gibson, M., 87, 88

Gilligan, C., 159, 174

Giroux, H., 88, 230

Gladden, R., 65

Goals 2000 Act (1994), 21

Godina, H., 117–131

Goffman, E., 89–91

Goldstein, B., 139

Good, T., 54

Gordon, M., 86

Gotbaum, B., 41, 42

Gottdiener, M., 60

Graduation: changes in rates of, 22; as criterion for evaluation of systems, 21–22; effect of repeating grades on, 26, 29; factors in failure to, 31, 34, 36–38; falling rates of, 29–31, 34, 36–38; homeschooling and, 37–38; migration and, 31, 34, 36; mortality and, 31; prison population and, 44, 45; private school enrollment and, 36–37

Graffiti: activating text of, 101; antigay, 103; as depersonalized form of harassment, 96; patriarchal relations and, 104; social character of ideology of "fag" mediated in, 101; text-mediated accomplishment of the ideology of "fag," 103–104; used to make public statements, 104

Grand Canyon (film), 128

Granovetter, M., 50

Grossberg, L., 122

Grubb, W., 66

Gruia, I., xii, 21–45

Gudykunst, W., 185

Gutek, G., 90

Gutierrez, K., 60

Gutmann, A., 215

Hafner, A., 193

Hall, E., 185, 188, 206

Hallinan, M., 50, 52, 56

Hammett, D., 119

Haney, W., xii, 21–45

Harlow, C., 45

Harrison, P., 53, 54

Hauser, R., 52

Hawaii: attrition rates, 23, 25*tab*; domestic/foreign migration in, 35*tab*; grade 9 bulge in schools, 29; graduation rates in, 30, 32*tab*

Hawk, Dee, 169
Haycock, K., 75
Haymes, S., 58, 60
Heath, S., 136, 137, 235
Henke, R., 37
Henriques, D., 41
Hess, R., 138
Heterosexuality: social relations of, 96
Higher Education Act (1965), 69
Higher Learning (Film), 128, 248
Hildenbrandt, H., 190
Hill-Collins, P., 58
History: in school, 239–242
Hochschild, J., 76
Holland, D., 165
Holmes, Leona, 170, 173, 176, 177
Homeschooling, 37–38
Home School Legal Defense
    Association, 37
Homesteading, 234
Homophobia, xii, 95–113
Homosexuality, 95–113. *See also*
    Students, gay and lesbian
hooks, b., 58, 60, 71, 150, 154, 166,
    270*n4*
Huckfeldt, R., 50
Hughes, Albert, 127
Hughes, Allen, 127
Hughes, Langston, 240
Huntington, S., 203
Hurtado, A., 133
Huston, J., 119

Ice Cube, 242
Idaho: domestic/foreign migration in,
    35*tab*; graduation rates in, 30, 32*tab*
Identity: "Americanized," 142; black,
    270*n4*; challenging, 60; collective,
    234; constructing, 236; creation of,
    60; cultural, 89–91, 159; defining,
    124; exploration, 58; formation, 57,
    118; ideology of resistance in, 58;
    minority, 58; national, 133, 213;

oppositional discourses of, 124; of
    oppression, 124; personal, 234; per-
    verse, 150; places of, 52; play, 265;
    racial, 204, 219, 222; student, 237;
    transnational communities and,
    205–206; white/nonwhite, 133
Ideology: of the middle class, 123
Ideology of "fag," 95–113; accomplish-
    ment in talk, 102–103; accomplish-
    ment of gay identity through, 105;
    embedded in social organization of
    heterosexuality, 107; entering,
    102–103; fag-baiting and, 108; gay
    consciousness and, 105–107; gossip
    and, 99–101; graffiti and, 103–104;
    identification as activity of male het-
    erosexual students, 99–100; identifi-
    cation gay students and, 102–103;
    lack of administrative intervention as
    acceptance of, 104; official silence of
    school and, 110–112; production of,
    101; relations of gender and,
    107–109; social character of labeling
    within, 100; social organization of
    stigma and, 99–101; teacher remarks
    and, 101; verbal abuse and, 102–103;
    work of passing in, 107, 109
Illinois: domestic/foreign migration in,
    35*tab*; graduation rates in, 30, 32*tab*
Immigrants: attitudes toward education
    and, 88; ideological whitening
    among, 140
Immigration: effect on attitude toward
    education, 85, 86; effect on graduation
    rates, 34; effect on racial composition
    of schools, 6; stigma attached to, 91
Income: access to education and, xii
Indiana: domestic/foreign migration in,
    35*tab*; graduation rates in, 30, 32*tab*
Integration: consequences of, 254; con-
    texts of, 254
Iowa: domestic/foreign migration in,
    35*tab*; graduation rates in, 30, 32*tab*

Jackson, Samuel, 128
James, C., 118, 120
James, Cyrillene, 174
Jameson, F., 122
Jason's Lyric (film), 242
Jet Li, 142
Johnson, A.J., 242
Jungle Fever (film), 128

Kagan, J., 189
Kamberelis, G., 238, 244
Kane, T., 73, 74, 78
Kansas: attrition rates, 23; domestic/for-
    eign migration in, 35*tab*; graduation
    rates in, 32*tab*
Karen, D., 76
Keith, M., 60
Kenny, L., 135
Kentucky: attrition rates, 23, 25*tab*;
    domestic/foreign migration in, 35*tab*;
    graduation rates in, 32*tab*
Khalidi, R., 205
Khayatt, D., 96, 97
Kim, H., 181–196
Kim, J., xiii
King, Martin Luther, 172, 239, 240, 241
King, Rodney, 124, 126
Kingsley, Doreen, 171, 172, 173
Kirkland, Renee, 172, 177
Kluger, R., 11
Koltyk, J., 142
Kreitzer, A., 39
Kroll, J., 128
Ku Klux Klan, 247–249

Lacan, J., 128, 129
Ladson-Billings, G., 55–59
Lafer, G., 66, 75
Lareau, A., 54, 85
Lasch, C., 118
Lavin, D., 79
Lee, C., xii, 3–20
Lee, S., xiii, 133–145

Lee, Spike, 128
Lei, J., 138
Lewis, B., 138, 203
Lewis, R., xiii, 163–179
Lieberman, P., 126
Lightfoot, S., 52
Lin, N., 50
Lindsay, C., 65, 190
Listening, xi. *See also* Talking; silence
    and dissent, xii–xiii
Loftus, G., 193
Logan, J., 4, 6, 12
Louisiana: attrition rates, 23, 25*tab*;
    domestic/foreign migration in, 35*tab*;
    graduation rates in, 30, 32*tab*
Lowe, L., 138
Loza, P., 63
Lubman, S., 181, 190
Ludwig, J., 76
Lussier, R., xiii–xiv, 217–231
Luttrell, W., 149, 150, 154, 273*n4*

MacLeod, J., 52, 53
Madaus, G., xii, 21–45
Mahiri, J., 235, 249
Maine: domestic/foreign migration in,
    35*tab*; grade 9 bulge in schools, 29;
    graduation rates in, 30, 32*tab*
Malcolm X, 172, 239, 240
Malcolm X (film), 241, 248
Maltese Falcon (film), 119, 120
Marginalization: silence and, xii
Marini, M., 52
Markus, H., xiii, 181–196
Maryland: attrition rates, 25*tab*; domes-
    tic/foreign migration in, 35*tab*; grad-
    uation rates in, 30, 32*tab*
Massachusetts: attrition rates, 25, 25*tab*;
    domestic/foreign migration in, 35*tab*;
    graduation rates in, 30, 32*tab*
Massey, D., 5
Matute-Bianchi, M., 86, 88, 92
McArdle, N., 15

McCarthy, C., xii, 90, 117–131, 204, 234, 235, 240
McDonough, P., 73
McNeil, L., 209
McPherson, M., 79
McQuillan, P., 85
Media: black realism and, 129; comic strips, 119; commodification of images of violence by, 126; commodification of inner city images in, 127; confirmation in, 128; construction of racial consciousness in, 242–246; creation of gulf between suburbanite/inner-city dweller and, 118; culture, 236; dealing with social troubles in, 120; discourse of crime in, 120; disregard of decline of opportunity and services in inner city, 127; fields of association and affiliation in, 118; languages of resentment in, 125–130; learning from, 247–249; literacy, 235; messages embedded in, xiii; nihilism in, 127; popular, xii; portrayal of inner city dangers in, 121–122; portrayal of suburbs as national interest/inner city needs as wasteful social agenda, 123; production of suburban anxiety and, 118; race-relations and, 118; racial antagonism and, 120; reflections of reality in, 125–130; representations of black youth, xiii; resentment and, 119–120; situated in cultural circuits, 118; triumph of suburban, middle-class values in, 117, 118; urban fables in, 120
Meecham, S., 117–131
Meeting the Challenge, 39
Mehan, H., 56
Mejía, D., 83
Melville, H., 119
Menace II Society (film), 127, 128, 242
Mercer, K., 124
Metz, M., 52

Miao, J., xii, 21–45
Michigan: attrition rates, 25, 25*tab*; domestic/foreign migration in, 35*tab*; grade 9 bulge in schools, 29; graduation rates in, 32*tab*
Mickelson, R., 76
Middle Income Students Assistance Act (1978), 69
Milliken v. Bradley, 268*n15*
Minami, M., 189
Minnesota: attrition rates, 23; domestic/foreign migration in, 35*tab*; graduation rates in, 30, 32*tab*
Mississippi: attrition rates, 25*tab*; domestic/foreign migration in, 35*tab*; graduation rates in, 30, 32*tab*
Missouri: domestic/foreign migration in, 35*tab*; graduation rates in, 33*tab*
Modern Times (film), 119
Montana: domestic/foreign migration in, 35*tab*; grade 9 bulge in schools, 29; graduation rates in, 30, 33*tab*
Morality: slave, 123
Morgan, S., 128, 129
Morrison, T., 119
Morsbach, H., 185
Mortensen, T., 69
Mortenson, T., 73, 75
Moscovici, S., 188
Movements: academic standards, 39, 40; civil rights, 172, 253; excellence, 40; minimum competency testing, 39
Mueller, J., xiii, 66, 163–179
Multiculturalism, 124
Mumpers, M., 70, 73, 75, 79

Nakamura, H., 184
National Association for the Advancement of Colored People (NAACP), 221
National Center for Education Statistics, 0
National College Access Network, 63

National Commission on Excellence in
Education, 39
A Nation at Risk, 39
Native Americans, 6, 268*n16*
Nebraska: attrition rates, 23;
domestic/foreign migration in, 35*tab*;
graduation rates in, 30, 33*tab*
Networks: information, 56; peer, 57;
social, 244
Nevada: attrition rates, 23, 25*tab*;
domestic/foreign migration in, 35*tab*;
graduation rates in, 33*tab*
New Hampshire: domestic/foreign
migration in, 35*tab*; graduation rates
in, 33*tab*
New Jersey: domestic/foreign migration
in, 35*tab*; graduation rates in, 30, 33*tab*
Newman, F., 64
New Mexico: attrition rates, 25*tab*;
domestic/foreign migration in, 35*tab*;
graduation rates in, 30, 33*tab*
Newton, Huey, 240, 243, 244
New York: attrition rates, 25, 25*tab*;
domestic/foreign migration in, 35*tab*;
grade 9 bulge in schools, 26; graduation rates in, 30, 33*tab*; student
exclusion from testing in, 41, 42
Nietzsche, F., 118, 121, 123
Nihilism, 127
Nisbett, R., 184, 187, 192
Nixon, Richard, 269*n29*
No Child Left Behind policy, 19, 40
Noddings, N., 83, 91
North Carolina: attrition rates, 25*tab*;
domestic/foreign migration in, 35*tab*;
graduation rates in, 30, 33*tab*
North Dakota: domestic/foreign migration in, 35*tab*; grade 9 bulge in
schools, 29; graduation rates in, 30,
33*tab*

Oakes, J., 48, 49, 51, 54, 56, 87
O'Connor, C., xiii, 64, 66, 87, 163–179

Ogbu, J., 52, 57, 86, 92, 157
Ohio: attrition rates, 25, 25*tab*; domes-
tic/foreign migration in, 35*tab*; grad-
uation rates in, 33*tab*
Oklahoma: domestic/foreign migration
in, 35*tab*; graduation rates in, 33*tab*
Olsen, L., 88, 133
Omi, M., 124, 125, 202, 204
Omnibus Budget Reconciliation Act
(1981), 269*n29*
Ong, A., 140, 141
Oppression, 53, 230
Oregon: domestic/foreign migration in,
35*tab*; graduation rates in, 30, 33*tab*
Orel, S., 41, 42
Orenstein, P., 174
Orfield, G., xii, 3–20, 251, 265
Ostrove, J., 71
the Other: culture embodied in, 138;
negation of, 123, 124; resentment
and, 240

Palestinian Americans, xiii. *See also*
Students, Palestinian-American
Panther (film), xiv, 237–250
Parenti, M., 117
Parents: educational level, 85; student
aspirations and, 52
Parks, Rosa, 172
Pastor, J., 156
Pataki, George, 74
Pedagogy: critical, xiv, 230; of the
oppressed, 230
Peer(s): background similarity and, 56;
culture, 91; networks, 57; opposi-
tion/support for academic achieve-
ment, 56–57; "pull" of, 56; student
aspirations and, 52
Pell Grants, 69
Penney, C., 193
Pennsylvania: domestic/foreign migra-
tion in, 35*tab*; graduation rates in, 30,
33*tab*

Perna, L., 75
Peshkin, A., 85
Peters, R., 191
Pettigrew, T., 254
Philips, S., 137
Pinar, W., 233
Placemaking, 58
Policy: college financial aid, 69–70; con-
    sequences of, 66; desegregation, 19;
    educational, xi; ethnographic, 66;
    federal, xii, 66; freedom of choice, 54;
    informing, xi; narrowing access to
    opportunity by, xi; neoliberal, 70;
    social, 7; state, xii, 66; student exclu-
    sion through, xii
Political: theory, xiii
Politics: of affect, 122–125; cultural, 123;
    global, xiii; of resentment, 124
Portes, A., 84, 86, 87
Postman, N., 117
Poverty: achievement levels and, 9; con-
    centrated, 9; correlation with race, 4;
    culture of, 138; dropout rates and,
    268n11; ideologies surrounding, 60;
    measuring, 268n24; segregation and,
    8–11, 10tab, 16–17, 18tab
Power: culture of, 150, 154, 157; of
    experience, 160; mobilization of, 123;
    organization of, 123; privilege and,
    54; relations, 47, 257–260
Pratt, M., 254, 255
Privilege: entitlement and, 54; intergen-
    erational transmission of, 54; legit-
    imization of, 54; power and, 54
Putnam, R., 86

Quinn, N., 182

Race: class overprediction by, 270n2;
    correlation with poverty, 4; decisions
    on course creation and, 51; exposure
    rates to whites by, 11tab; learning
    about, 133–145; median incomes

and, 75tab; as place of resistance, 58;
    popular culture and, 235; relations,
    219; representation in contemporary
    media, 117–131; segregation and,
    10tab; significance of class over, 135;
    as site of identification, 236; social
    construction of, 147; social order and,
    88; student aspirations and, 52;
    tracking and, 50
Race relations: affect and, 122; manipu-
    lation of difference in, 123
Racial: changeability, 234; consciousness,
    242–246; discrimination, 58; diversi-
    ty, 181; harassment, 217; hierarchies,
    133, 141, 144; hybridity, 234; identi-
    ty, 204, 219, 222; privilege, 159; pro-
    filing, 208; stereotypes, 208
Rapple, B., 42
Ravenel, Arthur, 223
Reagan, Ronald, 70, 269n29
Reality: of the inner city, 125–130;
    reflecting, 125–130; working class
    views of, 149–153
Reardon, S., 4, 5
Reauthorization of the Higher
    Education Act (1972), 69
Reed, A., 123
Reese, L., 83
Reform(s): academic standards move-
    ment, 39, 40; attrition and, 39–43;
    detracking, 48–49; equity-based, 47;
    high stakes testing and, 39;
    inequitable, 59; minimum competen-
    cy testing and, 39; negative conse-
    quences of, 40; redefining spaces of
    schooling and, 47–61
Reich, R., 215
Renier, T., 163, 164
Resegregation, 251; progression of, 7,
    8tab
Resentment: articulations of, 125; dis-
    course of crime, violence, suburban
    security and, 125–130; feeding,

125–130; forging identity through erasing the other and, 240; gaze of, 126; languages of, 125; politics of, 124; process of simulation and, 123, 124; production of, xii; social values and, 124; suburban, 121–122, 128, 129; as use of retributive morality, 123

Rhoades, K., 41

Rhode Island: attrition rates, 25, 25*tab*; domestic/foreign migration in, 35*tab*; graduation rates in, 33*tab*

Richardson, Tia, 170, 171, 173

Rodriguez, A., 117–131

Rodriguez, N., 90

Rofes, E., 95

Romeo Must Die (film), 142

Rosenbaum, J., 66

Rosewood (film), 241, 248

Ross, J., 49

Rothstein, R., 66, 75

Rudner, L., 37

Rumbaut, R., 139

Rury, J., 60

Rusher, W., 124, 125

Russell, K., 41, 170

Said, E., 203

Sanchez, S., 254

San Miguel, G., 89

Sares, T., 65

Sarroub, L., 206

Schooler, J., 193

Schooling: organizational features and production of minority identities, 88; subtractive, xii, 87–94

School(s): apartheid, 5; changing nature of enrollment in, 4; demographic changes in, 5–6; desegregation and, 3–20; gender relations of, 107–109; history in, 239–242; neighborhood, 19; opportunity to define "America" by, 144; racial composition of, 7*tab*;

racial hierarchies in, 133; racial transformation of, 5–6; re-segregation in, 4; segregation, 251; status of activities in, 136

Schools, segregated: curriculum in, 9; diminished opportunities in, 16; dropout rates in, 9; lack of resources in, 16; parental involvement in, 9, 16; teacher experience in, 4, 9, 16; teacher turnover in, 4, 9, 16, 268*n12*

Schramm-Pate, S., xiii–xiv, 217–231

Schumaker, Joel, 128, 129

Sefton-Green, J., 235, 236

Segregation, 267*n3*; busing and, 267*n9*; dimensions of, 5; dropout rates and, 9; economic, 4; increase in, 7; learning about, 251; in metropolitan areas, 3–20; parental involvement and, 9; patterns of, 4; post-*Brown*, 3–20; poverty and, 8–11, 10*tab*, 16–17, 18*tab*; race and, 10*tab*; racial variations in, 6–8; residential, 4, 12, 15; self, 257; self-perpetuating aspect of, 11; suburban, 4; teacher experience and, 4; teacher turnover and, 4, 9

Self: finding within diversity, 260–262; sense of, 237

Sennett, R., 71, 72, 76

Shakur, Tupac, 237

Shepard, L., 26, 39, 40

Shore, B., 182

Shweder, R., 182, 184, 192

Silence, xii–xiii, 181–196; appreciation of, 185; as choice, 257–260; cultural significance of, xiii, 183; of marginalized youth, 233; of privilege, 257–260; psychological consequences of, 183; respectful, xiii; structuring of, 233; understanding meaning of, 183; valued as way of demonstrating sympathy, 185

Simon, P., 80

Simpson, O.J., 124

Singleton, John, 125, 128
Skutnabb-Kangas, T., 87
Slavin, R., 54, 56
Slevin, K., 164
Smith, D., xii, 95–113
Smith, G., xii, 95–113
Smith, Susan, 124
Smolowe, J., 121
Snoop Doggy Dogg, 239
Social: ascendancy, 87; capital, 83, 91;
    class, 51, 64, 71, 139, 155; classifica-
    tion, 53; conflict, 124; divisions, 90;
    fictions, 120; inequality, 124, 230;
    justice, 124, 230; location, 150;
    mobility, 53; networks, 170, 244;
    order, 48, 88; organization, 95, 102;
    policy, 7; relations, 73, 183–188;
    reproduction, 88; status, 54; ties, 83;
    values, 124
Society: classless, 123
Solomon, R., 123
South Africa, 236
South Carolina: attrition rates, 23,
    25tab; domestic/foreign migration in,
    35tab; graduation rates in, 30, 33tab
South Dakota: attrition rates, 23;
    domestic/foreign migration in, 35tab;
    grade 9 bulge in schools, 29; gradua-
    tion rates in, 33tab
Space(s): alternative, 60; as collectives of
    difference, 251–266; constructed,
    255; of difference, 124, 255; free, xiv;
    homesteading, 234; integrated,
    251–266; meaningful, 234; placemak-
    ing and, 58; public, 58; racially inclu-
    sive, 264–266; redefining, 47–61;
    safe, 59; of schooling, 59–61; separa-
    tion of students by, 47; social, 254;
    territorialization of, 122; for young
    people, 234
Speech: antigay, 102; boundaries
    between public and private, 150; con-
    tent of, 188; cross-cultural differences

in, 186; as culturally saturated activi-
    ty, 182; as homophobic graffiti, 95; as
    part of democratic tradition, 184;
    silence and, 181–196; social organi-
    zation in, 95; as tool to enhance
    thinking, 182; as verbal abuse, 95, 96
Stage, F., 52
Stanton-Salazar, R., 50, 60, 83
Starr, D., 148, 150, 160
Steedman, C., 147
Stuart, Charles, 124
Stuart, G., 4, 15
Student(s): achievement gap between,
    47; activities chosen by, 136; average
    college debt of, 74tab; caring about
    school, 84, 85; desire for higher edu-
    cation, 66–69; detracking and, 47–61;
    disenfranchised, 53; disillusionment,
    53; equal learning opportunities for,
    48; expectations of, 48; networks and,
    50; rates of progress through system,
    21–45; shaping aspirations of, 52;
    status decided by whiteness, 136;
    teaching about Confederate Flag
    controversy, 217–231
Students, Asian: academic marginaliza-
    tion among, 136; adoption of hip-
    hop styles, 141, 142; cultural differ-
    ences among, 137, 138; dealing with
    culture of whiteness in schools,
    134–137; distribution in Boston
    (MA) area, 13, 14, 14tab;
    distrust/idealization of whites, 143,
    144; in ESL classes, 138; fear of
    teachers not valuing ideas by, 143;
    hiding culture to avoid being viewed
    negatively, 142; Hmong, 133–145; as
    "honorary whites," 136; identification
    with other minorities, 142; increase
    in enrollment by, 5, 13; integration
    of, 137; lack of trust in teachers, 143;
    learning about "America" by,
    133–145; as model minority, 136;

reluctance to speak about culture to outsiders, 142; responses to culture of whiteness, 141–144; school enrollments by region, 6*tab*; segregation levels in Boston (MA) area, 15–16; sense of cultural marginalization among, 141; silence and, xiii; social class and, 139; teacher response to, 137–141

Students, black: attitudes towards education, 76; choice of respect over detracking, 55–59; comparison of years completed with other ethnic groups, 76; detracking and, 53; distribution in Boston (MA) area, 13, 14, 14*tab*; exposure rates to whites, 11, 11*tab*, 12; increase in enrollment by, 5, 13; interpretation of media by, xiii; peer pressure among, 57; progression of desegregation/resegregation for, 3, 7, 8*tab*; rural integration and, 11; school enrollments by region, 6*tab*; segregation levels in Boston (MA) area, 15–16; silence viewed as hurdle, 181–196; vocational tracking and, 53

Students, gay and lesbian: avoidance of stereotypical behavior by, 106; being "out," 97, 98; dropping out, 97, 98; fag-baiting and, 96, 108; harassment of, 97; identification of, 102–103, 105–107; isolation of, xii, 102, 106; marginalization of, 104; ostracism of, 102–103; physical violence and, 102; relations with teachers, 111, 112; school experiences of, 95–113; self-identification and, 105–107; treatment of in schools, 95–113

Students, Latino: assimilation issues, 86, 87; attitudes towards education, 76; caring relations among, 91–94; choice of respect over detracking, 55–59; culturally negative messages and, 89; curriculum designed to

divest students of identity, 89–91; de-Mexicanization of, 83; devaluation of education as road to mobility by, 87; distribution in Boston (MA) area, 13, 14, 14*tab*; division between immigrant and U.S. born, 85–93; downward achievement and, 87; dropout rates for, 85; exposure rates to whites, 11, 11*tab*, 12; fluency in Spanish seen as "barrier," 89–91; generational status and orientation toward school, 86; immigrant attitudes toward, 86; increase in enrollment by, 5, 13; increase in segregation of, 8, 9*tab*; lack of course offerings corresponding to student needs for, 89–91–90; parental levels of education of, 85; re-segregation and, 3; revisions of names by faculty, 89–91; school enrollments by region, 6*tab*; schooling as mortification of self to, 89–91; segregation levels in Boston (MA) area, 15–16; subtractive schooling and, 83–94; tracking and, 87

Students, middle-class female, 147–161; acceptance of school hierarchy by, 155; culture of power and, 154; disregard for rules of meritocracy by, 158; indirect speech by, 154; privilege as a given, 159; relations with teachers, 153, 154; silence and obedience to authority by, 154

Students, Palestinian-American, 199–215; cast outside confines of "civilization," 202, 203; effect of global conflict on, 201–202; effects of September 11 attack on, 209, 210, 211; fears of, 202, 203; harassment of, 202, 203, 204, 208; hostile encounters with other students by, 202, 203; identity formation shaped with reference to contemporary politics, 201–202; limits of multicultural

Students, Palestinian-American
    (continued)
    education and, 206–211; loyalty to
    Palestine, 205–206; on-going conflict
    with Jewish students, 208; political
    debates and, 200; profiling and, 208;
    in programs with international per-
    spectives, 211–214; racialized dis-
    course and, 202–205; reactions to
    social inequality in school, 209, 210,
    211; silencing of, 200, 206–211; in
    transnational communities, 205–206
Students, white: distribution in Boston
    (MA) area, 13, 14, 14*tab*; drop in
    proportions of, 6; residential isolation
    of, 6; segregation levels in Boston
    (MA) area, 15–16
Students, working-class female,
    147–161; contradictions felt by, 158;
    denial of legitimacy to, 149; frustra-
    tion felt by, 159; reality of material
    locations of, 149; resistance by, 149,
    150; self-defined as oppositional cul-
    ture, 157; sense of difference among,
    150; struggles with teachers, 149,
    150, 151, 152; support for each other,
    157; view of selves as marginal, 151
Suárez-Orozco, M., 88, 205
Subtractive schooling, 83–94; caring
    relations and, 91–94; culture and,
    89–91; language and, 89–91
Supryia, K., 117–131
Swann, W., 187

Takaki, R., 191
Talking. *See also* Speech: concept of self
    and, 183–188; cultural meanings of,
    183, 193, 194; cultural model of
    group relational concepts, 183–188;
    cultural model of independent person
    and, 183–188; cultural practices of,
    181–196; differing cultural traditions
    and, 182; in education, 189–190;
    function and context in, 183; incor-
    poration of culture-specific models
    and, 182; intelligence and, 187–188;
    in multicultural world, 194–196; par-
    enting and, 188–189; psychological
    consequences of, 183; reasoning and,
    187; representations and practices in,
    182; responsibility on listener, 185;
    social relationships and, 183–188;
    social shaping of, 182; as thinking
    aloud, 193; thinking and, 192–194; as
    Western preoccupation, 184; in
    workplace, 190–191
Tamari, S., 207
Tate, Larenz, 128
Tatum, B., 258
Taylor, J., 174
Teacher(s): attitudes on diversity, 135;
    credentials, 9; in detracking, 48–49;
    experienced, 4; racialized construc-
    tions of students, 133; relations with
    gay students, 111, 112; turnover, 4, 9,
    268*n12*
Television. *See* Media
Tennessee: attrition rates, 25*tab*; domes-
    tic/foreign migration in, 36*tab*; grad-
    uation rates in, 30, 33*tab*
Tennis shoe registration, 54–55
Testing: appropriate use of results,
    40–41; computer use and, 41; deci-
    sionmaking based on, 40; disconnect-
    ed from reality of students, 233;
    effect on teacher attitudes, 136; errors
    in scoring/reporting, 41; high-stakes,
    xii, 39, 40, 44, 233; low-tech, 41;
    minimum competency, 39; sliding
    scale approach in, 41; standardized,
    39, 136, 233; student exclusion and,
    41, 42
Texas: attrition rates, 23, 25*tab*; domes-
    tic/foreign migration in, 36*tab*; grad-
    uation rates in, 33*tab*; student exclu-
    sion from testing in, 41, 42

on rates, 23;
ign migration in, 36*tab*;
in schools, 29; gradua-
3*tab*

1

47–61

255

50

: domestic/foreign migration
; graduation rates in, 33*tab*
n, K., 175, 176
192
rd, M., 50
., 56
nith, Candace, 172, 173, 176
xi–xiv, 60, 64, 219, 233, 234,
53, 254, 255
., xii, 11, 47–61, 56
rginia: domestic/foreign migra-
n, 36*tab*; graduation rates in,

ck, A., xii, 21–45, 48
less: representations of, xii
, B., 192
icka, A., 192
an, S., 219
ms, R., 118
, P., 52, 76
n-Brown, C., 117–131
er, G., 74
onsin: attrition rates, 23;
omestic/foreign migration in, 36*tab*;
rade 9 bulge in schools, 29; gradua-
ion rates in, 30, 33*tab*
men, black. *See also* Students, black:
age-related outlooks on success/inde-
pendence, 169–174; assumption of
responsibilities by, 164; awareness of
challenges to African Americans by,
173; awareness of risks of being
assertive on academic success, 174,
176, 177; constraints/opportunities
for success by, 167; coping with constraints, 174–177; demographics of,
168–169; documentation of
voices/experiences of, 166–174; educational success of, 166; effect of
other women on, 171, 172, 173; false
authenticity and, 270*n4*; family issues
in gaining education, 169, 170; family socialization of, 164; family sup-

Women, black *(continued)*
port for, 174–177; femininity and school success and, 163–179; gender-related narratives of, 167; orientation towards independence by, 164, 165, 169–174; physical indices of femininity, 169, 170; processes for commitment to school by, 167; recognition that blacks are not rewarded for school efforts by, 165; resilience of, 166; restrictions on body, 170, 171; self-esteem and, 165
Wood, J., 125, 126
Woodbine, B., 242–243

Wyoming: attrit
domestic/for
grade 9 bulge
tion rates in,

Yan, J., 185
Yassin, Ahlam, 2(
Yeo, F., 85
Yon, D., 235, 236
Yonezawa, S., xii,
Young, B., 4, 178
Young Lords part

Zimmerman, B., 1